Northeast India

Celebrating
30 Years of Publishing
in India

Also by the Author

The Braided River: A Journey Along the Brahmaputra

Northeast India

A Political History

SAMRAT CHOUDHURY

HarperCollins *Publishers* India

First published in the United Kingdom by
C. Hurst & Co. (Publishers) Ltd., 2023

First published in India by HarperCollins *Publishers* 2023
4th Floor, Tower A, Building No. 10, DLF Cyber City,
DLF Phase II, Gurugram, Haryana – 122002
www.harpercollins.co.in

2 4 6 8 10 9 7 5 3 1

P-ISBN: 978-93-5699-124-8
E-ISBN: 978-93-5699-119-4

Printed and bound at
Thomson Press (India) Ltd

FSC www.fsc.org
MIX
Paper from responsible sources
FSC® C010615

This book is produced from independently certified FSC® paper to ensure responsible forest management.

CONTENTS

The Indian Subcontinent, 1782

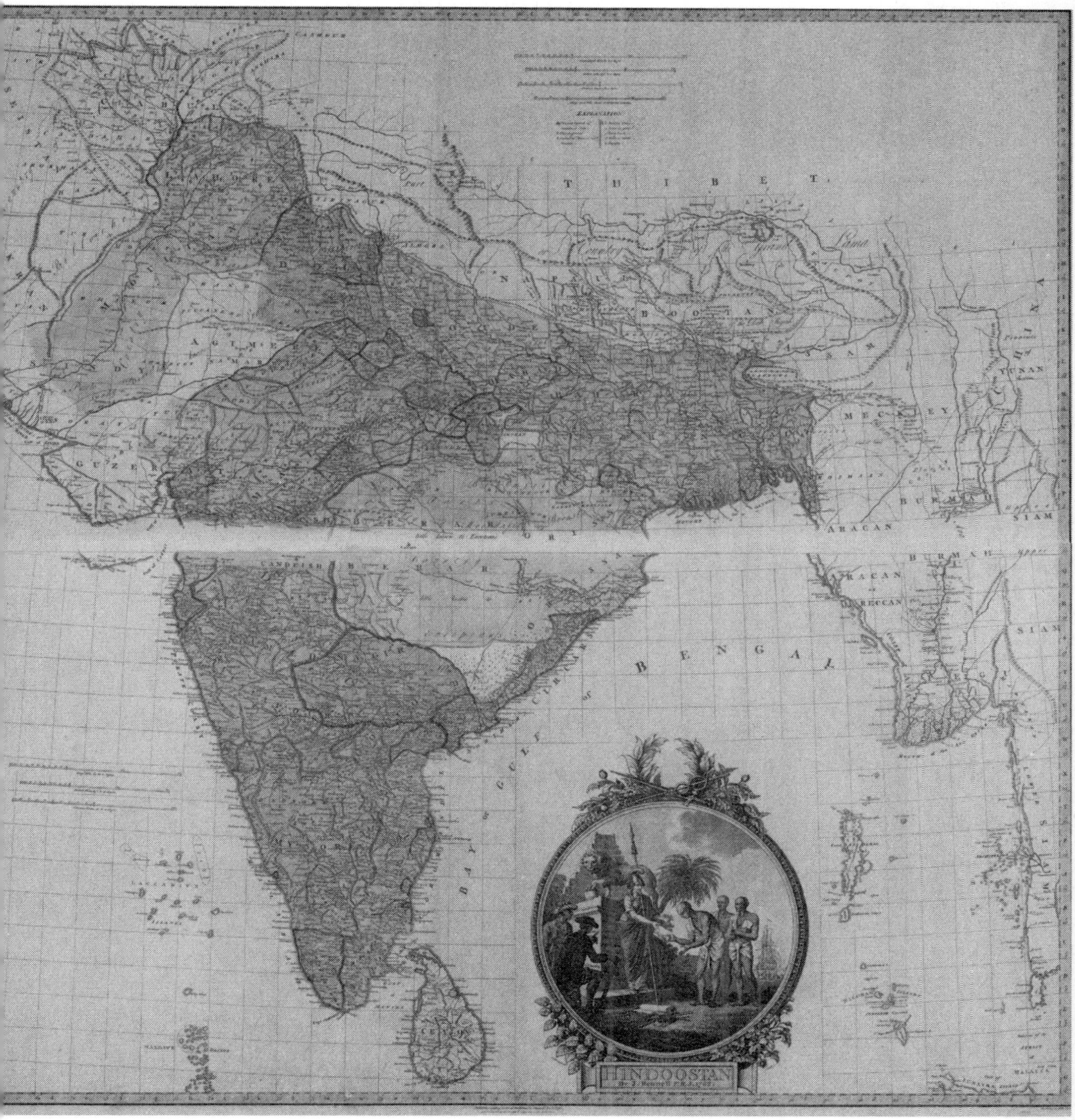

Source: Library of Congress, Geography and Map Division

ACKNOWLEDGMENTS

Writing a book is no easy task. Researching one such as this is especially difficult. For a writer with no institutional access to journals and libraries and no funding, the challenge becomes quite prodigious. Not only must one find the materials; but one must also find the time to use them. My thanks to open access resources such as the Internet Archive and JSTOR for making books and journals available to independent writers like me, and to the International Centre Goa and its Director, Dr. Pushkar, for offering me a month's stay as a Scholar in Residence to work on the manuscript.

Writing is a solitary activity, but a manuscript becomes a book through the efforts of many. My thanks to Michael Dwyer for his interest in publishing this book, and his suspicion that I might manage to write it. Thanks, also, to the anonymous reviewer who was its first reader, and to its editors, Lara and Rose. The raw manuscript was much improved by their efforts. Finally, my thanks to Daisy for seeing the manuscript through the production process all the way to the printed copy.

PREFACE

In contemporary maps of India, the Northeast is a protuberance that hangs on to the rest of the country by a slender thread, barely 21 kilometres wide at its narrowest point. It is a region surrounded by foreign countries. Tibet, now the Tibetan Autonomous Region of China, and the mountain kingdom of Bhutan, lie to its north and northwest. Myanmar and Bangladesh are to the southeast and southwest. The Himalayas stand tall as a formidable, but by no means impassable, natural barrier in the north. The southeast is lined by the hills and jungles of northern Myanmar. Flowing through it, down the middle, is the central geographical feature of the region, the Brahmaputra river. Throughout history, the fertile valley of this vast river has been at the heart of the region's politics. It was and is the most populous part of the land.

The geographical region is internally comprised of seven states of the Indian Union, which are often referred to as the 'Seven Sisters'. These are, in alphabetical order, Arunachal Pradesh, Assam, Manipur, Meghalaya, Mizoram, Nagaland and Tripura. The official region, however, also includes an eighth state, a late entrant that sits geographically separate from the rest—the former Himalayan kingdom of Sikkim, which became a part of India in 1975 and was inducted into the North Eastern Council, a government body of the region's states, in 2002. The Northeast as it exists now is therefore more of an administrative construct rather than a historical region with a shared past.

This book looks at the journeys through time by which each of these states entered modern India and acquired their present shapes. Since all of them border foreign countries, the making of some of those boundaries is also an inescapable part of the journey. The states now all share similar political and administrative structures under the Indian constitution. They are all run by governments headed by chief ministers and their councils of ministers, assisted by bureaucracies led by chief secretaries. These ministers must first win elections. They often do so with campaigns run by their parties on issues of identity, which remains a central matter in the politics of the region. Two of these are identities based on language and religion. The emergence of the current print vernaculars and the entry of major world religions into states of the region are therefore key parts of the story.

The sheer internal diversity in Northeast India is mind-boggling. Credible estimates put the number of languages spoken in the region at about 220, although there are claims for higher numbers. There are adherents here of all the world's major faiths. There are Hindus, of course, but there are also Christians, Muslims, Buddhists, Sikhs and animists. Only two of the states in the geographical region—Assam and Tripura—have clear Hindu majorities; two others, Manipur and Arunachal Pradesh, have roughly equal numbers of Hindus and Christians while three—Nagaland, Mizoram and Meghalaya—have Christian majorities.[1] About a third of the population of Assam, the most populous state in the region, is Muslim. This means that the Muslim population in the region exceeds the entire population of the Christian-majority states. By percentage, the highest concentrations of Buddhists in India outside the Union Territory of Ladakh are in the Northeast states of Sikkim, Arunachal Pradesh and Mizoram, where they constitute local majorities in certain areas.

Naturally, relations between these diverse communities, jostling for space and power, have not always been friendly. There are long, complicated and contested histories of ethnic, linguistic and religious tensions and conflicts between several of the region's communities, which continue to play an active part in today's politics. The fact that each of these communities has its own unique history and identity, and that there are several politically significant communities in even the smallest states, makes the task of writing any account of the region a difficult and fraught one. Moreover, there are also right-wingers of various hues who have long fought overtly and covertly on behalf of clashing nationalisms, big or small. What pleases the champions of one such group inevitably tends to annoy those of another, and vice versa.

It is not my aim to either please or displease anyone. I have therefore tried to report facts and events as honestly and accurately as possible, using standard sources, and have avoided interpretations of my own except in the concluding chapter. The language and worldviews of the original texts have been retained unchanged. This approach has the demerit of sometimes including outdated names and terms and reflecting old prejudices, but it also has the merit of reducing the anachronistic tendency to refashion the past using the values of the present.

My effort has been to write a readable narrative account guided by the two eyes of history, geography and chronology. Naturally, this effort is bound to involve simplification as well. The diversity of the region makes it nigh impossible for a single volume or author to chronicle the entire past of every community in detail. What I hope to have done with this book is provide for readers an accessible introduction to the political history of Northeast India.

1

TEA, CHRISTIANITY AND MODERNITY

ENTERING INDIA AND THE MODERN WORLD

What is now Northeast India lay far beyond the easternmost limits of the Indus Valley Civilisation, the oldest known civilisation on the Indian subcontinent. No empire of ancient India is known to have ever ruled the densely forested hills of this region which separates and connects South Asia with Southeast Asia and China. There is no evidence that the rule of the Mauryan empire, the first great Indian empire, extended so far east, although an ancient text, the Arthashastra, mentions products that suggest trade ties. The Gupta empire at its zenith extended as far east as Pundravardhana, corresponding to today's northern Bangladesh and the Indian area of North Bengal. The kingdom of Kamrup, associated with today's Assam, lay beyond this, further east. It finds mention in the Allahabad Pillar Inscription of Samudragupta, dated to around 350 CE, as a frontier territory whose ruler paid tribute to the great emperor—the first mention of the area in the historical record.

There is, however, an older kingdom of myth and legend to which the Kamrup kingdom is generally believed to be the inheritor. This was the kingdom of Pragjyotish, the land of eastern light. Its precise location and extent are unclear; there is mention of the eastern sea, and marshes, suggesting a southern boundary close to the Bay of Bengal and the Sundarbans. Its ruler Bhagadatta finds mention in the great epic, the Mahabharata, as chief of the Mlechchhas, the Brahminical term for 'barbarians' who did not observe distinctions of caste—thus placing them outside ancient Hindu society, and their territories beyond the cultural and social geography of Aryavarta, the 'land of the Aryans'.[1] Bhagadatta is described as a great warrior and a son of Naraka, king of the Asuras, who is himself characterised as a son of the earth goddess. Hindu mythology divides the world between the gods, known as Devas, and the Asuras, Rakshashas and Danavas, powerful and magical beings characterised as evil, who battled the gods. The tales in the Mahabharata include one of mortal combat between King Bhagadatta, fighting astride an armoured battle elephant, and the epic's hero, Arjuna, on a horse-drawn chariot with the god Krishna acting as his charioteer. In the end, Bhagadatta and his elephant are both slain—but not before Lord Krishna, one of the main gods of the Hindu pantheon, has had to break his vow of non-participation in combat in order to block a magical weapon hurled by Bhagadatta at Arjuna.

Curiously, the king Bhagadatta, in this account, was also said to be accompanied by Yavanas, a word that usually connotes Greeks, and was portrayed as being surrounded by peoples described as Kiratas and Cinas. The linguist Suniti Kumar Chatterji, in his book *Kirata-Jana-Krti*, published in 1951, wrote:

> It is the consensus of opinion among Indologists that in Sanskrit the term Kirata indicated the wild non-Aryan tribes living in the mountains, particularly the Himalayas and in the North-eastern areas of India, who were Mongoloid in origin. These Kiratas were connected with the Cinas or the Chinese, the Bhotas or the Tibetans, and other Mongoloid peoples.

According to Chatterji, 'With the single exception of the Khasis and the connected Jaintias (Syntengs) of Assam, the Mongoloid peoples who are found in India are all speakers of languages and dialects belonging to the Sino-Tibetan or Tibeto-Chinese speech family.'[2]

Chatterji estimated that the Tibeto-Burman speakers had dispersed from the area around the source of the Yangtze Kiang in China:

> In a similar way, the Chinese province of Yun-nan, to the east of Assam and Burma, formed the nucleus of the Thai (Dai) or Siamese tribes for their southward trek into Siam and Indo-China (Viet-nam). It seems quite probable that long before 1000 B.C. some of these early Tibeto-Burmans had penetrated within the frontiers of India, either along the southern slopes of the Himalayas, through Assam (and established themselves in the sub-Himalayan tracts as far west as Garhwal and Kumaon), or by way of Tibet, going up the Tsangpo or Brahmaputra and then crossing the Himalayan barrier into Nepal and Garhwal-Kumaon.[3]

Most of the tribal populations that inhabit Northeast India to this day speak languages from the Tibeto-Burman family.

The earliest literature that has been found to date of the people and lands in what is now Northeast India is the account of the Chinese Buddhist pilgrim Hiuen Tsang, who was in the kingdom of Kamrup in the mid-seventh century CE. Hiuen Tsang was studying the 'profound law of Buddha' at the Nalanda monastery in Magadha, in south Bihar, when Kumar Bhaskar Varman, the king of Kamrup, sent messengers to invite him to his capital. The pilgrim described 'going east 900 li or so' (about 240 kilometres) from the kingdom of Pundra-Vardhana, corresponding to northern Bangladesh and North Bengal, and 'crossing the great river'—the Karatoya, probably corresponding to today's Teesta or Brahmaputra—to arrive in Kamrup. Hiuen Tsang wrote:

> The country of Kamarupa is about 10,000 li [nearly 2,736 kilometres] in circuit. The capital town is about 30 li... The climate is soft and temperate...the men are of small stature and their complexion a dark yellow. Their language differs a little from that of mid-India... They adore and sacrifice to the Devas and have no faith in Buddha... There are abundant Deva temples, and different sectaries to the number of several myriads.[4]

The language of the people, according to Hiuen Tsang, differed 'a little from that of mid-India', meaning the Gangetic plains to the west.

The only written material to have been unearthed from the Kamrup kingdom from the remote past, apart from rock inscriptions, are the so-called Nidhanpur and Dubi copper plates, a bronze seal attached to the Dubi plates, and one clay seal found in Nalanda in Bihar. The Nidhanpur plate was found in the village of Nidhanpur in Sylhet district of today's Bangladesh, while the Dubi plate was discovered in a village called Dubi in Assam's Barpeta district. The Nidhanpur plates describe a renewal of land grants by the king, Bhaskar Varman, to a group of Brahmins. The Dubi plates and seal, also issued by the same king for a land grant renewal, trace the genealogy of the Varman kings from the asura Naraka and his son Bhagadatta. The language of the inscriptions is Sanskrit. However, Sanskrit, the language of scripture, was not the spoken language of the common people.

The linguist Suniti Chatterji wrote of Hiuen Tsang's account:

> it is curious that, according to him, the language of the Kama-rupa people 'differed a little' from that of mid-India... one would expect one and identical language to have been current in North Central Bengal (Pundra-Vardhana) and North Bengal and West Assam (Kama-rupa) in the 7th Century since these tracts, and other parts of Bengal, had almost the same speech, at least in morphology, in the 15th and 16th centuries, as can be seen from extant remains in Bengali and Assamese.

Chatterji surmised that 'perhaps the "differing a little" of the Kama-rupa speech from the speech of mid-India refers to those modifications of Aryan sounds which now characterise Assamese as well as North and East Bengali dialects'.[5]

The Varman dynasty was replaced by the Mlechchha dynasty started by a king named Salastamba, who claimed descent from Narak-Asura. His line ended and was replaced by one begun by a king named Brahma Pal around 1000 CE. In about 1198 CE, Bakhtiyar Khilji, a general in the army of the first Muslim sultan of Delhi, Qutubbuddin Aibak, having conquered Bihar and

Bengal, embarked upon an expedition through Assam to try and conquer Tibet. He faced little resistance on his way there. His advance was eventually checked by an army described as being of Mongol horsemen, and on his way back he found that the king of Kamrup had destroyed the stone bridge across the river Karatoya by which his army had crossed, and was preparing to attack him with overwhelming force. His forces were besieged and only Khilji himself, with a few hundred horsemen, managed to reach the opposite bank of the river.[6]

The course of history of the region was changed by a band that entered the area from the east rather than the west. In 1215 CE, a prince of the Tai kingdom of Mong Mao, from what are now the borderlands between Myanmar and Yunnan in China, left home with a band of around 9,000 men. They arrived, after thirteen years of wandering, in the upper reaches of the Brahmaputra valley. Here, Prince Siu Ka Pha (or Sukapha) began establishing a kingdom with its capital at Charaideo. This would in time become the great Ahom dynasty that ruled large parts of the Brahmaputra valley until the advent of the British East India Company, and that gave its name to the present state of Assam.

The next three centuries were marked by battles and wars between the Ahoms and the other kingdoms of the area, over all of which, eventually, the Ahoms prevailed. The Chutiya kingdom in the easternmost tracts of the Brahmaputra valley, and the Koch kingdoms at the western end, were the last of the local powers to be defeated. By the time this was accomplished in the sixteenth century, the Ahom empire had a new and far more powerful rival to contend with.

During the reign of Akbar the Great, the Mughal empire came to include nearly all of Bengal. A split in the Koch kingdom that ruled western Assam and north Bengal, and a civil war between the western Koch kingdom of Koch Bihar and its eastern cousin Koch Hajo, led, during the reign of Akbar's successor Jehangir, to the annexation of the lands west of the river Barnadi in today's central Assam, to the Mughal empire. The eastern Koch king sought assistance from their traditional rivals, the Ahoms, to stave off the Mughal challenge. A series of battles followed between

Mughal armies on the one side and the Koch and Ahom forces on the other. In the seventeenth century, during the reign of Jehangir's successor Aurangzeb as the Mughal emperor, his general Mir Jumla, a Persian from Isfahan who was then the Governor of Bengal, led an invasion of the Ahom kingdom. In March 1662, the Ahom capital Garhgaon fell to the Mughals, and the palace of the king, Jayadhwaj Singha, who had fled, was occupied by Mir Jumla. However, the rains and floods with their accompanying diseases—the scourge of all armies that invaded the Brahmaputra valley—had set in. The rising waters cut off Mir Jumla's communication and supply networks, and the Ahoms began a guerrilla resistance.

By the time the rainy season ended, Mir Jumla had fallen seriously ill. A peace treaty was concluded by which the Mughal forces agreed to withdraw, on payment of 20,000 'tolas'—more than 200 kilograms—of gold; six times that amount of silver; and the delivery of the Ahom king's minor daughter, Ramani Gabharu, to the Mughal imperial harem. Mir Jumla died of illness on his way back to Dhaka downriver via the Brahmaputra. A few years later, when hostilities resumed over unpaid war indemnities, the Ahoms under their celebrated general Lachit Borphukan successfully recaptured their lost territories by defeating the Mughal forces led by Raja Ram Singh of Amber, a principality near Jaipur in Rajasthan, at the Battle of Saraighat in 1671.

The Ahom rulers did not rule unchallenged for very long. Internal strife erupted in the kingdom, where there was a rebellion that involved religious and caste differences between adherents of two Hindu sects. The rebellion by followers of a Vaishnav[7] sect called the Moamaria destroyed the Ahom king's power between 1769 and 1805 in a series of revolts that left the kingdom ripe for invasion.

* * *

The story of the decline of the Ahom kingdom, and the birth of modern Northeast India, begins with religion—and cups of tea.

The place where it all started was Sivasagar (then Sibsagar), in the upper reaches of the Brahmaputra valley, around which the remains of a succession of Ahom capitals down the ages lie scattered.

Today it is a sleepy town where the main tourist attraction is an early eighteenth-century temple called the Siva Dol, dedicated to the god Shiva, the ascetic lord of destruction in the Hindu trinity. This large temple is flanked by two smaller ones dedicated to Vishnu, the preserver of creation, and Durga, a warrior-goddess, who is an avatar of Shakti, a Sanskrit word that means power or energy. They represent the three main sects of Hinduism—the Shaiva, Vaishnava and Shakta. The temples were built during Ahom rule in the early eighteenth century by a 'Bor Raja', or 'big king', who was not a king—she was a queen named Phulesvari.

When the Ahoms arrived in Assam in 1228, they had their own religion and spoke a language related to Thai and Lao. The royal family, the priests of the old faith, and the leading nobles of the king's court retained these for over 400 years. However, Hindu culture had begun to enter the Ahom court in the early 1400s during the reign of King Sudangpha, who was known as Bamuni Konwar, meaning 'Brahmin Prince', because he had been raised by a Brahmin couple. King Sutamla, also known as Jayadhwaj Singha, who ascended the throne in 1648, was the first Ahom monarch to formally adopt Hinduism. Despite this, there were subsequent conflicts between some Ahom rulers and the Vaishnav Hindu monasteries known as 'Sattras'. During the reign of King Gadadhar Singha in the late 1600s, according to the chronicles known as Tungkhungia Buranji, a golden idol was taken from the Dakhinpat Sattra and melted, with the gold being used for an Ahom temple in Charaideo. His successor Rudra Singha ended the persecution of the Vaishnav Sattras but also began to patronize their rival Sakta sect. The Hindu influence peaked under King Sutanphaa, also known as Siva Singha, who ascended the throne in 1714. He became a disciple of a Brahmin priest from Bengal, Krishnaram Bhattacharjee, who had been invited to the Ahom kingdom by his father, King Rudra Singha (or Sukhrungphaa). Siva Singha appointed Bhattacharjee chief priest of the famed Kamakhya temple in Guwahati. When Brahmin astrologers in 1722 predicted that his rule would soon come to an end, Siva Singha made large donations for building temples, including the ones in Sivasagar, in an effort to conciliate the gods. He also attempted to subvert the alleged decree of fate by declaring his queen, Phulesvari, a former temple dancer, as the king, and turning over the royal symbols of authority to her.

The queen was a staunch devotee of Durga and followed the traditions of Shakti worship, a distinguishing feature of which was blood sacrifices—in sharp contrast to the Vaishnava tradition of Hinduism which emphasises vegetarianism. 'She was even more under the influence of the Brahmans than her husband, and, in her consuming zeal for Shakta Hinduism, such as so often distinguishes new converts, she committed an act of oppression which was destined to have far-reaching and disastrous consequences', wrote Edward Gait in his *History of Assam*:

> Hearing that the Sudra Mahanta of the Vaishnava persuasion refused to worship Durga, she ordered the Moamaria and several other Gosains to be brought to a Sakta shrine where sacrifices were being offered, and caused the distinguishing marks of the Sakta sect to be smeared with the blood of the victims upon their foreheads. The Moamarias never forgave this insult to their spiritual leader, and half a century later, they broke out in open rebellion.[8]

In 1769, King Rajeswar Singha passed away and was succeeded by his brother Lakshmi Singha. The rebels, with the assistance of three disgruntled Ahom princes, rapidly took over the country up to the Ahom capital of Rangpur on the outskirts of Sivasagar, imprisoned the new king, executed many of the nobles and replaced them with their own leaders. However, in short order, the newly minted kings and nobles acquired the airs and vices of the old. The late Rajeswar Singha's queen, Kuranginayani, a princess from the neighbouring kingdom of Manipur further east, rallied the Ahom forces, killed the rebel chief Ragha Moran who had captured her for his harem, and retook the capital. The royalists successfully held off rebel counterattacks with the help of Manipuri cavalry that came to the aid of their princess.

A few years on, hostilities resumed again, with success for the rebels whose numbers were boosted by a tribe from what is now Arunachal Pradesh, the Nyishi, and their serfs residing in the border areas of the Ahom kingdom, known then as 'Dafla-bahatiyas'. The new Ahom monarch, Gaurinath Singha, was forced to flee downriver along the Brahmaputra from Rangpur to Nagaon in 1788. The king of Manipur again sent forces, but on this occasion, the Moamarias bested the Manipuri cavalry by surprising them in thick jungle. The Ahom king then escaped further downriver to Guwahati. There he found himself facing trouble from another set of rebels. A few hundred 'Doms', or fishermen, taking inspiration from the Moamarias—whose adherents were also largely drawn from similar castes considered low in the Hindu caste hierarchy—attacked the king's quarters and set it on fire.

The Ahom chronicle known as Tungkhungia Buranji recounts:

> The King, seized with fear in apprehension of a battle, crossed the stockade and proceeded down in a boat by the Brahmaputra to Nagarbera. One Rausch Saheb used to live in Bangalhat. The King had despatched to him Bika the Majindar of Gauhati [Guwahati], and Bhaba Kataki, with the request to arrange for the deputation of a contingent of sepoys from Calicata.[9]

And so it was that on a request from deposed King Gaurinath Singha, sent through a European merchant in Bangalhat near the modern town of Goalpara, seven companies of the East India Company under the command of Captain Thomas Welsh arrived from Calicata (or Calcutta) to save the Ahom king from his own subjects. This was the beginning of the end of Ahom rule, and the first step towards colonisation and the invention of modern Northeast India.

The well-armed and well-trained sepoys of the Bengal Native Infantry made short work of the rebel forces. The East India Company forces were soon withdrawn on the orders of the new Governor General, Sir John Shore, but before departing, Captain Welsh secured a treaty from the Ahom king that opened up free trade between the kingdom and neighbouring Bengal, of which the British were now the rulers. According to the Tungkhungia Buranji, while departing, Welsh and his men took with them the Ahom king's treasure, including a loot of 400,000 pieces each of gold and silver ornaments.

Barely twenty years later, fresh problems arose. The new teenage king Chandrakant Singha's powerful prime minister Purnananda Buragohain, and the Ahom viceroy in Guwahati, Badanchandra Barphukan, fell out badly. Barphukan, fearing for his life, made his way to Calcutta to seek military help from the Company Raj. His request was turned down. He then made his way to the court of King Bodawpaya of Burma, among whose consorts was a woman named Rangili Mepaya from Assam. Barphukan received a more helpful response from the Burmese ruler and in 1817 he invaded the Ahom kingdom at the head of a Burmese army. The Ahom forces were easily defeated and the new capital of Jorhat, along with King Chandrakant Singha, fell into Burmese hands in 1818. The king sent a princess from the royal family, Hemo Aideo, to the Burmese king's harem and made his peace with Burmese overlordship.

The situation did not last long. Barphukan was assassinated by a soldier at the instigation of the queen-mother. His rival Purnananda Buragohain had also died by then, and Buragohain's son Ruchinath now once again sought British help in retaking the kingdom. Although his request was also turned down, he managed to put together a militia, dressed them up like Company sepoys, and proceeded to invade Assam with some success. King Chandrakant's soldiers switched sides, and he was deposed. A new king, Purandar Singha, then a boy of ten, was installed in his place. The Burmese king, hearing of all this, and of the murder of Badanchandra Barphukan, once again despatched an army to Assam to restore King Chandrakant Singha to his throne. Burmese forces invaded Assam, defeated the divided Ahom forces, and put Chandrakant back on the throne. His rival Purandar Singha fled downriver on the Brahmaputra to Bengal. The Burmese, however, were now the real rulers of Assam. Chandrakant soon began to chafe at their overlordship and started moves to evict them. This did not escape their notice, and an even stronger force was despatched by the Burmese king to put an end to the repeated insurrections. Chandrakant, fearing for his life, fled to Gauhati and then on to Bengal at their arrival. Assam fell to the Burmese for the third time in 1821. They unleashed a reign of terror that is remembered to this day, called 'Maan'or din' in Assamese—the days of the 'Maan', meaning Burmese.

Although the two rival deposed Ahom monarchs, Chandrakant and Purandar, separately sought to retake the kingdom with British help, it was not forthcoming. When the British did finally intervene, it was for other reasons. The British East India Company's official history records that with Burma, 'differences had been occasioned at an early period by the incursions of a race of people called *Mhugs*'.[10] These people from the Arakan coast of Burma, after the conquest of their kingdom of Mrauk-U by the Burmese in 1784–85, had fled into adjacent British territories from where they mounted a guerrilla resistance. This led to clashes that spilled over into British territory. The British rejected Burmese demands for the extradition of the rebels and refused to check the raids.[11] In 1824, Burmese forces attacked and captured the island of Shapooree off Teknaf, in what is now Bangladesh, close to the Arakan coast. They were already masters of the kingdoms of Manipur and Assam by then. The Burmese forces now advanced into Sylhet 'and took post within five miles only of the town of Sylhet, and only two hundred and twenty-six miles from Calcutta'.[12]

The attack on British India's territories and subjects and the perceived threat to its towns and cities, including the capital, brought the Company Raj into direct confrontation with Burma. On 5 March 1824, the Governor General declared the government of Ava, meaning Burma, an enemy state, and a war began. When the fighting ended with the Treaty of Yandabo in February 1826, Assam, Manipur, Cachar and the rest of Northeast India with them entered the era of British overlordship.

War is expensive; the Burma war and a smaller conflict with the kingdom of Bharatpur in Rajasthan, along with the extension of the civil administration establishments into recently annexed territories, had contributed to pushing up what was called the 'registered debt of India' by more than £13 million between 1824/25 and 1827/28.[13] The East India Company was a commercial enterprise, primarily interested in revenues and profits. The Company's bosses in London strongly urged the need for retrenchments and cost-cutting.

On the basis of projected revenue earnings, the Company Raj annexed only the areas known as 'Lower Assam', corresponding to the territories in the lower or western part of the Brahmaputra's course, to its existing territories in Bengal. Coming as it did after the terror unleashed during Burmese rule, the arrival of the Company Raj was 'hailed with unbounded joy'.[14] The cost of holding, securing and administering the other areas was not thought to be worth the revenue benefits that would accrue. The agent of the Governor General for the North-East Frontier of Bengal, David Scott, became the ruler of Lower Assam. On his advice, Captain J.B. Neufville was appointed as political agent for the territory at the eastern extremity around Sadiya, although his base was 400 km west in Biswanath, in British territory.[15] The status of Upper Assam, which lay between Sadiya and Lower Assam, was not immediately decided. Purandar Singha, the principal rival of Chandrakant, was eventually made king of this area in April 1833, on promise of a payment of an annual tribute of Rs. 50,000. This proved too high an amount for the ravaged Ahom economy. When the new king began defaulting on his payments barely three years into his reign, he was removed, thus earning the dubious honour of having been deposed by both the Burmese and the British. On 16 September 1838, the British annexed the entire possessions of the erstwhile Ahom kingdom, bringing down the curtain on six centuries of the dynasty's rule.

It is perhaps not wholly accidental that the annexation of the Ahom kingdom coincided with the growing realisation in the corridors of the Company Raj power in London and India that Assam tea was a serious rival to Chinese tea. Tea from China, obtained in exchange for opium from India, was the business that had built the Company's fortunes. In 1833 the Company lost its vital monopoly on the tea trade with China. On 24 January 1834, Lord William Bentinck, as Governor General of India, issued a minute constituting a committee in Calcutta, 'for the purpose of submitting a plan for the accomplishment of the introduction of tea culture in India, and for the superintendence of its execution'.[16] The secretary of that committee went to China and returned in January 1835 with casks of tea seeds. Meanwhile, Captain Francis

Jenkins, an officer posted in Assam, had received from one of his subordinates, Lieutenant Charlton, who was posted at Sadiya in Upper Assam, a letter accompanied by a jar of leaves and a box of seeds of the tea plant that grew wild there. These he forwarded to Nathaniel Wallich, the botanist heading the committee established by Lord Bentinck, who concluded that the plant was indeed tea—and the committee officially reported this to Lord Bentinck on Christmas Eve 1834.[17] Wallich and two other experts arrived a few months later to study the plant in its natural habitat and assess the suitability of the area for the cultivation of tea. They reported favourably on both, as a result of which an experimental tea garden was established in Upper Assam. A small sample from this garden reached London in 1836. The first full shipment of twelve chests of Assam tea, of 40 lb each, was ready for despatch from the office of the Calcutta Tea Committee by March 1838, and reached London in November, to great excitement.[18] When eight of these were put up at auction, 'A competition of an unusual character ensued, which raised the price far beyond the most sanguine expectation that had been entertained.'[19]

The man who had overseen the growing of the tea crop in that experimental garden in Assam, the first 'Superintendent of Tea Culture', a Scot named Charles Bruce, left a short account of his pioneering efforts with a long title: *An Account of the Manufacture of the Black Tea as Now Practised at Suddeya in Upper Assam by the Chinamen Sent Thither for That Purpose. With Some Observations of the Culture of the Plant in China, and its Growth in Assam*. Published in 1838, this provided a descriptive account of the process of turning tea leaves into tea. It also contained 'A Dialogue between Mr C. A. Bruce and the China Black-Tea Makers', in which he quizzed them on the plant itself, how it was sown, where it best grew, how often to pluck it and so on. These were Chinese experts who had been brought in to cultivate the plant in Assam.

The only locals who had a culture of drinking tea at that time were the tribe called Singpho, who are known as the Kachin in Myanmar and the Jingpo in Yunnan in China. 'The Singphos have known and drank the Tea for many years, but they make it in a very different way from what the Chinese do', wrote Bruce:

> These Singphos pretend to be great judges of Tea. All their country abounds with the plant, but they are very jealous and will give no information where it is to be found, like the Muttack people. All the Singpho territories are overrun with wood jungle, and if only the underwood was cleared, they would make a noble Tea country. The soil is well adapted for the plant.[20]

The type of soil in the areas controlled by the 'Muttack people' of Bruce's telling was also in tea country. Most of these 'Muttack people' were the Moamarias, who had overthrown Ahom rule and carved out a little kingdom of their own, in the areas around what is now the town of Tinsukia, under a 'Bar Senapati', or 'big general', named Sarbananda Singha in 1805. At the time of Bruce's writing around 1836, Sarbananda Singha's son, Matibar Barsenapati, ruled the territory. 'The Muttack country, which I have traversed most, appears to me to be one vast Tea country, and I feel confident that not one half of its Tea tracts have been yet discovered', writes Bruce, adding that 'The whole of the soil of the Muttack country appears well adapted for Tea; I have taken particular notice of it, digging and examining it at every place where I have stopped. Great numbers of the tea tracts have been cut down by the natives in sheer ignorance and converted into paddy fields.'[21] He continues:

> South of the Burro Dihing river is situated Rajah Purandah Sing's country... There is plenty of tea in Rajah Purandah's country, but he is too lazy to trouble himself about it; he is not even acquainted with those places laid down in my map. I have lately heard of a very extensive tract in his country, said to be as large as a dozen tracts put together... All these tracts can be enlarged almost to any extent from the numerous seedlings that are found amongst the Tea plants, from the great number of seeds that can be collected every year, and from the immense number of cuttings that may be planted.[22]

The auction in London had established a high price for Assam tea. Bruce's report on the great suitability of Upper Assam for tea cultivation, and the unsuitability of the native rulers for the task, probably sealed the territory's fate. Matibar Barsenapati passed away in January 1839. After his death, the British authorities proposed dividing his domains and taking over the tea-growing areas known then as 'tea barees'.[23] The late king's counsellors refused those terms. What Bruce called 'Rajah Purandah Sing's country' had already been annexed in September 1838 and, subsequently, the adjacent Motok and Singpho areas were also annexed to British India.

The coming of the tea industry meant the clearing of uncultivated lands—labelled as wastelands—and forests for tea plantations. New rules were framed to parcel away wastelands—which often meant very useful land that was not under permanent cultivation—to planters on 45-year leases. The minimum size of the land grant would be 100 acres, and a quarter of this land would be revenue-free in perpetuity. Investors were naturally excited at the prospects. A new company, 'The Assam', was formed in London in 1839 with a nominal capital of a million sterling. Meanwhile, the firm of Carr, Tagore and Company in Calcutta had also set up a Bengal Tea Association and made preparations to enter the business. The London and Calcutta businessmen decided to join forces, and an amalgamated Assam Company was constituted. 'In 1840 they commenced operations, on a scale of expense in keeping with the existing idea that the profits of the undertaking would be so rapid and so enormous, as to render any attempt at economy imprudent and unnecessary', wrote W. Nassau Lees in an account of the Indian industry in 1869:

> Under the exciting influence of this false idea the most extravagant expenses were incurred and that nothing might be wanting to promote the enterprise, Government liberally transferred to the Company its superintendent and two-thirds of its own plantations and establishments. But alas, for the vanity of human expectations! Both the Government and the Company were doomed to disappointment. The soil in one place was not selected with reference to the requirements of the plant—labour in another was insufficient—the cultivation in a third was bad—the superintendence in a fourth was inefficient—ignorance everywhere was rampant—and to crown all, the tea, when manufactured, was pronounced by the London brokers to be bad![24]

This series of shocks obviously had a terrible effect on the business. As Lees recounted:

> The Assam Company, having, by the most reckless mismanagement, thrown away £200,000, the whole of its called-up capital, and about £20,000 more, was reduced to a state of insolvency so nearly verging on bankruptcy that £20 shares were sold in the Calcutta market for less than one rupee. It was proposed to wind up its affairs... The prospects of tea in Assam, so bright in the commencement, were now dimmed almost to extinction; and had it not been for the energy and perseverance of a few individuals, it is possible that the cultivation of the plant would have been abandoned altogether.[25]

The person who saved the enterprise from abandonment was a man named Henry de Mornay of the Assam Company. As Lees explained:

> On visiting the plantations this gentleman found them so choked with weeds that not a single plant was visible. Large sowings had been very regularly made, but, unfortunately, had as regularly been suffered to be destroyed by the jungle and rank vegetation which springs up in Assam with magic rapidity. The Company's capital had literally been poured out upon the earth, and there allowed to rot.[26]

The task of turning forests into tea gardens would require more than just vast capital. It would also require vast labour—and there was very little of the latter to be found locally in an Assam that had been depopulated by repeated Burmese invasions. The workers would have to be shipped in, the planters and government realised. Fortunately for them, recent technological developments had made this feasible. Steamboat travel had started in India on a commercial scale with the India General Steam Navigation Company in 1844. It revolutionised travel. A government steamer service from Calcutta to Guwahati started in 1847. It ran only once every six weeks, but reduced travel times from a minimum of three months to a snappy sixteen days. The growing connections between Assam and British India transformed the economy, society and polity. Before the advent of tea plantations and steamboats, of corporations and British rule, rural life in most of what is today Northeast India had been lived without much use of something that would soon become indispensable: money. The integration of the region into the capitalist economy now began in earnest.

* * *

The practical men who ran the affairs of the East India Company, perhaps more interested in certain profits on earth rather than uncertain rewards in heaven, had initially kept missionaries away from most of their territories in India for fear that meddling in religion might hamper business. The proselytising zeal of evangelists, though, was not easily thwarted. Although British India, with its teeming millions of heathens and pagans, remained largely off limits to the missionaries, they nevertheless found a foothold in the Danish settlement of Serampore near Calcutta. In 1812, a pioneering American missionary, Adoniram Judson, arrived at the Serampore mission established by the British Baptist missionary William Carey. Here Judson converted to the Baptist faith by immersion in the waters of the Hooghly river. He then headed to Burma and began his missionary task. His lonely efforts found support when a couple arrived from Boston via Serampore to Moulmein in June 1833. Judson's wife had by then passed away, and the arrival of Nathan and Elizabeth Brown with their young daughter Sophia made a welcome addition to his little mission compound. The Browns immediately threw themselves into the task of learning the local Burmese language. Two years later, when they had acquired some mastery over it, they were suddenly called away elsewhere. 'On 8th June an important meeting of the mission was held', wrote Elizabeth Brown:

> It had long been a cherished hope of the Board at home, as well as the missionaries in Burma, to introduce the gospel among the Shans—an interesting family of tribes inhabiting unexplored regions to the north and east—and through them it was expected by inland routes to reach China, whose seaports were at that time sealed against foreigners.[27]

The Company Raj in India had meanwhile become more welcoming of missionaries in the intervening years after a new royal charter forced this in 1813. As Elizabeth wrote:

> A proposal was now made by the Rev. W. H. Pearce of the English Baptist Mission in Calcutta, and several other friends of missions in Bengal, that the American Baptists should commence a work among these people in Assam, this country having become a part of the British dominions at the close of the Burman war. The proposal was the result of a communication received by Mr C. E. (afterwards Sir Charles) Trevelyan, one of the secretaries of the East India government, from Major Jenkins, Commissioner-general of Assam, inviting missionaries to come to Assam and promising them protection and assistance. The invitation was accepted, and Mr Brown was set apart to the task, to be accompanied by a printer with a press.[28]

The printer who accompanied them was a man named O. T. Cutter, along with his wife. They made their way to Calcutta on a merchant ship, and then began the more arduous journey to Assam in three boats that left Calcutta on 20 November 1835. The route was down the Hooghly, through the Sundarbans delta, and up the Jamuna and Brahmaputra rivers into Assam. By 15 January the following year they had reached Goalpara. Another month later, they were still travelling. 'Feb 15, Monday. We left Bishnath [Biswanath] on Saturday, but having a strong head wind and considerable rain, did not get on far', Elizabeth Brown recorded in her journal: 'March 2. Met Drs. Wallich, McLelland and Griffiths from Calcutta, who have been in Sudiya [sic] for several months, employed by the English government, searching for the tea plant... Mr C. A. Bruce from Sudiya was with them.' It took them another twenty-one days to get to Sadiya, where they set foot on 23 March 1836. The journey from Calcutta to Sadiya in eastern Assam had taken them four dangerous and exhausting months.

They were in for a shock. They had travelled so far to 'introduce the gospel among the Shans'—but there were no Shans to be found in the vicinity. As Elizabeth writes:

> The people immediately around the missionaries were the valley Assamese, hence still another tongue must at once be learned. It was a written language, but without a dictionary or grammar, and there was no interpreter. Pointing to an object, Mr. and Mrs. Brown would catch the name from the lips of a native, and write the sound in Roman letters.[29]

In this manner, they quickly picked up a rudimentary vocabulary. They occupied houses left empty by earlier British residents—with the Browns living in the house recently vacated by Andrew Charlton, the man who had sent the first jar of tea leaves from Assam—and were spared the effort of building from scratch. They set about constructing a schoolhouse of bamboo, with Mrs Brown instructing the little boys who came to see these strange new creatures, and Mrs Cutter teaching the girls.

The first book for use in the new schools was prepared by Nathan Brown in January 1837. It was 'a tract consisting of the parables of Christ, which was put into immediate use as a textbook in the schools, the pupils daily committing to memory lessons from the parables'.[30]

Their lonely efforts were supplemented later that year by the much-awaited arrival of another missionary, Miles Bronson. Bronson had started the journey from Calcutta with a Mr Thomas, who had died on the way when a tree fell on his boat. Bronson, who had been severely ill, somehow survived. He brought with him a baggage boat that contained a treasure not seen before in that part of the world: a printing press—the machine for whose use the printer O. T. Cutter had been sent from Burma.

The arrival of that machine would have a fateful and decisive impact on the future political history of Assam. The press travelled with the missionary establishment from Sadiya—which they were compelled to leave after a deadly attack by the local Khampti tribe in 1839—to a place called Joypore on the opposite bank of the Brahmaputra not far from the Naga Hills, before finally making its way to Sivasagar in late 1843. *The Baptist Missionary Magazine* of July 1844 recorded the reason for moving the establishment and the missionaries there rather than to Guwahati:

> The station which has come most into competition with Sibsagar is Gowhatti, at the eastern extremity of Kamrup district, of which it is the capital. This is the capital indeed of all Assam, at the present time, being the residence of the Commissioner of the Province, and having a population of 15,000 to 20,000 inhabitants. The principal objections to Gowhatti were the comparative sparseness of the Assamese population in its neighbourhood, and, especially, the fact, according to our best means of judging, that the Assamese spoken in that vicinity is a corruption of the pure Assamese, bearing nearly as close resemblance to the Bengali as to the Ahom.[31]

The Browns and the Cutters therefore settled in Sivasagar, and Brown's work on translating the New Testament into 'pure' Assamese continued. An older version of the text, translated by an Assamese pundit named Atmaram Sarma, had already been published by the Serampore Mission Press under the name 'Dharmapustak' in 1813—thus becoming the first published book in the language—but Brown persisted with his edition, because the earlier text had, in his view, too many Bengali words. He also put together and published, in 1848, a slim volume that had a vast impact. It was titled, after Adoniram Judson's work on Burmese, *Grammatical Notices of the Asamese Language*. Although the very first line of the book's introduction, on its first page, is that 'The following Notices do not claim to be regarded as a Grammar of the Asamese Language', that is exactly what it became.[32] The lasting influence of his book came about, arguably, owing to his other great work: the monthly newspaper he founded and edited called *Orunodoi*, the first in the Assamese language.

In the years immediately following the annexation of the various kingdoms that became part of the British province of Assam, these areas had been added to the Bengal Presidency. A new system of administration was required and officers and clerks were deputed from nearby Bengal. The languages they used in transacting official business were the existing official languages of revenue and judicial administration of Bengal Presidency—Bengali, Hindustani and Odia—which had been selected by the British rulers in January 1838 to replace Persian, the language of administration of the Mughal empire and the early days of the Company Raj. It was however the use of Bengali in education that triggered protests. When the judge A. J. Moffatt Mills arrived in Assam in 1853 to prepare a report on the revenue administration of the area since its annexation, he received a petition on the issue of language from a writer who was published in *Orunodoi*, a pioneering stalwart of the Assamese language movement named Anadaram Dhekiyal Phukan, seeking restoration of the Assamese language in education. 'Assamese is described by Mr. Brown, the best scholar in the province, differing in more respects than agreeing with the Bengalee, and I think we made a great mistake in directing that all business must be transacted in Bengalee, and the Assamese must acquire it', Mills wrote, while recommending Phukan's proposition for the favourable consideration of the Council of Education.[33]

The position of the missionaries was laid out in a letter from Miles Bronson, who was then posted at Nowgong, to James Halliday, the Lieutenant-Governor of Bengal. In the letter, dated 13 November 1854, Bronson wrote:

> It is now nearly twenty years since the establishment of the American Mission in Assam... We have also established two Printing Presses, and issued the whole New Testament, portions of the Old Testament, a number of elementary books for schools, and a monthly newspaper, all in the Vernacular. But in the prosecution of our efforts, and especially in the preparation of useful works in the Vernacular, one sore discouragement attends us. I refer to the substitution of Bengali for Assamese in all the Schools and Educational efforts of the Government, so that, instead of being able to bring our own Presses, and books and schools to act in concert with the efforts of Government, we find ourselves less favourably situated than we had hoped, for effecting immediate and permanent good for this long-neglected people.[34]

'Bengali', wrote Bronson, 'is not the Vernacular of Assam.'[35]

William Robinson, the Inspector of Government Schools in Assam at the time, and author of the first Assamese grammar, disagreed.[36] In a long note titled 'Some Remarks on the Use of Bengali in the Government Schools in Assam', he pointed out that the colloquial Bengali differed so much from place to place that 'Bengalis coming from distantly-situated zillahs are unable to understand one another except through the medium of the written language, or the language of the books.' Robinson argued that Brown's system of spelling had tended to widen the differences between Bengali and Assamese: 'It professes, I believe, to be a phonetic system, but where there is such a variety in the modes of pronunciation, it is to be inferred that Mr Brown has adopted that most common to his part of the country, and this has been set up as the standard.' Drawing a parallel with the English language, he provided an example of the dialect spoken by Lancashire peasants in the sentence 'Theyme sum uth granddist carpits has avur un clapt mee een un', and asked whether there was not 'some difference between this language and that used by Johnson'.[37] 'I am not aware of any objection having been made to me by any Native of the Province, Anondoram Phoken excepted, to the use of Bengali in the Government schools', Robinson wrote.[38]

A war of letters followed, with all the missionaries joining in to assert that the people of Assam simply did not understand the Bengali language, and Robinson firm in his view that the differences were those between dialects and not languages. He provided an example of a book, 'Friend of Young Assam', published by Anandaram Dhekial Phukan in 1849. A chapter of this was subsequently published as an extract in *Orunodoi*, the monthly newspaper run by Nathan Brown—the only newspaper in the province – in December 1852. The original book used spellings identical or similar to Bengali; the version published in *Orunodoi* was in the Assamese promoted by Brown.[39] Robinson added that by Brown's own admission, for the 'Dhekeries of Kamroop, the Kacharies, and other Tribes', Assamese was not the local vernacular. These sections then constituted about 890,000 from a population of 1,120,000—more than three-quarters of the population.

The British administration of the time found Robinson's arguments the more convincing, but the seeds of an enduring conflict of linguistic identities between the Bengali and Assamese had been sown. This would blow up in subsequent years, and remain a crucial force shaping the state's identity politics up to the present.

* * *

For the colonial administration, the issue of the language of education was soon overtaken by more urgent political concerns, an early intimation of which came in the form of two petitions that the judge Moffatt Mills had received during his Assam visit in 1853. One was from Kandarpeswar Singha, a descendant of the last Ahom king, Purandar Singha. The other was from Maniram Dutta Barbhandar Baruah, an enterprising aristocrat of the former kingdom popularly known as Maniram Dewan, because he had been a 'dewan', or agent, of the Assam Company that pioneered tea plantations. Both petitions requested restoration of the Ahom monarchy in Upper Assam.

Maniram wrote:

> By the stoppage of such cruel practices as extracting the eyes, cutting off noses and ears, and the forcible abduction of virgins from their homes, and by the removal of all wayside duties ... the British Government has earned for itself inestimable praise and renown. But by the introduction into the Province of new customs, numerous courts, an unjust system of taxation, an objectionable treatment of the Hill Tribes ... neither the British Government nor their subjects have gained any benefit.[40]

He proposed the reintroduction, with modifications, of the customs and institutions of the old days. One of the modifications he sought was the introduction of the office of Mahamantri (or Prime Minister), who would aid the king in running the country. Naturally, this was an office that he hoped to fill himself.

The petitions fell on deaf ears. Maniram, disappointed but persisting nonetheless, made the long journey to Calcutta to try and plead the case before the Lieutenant-Governor of Bengal. He was there when the sepoys of the British East India Company began to mutiny against their employers. 'What he could not achieve by prayers and entreaties, Maniram resolved to accomplish by sword and sword alone', the historian H. K. Barpujari. wrote: 'Through his letters, couched in the most seditious terms, Maniram goaded Kandarpeswar Singha to unfurl the standard of revolt with the aid of the local sepoys and through his friend Madhu Mallick, a Bengali muktear [a kind of lawyer] he prepared the ground for insurrection.'[41] Mallick arrived in Jorhat from Calcutta and began to 'assemble certain of Booroahs [Baruahs] and Phookans around Joorhat and acquaint them the contents of Maniram's letter'. Baruah and Phookan were titles of the erstwhile Ahom aristocracy; the holders of those offices, who had lost their former privileges under the new dispensation, were being sounded out for restoration of the monarchy. One among them, Mahesh Chandra Phookan (or Pealie Phookan), was deputed to go to Sivasagar to recruit more nobles to their cause.

A rebellion against East India Company rule was then stirring through large parts of the country. In 1848, the British Governor General, Lord Dalhousie, had introduced a 'doctrine of lapse' that enabled the annexation of princely states whose rulers did not have natural heirs, thus contributing to the grouses of the old elites. To this was added the growing discontent of both Hindus and Muslims among the sepoys serving in the Company's army over issues related to religious taboos. A rumour had spread that the cartridges for the new Enfield muskets they were to use were greased with the tallow of beef, forbidden for Hindus, and the lard of pork, forbidden for Muslims. By April 1857 the sepoys were up in arms.

In Assam, the uprising was planned to coincide with the annual Durga Puja festivities in the autumn, when the goddess Durga is worshipped in numerous public ceremonies in towns and villages. The British officials, however, got wind of it before it could be put into action:

> The Commissioner of Assam was roused from his torpor when in the middle of August 1857, he received from Holroyd the intelligence that several officers of the Assam Light Infantry with the detachment at Golaghat had entered into a conspiracy with

> the young prince Kandarpeswar offering him the assistance of the regiment to reinstate him on his throne and maintain the country for him.[42]

A small European force of 104 men was urgently sent to Assam. In the meantime, the ranking officer on the spot, Major Hannay, called in detachments of Rabha, Manipuri, Nepali and other 'non-Hindustani' troops to guard the military lines at headquarters. The would-be mutineers were apprehended before they could put their plan into action. Kandarpeswar Singha himself was arrested, as were Maniram Dewan and his fellow conspirators, including Peali Phookan, Madhu Mallick and a Muslim man from Jorhat named Farmud Ali. Dewan and Phookan were hanged. Mallick got life imprisonment. Ali received what was a terrible punishment then, and is a dream retirement plan now. He was exiled to the Andaman Islands.

* * *

The failed revolt of 1857 heralded the end of East India Company rule. The following year, the control of India was taken over by the British Crown. Administrative authority in London shifted from the East India Company to the office of the Secretary of State for India, while legislative authority was now with the British parliament. In India, the Governor General, now with the added title of Viceroy, represented the Crown and ruled with civil, military and legislative powers. The first step towards some form of representation in government came soon after. The Indian Councils Act of 1861 transformed the Viceroy's Council into a kind of cabinet with executive and legislative powers. Provincial legislative councils, which had existed until 1853, were also revived. The foreign rulers felt the need for a 'native element' in the Viceroy's Council; the Maharaja of Patiala and two other royals, Raja Dinkar Rao of Gwalior and Raja Deo Narayan Singh of Benaras, were admitted to the council as members. Membership was by nomination, with the Viceroy, the Secretary of State and the Crown doing the nominating. Naturally, rulers who had supported the British during the revolt of 1857 were preferred. The idea that commoners, and natives of India at that, could rule themselves was still quite inconceivable to the European rulers. They could, however, keep their neighbourhoods and villages clean—and that is where the beginnings of representative democracy in India began, at the bottom of the administrative and legislative ladder, with experiments in municipal administration. The Bengal Municipal Act was passed in 1864. Madras and Bombay passed similar legislation. In Punjab, Lieutenant-Governor Sir Robert Montgomery introduced municipal committees in all the principal inhabited places. The committee members were to be selected from among themselves by the local people.[43]

The political changes, from municipal committees at one end to the British Crown and parliament at the other, came at a time when the economy was changing. New technologies had come that changed the meaning of 'far' and 'near'. The journey to Assam from Calcutta that had taken Nathan and Elizabeth Brown four months in 1835 was now only sixteen days by steamer. The frequency of steamer services had also increased to once a month instead of once every six weeks. Railway lines had been laid at places across the country. The tea plantations, after their initial struggles, were now profitable, and there was a rush of capital into the business. The expansion required more labour, and this labour was acquired through 'coolie-catchers' who lured poor tribals from the Chota Nagpur plateau with false promises of the great wealth that awaited them at the end of the journey to Assam. The population of Assam which had been decimated during the years of Burmese invasions—in 1826 the population of the Brahmaputra valley was estimated at 830,000—rose rapidly.[44] Tea garden labourers were by far the largest number of new immigrants.

In 1872, the first census report for India was released. It had force-fitted the chaotic variety of India's peoples into neat categories based on religion, language and caste. Assamese, thanks largely to the pioneering efforts of the American Baptist missionaries, was finally recognised by the British administration as a separate language rather than a dialect of Bengali. The Browns had left years ago, but Miles Bronson, their old colleague, was still at work in Assam. In March 1872 he presented a memorandum on behalf of the Assamese community of Nowgong to the Lieutenant-Governor of Bengal, Sir George Campbell, arguing yet again that Assamese was the vernacular of the people, was taught in the missionary schools, and had books and a dictionary published in the language. The following month, the long struggle finally bore fruit: on 9 April 1873, Campbell ordered that Assamese should be introduced in the courts and schools of the Brahmaputra valley.

By then, the British rulers of Bengal and India were seriously examining the prospect of separating Assam from Bengal for administrative reasons. Campbell found his duties too onerous. As the 1872–73 *Report on the Administration of Bengal* said:

> It has always been the Lieutenant-Governor's decided conviction that if the Bengal provinces are not to be divided or very largely reduced, it is most necessary to strengthen the Government: so great a government cannot efficiently be carried on by one man alone. The Government of India has preferred the alternative of diminishing the Government, and Sir George Campbell has not objected to the proposal which has been made of separating Assam and the adjacent districts from Bengal. To the province of Assam, it is proposed to add Goalparah and the Garo Hills to the west, and Sylhet and Cachar on the south, with Muneepore on the south-east.[45]

Steps towards a bout of map-making followed. The next year, the Bengal Eastern Frontier Regulation Act of 1873 was passed. It was the first law passed specifically for the territories that subsequently became Northeast India, and like the Punjab Frontier Crossing Regulation of 1873 that was applicable at the western end of the British Indian empire, it sought to control the movement of British subjects out of the administered areas into tribal territories, and the movement of people from the tribal areas into British-administered lands. Tribal raids to carry away people as slaves, or to take their heads in headhunting raids, were then a common problem across large tracts of the eastern frontier of Bengal. The booming plantation economy meant that tea gardens were now pushing into the foothills on all sides of the Brahmaputra valley, in what were traditionally tribal lands, and this often provoked retaliatory raids. Moreover, while slavery had been abolished by the East India Company Raj in 1843, the decision was naturally unpopular with those who held slaves—such as the chieftains among several tribes in Northeast India, or what was then called the eastern frontier of Bengal. The carrying away of British subjects as slaves led to clashes that inevitably ended, after a spiral of escalation, in costly punitive expeditions by columns of soldiers marching into the hills. The Bengal Eastern Frontier Act tried to reduce these problems by demarcating an 'inner line', to go beyond which its subjects would require an 'inner line permit'. There was no formal 'outer line' to match the inner line; the external boundary of British India in several places was still rather vague, not least because places such as the far ends of what are now Arunachal Pradesh and Eastern Nagaland were still unexplored blanks on the map.

Assam became a separate province under a Chief Commissioner in 1874. As planned, Goalpara, Sylhet, Cachar and the Garo Hills were added to it at this time, though the idea of adding Manipur as well was dropped. The area of the newly created Chief Commissionership of Assam was 67,267 square kilometres. Its total population was 4,132,019, out of which the three districts of Sylhet, Cachar and Goalpara, which were transferred from Bengal to the new province, accounted for 21,924 square kilometres of territory and a population of 2,702,327 souls, as per the census of 1872.[46] The transfer of these territories with their large Bengali-speaking populations to Assam pleased neither the Bengalis nor the Assamese. An association of big landlords in Goalpara, the Goalpara Zamindars' Association, a Sylhet People's Association and a Cachar People's Association all petitioned the government against the merger of their districts with Assam.

After the transfer, the tensions between the Bengali and Assamese linguistic identities grew. An Asamiya Sahitya Sabha (Assamese Literary Society) had been founded in Calcutta in 1872.[47] In 1888, an organisation called the Axomiya Bhaxa Unnati Xadhini Xobha (Association for the Development of the Assamese Language) was founded in Calcutta by Assamese students who were studying in what was then the capital city of colonial India. The establishment of this organisation is said to be a landmark in the history of Assamese language and literature. Among its most important projects was the standardisation of the Assamese language.[48] This and the Asamiya Sahitya Sabha were the forerunners of a powerful organisation called the Asam Sahitya Sabha (Assam Literary Society) founded in 1917 that subsequently played a central role in the state's politics of culture and identity.[49]

2

THE POLITICS OF REPRESENTATION

WORLD WARS, PARTITIONS AND INDEPENDENCE

Among the things the Assam government concerned itself with in the early years of its existence was the encouragement of local self-government. Elections in the United Kingdom had brought a Liberal government to power in London. A new Viceroy, Lord Ripon, of suitably reformist temperament, was sent to rule India in 1880. He passed a resolution in 1882 that gave a major impetus to the establishment of local self-government across India. District councils and local boards were established. The elective principle had already been tried piecemeal in different provinces at the municipal level. This now came to be applied at scale. This top-down gift of democracy was supplemented by the stirrings for representative politics of another kind. It came about, as is often the case, as a result of unintended consequences. In 1879, a senior officer who had spent his lifetime serving the British Raj in India was superseded and sidelined. Generally reputed to be an upright, honest and competent officer, as well as a keen ornithologist, Allan Octavian Hume had apparently managed to offend the then Viceroy, Lord Lytton, by his excessively frank speech. After his retirement, believing the government to be out of touch with the Indian people, Hume set about establishing what would become the Indian National Congress—the political party that later led India to independence.

At the time of its founding, neither Hume himself nor the Indians who were part of the organisation seem to have had any notion that India's independence as a country was possible or even desirable. The first speaker on the first resolution at the first session of the Congress held in Bombay in December 1885 was Subramania Aiyar of Madras. After declaring that 'by a merciful dispensation of Providence' Britain had rescued India from centuries of external aggression and internal strife, Aiyar summed up the benefits of British rule 'in one remarkable fact, that for the first time in the history of the Indian populations there is to be beheld the phenomenon of national unity among them, of a sense of national existence'.[1] He was commending the British Raj for having invented the idea of an Indian nation. The Indian as a political identity followed.

The Congress sought a voice for Indians in the councils of power. Responding to its pressures, the British parliament passed a new version of the India Councils Act in 1892 that increased the representation and powers of different interest groups, such as associations based on common professional, commercial or territorial interests, in the provincial and central legislative councils.

A robust press, both in English and in local vernaculars, had meanwhile developed across India. An educated elite, mostly male—women going to schools and colleges was still rare—had emerged. Many of this new elite were fluent in English, and adopted the fashions of Englishmen, discarding their traditional 'dhoti' wraps for trousers, and their long, flowing 'kurtas' for shirts. Sons of wealthy Brahmins changed their hairdos, dispensing with the pig-tails that had for centuries been a symbol of caste pride. Home decor had also begun to change; the dining table with chairs was challenging the age-old practice of eating seated cross-legged on the floor. Some brave and wealthy souls from the higher castes even broke the taboo that prohibited sea voyages, which it was believed caused Hindus to lose caste. Many indigents from the lower castes and classes, driven by poverty and with little to lose, also broke this taboo by signing up to become indentured labour in the far corners of the empire. Taboos of food and drink, mandated by religion and caste, however, remained. The tastes of the white rulers were beyond the pale for both the Brahmins, who in most parts of India largely abjured meat, and the Muslims, who ate no pork. The cow, of course, was holy to Hindus, who called it 'cow mother', and eating beef was therefore a sin of the worst kind.

On the consumption of one item, however, the British administration and the new elites found themselves in broad agreement. Consuming opium had been a part of local culture in Assam at least since the days of the Mughal invasion led by Raja Ram Singh in 1669. People grew the poppy flower and made their own drugs. The British government decided to put a stop to this. Local cultivation was banned, and a system of supply from government depots against cash payments was introduced. The peasants did not like this; they did not have cash to spare, and couldn't fathom having to pay for what had always been theirs to grow for free. Their unhappiness increased further as the revenues demanded of them kept rising. They broke out in revolt in December 1893. Although they were subdued by force of arms, the government reduced its revenue demands. The opium habit, however, was gradually driven from socially acceptable norm to criminal opprobrium. The new rulers demanded workers who would jump to it, working as wage labour or cultivating their lands and thus increasing revenues; lazy addicts were useless for the new capitalist economy.

However, the government was also starting to face the opposite problem, that of excessive hard work and enthusiasm on the part of some native people. The new elites emerging with degrees from the colleges and universities established after the revolt of 1857 had notions of equality and freedom in advance of the times. Particularly in Bengal, where a section of the Hindu Bengalis had been early adopters of English education—the old Muslim Bengali elite stuck to Persian and eschewed the new system of education for a generation or two longer—there were stirrings of unrest. The natives wanted equal opportunity for representation in the elite Indian Civil Services bureaucracy which administered the country. They wanted to become lawyers and judges, and those who became judges wanted to pass judgments even in cases involving white people, upsetting the then widely accepted notion of white racial supremacy.

The new Viceroy, Lord Curzon, embarked upon a fresh round of map-making to cut Bengal and its troublesome inhabitants down to size. Despite protests against the scheme from the moment it was first announced in 1903, he went ahead with dividing the territory on the basis of religion, between a predominantly Muslim east and a mainly Hindu west. Assam was tagged on to East Bengal to form the province of Eastern Bengal and Assam. Protests immediately began across both Bengal and Assam. The Indian National Congress was drawn into these protests and was transformed by the experience from being a party of middle-class gentlemen, politely requesting relatively minor reforms, into a party of freedom fighters with a mass base seeking radical change. In Bengal, a boycott of foreign goods and a 'swadeshi', or national movement, began. At the 1906 Congress session held in Calcutta, for the first time the demand for 'swaraj' or self-rule, meaning independence, was adopted. 'Vande Mataram', meaning 'hail the mother', a slogan from a Bengali novel by Bankim Chandra Chattopadhyay, became popular and was banned. The painter Abanindranath Tagore, a brother of the writer Rabindranath Tagore, painted an image of Bengal as a Hindu goddess, which he initially called 'Banga Mata' or 'Mother Bengal'. The original painting had no map in the background, but it soon morphed into Bharat Mata, and was eventually appropriated by Hindu nationalists with the expansive cartographic imagery so dear to them now.

The protests against the partition of Bengal were led by the Hindu Bengali intelligentsia and had a distinctly Hindu tone. Muslim opinion, however, largely supported the divide, which devolved power to Dhaka away from Calcutta. In 1906, India's Muslim elites came together in Dhaka to form the All-India Muslim League, with Khwaja Salimullah, the Nawab of Dhaka and the architect of the organisation, as one of its vice-presidents. The Aga Khan, Sultan Muhammad Shah, who did not attend the event, was made president in absentia. The stage was now set for the accelerating spiral of events that would eventually lead to the partition of India, and of Assam. There, in April 1903, an organisation called the Assam Association had been formed 'to give its loyal support to the British Government to ameliorate the condition generally of the people of Assam by taking up social, commercial and economic questions, and ventilate their grievances or take such measures as may lead to their removal'.[2] Its first president was the zamindar of Gauripur estate, Raja Prabhat Chandra Baruah.[3] Jagannath Baruah, leader of an older organisation from Jorhat in Upper Assam, the Jorhat Sarvajanik Sabha, was vice-president. The general secretary, described by historian H. K. Barpujari as the 'soul of the Association', was an energetic man named Manik Chandra Barua. With the partition of Bengal, and its own amalgamation with East Bengal, the Assam Association, which had carefully avoided any mention of taking up political questions in its founding document, now found itself compelled to declare its opposition to the scheme.

There was also strong protest from another quarter in Assam. Since 1874, when Sylhet became part of Assam, the province had comprised two river valleys—the Brahmaputra valley, dominated by Assamese speakers, and the Surma or Barak valley, dominated by speakers of the Sylheti dialect of Bengali. The leading political light of the Surma valley at that time was a man named Bipin Chandra Pal, one of a nationally renowned troika of hardliners known as 'Lal, Bal, Pal'. 'Lal' was the shortened name of Lala Lajpat Rai, from Punjab. 'Bal' stood for Bal Gangadhar Tilak, from Bombay Presidency. This trio popularised the ideas of 'swaraj', or independence, across the country. Pal, then a Congress leader of national stature, travelled around the country spreading the message of what was then called the 'New Movement', the mantra of 'swadeshi' and 'swaraj'. Naturally, he included his home turf of Sylhet in Assam in his travels.

The government decided that there was a need to 'control and canalise the now fast-flowing current of Indian nationalism'. The chosen method was further reform of the Indian Councils Act, and this came to fruition in 1909. The new liberal Secretary of State for India, John Morley, and conservative Governor General, Lord Minto, agreed 'on the one hand that extremism should be firmly checked and on the other that a new move should be made to satisfy the moderates and ensure their continued cooperation with the Government'. They decided to recognise and legalise the principle of election for both the Central and the Provincial Councils, and to enlarge them all once more, conceding majorities for nominated and elected members rather than government officials in the Provincial Councils. Voting and membership were restricted to adult males. The councils, which previously had no real powers, were newly authorised to discuss and pass resolutions on any matter of public interest, including the government's budget policy. According to rules made under the act, besides local government bodies and universities, chambers of commerce, landowners and minority religious communities, of which the most important were the Muslims and Sikhs, were represented. Crucially, responding to a petition from the Muslim League's founding president, the Aga Khan, separate electorates were constituted for Muslims—with historic consequences.

The unrest created by the partition of Bengal persisted. The new Viceroy, Lord Hardinge, proposed a fresh redrawing of maps to put an end to the agitation. In 1911, the capital of India was shifted out of Calcutta to Delhi. A grand durbar was held in that city at which King George V announced the reconstitution of Bengal as a unified province under a governor. Bihar, Orissa and the Chota Nagpur plateau, which had previously been made parts of British Bengal, were separated from it. So, once again, was Assam, which now became a province with its own legislative council. The territories added to it from Bengal in 1874—Sylhet, Goalpara and Cachar—remained with it. This did not please all sections. In Sylhet, there were protests in favour of amalgamation with Bengal, but the government was done with placating protesters. The demand for reunion which they made in a memorial to the Viceroy, Lord Northbrooke, on 10 August 1874, was rejected by the government.[4]

Assam thus continued its journey with a large Bengali population transferred to the province, along with their lands, and a growing resentment among the Assamese against these people who seemed to take up all the sought-after clerical jobs in the colonial administration. To make matters worse, from their perspective, an influx of Bengali Muslim peasants from the district of Mymensingh in Eastern Bengal had begun when Assam and East Bengal were joined together as one province in 1905.

* * *

Ever since the early days of its rule in Assam, the British administration had been troubled by the shortage of labour in the province. The initial struggle had been to import labour for the tea plantations, but in time, the unexploited economic potential from cultivation of rice and jute in the vast floodplains of the Brahmaputra made the import of cultivators for these crops lucrative. The need for labour found mention in administrative reports. 'Sir George Campbell [then Lieutenant-Governor] thoroughly recognizes that the great want of Assam is population', noted the *Report on the Administration of Bengal, 1872–73*, when the province of Assam was being formed.[5]

The administration's hopes that the population shortage would be addressed by cultivators from neighbouring areas of Bengal migrating to Assam were belied in the initial years. The census report for 1891, authored by the then Census Commissioner, the historian Edward Gait, noted the enormous demand for labour of the tea industry, coal mines and the Public Works Department, and complained:

> It might have been thought that the amount of cultivable land, the fertility of the soil, and the low rents prevailing would have induced some portion at least of the overcrowded cultivators of Bengal to find their way to Assam and take up land there. But this does not appear to be the case.[6]

Suddenly, after 1905, when Assam and East Bengal were joined into one province, the situation began to change. The census report for 1911 for the first time noted the vast improvement in communications to Assam owing to the extension of railway lines and an 'extraordinary in-course of settlers to the char lands of Goalpara from the Bengal districts of Mymensingh, Pabna, Bogra and Rangpur'.[7] The number of such immigrants was reckoned at around 51,000. The recent constitutional reforms had created a legislative council for Assam in the new capital, Shillong, and the matter of this immigration came up for discussion there.

The 1911 Census also wrestled with a question of great and enduring political significance: the definition of the people who could be called Assamese. Referring back to the previous census report, the Census Commissioner J. McSwiney wrote:

> an Assamese is not necessarily a person born in Assam, for the term can properly be applied only to a native of the Brahmaputra Valley and even there excludes all descendants of immigrants: nor can we identify him by his language, because large numbers of coolies and ex-coolies, especially in the eastern end of the Valley, have returned Assamese as their language.[8]

His report had a table on 'Indigenous Castes and Tribes' organised, as the name suggests, by caste and tribe rather than by linguistic community—an important distinction, since Hindus from any linguistic community can belong to the same caste.

The question of who is Assamese is still being debated in the politics of the state today. Several successive governments of the state, up to and including the present one, have attempted to find an acceptable legal definition. Over time, the matter has become one of critical importance to the lives of millions of inhabitants of Assam, as the politics of evicting illegal immigrants has become central to the state's politics.

Back then, bigger questions were about to roil the country and reshape the human world. The First World War began in 1914, and India was drawn into the war effort. Men and materials were sent from everywhere. Northeast India, too, contributed. It was the first exposure to the wider world for tribesmen from villages in the hills, who having generally never ventured even as far as 'mainland' India, were suddenly ferried to distant countries. In the midst of this, a Gujarati lawyer and activist based in South Africa named Mohandas Gandhi returned to his homeland and joined the Indian National Congress. Two years later, in 1917, a year marked by the Russian Revolution, Gandhi set off for his first major political action in India to a place called Champaran in Bihar, to lead the resistance of peasant indigo cultivators against their overlords.

This became the first successful example of Gandhi's methods of peaceful mass resistance and civil disobedience in India.

The tumultuous events around the world accelerated the pace of political change. Repression and resistance fuelled one another. In 1919, there was the infamous Jallianwala Bagh massacre in Amritsar, when soldiers shot dead at least 379 unarmed civilians who were protesting a new law that allowed for imprisonment without trial. The country erupted in outrage. Britain's parliament responded by passing a new Government of India Act. In his royal proclamation issued on 23 December 1919, King George V, whose titles included that of Emperor of India, announced: 'The Act which has now become law entrusts elected representatives of the people with a definite share in government and points the way to full representative Government hereafter.' The franchise was still restricted to lobbies selected for their wealth and social influence, but the principle of representation by separate electorates for communal minorities was extended from only Muslims to Sikhs, Indian Christians and Europeans. A bicameral legislature at the centre came into existence, which became the kernel of the future Indian parliament. The strength of provincial assemblies was also increased.

Assam was initially not considered a fit case for extension of this scheme. The Assam Association took up the matter. There were also fresh demands from leaders in Sylhet and Goalpara for separation from Assam and reunification with Bengal. The movement had the support of the zamindars of Goalpara, among whom Prabhat Chandra Baruah, the zamindar of Gauripur estate and founder president of the Assam Association, was a leading light; Baruah now demanded that Goalpara return to Bengal. The separatist movement became a life and death question which the Assam Association was called upon to tackle when it met at Goalpara under the leadership of Tarun Ram Phookun on 27–29 December 1918. Feelings were then running so high between the Assamese and local Bengalis that the latter not only boycotted the reception but withheld cooperation with the organisers of the conference.[9] The Assam Association when it was founded had included both Bengali and Assamese speakers. By this time, almost all Bengali-speaking members had already severed their connections with the Assam Association.

A sense of growing threat due to unchecked immigration of Bengali-speaking Muslim peasants from Mymensingh was also building up. The Census of 1921 clarified the scale of what had become a problem of plenty. 'The influx of immigrants from Eastern Bengal has formed the subject of questions and unfavourable comment in the Legislative Council by members representing certain Assam Valley constituencies', Census Commissioner G. T. Lloyd wrote.[10] 'In the last decade the movement has extended far up the Valley and the colonists now form an appreciable element of the population in all the four lower and central districts', he continued. 'About 85 per cent are Muhammadans and 15 per cent Hindus.' The population of these settlers in the Brahmaputra valley had increased from 54,000 in the 1911 Census to 258,000 in the 1921 Census: 'If we add the children born after arrival in Assam ... the total number of settlers in the valley must come to at least 300,000.' The census also recorded another number that was becoming increasingly important: the percentages of Bengali and Assamese speakers. The Bengalis had decreased from 48.1 per cent in the 1901 Census to 44.1 per cent in 1921. Curiously, the Assamese had also declined, from 22 per cent in 1901 to 21.6 per cent in 1921.[11]

The British authorities were initially quite pleased with the East Bengali peasant influx. 'They are hard-working and good cultivators who cannot fail to benefit the country', wrote Lloyd. A. H. W. Bentinck, the Deputy Commissioner of Kamrup, was more effusive. 'They have reclaimed and brought under permanent cultivation thousands of acres which the local cultivators had for generations past merely scratched with haphazard and intermittent crops or recognized as exigent of efforts beyond their inclination', he wrote.[12] Relations between the locals and the immigrants, Bentinck indicated, were not the best:

> They do not at present mix well with the local population: the latter in a great many instances sold the newcomers sarkari [government] lands at rates highly profitable to the sellers and

> the discovery of this has left a not unnatural soreness. The local cultivators on the other hand regarded the newcomers as savages, whose pernicious habits were only partially redeemed by their ignorance of local land-tenures.[13]

The district officials in several districts had found it necessary to come up with administrative measures to separate the two groups by a 'Line System' that demarcated areas where the new settlers were allowed to settle from those where they were not.

The issue found expression in the emerging popular politics. An organisation called the Axom Xonrokhwini Xobha (Assam Preservation Society) was formed by a local Congress leader named Ambikagiri Raychaudhuri in 1926 to promote Assamese interests.[14]

By the time the 1931 Census came around, the welcome for the immigrants, even among the British officials, had worn quite thin. The Census Commissioner now was an Indian Civil Services officer named C. S. Mullan. He began his report with the words, 'Mega biblion, said a famous librarian of the ancient library of Alexandria, mega kakon—a great book is a great evil.'[15] The 'great book' he had in mind was the one whose introduction he was writing, the census report of Assam for the years 1921 to 1931. Mullan's book would not meet the criteria for literary greatness—he probably used the word to indicate its size—but it did become the source of considerable trouble in the years and decades to come.

An examination of the population is the core concern of any such census, and naturally Mullan looked at the numbers. In the preceding decade of 1911–21, he noted, three factors had accounted for the increase in the population of Assam: '(i) The natural growth of the population, (ii) The large expansion of the tea industry which imported 769,000 coolies into the province, and (iii) The immigration of Eastern Bengal colonists and Nepalis.' Against this was the abnormal decrease of the population that had been wrought by the global influenza pandemic of 1918–19, 'which was estimated to have carried off 200,000 people'. The net result was that 'the population of Assam had increased in 1911–21 by 13.2 per cent or 929,725 persons of whom 411,941 were gained by migration and 517,784 represented the increase in natural population. Immigration, therefore, accounted for nearly half the total provincial increase in that decade.'[16]

The population in the next decade of 1921–31, for which he was writing the census report, had increased by a record 1,257,611 persons. Mullan concluded, after looking at the increases in the various regions of Assam, that 'It appears prima facie that the large increase at the present census is due much more to the natural growth of population than it was in the previous decade.' He estimated that of the 1,257,611-person increase in population, 1,135,963 was due to natural increase and the gain by migration was 121,648, and concluded that 'the gain by migration has been small and the variation in the natural population has been large'. In other words, the abnormal spike in migration in the decade of 1911–21 had fallen sharply in the decade of 1921–31.

Mullan, however, raised a belated alarm:

> Probably the most important event in the province during the last twenty-five years—an event, moreover, which seems likely to alter permanently the whole future of Assam and to destroy more surely than did the Burmese invaders of 1820 the whole structure of Assamese culture and civilisation—has been the invasion of a vast horde of land-hungry Bengali immigrants, mostly Muslims, from the districts of Eastern Bengal and in particular from Mymensingh.

Continuing with the rhetoric of invasion and conquest by the Bengali peasants, he looked at the figures for number of persons born in Bengal in each district of the Assam valley, and concluded that they illustrated 'the wonderful rapidity with which the lower districts of the Assam Valley are becoming colonies of Mymensingh'. Unlike his predecessors who had actively encouraged this migration, Mullan saw no redeeming features in the migrants. 'Wherever the carcase, there will the vultures be gathered together—Where there is waste land, thither flock the Mymensinghias', he wrote.[17]

His words, written in a colonial context remembered for its unofficial politics of 'divide and rule', have played a fateful role in Assam from then until now. It raised a fear among the locals that they would be overrun by migrants, and instituted a politics whose cornerstone was stopping immigration into the province and evicting 'Bongals', or outsiders, a word that in actual practice in Assam often led to the targeting of Bengalis, Muslim or Hindu, irrespective of citizenship. The effects of that politics are still being felt by millions of people in the state, which is the only one in India where an exercise to draw up a National Register of Citizens was completed in 2019. More than 1.9 million people were excluded from the register. As of January 2023, their fates still hang in the balance between citizenship and statelessness.

* * *

The importance of numbers, in the council and in the population, was well understood by everyone by the time Mullan published his report in 1932. Majorities meant power. Naturally, no group wanted to be a minority.

In 1928, when a delegation of seven British members of parliament comprising the Indian Statutory Commission, better known as the Simon Commission after its chairman Sir John Simon, arrived in India to examine the issue of further constitutional reform—a promise mentioned in the Government of India Act of 1919—the government was inundated with petitions of all sorts clamouring for greater representation. Among the petitions it received in Assam, apart from those representing the tea industry and associations such as the Ahom Association, was one from the Assam government itself that included some newspaper excerpts. 'There is a persistent rumour here (at Shillong) that two Surma Valley members have earned quite a fair deal in cash in the matter of overthrowing the Minister and that two other members have got hopes for appointment of their near relatives to Government service', said one extract, titled 'Translated from a Bengali Newspaper in 1928'.[18] Another similar passage, this time translated from an Assamese newspaper from 1927, read: 'It is known that on the 30th August last, the Nomination Board to select a candidate for Deputy Superintendent of Police sat in Gauhati. For this post the candidate has previously been selected. The Board is but a farce.'[19] In other words, structures and norms familiar to Indians today were already established.

Apart from nepotism and corruption, a feeling of communal discrimination in the matter of selection for jobs and government favours generally had also grown. A translated excerpt from an Assamese newspaper of 1928 complained that the government was appointing too many Bengali officers in the district of Goalpara:

> A Bengali clerk was recently appointed in the office of the Civil Surgeon and it is understood that this clerk bears some relation to the Civil Surgeon. He was at first taken temporarily but he has now been made permanent. Both the head clerk and the sheristedar [chief administrative officer of the district court] in the office of the Deputy Commissioner are Bengali. The head clerk is trying his best to employ his relatives in his office.[20]

These high emotions over competition for jobs in the new administration, and for representation in the new politics, hid a basic reality. It was a contest purely between different elites.

The franchise in those days was severely restricted. Only those who owned property and paid taxes could vote. Certain minimum amounts of tax were specified to qualify as an elector to one or the other of the constituencies, which were organised by community as well as geography. For the seats reserved for zamindars or landlords in the Provincial Council, for example, electors needed to 'hold Government titles not lower in rank than that of Raja or Nawab', meaning they had to be not mere landlords, but big or small kings. The restrictions effectively barred women from voting. The electorate at the 1926 election in Assam was 4.3 per cent of the population of the constituencies, excluding the population in tea gardens, where the owners and managers had seats and votes, but the workers, of whom there were an estimated 1 million, had neither. 'The fraction of the female vote enfranchised is infinitesimal', the Assam government's memorandum to the Simon Commission said: 'Outside Shillong [then the capital of Assam] the highest known percentage of women voters to female population was 0.27 and the lowest 0.01.'[21]

The caste composition of the elected members revealed that 'On a classification of Hindu candidates by caste it appears that there were no candidates from the lower orders save for the first election.' Brahmins and Kayasthas, the traditional castes of priestly pundits and scribes, both Bengali and Assamese, had secured the bulk of the seats, far exceeding their proportions in the population. The Kalitas and Ahoms were also well represented. However, the lower castes in the traditional caste hierarchy, classified in the government report as Sudras, were entirely missing. So, too, were all the indigenous tribes except the Koch. The hills had been by and large 'scheduled districts' since 1874, when the British province of Assam came into being, and by virtue of this categorisation, were administered directly by the governors, with no system of popular representation. Essentially, the fight for representation and government jobs was thus a three-way contest between the caste Hindu elites among the Bengalis and Assamese, and the Muslim upper classes, who also came disproportionately from elite castes such as Saiyyid and Shaikh.

The Simon Commission recommendations, followed by a series of three Round Table Conferences between 1930 and 1932 held in London, resulted eventually in the Government of India Act of 1935 being passed by the British parliament. This was the piece of legislation that established India as a federation with a parliament at the centre, set up provincial assemblies, and significantly expanded the electorate by relaxing the qualifying rules to be a voter. The 1935 reforms also started something else: the process of separating from India some of the territories that had been added to it during the years of British rule. Aden in the west and Burma in the east were separated from the sprawling multi-ethnic empire of British India. The separations took effect in 1937. In the case of Burma, the separation established a border between the countries that ran through places in what is now Northeast India where the concepts of maps and nations had not existed when they fell under British rule.

Electoral politics, starting with the elections held in 1937, accelerated the rift between Hindus and Muslims that led to the partition of India. In the 1937 elections, the Congress won all the Hindu-majority provinces—but the Muslim League fared rather poorly in the Muslim majority provinces, where local Muslim-led parties won. The League, according to historian and former administrator Penderel Moon, expected that they would be invited by the Congress to form coalition ministries in some of the provinces, such as in what was then the United Provinces in north India. Instead, the League members were told by the Congress to 'cease to function as a separate group' and to join their party. 'This proved to be a fatal error—the prime cause of the creation of Pakistan—but in the circumstances it was a very natural one', wrote Moon.[22] The Congress had the numbers, and had no need to invite its principal opposition into the ministry. Its superior attitude, however, outraged the League leadership. 'Jinnah himself, who before the elections had been saying there was no substantial difference between the League and the Congress, at once began to adopt a very different tone', wrote Moon. Muslims could expect neither justice nor fair play under a Congress government, Muhammad Ali Jinnah—a former leading light of the Congress Party—now warned. The fear of being reduced to a permanent minority under a dominant Hindu majority resounded with Muslims around the country. The local Muslim-led parties in the populous and powerful provinces of Punjab and Bengal made common cause with the League, strengthening it enormously.

In Assam's politics, 1937 was a momentous year. The province had now got its own Legislative Assembly, and 108 members from 14 parties had been elected from across the state in the first-ever assembly polls. The elections had thrown up a divided verdict. The Congress, with thirty-three seats, was the single largest party, but fell well short of the halfway mark and declined to form a minority government.[23] The Governor of Assam, Sir Robert Reid, recounted in his memoirs what happened next:

> The question of all questions to be faced was formation of a Ministry on 1 April, when the Act of 1935, giving full provincial autonomy, would come into force... From the first ... my hopes had centred on Sir Muhammad Saadulla, an experienced Assam Valley Muslim who had been an Executive Councillor under the old Act. He had returned to a lucrative practice at the Calcutta Bar, but we heard he was prepared to be public-spirited. On 15 March he saw me and said he would try to form a Ministry; a

> few days later he told me he would burn his professional boats in Calcutta and settle again in Shillong.[24]

Saadulla, Governor Reid's pick for the job, was able to cobble together a majority with support from the European planters, four different Muslim parties, and others including a Khasi pastor who had been elected from Shillong, J. J. M. Nichols-Roy, and the Assamese leader from Guwahati, Rohini Kumar Choudhuri. He thus took office on 1 April 1937 as the first prime minister of Assam—that being the designation for the head of the province under the Government of India Act.

The numbers were stacked against his government from the start. When the budget session of the assembly started on 3 August, the government began to suffer defeat after defeat. The Muslim League by then had ten members in the assembly, mainly from the Bengali-dominated Surma valley. To Saadulla's discomfiture, they were siding with the Congress. 'This trying situation forced Saadulla to woo the Muslim League. He attended its all-India conference held at Lucknow in October 1937. There he committed himself to advising his party's Muslim members to join the League', wrote historian Amalendu Guha.[25] Saadulla resigned in February 1938 and formed a fresh government, this time including ministers from the Muslim League. His majority, however, was still wafer-thin; his government survived a no-confidence motion by a single vote. Naturally, this unstable state of affairs could not continue for long. Facing increasing unrest, Saadulla finally resigned.

The trouble was that the Congress did not have the numbers either. The Congress president, Subhas Chandra Bose, immediately rushed to Shillong along with Maulana Abul Kalam Azad to try and assist the local Congress, led by Gopinath Bordoloi and his senior, the veteran Tarun Ram Phookun, in cobbling together a majority in the teeth of opposition from the British government and the European planters, who much preferred Sir Saadulla. The journey from Calcutta, which had taken four months a century earlier, was now a matter of hours. No less important, it had become possible to talk to people across the country and world in real time. A revolutionary invention, the telephone, had become available. Hurried telephonic consultations were held with Rajendra Prasad and Sardar Vallabhbhai Patel.[26] The efforts of Bose and Patel—Azad and Prasad disagreed with them on the strategy to be adopted—led to the installation of the first Congress ministry in the province, led by Bordoloi as prime minister, on 19 September 1938.

Bordoloi was a politician of considerable skill. A lawyer and graduate in history from Scottish Church College, Calcutta, he had joined the Congress in 1921 when Gandhi visited Assam. He developed differences with the Congress over the issue of the Non-Cooperation Movement, because he did not think it was a good idea to vacate public offices, and resigned from the presidency of the Assam Congress in February 1930. He and his senior colleague Tarun Ram Phookun then revived the Assam unit of a party with which they had been associated in the past, the Swaraj Party, a breakaway faction of the Congress that briefly achieved prominence in the 1920s under the leadership of Chittaranjan Das, a stalwart of Bengal politics, and Motilal Nehru, a Kashmiri pandit lawyer settled in Allahabad and the father of Jawaharlal Nehru. Bordoloi returned to the Congress before the first assembly elections of 1937 at a time when the older generation of Assam Congress stalwarts had passed away, and rose to the party's leadership in a very short span of time. His ministry fell in just a year because of global events. The Second World War broke out, and the British government declared India a participant without the assent of any of its elected bodies. In protest, the Congress, which had supported the war effort during the First World War, asked all its governments to resign. Bordoloi's government in Assam was the last Congress government to do so, eventually putting in its papers on 16 November 1939.

A second Saadulla ministry followed. It did not last very long. When Japan entered the war in December 1941, his government ordered the participation of students in a War Fund Exhibition held in the Judge's Field in Guwahati. Students of the nearby Cotton College protested, and were attacked by police with sticks. The Assamese leader Rohini Kumar Chaudhuri, who was then education minister in the coalition government, resigned in protest against the police atrocities and formed a new party. According to V. P. Menon in his book *The Transfer of Power in India*, Chaudhuri felt he could form a government with Congress support, but 'the refusal of two successive Governors—Sir Robert Reid and Sir Andrew Clow—to accept a ministry which depended for its support on a party which refused to cooperate in the war effort destroyed Chaudhuri's hopes'.[27] Assam went under governor's rule until August 1942, when a third Saadulla ministry managed to take office with help from the British authorities. 'The internment of about half the number of Congress members of the Assembly by the end of that year made his position secure for the time being', wrote Menon.

* * *

The Congress move to quit offices in 1939 was seized upon by Jinnah and the Muslim League, which now assumed power in the provinces. In 1940, the Muslim League passed the historic Lahore Resolution calling for the areas in which Muslims were a numerical majority to be constituted into an independent state. This became the basis of the partition of India and the birth of Pakistan. The Congress leaders, meanwhile, were mostly under arrest. There was also internal dissent within the party. Its president, Bose, after winning the organisational polls for a second term against a candidate backed by Gandhi, had been compelled to resign. In January 1941, Bose, who was a leftist during his time in the Congress, escaped from house arrest in Calcutta and made a remarkable journey from there to Kabul and then to Communist Moscow, disguised first as a Pathan insurance agent and then as an Italian count, to seek support for militarily overthrowing the British government of India. The Soviets—then still officially neutral in the World War—were not helpful, but allowed him to transit to Rome. Bose reached Berlin in April 1941. After months of waiting, he eventually met Adolf Hitler, but he got little in the way of material aid. Bose then made another remarkable journey, this time by submarine, from wartime Germany to Japan. The army that he came to lead, called the Indian National Army, would eventually invade Northeast India from Burma along with the

Japanese Army in 1944, before being halted following the epic battles of Kohima and Imphal.

The increasing disaffection among their Indian subjects in the midst of a world war was a bother that the rulers were keen to avoid. In March 1942, Sir Stafford Cripps, a member of the War Cabinet, was sent on a mission to secure Indian cooperation in the war effort with a promise of awarding India the dominion status it sought at the end of the war, in exchange for its full support. Gandhi dismissed the offer, calling it a 'post-dated cheque on a crashing bank'. The war at the time was not going well for the Allies; the bank was indeed in dire straits. The Congress now issued a call to the British rulers to 'Quit India'. The Muslim League was far more accommodating. The Indian Army of 2.3 million mostly Indian men also remained loyal, fighting on behalf of the Allied forces in battlefields around the world. India's resources contributed greatly to the war effort—at immense cost to the people of some parts of the country. Bengal suffered a terrible famine in 1943, whose miseries were compounded by the policies of the government under Prime Minister Winston Churchill, which were aimed at bolstering the war effort. In April 1942, the Governor of Bengal, a military man, had ordered the seizure of grain from cultivators and the destruction of country boats to defend against a possible Japanese invasion. An estimated 3 million people died of starvation partly as a result of this.

Elections to the British parliament after the war had ended in the West brought the Labour Party to power. The new prime minister who replaced Winston Churchill was Clement Attlee, who had visited India in 1928 as part of the Simon Commission. Attlee despatched a delegation consisting of Sir Stafford Cripps, A. V. Alexander (then First Lord of the Admiralty) and Frederick Pethick-Lawrence, Secretary of State for India and Burma. The group reached New Delhi in March 1946, and set about meeting with leaders of the Congress and Muslim League. Aiming to preserve the political and economic unity of India, they proposed a federal solution, which was announced by Prime Minister Attlee in May: a government of three tiers, provincial, regional and central, under a common constitution. The basic idea was that contiguous provinces would be grouped together into three regional groups and all groups would be under a common central government with powers over defence, foreign affairs and communications, and with the powers necessary to raise the finances for these. The groups of provinces would determine what subjects they wanted to be taken in common at the regional level. All residuary powers would rest with the provinces themselves. The provincial assemblies would have the power to vote for a reconsideration of the constitution after an initial period of ten years.

Assembly elections held in December 1945 and January 1946 had brought the Muslim League to power in Bengal, Punjab and Sindh. In most provinces it won between 80 and 100 per cent of the seats reserved for Muslims. The sole exception was the North-West Frontier Province (NWFP), where it won less than half the Muslim seats in the predominantly Muslim province bordering Afghanistan. The Congress, led by the Pashtun leader Khan Abdul Jabbar Khan and his brother Khan Abdul Ghaffar Khan, won a majority there. In Assam, where the Congress had won, Bordoloi was back in power as premier. The Cabinet Mission Plan's scheme of grouping provinces created an immediate problem for the Congress in these two provinces. The group scheme put NWFP in the same basket as Punjab, Sindh and British Balochistan. More troublingly, Assam and Bengal were grouped together, which would have meant representatives of both would have to sit together to draft the constitutions for the provinces and the common 'group constitution', and determine what subjects the regional government should have. Any province could opt out of a group, but only after the constitution had been drafted. This raised alarm bells in the Congress leadership in Assam and Delhi.

On the very day that the Cabinet Mission Plan was announced, 16 May 1946, the Assam Provincial Congress Committee, which was in session in Guwahati, sent a telegram to the Congress Working Committee in session in New Delhi, 'intimating the universal feeling of apprehension of the people of Assam, and lodging emphatic protest against the Grouping clauses'.[28] Gopinath Bordoloi, who was then in New Delhi, was also 'instructed telegraphically to meet Congress Working Committee and represent Assam's case, and acquaint the Committee with Assam's strong opposition and her refusal to accept the Grouping Plan'.[29] Bordoloi met the CWC and submitted a memorandum three days later, criticising the Plan's proposals for 'falling far short of the Congress claim that the Constituent Assembly was the sovereign authority' and for the manner in which it would 'perniciously affect the province of Assam'. Assam, Bordoloi pointed out, would be forced to enter into Group C along with Bengal, and her constitution would be framed by the majority of members in that section, with no room for revision.

Meanwhile, the big picture was changing. The Muslim League Council, after three days of consultations, voted unanimously in favour of accepting the Cabinet Mission Plan after Jinnah told them it represented the maximum that he could secure. Jinnah and the League at this point therefore dropped their demand for partition and Pakistan in favour of an undivided federal India. The regional part of the scheme represented, to them, an acceptable compromise to the demand for Pakistan. The Congress, under the leadership of Maulana Abul Kalam Azad and Sardar Vallabhbhai Patel, also formally accepted the Cabinet Mission Plan by passing a resolution on 26 June 1946 that took note of the unfairness of the scheme to NWFP and Assam, and to the Sikh minority, but nonetheless saw merit in the Plan as a whole. Moves began to establish an interim government of India with twelve ministerial portfolios, of which the Congress and Muslim League were to get five each, with the remaining two reserved for a Sikh and Christian or Anglo-Indian representative.[30] Haggling over the number of portfolios—the Congress wanted an additional portfolio for its backward caste representative Jagjivan Ram—and the exact ministries began between the parties. The process to elect members to the Constituent Assembly of an undivided India commenced.

The All-India Congress Committee met in Bombay on 6–7 July 1946, and formally ratified the earlier resolution of the Congress Working Committee, accepting, with certain reservations, the Cabinet Mission Plan. Maulana Azad—the outgoing president of the Congress, having decided to quit his position which he had held since 1940—moved the resolution for its ratification, which was seconded by Sardar Patel, who had said 'We place this Resolution before the House for ratification. Either you accept it or reject it in toto.'[31]

It was accepted.

At this critical juncture, Nehru, the incoming Congress president, who spoke at the meeting the day after the ratification, struck a different note. 'When India is free, India will do just what she likes', he said. This was the line adopted by Mahatma Gandhi earlier. On 23 June 1946, Gandhi had told the audience at his evening prayer meeting: 'Let us not look to the British Cabinet Mission, but let us ourselves become a cabinet mission and develop that power and authority.'[32]

Nehru elaborated on this at a press conference in Bombay on 10 July, where he said that the Congress would enter the Constituent Assembly 'completely unfettered by agreements and free to meet all situations as they arise'.[33] He added that the Congress had only agreed to participate in the Constituent Assembly, and considered itself free to change or modify the Cabinet Mission Plan as it thought best. 'We have committed ourselves on no single matter to anybody', he said, adding, 'The big probability is that, from any approach to the question, there will be no grouping.'[34] The NWFP and Assam would go against grouping and hence the groups would collapse, he said. 'Assam will not tolerate it under any circumstances whatever', was his position.[35] Azad, in his autobiography *India Wins Freedom*, recounted this event and wrote: 'I must place on record that Jawaharlal's statement was wrong.'[36] The Congress, as was abundantly clear, had in fact formally voted to accept the Plan, and the commitments that came with it.

Nehru's press conference, probably intentionally—he was after all a fine lawyer and a seasoned politician—torpedoed the Cabinet Mission Plan. Jinnah reacted to the press statement by saying that Nehru's declaration meant that the Congress had rejected the Plan. He called an emergency meeting of the Muslim League Council at which he now stated that Pakistan was the only course left to the Muslim League. The Council passed a resolution rejecting the Cabinet Mission Plan and called for 'direct action' to press for the demand for Pakistan. This led to 'Direct Action Day' on 16 August 1946, when terrible Hindu–Muslim riots broke out in Calcutta before spreading to the rest of Bengal, the plains areas of Tripura, and Bihar. The riots, which left thousands of people dead, finally cemented public opinion, both Hindu and Muslim, in favour of partition.

The process of electing a Constituent Assembly and setting up an interim government as envisaged by the Cabinet Mission Plan, however, went ahead, and so India's Constituent Assembly ended up being elected on the basis of a plan that had already failed. The League participated in the elections to the Constituent Assembly and won 73 seats, but boycotted attending the sessions. The princely states, numbering around 562, then constituted about half the territorial area of undivided India, and they sent representatives for their 93 seats. The Congress won 208 seats. When the Constituent Assembly of India met for the first time on 9 December 1946, it had 207 representatives in attendance out of a total membership of 389. Members from the Congress and some smaller parties, such as the Scheduled Caste Federation, were present. The SCF leader, Bhimrao Ambedkar, who was later hailed as the 'Father of India's Constitution', had been elected from East Bengal owing to the efforts of the Dalit leader Jogendranath Mandal, after failing to win a seat from his home province of the Bombay Presidency due to the Congress's opposition.

The formal burial of the Cabinet Mission Plan, however, had not yet happened, and this remained a cause of concern to the Assam Congress. Bordoloi sent two of his colleagues, Bijoy Chandra Bhagabati and Mahendra Mohan Chaudhuri, to meet Mahatma Gandhi for advice on 15 December. Gandhi told them: 'If Assam keeps quiet it is finished... It must become fully independent and autonomous... [A]s soon as the time comes for the Constituent Assembly to go into sections, you will say, Gentlemen Assam retires. For the independence of India, it is the only condition.'[37] The Assam Congress, thus bolstered by the Mahatma's backing, passed a resolution announcing its decision to stay out of the grouping scheme with Bengal and rejecting any notion of a group constitution. 'It drove, as it were, the final nail into the Cabinet Mission Plan's coffin', wrote Satish Chandra Kakati, former editor of *The Assam Tribune*, in a tribute to Bordoloi titled 'The man who saved India from disaster'—the 'disaster' being an undivided and federal India. This piece was reproduced in a biography of Bordoloi edited by his daughter, Lily Mazinder Baruah.[38]

According to Kakati, two pertinent questions arose in this regard. First, who was the man behind the partition of India? And second, was partition the better alternative? The jurist H. M. Seervai in his book *Partition of India: Legend and Reality*, had held not Jinnah but Gandhi, Nehru and Patel responsible, Kakati pointed out. 'However even a cursory study of how Gopinath Bordoloi ran from pillar to post while the hectic discussions on the British Cabinet Mission Plan were on to plead for its rejection will point towards the fact that the man behind the Partition of India was Gopinath Bordoloi', he wrote. He continued: 'Had not Bordoloi persevered in his opposition to the grouping scheme, the history of India would have been different today.'[39] Answering his second question, Kakati considered that partition was the better alternative because an undivided India with a weak centre would have risked breaking up into more than two pieces.

Perhaps Kakati gives Bordoloi too much credit for the role he played in bringing about the partition of India. There was already acceptance for partition in influential sections of the Congress leadership by 1942, when it rejected the Cripps Mission proposals. The Congress Working Committee had then passed a resolution stating that it could not 'think in terms of compelling the people of any territorial unit to remain in an Indian union against their declared and established will'. As the historian Rajmohan Gandhi, who happens to be Gandhi's grandson, noted in his book *India After 1947*, the Committee significantly added that 'acceptance of this principle' inevitably ruled out any 'compulsion being exercised on other substantial groups within that area'.[40] The first sentence, according to Rajmohan Gandhi, conceded the possibility of separation of certain territorial units; the second sentence allowed for portions within the seceding unit to remain in the union.

The former British administrator Penderel Moon wrote in his account *Divide and Quit* that in 1944, at the instance of C. Rajagopalachari, the Congress premier of Madras Presidency—

to whose daughter, Lakshmi, Gandhi's son Devdas was married—Gandhi had offered Jinnah 'a Pakistan consisting of those contiguous areas in the north-west and north-east of India in which Muslims were in a majority. On this principle, Pakistan would be shorn of nearly all Assam and of large parts of the Punjab and Bengal.'[41] Jinnah's demand was for six whole provinces—Punjab, Sind, Balochistan, NWFP, Bengal and Assam—and he rejected this offer of what he called a 'moth-eaten' Pakistan. It was what he eventually got, thanks to the collapse of the Cabinet Mission Plan.

On 3 June 1947, Lord Mountbatten, India's Governor General and last Viceroy, announced the partition of India into two parts: India and Pakistan. Bengal, like Punjab, was to be divided—despite the last-minute efforts of the Muslim League premier of the province, Shaheed Suhrawardy, and the Congress leader Sarat Chandra Bose, brother of Subhas Chandra Bose, to preserve a united, independent Bengal. Mountbatten also brought forward the date for both partition and India's independence by ten months, from June 1948 to 15 August 1947—barely two months from the date of his announcement. The task of drawing up the maps for the new countries was given to a lawyer, Sir Cyril Radcliffe, who had never been to India. Radcliffe was flown into India in July and given five weeks to do the job. The cavalier manner in which the country was finally divided led to the holocaust of partition in which an estimated 1 million people—mainly in Bengal, Punjab and Jammu and Kashmir—died, and another 15 million became refugees.

* * *

According to Mountbatten's 3 June announcement, only two parts of undivided India would have referendums to decide which of the two countries they would join. One was the North-West Frontier Province. The other was not a province at all, but a portion of a province—the Sylhet district of Assam. Uniquely in the entirety of undivided India, this was the only case of a district having a referendum to decide its fate. The issue of migration from Bengal had mounted during the war years, when Saadulla was in power. Communal tensions between Hindus and Muslims were running high. So, too, were feelings of difference between the Assamese and Bengalis. The Assam Pradesh Congress Committee, in its 1945 election manifesto, stated:

> Unless the province of Assam is organised on the basis of Assamese language and Assamese culture, the survival of the Assamese nationality and culture will become impossible. The inclusion of Bengali speaking Sylhet and Cachar and immigration or importation of lacs of Bengali settlers on wastelands has been threatening to destroy the distinctiveness of Assam and has, in practice, caused many disorders in its administration.

The desire to not have Sylhet in Assam on the part of the Assam Congress was therefore one that was well known to the party's top leadership and the British authorities, including the Viceroy who preceded Mountbatten, Lord Wavell.

Sylhet district had a 60 per cent Muslim population, and with the League undertaking a vigorous campaign not matched by the Congress, the referendum result went along expected lines. The vote may have been closer if the tea garden labourers, a population of close to 200,000, had been allowed to vote; they were denied the right. Over 56 per cent of valid votes went in favour of the district joining Pakistan. There were, unsurprisingly, allegations and claims of unfairness in the process from the biggest losers from the referendum, the Sylheti Hindus, who overnight were reduced to being refugees who were unwelcome on either side of the new border—in their original homeland for their religion, and in Assam next door for their language. However, the deed was done, and the Surma valley, which had been made part of Assam by administrative fiat, despite protests by its residents in 1874, was now sent back to East Bengal, minus an area of 709 square kilometres, where Hindus constituted a thin majority. This was awarded by the Radcliffe Boundary Commission to Assam, and now forms the Bengali-speaking Barak valley area of the state.

After the referendum, which was held on 6 July, and partition and independence the following month, deadly riots pitting Hindus and Sikhs against Muslims broke out. The worst of the violence was in the western areas of the country, but there was trouble in the east and northeast too. A stream of mainly Sylheti

Hindu refugees, estimated in the 1951 Census to number around 275,000 people, flowed into Shillong, Guwahati, Dibrugarh and other towns of Assam. By this time, tensions between Bengali and Assamese speakers had already existed in the state for decades. The influx of refugees set the stage for an escalation of the anti-immigrant sentiment—primarily directed against migrants from East Bengal—that was already present in the politics of Assam.

The following year, parliament enacted the Immigrants (Expulsion from Assam) Act in March 1950. It empowered the Government of India to order the expulsion of any person or group from outside India that had come into Assam, if 'the stay of such person or class of persons is detrimental to the interests of the general public of India or of any section thereof'. The law, however, would not apply to 'any person who on account of civil disturbances or the fear of such disturbances in any area now forming part of Pakistan has been displaced'. This law contained in kernel the ideas that led to the National Register of Citizens published in 2019, and the no less controversial Citizenship (Amendment) Act, which allows for faster citizenship for six non-Muslim communities from certain neighbouring countries, passed the same year.

In April 1950, Nehru signed an agreement with Pakistan's prime minister, Liaquat Ali Khan, in which the governments of India and Pakistan solemnly agreed that each would 'ensure, to the minorities throughout its territory, complete equality of citizenship, irrespective of religion, a full sense of security in respect of life, culture, property and personal honour, freedom of movement within each country, and freedom of occupation, speech and worship, subject to law and morality'. The treaty has been observed more in the breach, first in Pakistan and later in India as well, but at that moment, one clause of the pact had the effect of sending many Muslim refugees in East Pakistan back to their homes in Bengal and Assam, to the annoyance of many. A lot of property left by fleeing refugees was simply occupied by others in those troubled days. The agreement provided for the return to refugees of immovable property that they had left behind if they returned by 31 December 1950.

Bordoloi passed away in August 1950 at the age of sixty. He had achieved a great deal for the Assamese people as the helmsman of the state during the crucial period immediately before and after independence. At the time of his death, Assam was larger than it had ever been during the centuries of Ahom rule. It was a vast province that included all of Northeast India barring the two small princely states of Manipur and Tripura and a portion of the Khasi Hills. The dream of crafting an 'Assam for Assamese' which he voiced in the state assembly soon after independence was greatly advanced under his able leadership.

Partition put an end to the political career of his rival Saadulla. The former premier had chosen to stay back in India rather than go to Pakistan. Bordoloi's senior by five years, he was ailing by then. Saadulla died in 1955.

One prominent Muslim member of the Assam Assembly did move to Pakistan. The peasant leader Maulana Bhashani, who had come up the river Brahmaputra from Sirajganj to Dhubri and Goalpara in Assam, went to East Pakistan. He subsequently became one of the founders of the Awami League which helped to liberate East Pakistan from its western wing, now known simply as Pakistan, and create the country of Bangladesh. Bhashani was the man who issued a call to citizens to fly the Bangladesh flag on Pakistan's Republic Day in March 1971. The Pakistan Army of military dictator Yahya Khan launched a genocide two days later, leading to civil war, and the emergence of Bangladesh as a country after India entered the war on the side of the Bengali rebels.

The Sylheti Hindu community became permanent refugees after partition. Its members found themselves unwelcome both in Pakistan and Northeast India—in one place for their religion and in the other for their language.

The triumphal assertion of the Assamese linguistic identity soon became a political issue in Assam. Demands for making Assamese the sole official language of the state began to be voiced by organisations such as the Asam Sahitya Sabha, the influential literary society whose anthem is 'my mother language—my eternal love'. This was greeted with dismay in the hills of Assam, which were inhabited by tribes who spoke their own languages.

The matter came to a head after the Assam government, under political pressure, passed the Assam Official Language Act in 1960 that made Assamese the official language of the state. This gave an immediate fillip to demands for separate hill states to be carved out of Assam, details of which are contained in some of the following chapters. One state, Nagaland, was carved out of the Naga Hills, then administered by Assam, in 1962. A whole bunch of others followed, in a substantial redrawing of the map of Assam and Northeast India after the Bangladesh War of 1971.

The war was won by India and the Bengali rebels despite the efforts of the American administration of President Richard Nixon and his national security adviser, Henry Kissinger, to prevent it. The US at the time backed the Pakistani military dictator Yahya Khan, who was presiding over a genocide in East Pakistan.[42] India found support from the Soviet Union. When a Pakistani military defeat appeared imminent, the US sent an aircraft carrier group from Vietnam to threaten India, but it was too late. Indian forces took Dhaka, and East Pakistan emerged on the world map as Bangladesh. Prime Minister Indira Gandhi, who had survived being expelled from the Indian National Congress only two years earlier—she split the party and won a majority of members to her side—now emerged as the powerful leader of a country that had won a famous victory in war. Within two years, however, the euphoria waned. Protests against her government began in the western state of Gujarat, whose most influential leader at the time was the former deputy prime minister, Morarji Desai, who Indira Gandhi had fired from her cabinet in 1969. Desai would later be named by the American investigative journalist Seymour Hersh—citing information from multiple independent sources—as one of the most important assets of the Central Intelligence Agency.[43] Desai sued Hersh for libel in the USA, and lost.

Gujarat at the time was run by a Congress regime notorious for its corruption. 'The Chief Minister, Chimanbhai Patel, was popularly known as Chiman chor [thief]', wrote historian Ramachandra Guha in his book *India After Gandhi*. A powerful student-led protest movement demanding his removal called Nav Nirman (Movement for Regeneration) began. Patel was compelled to resign. This inspired students in Bihar to launch a protest movement in their own state.[44] They found an inspiring leader in a veteran freedom fighter named Jayaprakash Narayan. The movement against Indira Gandhi's government now went national. The increasingly embattled prime minister alleged that this was the work of a foreign agency. In 1975, facing political pressures from both the right and the left, she declared a national emergency. The following year, she had the preamble of the constitution amended to include, in the description of the Indian republic, two words that rang alarm bells in the West during the Cold War: the words 'socialist' and 'secular'. For the next two years, India experienced a spell of dictatorial rule. In 1977, Indira Gandhi called fresh elections and for the first time in the history of modern India, a party other than the Congress came to power. This was the Janata Party, containing the seeds of its successor, the Hindu nationalist Bharatiya Janata Party. Her old rival Morarji Desai now became prime minister.

* * *

In Assam, the fresh wave of refugees that had entered the state fleeing genocide and war in neighbouring Bangladesh in 1971 triggered strong anti-refugee sentiments. The issue of sending back refugees from East Pakistan was high on the All-Assam Students' Union's agenda immediately after the Bangladesh Liberation War.[45] In 1978, Assam got its first non-Congress government under the Janata Party, and a leader named Golap Borbora, who had been jailed during the Emergency, became chief minister. Soon facing dissidence, Borbora made a tactical statement in the Assam Assembly on 16 March 1979, stating that the influx of migrants from Bangladesh and Nepal was assuming alarming proportions and that his government had taken a firm stand on the matter.[46] Not long after, a member of parliament from his party from the Mangaldoi constituency passed away. The Election Commission began a revision of the constituency's electoral rolls for holding a by-election amid rumours that Indira Gandhi, who had lost her parliamentary seat in 1977, might contest from there. At this stage, national politics and state politics began to merge. The All-Assam

Students' Union, under the tutelage of the state's border police, filed complaints against 47,658 voters of the constituency with the Election Commission demanding their names be removed from the electoral list because they were foreigners.[47] It was widely rumoured that these alleged illegal immigrants, mainly Bengali Muslims, had been encouraged to settle in Assam by the Congress. The issue rapidly snowballed into a popular movement to evict illegal immigrants. The Assam Movement, as it is called, lasted from 1979 until 1985. It was often violent, with casualties on all sides; 855 Assamese youngsters, now remembered as martyrs of the Assam Movement by the students' union, were killed mainly in police action. At least 2,191 Bengali Muslims were hacked to death overnight by supporters of the movement in a village called Nellie in February 1983. In the same month, there was a massacre of Bengali Hindus, also by supporters of the movement, in a village called Khoirabari, in which roughly 500 people were killed.[48]

The movement ended with the leaders of the students' union signing an agreement called the Assam Accord, under which the Government of India promised that 'Foreigners who came to India on or after March 25, 1971 shall continue to be detected, deleted and expelled in accordance with law.'[49] The date coincided with the start of Operation Searchlight, the Pakistani military operation that began the Bangladesh genocide. One of the three leaders of the agitation who signed the Accord, Prafulla Kumar Mahanta, became chief minister of Assam after its signing in 1985. The euphoria of the moment, as he and his fellow student leaders moved out of university hostel rooms into ministerial bungalows, soon began to give way to disenchantment. In this situation, a militant group called the United Liberation Front of Assam (ULFA) that sought to separate the state from India began to take root. According to author and social scientist Hiren Gohain, 'Mahanta knew many of the top leaders of the militant and armed outfit from the days of the Assam movement, and took a rather indulgent view of their activities.'[50] The youthful leaders 'recklessly concentrated on the privileges brought by power, distributing largesse, showering rewards and favours on hangers-on and sycophants', wrote Gohain, and 'nepotism and corruption engulfed the leadership'.[51]

As the former student leaders fell sharply from grace, the ULFA stepped into the political vacuum. They were at once acclaimed by the supporters of the Assam Movement as new saviours.[52] The militant group unleashed a wave of extortions, kidnappings and summary executions. Assam's famed tea industry was especially badly affected. Hindustan Lever Limited, the Indian subsidiary of the multinational Unilever, owned several gardens in Assam from where it produced tea for brands such as Brooke Bond and Lipton. When its managers faced death threats following a demand for extortion money that they could not pay, pressure built up in the corridors of power in London and Delhi. The managers were evacuated overnight on a secret flight from a small Second World War airstrip that was organised by Indian intelligence agencies.

Mahanta's government was dismissed days later, and on 27 November 1990, an Indian Army operation commenced to clear out the ULFA.[53] The shooting began in earnest from both sides. The powerful Indian state's pressure soon began to tell. In 1992, the group suffered a split as one faction surrendered. More military operations in India and Myanmar followed. However, the ULFA's firepower was destroyed only after 2003, when the Indian and Bhutanese militaries jointly hit ULFA bases in Bhutan. The last straw for the ULFA and several other militant outfits in Northeast India came in December 2008, when elections in Bangladesh brought Sheikh Hasina of the Awami League to power. She reversed her predecessors' policy of allowing the militants to function from safe havens in Bangladesh. A large number of top leaders, including ULFA's chairman, Arabinda Rajkhowa, were nabbed and handed over to Indian agencies. Only one key militant, Paresh Baruah, escaped. News filtering out from Indian agencies said he had managed to find covert Chinese protection in Yunnan near that country's border with Myanmar. It is perhaps a coincidence of history that this was the area from where the first Ahom king, Siu Ka Pha (or Sukapha), and his band of followers, according to the Assam Buranji, had come some 800 years before.[54]

The politics of Assam since the heyday of the ULFA has seen a sharp turn from separatism to Hindu nationalism with an Assamese twist. The state is now run by the Bharatiya Janata Party of Prime Minister Narendra Modi. In August 2019, it published a National Register of Citizens for Assam—an official register of all residents of the state recognised as Indian—from which 1.9 million of the state's 32 million people had been excluded. A massive bureaucratic exercise had been conducted over the previous five years to sift through documents of all the state's millions of inhabitants in order to separate those who had paperwork to prove they or their ancestors were in Assam before midnight on 24 March 1971, the cut-off date agreed upon in the Assam Accord, from those who could not. The exercise followed fresh efforts by the All-Assam Students' Union dating back to 2005 for proper implementation of the Accord, the cornerstone of which was the mantra of 'detect, delete, deport': detect illegal immigrants, delete their names from electoral rolls, and deport them. The conclusion of the exercise which had left 1.9 million residents of Assam, a majority of them Bengali speakers (Hindu and Muslim), facing statelessness, was greeted with howls of protest. As the AASU general secretary, Lurinjyoti Gogoi, said, 'The figure of 19 lakh NRC-rejects is not what we expected, given the history of large-scale influx into Assam. This NRC has turned out to be incomplete and error-prone. We will appeal to the Supreme Court to remove the faults and discrepancies.'[55] They had expected a much larger number of exclusions.

The efforts to push up that number are currently ongoing. The issue is complicated by the desire of Hindu nationalists to exclude only the Muslims from the NRC, while the AASU and other Assamese nationalist organisations—whose nationalism is linguistic rather than religious—would prefer to see all immigrants from East Bengal, Hindu and Muslim, out. Debates continue about pushing back the cut-off date from 1971 to 1951, although that would not satisfy the Assamese nationalist hardliners who want 1826, the year when Lower Assam first became part of British India, to be the cut-off year. They want everyone who came after 1826, along with their descendants, to be evicted or at best tolerated as officially second-class citizens with restricted rights.

The politics of migration, which began in Assam long before the independence of India in 1947, is still going strong a hundred years later. The identity politics which fuels it—now in a tango of simultaneous collaboration and conflict with Hindu nationalism—is still largely based on tussles over languages, religions and identities that began long ago, during the years of colonial rule.

3

THE NAGA REBELLION

THE LONG FIGHT FOR FREEDOM

On 14 August 1947, on the eve of India's independence from British rule, the British Deputy Commissioner of what was then the Naga Hills district of Assam, Charles Pawsey, received a curious telegram—addressed not to him, but to the United Nations, with copies marked to Prime Minister Jawaharlal Nehru and newspapers in Calcutta and Delhi. The message was quite straightforward. 'Benign excellence', it read, 'Kindly put on record that Nagas will be independent.'[1] It was a communication sent by the leaders of an organisation called the People's Independence League. The local postmaster, on reading the message, referred it to Pawsey for clearance. The telegram never left the district capital of Kohima, but its suppression did nothing to change the intent of those who had sent it.

It is doubtful that there would have been much of a reaction even if the telegram had reached its intended recipients. The precise location of the Naga Hills themselves was then a mystery to most people in the distant national capital of Delhi, who in any case were preoccupied with the independence of India and its partition. What lay within the Naga Hills was remote even to most of their neighbours in the lower reaches of the Brahmaputra valley of Assam. Parts of the foothills near the upper reaches of the Brahmaputra valley had come under the influence of Ahom kings and the British who succeeded them in preceding centuries, and there were trade interactions as well as occasional skirmishes between the Nagas of those areas and the Ahoms, but the further hills in the direction of Burma had remained beyond all outside administration until the final decade of British rule.

The anthropologist Christoph von Fürer-Haimendorf, in the opening of his book *The Naked Nagas*, published, with rather poor timing, in the first week of the Second World War in 1939, wrote:

> An icy wind sweeps over the hills, forcing the coolies to crowd closer round the camp-fires. Wrapped only in thin cotton cloths they seem curiously content with this one-sided warmth, while we shiver even inside our bamboo hut, which offers at least some protection against the intense cold of the November night. The maps of the survey operations of 1924 lie spread out on the improvised table. So far, they have served us well, but now we have come to the edge of mapped territory; before us lies unexplored country. Irregular white patches indicate its extent and a line boldly drawn through land where no European has yet been marks the probable frontier between Assam and Burma.[2]

Fürer-Haimendorf had visited these areas in 1936 armed with letters of support from the Viceroy of India, Lord Linlithgow.

The Viceroy's letters obviously meant little to people who could not read. Beyond the camp at the 'edge of mapped territory', Fürer-Haimendorf's passage was guided by Chingmak, a tattooed headhunter, and secured by armed sepoys accompanying the expedition under the leadership of J. P. Mills, the District Collector of the Naga Hills. Mills, a popular local administrator, had managed to secure Chingmak's cooperation for the expedition whose ostensible mission was to secure the release of six Naga captives taken as slaves by the men of a village called Pangsha further east. The trouble was, no one knew where exactly Pangsha was, not even Chingmak.[3] Nagas in the areas beyond British administration did not generally venture far from the territories controlled by their own villages in those days, owing to headhunting raids between villages. Naturally, this situation did not encourage travel across long distances, which had to be done on foot through difficult terrain in hostile territories, with one's head being the possible object of covetous attention of warriors who were eager to add to their trophy collections. The imaginations of territory and identity were thus very local. The principal units of identity were the family and clan. Beyond this was the territorial identity which came from the village ward or 'khel' and the village itself. The largest unit was the tribe. The construction of a larger Naga nation uniting the numerous tribes, each with its own language and identity, is a modern project that began after the advent of British rule.

The tribes called Naga 'defy a common nomenclature', according to former Nagaland chief minister Hokishe Sema. 'There are no composite Naga people, and among them there are many distinct tribes having more than thirty dialects, with almost every tribe constituting a separate language group', he wrote in his account on the emergence of Nagaland.[4] Their cultural and social setups varied greatly, Sema wrote, and even in physique and appearance there were differences from group to group and place to place. He continued:

> The nomenclature 'Naga' is given to these tribes by the outsiders... In fact, for long this appellation of 'Naga' was resented by these people, till political expediency caused it to be accepted as describing the separate identity of these people as distinct from other ethnic tribal people and also from the people in the country at large.[5]

According to Sema, each tribe has its own name, although some tribes living in close proximity have combined over time, forming new composite tribes such as the Zeliangrong, a mix of the Zemi, Liangmai and Rongmai tribes, and Chakesang, a combination of the Chkru, Khezu and Sangtam tribes.

The origin of the word 'Naga' itself was a matter of much debate, he noted. He offered two 'largely accepted viewpoints' on the etymology of the word: 'In Burma, the Naga tribes are called Na-ka which in Burmese means people or men or folk with pierced ear-lobes.' Since most Naga tribes had migrated to the Naga Hills via Burma, one possibility was that the name had originated there, Sema wrote. The other theory on the origin of the word was that it came from Assamese, in which language the word means 'naked'. It was the word 'used for the naked people of the hills who often came in contact with people of the plains of Assam'. Where these people of the hills came from, and when, is lost to history. Nor is it clear how many such tribes there were or are; the number is hotly debated to this day. Different documents put the number of Naga tribes within Nagaland between fourteen and seventeen, with sixteen being a broadly accepted figure; but there are also at least as many Naga tribes outside Nagaland. According to the Naga author Charles Chasie, 'Each tribe is distinct in terms of language, customs, culture and traditions, system of governance etc. Quite often people mistakenly describe the Naga tribe languages as "dialects" but they are not. Even within the same tribe language, the dialects are often so different as to render communication impossible!'[6]

The Naga tribes were oral cultures, and had no writing before colonial rule. There are stories that speak of a migration from China or Mongolia via Myanmar more than 2,000 years ago, but it is impossible to tell how old these stories themselves are. Other stories, based on old songs, speak of an origin place called Chungliyimti located somewhere in today's Thailand, although there is also a Naga village of that name in Tuensang district of Nagaland.[7] Not all the Naga tribes share the same origin myth. Chungliyimti is claimed as the origin place of the Sangtam and Ao Naga tribes. The Chang tribe has songs that speak of an origin in a place called Mongkonyu. There are also tales of dispersal of some of the tribes from a place called Makhel, in the hills of Manipur bordering Nagaland.[8]

When the founder of the Ahom dynasty, Siu Ka Pha, or Sukapha, passed through hills inhabited by Naga tribes on his way into Assam in the thirteenth century, he had to fight his way in.[9] In later years, friendlier commercial and political ties also developed between the Ahoms and Nagas. There were land grants to Nagas in the plains, some Nagas fought in the Ahom armies and Nagas sheltered Ahom princes fleeing from court conflicts.[10] The royal chronicles of neighbouring Manipur also include tales of conflict with the Nagas, dating to the reign of a king named Punsipa, who ascended to the throne in 1404.[11] There are also again signs of more fraternal ties at other times.

It is widely accepted among both Naga intellectuals and the general public that in former times—and even to some extent today—the essential element of identity has been the village. One often hears that the Nagas lived in self-sustained village-republics, which had relations, friendly or hostile, with other, at times quite distant, villages. A second important element of identity was and is the clan.[12] The broader identity of tribes as they exist now does not appear in early colonial accounts. The 1841 report of W. Robinson, for instance, speaks of Namsangiya, Borduwaria and Paniduwaria Nagas who were 'in possession of brine springs of considerable value, and further, were always supposed to pay allegiance to the Rajas of Assam'.[13] All these names relate to particular places of habitation, Namsang, Borduwar and Paniduwar, and the names themselves are exonyms, by which their Assamese neighbours recognised these people who inhabited the foothills nearest to them. The Nagas from the further hills, who were completely independent of Ahom rule, were known then by the generic term 'Abor'—a word that in later years became the name of a similarly independent tribe from what is now Arunachal Pradesh.

There is great diversity in the traditional political arrangements of the Naga tribes. According to Chasie:

> The cultures, values, and systems of governance among the tribes are so different… Just to have a taste of the cultural pot-pourri one could mention the autocracy of the Konyak tribe, where commoners may not even stand straight before the Chief. Slightly lower in scale we have the chiefship of the Sumi [Sema] tribe where the chief's word was still considered law. Then we have a kind of Republican system, with elections, among the Ao tribe. And, finally, there is the 'pure democracy' of the Angami tribe where the search for consensus was the norm and election through majority decision was unknown.[14]

Contact between the Naga tribes and the wider world increased after the establishment of British rule in Assam and Manipur in 1826. The new rulers wanted to open up a road between Assam and Manipur, and in January 1832, Captains Jenkins and Pemberton led an expedition of 700 Manipuri troops that had to fight their way through the country. That winter, Raja Gambhir Singh of Manipur, accompanied by a force under Lieutenant Gordon, again passed through the same lands, and once more had to fight 'almost every step of the road'.[15] Naga raids into areas which had become British Indian territory after the Treaty of Yandabo were then a common occurrence, and the initial British notion that the tribes could be controlled by Manipuri kings in Manipur and Cachar having produced little effect, in 1839 a force under a British official, Mr Grange, was sent from Nowgong in Assam into the Angami Naga areas to 'investigate fully the causes of the Angami raids' and 'endeavour to punish the Chiefs of the large villages of Konemah and Mozemah who were known to be implicated in these outrages'.[16] He discovered that 'a great trade in slaves was carried on by the Angamis with Bengali merchants: and that one main object of the raids was to procure supplies of such slaves'.[17]

Negotiations on the fixing of boundaries between Manipur, the Naga territories and Assam commenced. Over the next few years, a stockade and market were established near the modern town of Dimapur at a village known then as Samaguting, and now as Chumukedima. An Indian police official, Bhogchand Daroga, was posted there. In 1849, he tried to arrest a group of Naga and Cachari men for murder, and was speared to death for his troubles.[18] A series of punitive military expeditions on the one side, and retaliatory headhunting and slaving raids on the other, followed. In the absence of roads and supplies, attempts to occupy the country for any length of time failed. After ten expeditions up to 1851 had failed to 'pacify' the Nagas, British forces were finally withdrawn from Naga territories under orders of the Governor General, Lord Dalhousie. 'I dissent entirely from the policy of what is called obtaining a control,' he wrote, 'that is to say, of taking possession of these hills, and of establishing our sovereignty over their savage inhabitants. Our possession could bring no profit to us, and would be as costly as it would be unproductive.'[19]

Leaving the Nagas alone, however, was easier said than done. Tea plantations in Assam had begun to push further and further into what had until then been remote areas, in many cases into lands in the plains known since Ahom times as 'Naga khat', that the local Naga tribes considered to be theirs. The desire on the part of one side to occupy these lands, and on the other to capture slaves and take heads in retaliation, made conflict inevitable. In 1865, the Lieutenant-Governor of Bengal, Sir Cecil Beadon, pointed out that the treaties with Burma and Manipur recognised no intermediate independent territory, and 'while the wild tribes who inhabit the southern slopes of these hills are subject to Burmah and Manipur, those who inhabit the northern slopes are subject to the British Government'.[20] He proposed bringing these territories under British administration and control. The Government of India under the new Governor General, Lord Lawrence, seeing much cost and little revenue potential in the proposal, shot it down. The only advance the Governor General allowed was the establishment of a permanent military post at Samaguting, the place where Bhogchand Daroga had been posted before his murder.

The Naga Hills (administered) District was established in 1866 with its headquarters in Samaguting.[21] It included most of the Angami, Rengma, Sema, Lhotha and Zemi Naga territories, a part of North Cachar and—briefly—the Khasi and Jaintia Hills of what is now Meghalaya.[22] A system of issuing police passes was initiated, by which Nagas entering the plains had to deposit their weapons at the police post and secure a pass. Seven salaried Naga delegates representing different 'khels', or village wards, were attached to the office of the Deputy Commissioner as 'dobashis', or interpreters. After 1871, this was changed to ten representatives from ten powerful Angami Naga villages such as Kohima and Khonoma.[23]

Territorial boundaries then were still rather fuzzy, and so, in 1869, the government ordered a survey to settle the boundary between the Naga Hills District and neighbouring Manipur. Even before the survey could begin, the king of Manipur at the time, Chandrakirti Singh, claimed that Manipur extended well into the

Naga Hills and included even the largest Angami village, Kohima.[24] The claim rested on the alleged conquest of these villages by past kings of Manipur, which a British political agent in Imphal, James Johnstone, later mentioned. 'Ghumbeer Singh reduced several villages to submission, including the largest of all, Kohima, at which place he stood upon a stone and had his footprints sculptured on it, in token of conquest', wrote Johnstone in his memoirs, which carries an illustration of this 'Kohima Stone'.[25]

After the Manipur king's objection there was a delay. The survey finally began on 5 January 1873. Days later, on 16 January, a Manipuri force of some 400 troops, led by a Major Roma Singh, appeared, and he 'announced that he had received orders from the rajah of Manipur to knock down all the boundary pillars being erected by survey party'.[26] Owing to the dispute with Manipur, the survey made little progress. The next year, however, surveying work resumed. The surveyors now faced hostility from the Nagas. Naga Hills Deputy Commissioner Captain John Butler, leading one of the survey parties, died of his wounds after being speared in an ambush near Wokha in the Lotha Naga lands in December 1875.

Raids on villages within British-ruled Assam were still a frequent occurrence, and finally the Government of India decided that permanent occupation of the Naga Hills was the only solution to this state of affairs. In March 1878, Kohima in the Angami Naga country was identified as the site for the headquarters where a Political Officer would be stationed. Wokha in the Lotha Naga territory was also to be occupied. British district officials had begun offering protection from headhunting and slaving raids by their neighbours to the relatively weaker ones among Naga villages, on condition they pay taxes. The Government of India, in July 1878, finally communicated a change of policy to the Chief Commissioner of the new province of Assam, of which the Naga Hills district had become a part since 1874. The forward policy of extension of authority, village by village, advocated by Colonel Richard Keatinge, the Assam Chief Commissioner, was approved.[27]

It did not proceed smoothly.

In October 1879, the newly appointed Political Officer for the Naga Hills, G. H. Damant, walked up the steep hill atop which sits the powerful Angami Naga village of Khonoma. He was accompanied by an armed escort of twenty-one sepoys and sixty-five policemen. Damant had not anticipated the reception he got; he was greeted with a bullet to the head as he approached the village gate.[28] Of his guard, thirty-five were cut down. The Nagas then attacked the British stations in Kohima and Samaguting, both of which were besieged. News of this reached the British political agent in neighbouring Manipur via a Naga messenger. A force marched from there to lift the siege. News of the killing of Damant and his party had also reached Shillong in the Khasi Hills, which by then had become the capital of Assam. From there, a military expedition under a Brigadier General was organised. Columns of soldiers of the Sylhet Light Infantry and the Assam Light Infantry armed with artillery were sent to extract revenge. They reached Khonoma to find the village abandoned; the villagers had retreated to a strongly fortified position on the crest of a nearby hill. In order to get there, the soldiers had to cross other Angami Naga villages, which they attacked and destroyed. They then laid siege to the Khonoma villagers. However, a band of Naga warriors managed to slip through the siege, march to Cachar—a distance of 129 kilometres as the crow flies—and attack and destroy a tea estate there, killing the British manager, among others, before returning. The British forces maintained their siege. Eventually, in March 1880, the Khonoma Nagas were forced to capitulate. Attempts to confiscate their lands failed; none of their neighbours dared take them. The British then left after securing a promise of a token revenue payment from Khonoma of 1 rupee and 1 maund (roughly 38 kilograms) of rice a year.

* * *

The transformative arrival of British rule in the years after the Anglo-Burmese War broadly coincided in the Naga Hills, as in Assam, with the arrival of Christianity. It was from neighbouring Assam, where the American Baptist missionaries had set up base in Sivasagar, that Christianity made its way into the Naga Hills. 'As each cold season came around, hill men came in for trade and sight-seeing', wrote Mary Mead Clark, wife of the missionary

E. W. Clark who succeeded the Browns and Bronson in Sivasagar in 1868:

> Our press building with its typesetting, printing, and binding of books was for them the wonder of wonders. Some of the great men, dressed in their military costumes, came one day to our schoolhouse door, and manifesting much interest in what we were doing, were asked, 'Wouldn't you like us to come up to your village and teach your children as you see these being taught?' A chief replied, 'Yes, and we will send our children to learn'. There was however a concern that needed to be addressed. 'But we hear that you take heads up there'. 'Oh yes, we do', he replied, and seizing a boy by the head, gave us in a quite harmless way an object-lesson of how they did it.[29]

Naturally, this was a dampener, but the Naga Hills, visible daily from the mission press compound, beckoned. The first step in their direction was taken by Godhula Barua, an Assamese convert who had been christened Godhula Rufus Brown after Nathan Brown. A former soldier, he converted in 1860 through baptism in the Sivasagar tank next to the Siva Dol temple. The missionaries found an Ao Naga living near Sivasagar who was persuaded to visit Godhula in the evenings and teach him a bit of the Ao language. In the winter of 1871, Godhula and his Naga companion set out for the tea gardens at the base of the Naga Hills. At the Amguri Tea Gardens, he met Naga men from a village that Mary Clark in her account called Dekha Haimong. He persuaded these men to take him with them to their village. There, upon arrival, Godhula, though unharmed, was made a prisoner, but he had a good singing voice and gradually won the villagers over with his singing.[30] When he finally returned to the Sivasagar mission compound, it was in style—with an escort of forty armed Ao Naga warriors. The following April, Godhula and his wife Lucy, another early convert, went up to spend the rainy season in the Naga village. They set up a bamboo chapel there and returned in November with a band of 'wild men, battle-axe and spear in hand', of whom nine were baptised in the Dikhow river in front of the Sivasagar mission's bungalow.

Mary Clark wrote:

> These Naga Christians, now very desirous of taking Mr Clark up to their mountain home, and having no calendar save the wet and dry season, seed time and harvest, and the moon's changes, fixed upon a certain phase of the next moon as the date when they would come and take him up to their savage wilds. At the appointed time sixty warriors appeared to escort him.[31]

Mr Clark was taken up to the same village, a distance from Amguri of about 40 kilometres as the crow flies, which was reached on the second day of the march. He returned after twelve days, but from then on, Godhula and his wife began to spend part of the year in the Naga village, with Clark making occasional trips. In 1876, Clark decided to move there. As Mary Clark explained, 'To live beyond the English flag at that time required a permit from the Viceroy of India, residing in Calcutta. On making the application, Mr Clark received the reply that he must do it at his own risk, with no expectation whatever of protection from British arms.'[32] Clark was not dissuaded; he went. It was a decision that would have an impact on the history of the Naga Hills that was no less significant than the influence Brown's battles on behalf of the Assamese language had on the history of Assam.

The increasingly peaceful Ao Naga areas came under the British flag in December 1888, when the Governor General finally gave his consent to extend administration to these areas. By then, some Lotha and Angami villages had also come under British administration—a process that began in 1874, when Captain J. Johnstone, officiating for Captain Butler, took three villages under his protection on condition that they pay revenue to the government. Creeping village by village and tribe by tribe, more and more of the Naga Hills gradually came under British rule. It was a process that continued despite opposition from senior officers in the British administration then and for several years after. On 25 November 1896, Sir William Ward, the Chief Commissioner of Assam, wrote a letter which runs as follows:

> I have always been opposed to extending our area of political control, which is always followed by annexation, as in the case of Mokokchung subdivision [the Ao Naga area]. To annexation

> succeeds a further area of political control, and further annexation, etc. All this annexation means further expenditure. North Lushai [in the Mizo Hills] is bad enough, with its expenditure of 5½ lakhs [Rs. 550,000] a year and revenue of Rs. 7,000 only...[33]

His successor, Sir Henry Cotton, endorsed this position. 'I agree entirely with Sir William Ward's views, and would object strongly to any extension of political control, if it can possibly be avoided', he wrote, 'But there is always the risk of our hands being forced at any time.'[34]

The hands of officials at the local level apparently continued to be forced every now and then. Under the growing influence of the Church, on the one hand, and the expanding British administration on the other, the days of headhunting and feasts of merit in Naga villages gradually began to recede. The written word entered the formerly oral culture. Languages were, as everywhere else, standardised by the advent of the printing press. Education followed. Dress began to change. With the end of headhunting raids in the administered areas, travel became safer. The sense of larger identities, going beyond clan and village, began to grow. The economy changed completely, from barter and self-sufficient villages to money and the ideas of capitalism. The First World War widened horizons further. Towards the end of the war, in 1917, the Secretary of State sent a request for labourers from India to work on the battlefields of France. The Assam government proposed to exempt from house tax those who volunteered. In March 1917, a Naga Hills Labour Corps was raised. 'All the Lhotas and the majority of the Semas made a good response, the latter sending 1,000 men. The Aos sent men too, if a little slowly. Angamis, Kacha Nagas and Kukis would not volunteer', wrote Robert Reid, a future Governor of Assam, in his account.[35] It was the first known brush of the Nagas, whose contacts had historically been limited to adjoining areas of Burma, Assam and Manipur, with the wider world beyond the seas.

The survivors returned home after the war. By then, the British town of Kohima in the Angami Naga Hills, facing the old village of Kohima, was already forty years old and well established. The office and bungalow of the Deputy Commissioner were the centres of administration around which the new way of life had taken root. A number of Naga employees, mostly Angami Nagas from the surrounding hills, worked at the DC's office, including some who were dobashis or interpreters. They were an influential group in the emerging society, and pioneered its journey into modern politics through the formation of a 'Naga Club' in 1918. The idea for such a club had apparently come about because of the European Club, where the white sahibs used to gather for drinking and eating, to which the natives were, as was usual in those times, denied entry. The Naga Club was given use of a canteen in a building previously used by the Assam Rifles.[36]

When the Simon Commission came to India, among the places it visited was faraway Kohima. The members of the Naga Club, with the prodding of the Deputy Commissioner, J. H. Hutton, and a Khasi assistant of his from Shillong, Hari Blah, put together a petition. There was at the time only one Naga in Kohima sufficiently lettered in the 'white-man's language' to do the drafting. This was a teacher at the Kohima Mission School named Ruzhukhrie, who had passed high school in Calcutta. The Naga Club members made a beeline to his house one winter's morning in January 1929. The DC had told one of them that a very high-ranking visitor was coming to find out how they would like to be governed in the future. Ruzhukhrie put together a draft in pencil and took it to the DC's office.[37] The final petition, which had passed through the editorial scrutiny of Blah and Hutton himself, was a well-crafted document that marked the beginning of the politics of representation in the Naga Hills, and of the subsequent Naga struggle for independence from India.

'Sir', it begins,

> We the undersigned Nagas of the Naga Club at Kohima, who are the only persons at present who can voice for our people, have heard with great regret that our Hills is included within the Reformed Scheme of India without our knowledge, but as administration of our hills continued to be in the hands of British officers, we did not consider it necessary to raise any protest in the past.[38]

The petition goes on to say that they lived in a state of intermittent warfare with their neighbours, the Assamese and the Manipuris. 'They never conquered us, nor were we ever subjected to their rule. On the other hand, we were always a terror to these people', it declares:

> Our country within the administered area consists of more than eight regions, quite different from one another with quite different languages which cannot be understood by each other, and there are more regions outside the administered area which are not known at present. We have no unity among us and it is only the British Government which is holding us together now.

There was no one, the petition said, who could represent all Nagas in any council of a province. Moreover, their population of 102,000 being very small in comparison to the plains, any representation they secured would be negligible:

> Our language is quite different from those of the plains and we have no social affinities with Hindus or Mussalmans. We are looked down upon by one for our beef, and the other for our pork, and by both for our want of education which is no fault of ours.[39]

The petition concluded with an appeal to be placed directly under British protection:

> If the British Government, however, wants to throw us away, we pray that we should not be thrust to the mercy of people who could never have conquered us themselves and to whom we were never subjected; but to leave us alone to determine for ourselves as in ancient times.[40]

The petition was signed by twenty members of the Naga Club.

The desire to be left alone was also expressed without any British assistance and in a quite different manner by another set of Nagas at around the same time. These were the Rongmei Nagas from the hills of Manipur adjoining Cachar in Assam, who in those days used to be known as 'Kacha Nagas'. There, a rebellion broke out due to the activities of a local holy man named Jadonang and his successor, a young woman named Gaidiliu. Jadonang was hanged for murder and Gaidiliu was eventually arrested after quite a chase.[41]

The future of the Naga Hills—and of India—was still undecided when the Second World War began. The war reached the gates of India when Burma fell to the Japanese in 1942. Suddenly, the tracts of the eastern Naga Hills and the valley of Imphal in the kingdom of Manipur were all that lay between British India and the Japanese Army. The tide of war had already turned by the time the Japanese attack finally came. In March 1944, the Japanese, together with the Indian National Army led by Subhas Chandra Bose, made a desperate thrust towards British India via Manipur and the Naga Hills. Japanese forces entered Manipur, and the Indian National Army flag was raised at Moirang, less than 50 kilometres from the capital, Imphal. The Japanese also reached Kohima. The battle there reached its deadliest at the Deputy Commissioner's bungalow on a hill in the middle of the town, where the Japanese had dug in on one side of the tennis court. The British were on the other side. Bloody, relentless trench warfare continued at close quarters for months, until finally the British managed to bring up tanks on their side. The Japanese infantry continued to attack the tanks until they were mowed down. The defeat of the Japanese forces in Imphal and Kohima prevented their advance into the plains of India where they would have been far harder to stop, especially in the likely event of local support for Bose and his army.

Most Nagas aided the British in the war, acting as guides, spies and porters, and occasionally ambushing Japanese columns, for which they received high praise from Field Marshal William Slim in his 1956 account, *Defeat into Victory*. Among the rare individuals who did not was an Angami Naga man named Zapu Phizo who happened to be in Rangoon with his brother Kevi Yalley when the war reached there. He met Bose there, and became an ally in his war effort. After the war he was arrested and imprisoned in Insein jail near Rangoon. The following year, 1946, he was let out of prison and took a ship to Calcutta, from where he made his way back to the Naga Hills. Political developments had accelerated and independence was on the horizon. The Naga Club had grown, under the tutelage of the new Deputy Commissioner, Charles Pawsey, into a body called the Naga Hills District Tribal Council. This organisation morphed into the Naga National Council, which held its first meeting in Wokha in the Lotha Naga areas in February 1946.

In February 1947, the Naga National Council presented a memorandum to the government through Deputy Commissioner Pawsey, seeking self-determination. 'The Nagas have had no connection with the policies of different groups of Indian politicians... [A] constitution drawn up by the people who have no knowledge of the Naga Hills and the Naga People will be quite unsuitable and unacceptable to the Naga people', said the memorandum, signed by the NNC secretary T. Sakhrie. Like several of the veteran British administrators in Northeast India, including his predecessor Hutton and former Assam governor Robert Reid, Pawsey had favoured a plan to create a British protectorate in the belt of tribal lands between India and Burma. The crown colony, as it was envisaged, would have included the hills of Northeast India, northern Burma, and the Chittagong Hill Tracts that later went to East Pakistan, a population of roughly 2.5 million, and would be ruled by a governor reporting to Whitehall. Assam premier Gopinath Bordoloi, on hearing of this secret plan, raised the alarm with the Congress leadership in Delhi.

As India hurtled towards independence and partition, a sub-committee of the Constituent Assembly of India, led by Bordoloi, visited the Naga Hills in May 1947. The crown colony plan had by this time been abandoned by the British authorities as impractical. The Bordoloi Committee, with the Khasi leader J. J. M. Nichols-Roy and the Bodo leader Rup Nath Brahma among its members, managed to co-opt Aliba Imti, secretary of the Naga National Council, to join them after their first Naga member Mayangnokcha Ao resigned. On the first day of depositions on 19 May in Kohima, Aliba Imti clarified his position, saying that 'As far as the political attitude is concerned, I will be the last man to deprive the political privilege from the Naga people. I am always for a united Naga people. I am always for a free Naga people. I am always for an independent Naga people.' The following day, Bordoloi raised the issue of the NNC memorandum demanding an interim government for the Naga Hills, asking 'can you give us an idea of what an interim government would imply in full?' Kevichusa of the NNC responded, saying 'By Interim Government we mean a Government of the Naga people by the Naga people and that the people would run their own show with little or no disturbance from outside and during the period of these 10 years we should be able to make a responsible choice.'[42]

Ramadhyani, the secretary of the sub-committee, raised two questions on issues of territorial boundaries, especially with Manipur, and concerning the presence of other minority tribes, especially Kukis, in some of the areas in question. 'It is quite true that the Nagas are possibly ethnologically different from others', he said:

> But if you look at the whole of India, it consists of many numbers of races speaking different languages... If you take a man from the south of the India peninsula you will find him speaking a totally different language and altogether, even racially, completely different, from a man from the Punjab or N.W.F.P. or Bengal or Assam.

The Nagas themselves have several different languages, he pointed out, and this did not prevent them from discussing a common future. He therefore did not consider the uniqueness of the Nagas a sufficient case for separation. The one point raised in the NNC memorandum he did concede was that a constitution framed by those with no knowledge of the Naga Hills and Naga people would be unacceptable to them. 'That is exactly the reason we have come to you', he said.[43] The NNC was not convinced.

A month after Bordoloi and company departed from Kohima, Assam governor Akbar Hydari arrived there to meet the NNC. He had Deputy Commissioner Charles Pawsey on his side, and was able to hammer out an understanding. Called the Nine-Point Agreement, this document, signed in June 1947, asserts that in legislative matters, 'No laws passed by the Provincial or Central Legislature which would materially affect the terms of this agreement or the religious practices of the Nagas shall have legal force in the Naga Hills without the consent of the Naga Council.' It also agrees that administrative divisions should be modified so as 'to bring under one administrative division as far as possible all Nagas'. For executive matters, the general principle was accepted that 'what the Naga Council is prepared to pay for, the Naga Council should control'. The agreement was for a period of ten years, during which time the Governor of Assam would have 'special responsibility', after which 'the Naga Council will be asked whether they require the present agreement to be extended for a further period or a new agreement regarding the future of the Naga people arrived at'.

His intervention in this and other matters did not go down well with Bordoloi, who wrote to Sardar Patel accusing Hydari, who was Muslim, of trying to turn Assam into Pakistan. However, Hydari himself seems to have been trying to turn the Naga Hills into India, because on 5 August 1947, nine days before partition, he sent a telegram to Nehru with the following message:

> My telegram 25 July Pawsey Deputy Commissioner Naga Hills telegraphs as follows begins 'Zaphu Phizo and friends from Khonoma excluding the Themova clan are enroute Delhi to oppose Naga National Council. They should be completely ignored as they represent unimportant minority'. Suggest you warning Mahatmaji and Sardar Patel against giving them any encouragement. Also, Congress press should be required not to give these people any publicity.[44]

Perhaps Hydari's telegram arrived too late, because the story has passed into legend among the Nagas that Phizo and his delegation of eight met Gandhi in Delhi in July 1947. They asked him if the Government of India would force the Nagas to join India, to which Gandhi apparently replied 'No, not if I am alive. I will go [to] the Naga Hills and say that you will shoot me before you shoot a single Naga.'[45]

A month later, on 14–15 August, India and Pakistan became independent, and the British Indian empire broke into three parts: India, West Pakistan and East Pakistan, corresponding to today's Bangladesh. A day before the new India was born, on 14 August, the People's Independence League—a group from Khonoma led by Phizo—sent the undelivered telegram of hope and defiance announcing its resolve to lead a free Naga nation. It is a resolve that has led to decades of armed insurgency, and violent reprisals by the Indian state.

* * *

The little war escalated gradually, and then suddenly.

In the immediate aftermath of partition and independence, vicious riots consumed the new countries of India and Pakistan. Long lines of refugees, bearing what scant possessions they could on their heads and backs, trudged hundreds of miles, often coming under attack. Around a million men, women and children died. A right-wing extremist associated with the Hindu Mahasabha and the Rashtriya Swayamsevak Sangh assassinated Gandhi. The Naga Hills were then a distant oasis of relative calm in comparison to the madness outside. Yet, the seeds of further conflict had already been planted, and they were starting to sprout.

The constitution of India was in the process of being drawn up. The fate of the Naga Hills and other tribal areas of Northeast India was being determined. In the case of the Nagas, two competing ideas of the terms of future governance of the place existed: those of the Bordoloi Committee report, which the NNC had not acceded to, and the more generous terms of the Nine-Point Agreement, which they had signed.

In May and June 1948, Naga representatives travelled to Shillong to meet with Assam governor Hydari and premier Gopinath Bordoloi. Nari Rustomjee, who arranged the meeting, mentioned only one person: Phizo. 'I have known Phizo and his family for over twenty years', he recalled in his memoirs:

> I first met him when he called in at my office one afternoon and wanted me to confirm that the Nine-Point Agreement entered into by Sir Akbar still held good. He also wanted confirmation that the agreement had the approval of Assam's Chief Minister, Gopinath Bordoloi, and would be honoured by him. I consulted Sir Akbar, and it was decided that Phizo should meet Sir Akbar and Bordoloi at Government House for a personal discussion.

> What struck me about Phizo at my first meeting was his extraordinary thoroughness and pertinacity. He was armed with neatly typed, systematically serialised copies of all documents relevant to the Naga problem and he gave the impression of carrying single-handed, in his little brief case, the destinies of the entire Naga people.[46]

Following the assurances and protestations of good faith on the part of the government, the next month Phizo was arrested in Calcutta and imprisoned in Presidency Jail. He got out a few months later, on compassionate grounds, after the death of his son in a road accident.

Hydari, architect of the Nine-Point Agreement, passed away suddenly following a stroke in December 1948. With his demise, his agreement with the NNC lost its most powerful champion in the Indian government. The debate in the Constituent Assembly on the 'Provisions as to the administration and control of Scheduled Areas and Scheduled Tribes' took place in September 1949. The Sixth Schedule that entered the Indian constitution was based on the Bordoloi Committee report rather than the NNC-Hydari Nine-Point Agreement. Its passage provoked a suspicion of betrayal in the NNC, which immediately shot off a letter to Sri Prakasa, the Governor of Assam. The letter, dated 22 September 1949, says

> The Sixth Schedule of the Indian Constitution is far from satisfying the Nagas. Two years ago, late Sir Akbar Hydari, the then Governor of Assam, gave some extra promises to the Nagas. Where are the promises? The honourable Prime Minister of Assam had also given a written assurance to the Nagas that the Agreement arrived at between the late Governor and the Naga National Council would be fully implemented. Where is the assurance?[47]

The Indian constitution came into force on 26 January 1950, the day now celebrated as India's Republic Day. In December the same year, Phizo became president of the NNC. The betrayals he had feared had happened, and it was now his turn to respond. On 1 January 1951, he wrote to the President of India, declaring that a voluntary plebiscite would be taken by the people of Nagaland on the issue of Naga independence. On 11 April, he followed up with another letter saying: 'We have great pleasure to let Your Excellency know that the Naga National Council has now come to a position to fix a date for the commencement of the said Plebiscite.'[48] The date he announced was 16 May 1951, starting at 10 am, and the process was to last two to three months. The NNC invited the government to send observers.

Khodao Yanthan, a Lotha Naga associate of Phizo's from Wokha, was one of the people involved in organising that plebiscite. 'I went to meet Mr Phizo in Kohima', he recalled many years later:

> He told me, 'Khodao, take this petition and go around not only in the Lotha area, but also in the Ao and Rengma areas, and make sure everyone knows about this petition'... In the plebiscite form, every Naga had two options: either to be independent or to join the Indian Union. I put my thumb impression in blood for independence.[49]

The NNC plebiscite was held only in the Naga Hills district areas. The areas that had remained outside British administration until 1947 were presumed to be outside the successor Indian government's rule as well. More than 99 per cent of Nagas, according to the NNC, voted for freedom in this plebiscite. The date 16 May 1951 is still commemorated by Naga separatists as Naga Plebiscite Day.

Independent India held its first general elections from October 1951 to March 1952. The NNC called for a boycott of these polls, and of the first elections for the Naga Hills District Council that had been constituted under the Sixth Schedule. As Hokishe Sema, a chief minister of Nagaland state and a political opponent of the separatists led by Phizo, later acknowledged, 'To keep the record straight it must be mentioned that not a single vote was cast.'[50]

The Indian government simply ignored all this. So, in 1952, according to Yanthan, three of them—Phizo, Yanthan and another Naga leader named Imkongmeren—travelled to Delhi to meet Prime Minister Jawaharlal Nehru with their plebiscite results. 'We waited and waited and waited', he recalled. Eventually they were given an audience: 'There was no one else in the room except his private secretary. We explained everything. He got angry. He said it is inconceivable for Nagas not to join the Indian Union. So, we invited him to come to Nagaland and see for himself.'[51]

The following year, Nehru went to the Naga Hills to see things for himself, as the NNC had requested. He invited his Burmese counterpart U Nu to accompany him. The two prime ministers arrived in Kohima by road from Imphal on 30 March 1953, and proceeded to a football ground in Kohima to address a crowd. What happened next was reported around the world. *The New York Times* the following day carried a small, single-column report headlined 'Booing tribesmen walk out on Nehru', by a correspondent then in Kohima, who reported:

> Prime Minister Jawaharlal Nehru suffered a public snub by 3,000 Naga tribesmen who walked out booing and waving spears from a meeting he addressed today... Almost the entire group of the tribesmen present left the football field as Mr Nehru was coming to the platform. They refused even to turn around as the prime minister, who is accustomed to holding crowds of hundreds of thousands, began to speak... The ordinarily polite Nagas, some of whom had travelled up to 150 miles to see the two statesmen, retired to hillside thatched mud-and-bamboo huts in a huff after the local district commissioner had refused to receive a petition for 'Nagaland' that colourful feather-helmeted chiefs had prepared for Mr Nehru.[52]

Isak Chishi Swu, who would later go on to become chairman of the largest Naga insurgent group, the National Socialist Council of Nagaland (NSCN), was present there that day. 'I was there as a cameraman', he recalled: 'The Naga National Council wanted to present a memorandum to the Indian prime minister but the deputy commissioner refused to let us present it. So, we left and asked everyone to leave.'[53] The Deputy Commissioner, an official from Assam, took the blame for this—although it is not clear whether he acted on his own or on advice from his superiors—but the damage had been done. Neither *The New York Times* nor Swu mentioned an additional detail: that it was still common for large numbers of the Naga tribesmen in 1953 to wear loincloths, and that they had turned around and thumped their bare bottoms at the two prime ministers before walking out. 'What Nehru saw, to his everlasting chagrin, was hundreds of Nagas whacking their backsides as they left', wrote Charles Chasie and Sanjoy Hazarika in a paper titled *The State Strikes Back*.[54]

The bum salute, in front of a foreign dignitary and the international press, did not go down well with Prime Minister Nehru, and left the Assam government, led by Chief Minister Bishnuram Medhi, deeply embarrassed. The police were sent to raid homes of the NNC leaders. They failed to find them. The government prepared itself for harder measures. The Assam Maintenance of Public Order (Autonomous Districts) Act was passed in May. Under this the state could, 'if satisfied with respect to any particular person that with a view to preventing him from acting in any manner prejudicial to the public safety and the maintenance of public order it is necessary', extern the person from an area, ask him or her to reside elsewhere and report his movements to the authorities, who could also restrict his employment, business, association with others, dissemination of views and use of articles that could be specified in an order.[55] It also empowered the government to 'regulate the conduct' of any such person. These harsh actions began. The NNC believed this was all Nehru's doing. According to Khodao Yanthan, Phizo's closest associate for many years, 'Even before he left Kohima, he ordered the arrest of all NNC leaders. Nehru's policy was to finish off the Nagas. Nehru told U Nu to treat the Nagas in Burma the way he treated them in Assam. So, it was a conspiracy.'[56] A section of the NNC now began preparing for armed struggle.

In the winter of 1953, Phizo, with two of his aides, made a tour of villages in the unadministered areas along the eastern boundary of the Naga Hills district, and arrived in what is now called Aghunato subdivision, inhabited by Sema, Sangtam and Yimchunger Nagas. 'The independence of the Nagas as a nation distinct from the Indian nation was the essence of the speech of all three speakers', Ihezhe Zhimomi, who later became a member of the Nagaland Legislative Assembly from Aghunato recalled many years later.[57] Zhimomi, then a teenager, described how

> people were told not to fall into the trap of the government of India by accepting its handouts like red blankets, free salt, jobs, etc. The audience was told in a very authoritative manner that acceptance of any of the benefits of the government of India would ultimately result in their bondage by imposition of unbearable taxes like land tax, animal tax, tax on wives for people with more than one wife, tax on families with many children, tax on property, tax on feasts of merit, etc.[58]

Phizo's speech had an electrifying effect on the audience. The chiefs, who tended to have the most animals, wives, children and feasts, pledged their support for Phizo and the NNC. A few months later, when an Assam Rifles detachment set up camp on the outskirts of a village in that area to guard a road-building team, without permission from the locals, it annoyed the villagers greatly. 'On one late evening three of the Assam Rifles personnel entered the village to have their fill of the local brew. The villagers pounced on the three and beheaded them', Zhimomi recounted.[59] Other similar incidents followed. The Assam Rifles, in response, began to raid Naga villages. The Nagas raised a formal military organisation allied to the NNC, the Naga Safe Guard, with a Sema Naga warrior named Kaito as general. They in turn started ambushing the Assam Rifles from their base in a village called Khekiye.

The army and the Assam Rifles retaliated in September 1954, attacking and capturing Khekiye. To the Nagas, it signalled the start of a war. The Indian government, however, saw it as a small and hopefully transient problem, and a politically inconvenient one best kept out of public discourse. It was not until matters were well out of hand that Nehru finally made a statement in parliament about the situation in August 1955. 'During the last few months, there have been sporadic outbreaks of violence by certain elements on the borders of the Naga Hills district and the south of the Tuensang division', said Nehru:

> These consisted of ambushes in which some Assam Rifles men as well as a number of tribal interpreters and other villagers were killed, some school buildings, houses and some villages were burnt, and medical supplies were looted. Government thereupon

> sent two companies of the Shillong Brigade in May this year for garrison duty at Tuensang to relieve Assam Rifles for rounding up the violent elements. Troops were used only for garrison duties and not for operations.[60]

The Political Officer in Tuensang, who was himself a Naga, had reported the presence of 'organised armed gangs, totalling a few hundred in this area' and requested military aid, Nehru told parliament, so the government had 'agreed to send a battalion of the army to the Southern sector of the Tuensang Frontier Division'.

The army, as it turned out, was going to have a bit of work to do for a few decades more. Phizo was preparing for war. The Indian government was not his sole opponent. A rift had opened up in the NNC between himself and the organisation's secretary Theyieu Sakhrie. It was a classic hardliner-vs-moderate clash that had been simmering in the NNC for years; Sakhrie and his supporters wanted a peaceful political struggle but Phizo and his men did not believe this would yield any results. This led to a showdown in which Phizo denounced Sakhrie as a traitor. Sakhrie was murdered not long after. He was also an Angami Naga from Khonoma, like Phizo, and his killing immediately started a blood feud between his clan and Phizo's. With Sakhrie out of the way, Phizo, who had now gone underground, moved quickly. In March 1956, under his leadership, a Naga federal government was formed with Khriesanisa Angami as president. It adopted a constitution called the Yehzabo and formed a parliament called Tatar Hoho. The NNC was to be the only recognised political institution in Nagaland, which was to be the name of the new independent Naga country.[61] This was followed by an audacious military move. On 10 June 1956 the Naga Army attacked Kohima. They were initially successful, and even managed to occupy the headquarters of the Indian Army's operational base in Kohima, but were eventually defeated and driven out, aided by differences between the Naga generals Kaito Sema and Thangti Chang. Yet, even in its failure, the Naga Army's siege of Kohima was to lay the seeds of India's longest insurgency.

A month after the attack on Kohima, an old and highly respected resident of the town, and the first Naga to become a doctor of modern medicine, Dr Harielungbe Haralu, went out to visit his grandchildren who lived nearby. An Indian Army patrol that had come in for attack the previous night accosted him, and clubbed him close to death with rifle butts, finally shooting his near-lifeless form. His body was flung over a cliff but became caught in a tree, where it remained for the local residents to see.[62] Members of Dr Haralu's family worked in important positions for the Indian government. His son Thepfurüya was working as Assistant Political Officer in the Naga Hills while his daughter Nikki, who later became an ambassador, was working in the Ministry of External Affairs. The brutal killing of Dr Haralu immediately swung Naga public opinion, then divided between followers of the moderate Sakhrie and the hardliner Phizo, firmly in Phizo's favour.

The incident led, belatedly, to a full discussion of the situation in the Naga Hills in parliament. The Nehru government, after consistently underplaying the magnitude of the crisis, was forced to acknowledge at least some part of all that had been happening. There was no representative from the Naga Hills and the siege of Kohima by the Naga Army was mentioned only briefly by the member of parliament who probably knew best what was really going on: Rishang Keishing, then a young MP from the hills of neighbouring Manipur. A Tangkhul Naga, Keishing was in touch with the NNC leaders. In the course of the debate in parliament, he read out parts of a letter that Sakhrie had sent him in 1953, after Nehru's disastrous Kohima visit, in which the NNC's moderate leader lamented that they had heartily welcomed the prime minister's visit, 'because we felt that we could get the opportunity to have a heart-to-heart discussion on all outstanding issues between the Nagas and India. That opportunity came and went like a mirage.'[63] After the walk-out by the crowd from Nehru's public meeting in Kohima in 1953, some eighty of them had been arrested, Sakhrie wrote.

'It was after this sad occurrence that the Assam Government took police measures and repression started', said Keishing. 'The police indulged in ravaging houses and destroying crops and there were cases of raping as well.'[64] While all this was going on, the NNC made repeated attempts to have discussions with the government, he pointed out, but these efforts were scotched because the government always insisted on 'some condition'. Finally matters had blown up and the situation was that 'most of the homesteads in the villages have been burnt to ashes by our Army, who put to flames more than 30 villages out of the 54 villages in Mokokchung sub-division alone, and also destroyed more than 60 per cent of the villages in the other areas'.[65]

An orgy of gruesome murders and ruthless oppression had been let loose, said Keishing, referring to the murder of civilians such as Dr Haralu and hundreds of others; and even children as young as one were being put in jail. The army had shown complete disregard for the sentiments of the Nagas, Keishing alleged. The naked bodies of dead Nagas had been carried bound by their hands and feet from bamboo poles. The bodies were burnt, contrary to Naga funerary rituals.[66] None of this was having any positive effect on security, he pointed out, because 'the headquarters of the military operations at Kohima was occupied and looted for about a week in June'. A convoy of passengers bound for Imphal was attacked and looted just 2.5 miles from Kohima, he added. A member of parliament from the Imphal valley of Manipur, L. Jogeswar Singh, who had moved the motion for the discussion, was in that convoy, and had been fortunate to survive. He was relieved of his belongings and was briefly held captive like the other passengers before being released.

What Keishing said next, on that day in 1956, proved prophetic:

> As a matter of fact, the issue has been so much entangled that no amount of administrative and military action can solve it. It may be that the rebel Nagas will have to admit defeat, very soon, at the hands of the far superior military strength of the Army. But that does not solve the problem. Those who know the mind of Nagas will tell you that the spirit of revenge for all the killings that are going on will persist for generations… I want to make it clear to all concerned that this problem is not an administrative problem. It is a wholly political problem, and it must be viewed in that perspective.[67]

Replying to the debate, Bimala Prasad Chaliha, an MP from Assam and later chief minister of the state, said that 'the police operation or the military operation or the outbreak of violence and all other unpleasant happenings are only offshoots which have arisen from the demand for complete independence'.[68] After praising the Nagas as a 'great people', Chaliha went on to say that as violence had in fact broken out, 'the Government, as the authority responsible for law and order, have to bring the situation under control'.

Nehru himself said the problem was not being treated as a purely military one, and he believed the government would not succeed without winning the goodwill of the people. 'But then, what exactly do you do when other people start killing? Do we send them messages of goodwill, or do we try to stop the killing?'[69] Referring to the allegations of atrocities that Keishing had mentioned, Nehru acknowledged that 'obviously in military operations and the rest, I cannot get up here and say that everything that is being done was as if we were sitting in a drawing room and that everything that was done can be justified completely'. Mistakes had been made, Nehru reluctantly conceded, and one such mistake that had distressed him exceedingly was the killing of Dr Haralu. He also acknowledged the burning of large numbers of villages, but said that most of those were burnt by the Naga insurgents themselves, or caught fire in the course of fighting. The question of the NNC-Hydari agreement and the dissatisfaction of the NNC with the Sixth Schedule of the Indian constitution had been raised 'off and on in the last eight or nine years', said Nehru. 'On three occasions I met Mr Phizo', he said,

> and at least once or maybe twice I met other Naga leaders... [A]t least four or maybe five times I have discussed this matter with them and pointed out to them that we are always prepared to consider any constructive proposal for amendment to the provision regarding these areas, but it is no good talking to me about independence.[70]

Phizo, who was now the main target of the military operations in the Naga Hills, had, however, given up on the idea of talking. Along with his associate Khodao Yanthan, he set out in December

1956 to try and escape to East Pakistan. The army presence was heavy, and they decided eventually to travel separately to avoid detection. Both of them successfully made their way to Dhaka, now the capital of Bangladesh, which was then East Pakistan. 'They asked me why I had entered Pakistan so I explained to them that Indian Armed Forces had occupied Nagaland and we needed protection, so after that Pakistanis and Nagas shook hands. The Pakistanis said they would help us and so would the Chinese', Yanthan recounted years later.[71] They were 'guests' of the Pakistanis for the next four years.

The added international dimension hastened political activity on the Indian side of the border. The Nehru government moved to organise those Nagas who were friendly towards it. An All-Tribes Naga People's Convention (NPC) was held in August 1957, which passed a unanimous resolution for a political solution within the Indian Union. The NPC proposed the formation of a separate administrative unit by merging the Naga Hills and Tuensang division of NEFA. The Government of India acceded to this with alacrity, and in December the same year a new administrative unit called Naga Hills and Tuensang Area, to be administered by the Governor of Assam through the Ministry of External Affairs, was inaugurated. A second meeting of the NPC was held in May 1958, and this time, the NPC decided to reach out to their pro-independence brethren. The outreach was met with a rebuff; Phizo and his supporters demanded recognition of their Naga federal government as the starting point of negotiations. The Government of India, which had already unleashed the army and deployed special provisions of law—the Assam Disturbed Areas Act had been imposed on the Naga Hills since January 1956—decided to strengthen the military's hand further. A harsh new law called the Armed Forces (Special Powers) Act (AFSPA), specifically applicable only to Assam and Manipur, was brought in as an ordinance in May 1958, before being passed into law by parliament. It empowers any officer of the army operating in a disturbed area to shoot to kill, if he is 'of the opinion that it is necessary to do so for the maintenance of public order'.[72] Soldiers could also destroy any structures from which they thought armed attacks were likely to be made, which in practice meant every house in every village. They could arrest any person without warrant on suspicion and were free to use whatever force they considered necessary to effect such an arrest. They could also, naturally, enter and search any premises without a warrant. No prosecution, suit or other legal proceedings could be instituted, except with the previous sanction of the central government, 'against any person in respect of anything done or purported to be done in exercise of the powers conferred by this Act'.[73]

It was a law conferring unlimited impunity on the armed forces. Not even the colonial British Raj, through the decades of India's independence struggle led by freedom fighters, including Nehru, had come up with anything quite so extreme.

When the bill was brought before parliament on 18 August 1958 by Home Minister Govind Ballabh Pant, he described it as 'a very simple measure'.[74] He faced a straight question from the Speaker, M. A. Ayyangar, who asked whether any person could be deprived of his life by any commissioned officer under this law. Pant replied, not quite honestly, 'No, no. In accordance with the law, that is, the law passed by this House.'[75] Mafida Ahmed, an MP from Jorhat in Assam, asked whether the government of Assam had been consulted before introducing the bill. 'In fact, the Government of Assam made a request to us', replied Pant. It was left to an MP from Orissa, Surendra Mahanty, to express the truth about the AFSPA in plain terms. 'This is a unique legislation, the kind of which has never been contemplated since this Indian Parliament came into existence', he said.

> This is martial law as defined in Article 34 of the Constitution… A havildar can shoot a person without order from a magistrate. He can attack any property. He can destroy any building. He can put any person behind bars or in a concentration camp. For all this, no action can be taken against him except with the permission of the Government of India.[76]

It was high time, Mahanty said, that the Government of India 'took us into confidence and let us know what is the real nature of the Naga trouble'.[77]

The Deputy Speaker, the Sikh leader Sardar Hukam Singh from Punjab—then a member of Nehru's Congress Party—took up Mahanty's argument: 'We do not want a free India with barbed wire and concentration camps, where havildars can shoot at sight any man. If that is the concept of free India, I think I may as well be a traitor.'[78] Laisram Achaw Singh, a socialist MP from the Manipur valley, also opposed the bill, saying 'I have found that the military authorities have committed excesses in many cases'. He referred to instances of rape, saying 'it is dangerous to invest the military authorities with extraordinary powers and of killing and arrest without warrant and of house-breaking... This is an act of provocation on the part of the Government... This is a lawless law.'[79] The sole Naga MP who spoke in the debate was Rungsung Suisa, a Tangkhul Naga from the Manipur Hills who had been elected on a Congress Party ticket. He also said the ordinance was not necessary in Manipur, because the Nagas of the Manipur Hills were not part of Phizo's movement. 'If we want to join the rebels then who can prevent us?' he said. 'Then, the Indian armed forces can kill us, but they cannot prevent us. I am not going to be afraid of offending anybody, it is what it is.'[80]

The only clear support for the bill came from the members from the plains of Assam, who spoke in its favour, rallying behind the then prime minister and home minister—although there were expressions of concern even from some among them, such as D. Basumatari, a Bodo tribal. Nehru and Pant, however, had made up their minds. The Armed Forces (Special Powers) Act passed into law. Incidents of murder, rape and the burning of villages by Indian Army forces would soon follow. The usual argument then and now by those in favour of the law was that the excesses were the acts of bad apples; but even the rotten apples were not brought to justice, even when they committed crimes such as rape. Despite numerous documented cases of such excesses over the decades, and a recommendation by an expert committee constituted by the Government of India for repeal of the law, AFSPA remains in force to this day, an enduring blot on Indian democracy. It has been more than six decades since it was brought into use in the Naga Hills and Manipur, but in a testimony to its failure to restore peace, those areas are still routinely declared to be 'disturbed areas' by the government, because the AFSPA can only apply in an area officially notified as 'disturbed', and this notification comes up for renewal every six months. After Northeast India, the 'lawless law' was used in other places such as Sikh-majority Punjab and Muslim-majority Jammu and Kashmir, but it has never been used anywhere in the Hindi-speaking, Hindu-majority Indian heartland—despite statements by senior political leaders and security officials under both Congress and BJP governments that identified left-wing extremism in Central India as the country's biggest internal security threat.

* * *

When it started back in 1958, the military repression was accompanied by swift political concessions for those Nagas willing to throw in their lot with the government. A third meeting of the Naga People's Convention was held in October 1959 in Mokokchung, an area dominated by the Ao Nagas several of whose leaders had long favoured a settlement with India. At this meeting, a Sixteen-Point memorandum was presented that envisaged the creation of a new state of Nagaland within the Indian Union. This was presented to Nehru and led to the signing of a historic agreement the following year between the Government of India and the Naga People's Convention. 'The territories that were heretofore known as the Naga Hills-Tuensang Area under the Naga Hills-Tuensang Area Act, 1957, shall form a State within the Indian Union and be heretofore known as Nagaland', it announced.[81] The new state would have a legislature, and an elected council of ministers led by a chief minister, but it would function under the Ministry of External Affairs of the Government of India, and executive powers would be vested in the Governor of Nagaland, who would receive the advice and assistance of an executive council headed by the chief minister and his council of ministers. The arrangement was understood to be transitional, with full statehood on the menu.

The biggest obstacle to this political settlement, meanwhile, had reached London.

After spending four years in Dhaka and Karachi, Phizo had finally managed to make his way to Zurich on an El Salvador passport obtained with Pakistani help. There he was detained, but a year later got to London with the help of a peace activist and Anglican priest, Reverend Michael Scott. Back in the Naga Hills, his followers reacted with predictable fury to the moves towards a Nagaland state within the Indian Union. It was, from their perspective, a sell-out, not only for settling for less than independence, but also for less than all the areas inhabited by Naga tribes. Several of these tribes lived in the hills of Manipur, and there were also populations in Assam, parts of what is now Arunachal Pradesh, and, across the international border that had been drawn into nineteenth-century colonial maps, in neighbouring Myanmar.

In August 1961, Dr Imkongliba Ao, the first president of the Naga People's Convention, who had led the delegation to Nehru to present the Sixteen-Point memorandum, was shot dead by an unidentified gunman. In another attack, the rebels also managed to shoot down an Indian Air Force plane and take captive the pilot and crew, who had survived the crash-landing. The Indian security forces had not been idle either. In January 1962, Phizo held a press conference in London in which he accused the Indian Army of causing the death of roughly 75,000 Nagas, mostly civilians, between 1955 and 1959. He sought an inquiry by the Geneva-based International Commission of Jurists. K. L. Mehta, joint secretary in India's Ministy of External Affairs, responded to this with a note marked 'Secret' addressed to the Indian consul-general in Geneva, in which he said Phizo's allegations were grossly exaggerated. Up to December 1961, altogether 306 members of the security forces had been killed and 692 wounded in hostilities in Nagaland, he wrote, while the 'Naga terrorists have lost 1595 men during the same period.'[82]

In the midst of all this, Nagaland emerged as a state of the Indian Union. Prime Minister Jawaharlal Nehru moved the bill in parliament for its creation in August 1962. Speaking on the occasion, he said an agreement had been reached with Dr Imkongliba Ao in July 1960, following which a Naga Council was formed, 'and during the last two years it has been functioning as a preliminary to the changeover'. This council of five members was drawn from an interim body of forty-five members drawn from the tribes of Nagaland, said Nehru: 'Elections to the village, range and tribal councils had been held and the administration of Nagaland has increasingly become the responsibility of the representatives of the Naga people themselves.'[83]

His colleague Renu Chakravartty, an MP from West Bengal, spoke in favour of a constitutional amendment giving special status to the proposed state of Nagaland, by which no act of parliament in respect of Naga religious or social practices, customary laws and the transfer of land would apply to Nagaland unless the Nagaland Legislative Assembly accepted it. The debate saw speaker after speaker rising to support the bill. The sole Naga voice among those was that of S. C. Jamir, who later became one of the longest-serving chief ministers of Nagaland. Jamir, in his speech, gave a small history lesson on the background of the Naga movement for independence from India. Not everyone supported the move. P. C. Barooah, a member from Assam, pointed out that the Assam Assembly had passed a resolution saying:

> This Assembly is of the opinion that in the interest of national solidarity and also with a view to bringing about a co-ordinated development and greater political stability of the eastern region of India, there should be an integrated political and administrative set-up of the various units within this area and that nothing should be done which may have an effect of weakening this unity... This Assembly is of the view that the provisions of the State of Nagaland Bill, 1962, are not conducive to the aforesaid objectives.[84]

Among the seven legislators who voted against the creation of Nagaland was Gujarat's Umashankar Trivedi of the Bharatiya Jana Sangh, predecessor of the Bharatiya Janata Party, because he favoured assimilation of the Nagas, rather than their existence as a separate community. In his speech in parliament, he blamed Christian missionaries for 'tutoring the Nagas that they were a separate nation'; said 'it is a fight of one religion against the other, it is not the fight of a tribe'; expressed his great sorrow for the fact that the violence unleased by the Naga militants could not be 'put down' militarily; and wondered why murder charges had not been brought against Phizo, and sought his extradition from the UK.[85]

Despite the guarded opposition from Assam and the open opposition from the Hindu right, the new state of Nagaland was inaugurated by President S. Radhakrishnan on 1 December 1963, with P. Shilu Ao, who had headed the interim Executive Council, as the first chief minister. The inauguration of the state, and the warm reception this got from several of the Naga tribes, became a problem for Phizo and his supporters. 'They were perturbed over the fact that the fighting arm of the Underground from the Sema and the Tuensang areas was parting company from them. Shilu was considered to be too crafty and parochial and capable of influencing the Aos thereby leaving the Chakesang and Angamis in the lurch', wrote Hokishe Sema, who was one of the ministers in that first Nagaland cabinet.[86] 'They also knew that if Shilu and his party won the majority in the elections then the return of Phizo would become an impossibility', he continued.

Phizo himself took the initiative, sending a letter to Nehru through Reverend Michael Scott in which he proposed peace talks. Meanwhile, the first elections for the state assembly were announced, and two local parties, one led by Shilu Ao and another by Vizol Angami, entered the fray. Neither party was officially registered yet, so all candidates stood as independents. Ao's Naga Nationalist Organisation, which was essentially the Naga avatar of the Indian National Congress, won twenty-six of the forty-six seats, half of them unopposed. The Democratic Party, which was friendly towards Phizo, won twelve. Independents won two. The remaining six seats were reserved for the Tuensang area's representatives, who were to be nominated by the Tuensang Regional Council. There were at that time only three districts in Nagaland—Kohima, Mokokchung and Tuensang—and the administration of Tuensang remained the responsibility of the Governor. There was a buzz that Phizo would return for peace talks before the elections, but he failed to put in an appearance, leaving his supporters dejected. The defeat of the Democratic Party in those first polls, coupled with Phizo's absence from the scene, essentially cemented the status of Nagaland state as a partial political solution to the Naga issue.

All the Democratic Party MLAs resigned from the assembly in December 1964 when peace talks were announced between the Naga rebels and the Indian government.

After the 1964 assembly elections, the Nagaland Baptist Convention adopted a resolution requesting the governments of Nagaland and India to establish a Peace Mission. The government responded, and the first peace talks between the two sides took place, with the Peace Mission delegation, comprising of veteran activist Jayaprakash Narayan, Assam Chief Minister B.P. Chaliha and Reverend Michael Scott, playing referee. All they produced was a temporary ceasefire.

Nehru died in May 1964. The peace talks, with an Indian government led by Nehru's daughter, Indira Gandhi, carried on till 1966, when there were two bomb blasts in the railway stations in Diphu and Lumding, in which more than 100 people were killed. Scott was denounced by Foreign Minister Swaran Singh in parliament for writing letters to the United Nations Secretary-General U Thant of Burma, and to the Burmese government, on behalf of the Nagas. Despite all this, Indira Gandhi held a third round of talks with Kughato Sukhai, who was head of the underground Naga government, and with members of his delegation including Isak Swu, who later became chairman of the National Socialist Council of Nagaland. Scott, meanwhile, was served with a two-day notice asking him to leave India. A solution seemed imminent and a delegation of two Naga leaders, Vizol and the Tangkhul Naga MP Rungsung Suisa from Manipur, went to London to meet Phizo, but Phizo remained adamant in his refusal to visit India. The talks failed, and this time, a section of the underground leaders decided to make their way to Communist China, seeking weapons and training. Phizo himself visited USA seeking help, but had to return empty-handed. A further round of talks was scheduled for 1967, but by then the long march to China had begun. Isak Swu and a young Tangkhul Naga leader from Suisa's village, Thuingaleng Muivah, were among those who made that journey. The next phase of Naga underground politics was about to begin, and it would be led by these two men and their powerful ally and rival, the Burmese Naga S. S. Khaplang.

Phizo remained in exile in Bromley near London until his death in 1990. The movement had slipped from his grasp long before.

* * *

A group of 130 Nagas led by Muivah and Thinoselie Keyho, who later became general of the underground Naga Army, made the journey on foot through Mon in the Konyak Naga area, via Burma to China in the winter of 1966. There they ran into the Burmese Army but managed to talk their way through, eventually reaching a Chinese People's Liberation Army border post in Yunnan in January 1967. 'It had taken us ninety-three days in addition to the three months we had spent in Mon district', Keyho later recounted. The Chinese gave them a camp to stay in, and interrogated them for a good eight or nine days: 'After that Muivah and I were taken to Peking where we met the deputy chief of the PLA.'[87] The Chinese gave them some small arms and training, then sent the group back. Muivah stayed behind. A second, larger group of fighters reached him there in 1967. The rebels found their way blocked by the Burmese military on their way back, and had to fight their way through, suffering considerable losses.

Further internal fissures had developed among the Naga rebels in the meanwhile; there were differences between the Sema Nagas and the rest. The external situation, too, was changing, and it transformed dramatically in 1971 when the Bengalis of East Pakistan rose in revolt against West Pakistan. A genocide by the Pakistani military and a civil war followed. India entered the war on the side of the Mukti Bahini rebels fighting for an independent Bangladesh. The Pakistani forces were swiftly defeated, and forced to surrender. Among those who surrendered was a group of Naga rebels led by Keyho, who after rounds of interrogation in Calcutta and Delhi eventually wound up in jail in Shillong.[88]

The Bangladesh War and the end of East Pakistan, which heralded the emergence of Bangladesh as an independent country, led to a total transformation of the security dynamics as well as politics of Northeast India. Prime Minister Indira Gandhi and her advisers redrew the map of the entire region. The creation of Bangladesh with Indian help wiped out safe havens in what, as East Pakistan, had been an easy go-to place for all the region's rebels. Internal strife within the Naga separatist movement, under pressure from the Indian government, escalated.

The different Naga tribes with their different languages and distinct territories had long tended to see themselves as Ao, Sema, Angami or Lotha first. Over the years, differences had accrued and hardened in the positions of the various tribes. After Sakhrie's murder, Ao leaders had led the way towards accommodation with India, and one of them—Imkongliba Ao, the first president of the Naga People's Convention—had been killed by gunmen suspected to be working for Phizo. A subsequent killing in Kohima in 1968, that of the Sema general Kaito, brother of Kughato Sukhai, also ascribed to Phizo's supporters, took most of the Sema forces out of Phizo's leadership. This left Phizo leading a largely Angami and Chakesang Naga movement, but even within this there were differences, because of the murder, years earlier, of his rival from his own Khonoma village, T. Sakhrie.

The government, fresh from its great victory in the Bangladesh War, now unilaterally withdrew the tattered ceasefire with the Naga underground that had come into force when peace talks began, and the shooting started again. Elections were held for the Nagaland Assembly in the midst of this, but the elected government was soon dismissed and the state came under president's rule. This was followed by the declaration of national emergency by Indira Gandhi in June 1975. The attempt to forcibly bring an end to the Naga conflict began in earnest. For the Naga rebels, weakened by internal divisions, the pressure was too much. In November 1975, Phizo's brother Kevi Yalley, along with five other top leaders of the Naga insurgent underground, signed a peace deal in the town of Shillong, capital of Meghalaya. It had only three clauses: that the signatories from the Naga underground had decided to accept the Indian constitution; that they would surrender arms; and that they would have 'reasonable time to formulate other issues for discussion for final settlement'. It was, quite naturally, seen as a surrender, one about which Phizo maintained an uncharacteristic silence.

The Shillong Accord was condemned by two of the next generation of leaders of the Naga underground who had managed to escape the Indian military dragnet: Muivah and Swu. Both were in China at the time. They had begun their journey in September 1974 with a band of around 200 followers, and after a difficult trek through Burma, had managed to get once again to China. 'I was in China when we heard over the radio that the Shillong Accord had been signed', recalled Muivah. By then a second band had reached them and they were attending 'military training and political classes'. Muivah and his supporters returned to the Naga Hills on hearing of the Shillong Accord and held a 'National Assembly' condemning it. They also formed a new government in exile, with Phizo as the symbolic president in absentia, Isak Swu as vice president and Muivah as general secretary, and set up base in the Naga-inhabited area of Burma, taking on board the Burmese Naga leader S. S. Khaplang. The pro-Shillong Accord group, according to Muivah, came to their camp and, in August 1978, took them captive. 'They had plans to do away with us', recalled Muivah.[89] The plan went awry and the captors wound up dead, courtesy of Khaplang, whose turf it was. In January 1980, the Eastern Nagaland Revolutionary Council, representing Burmese Nagas, and those from the former NNC who were opposed to the Shillong Accord agreed to a merger. A new organisation, the National Socialist Council of Nagaland, was born on 31 January 1980, and a new government in exile called the Government of the People's Republic of Nagaland was formed. A 'collective leadership' of Muivah, Swu and Khaplang took charge of the NSCN and the parallel government it set about establishing.

The organisation has suffered numerous splits since then. First, in 1988, a major break happened between a faction led by Khaplang and another led by Muivah and Swu. This led to the creation of two organisations, the National Socialist Council of Nagalim (Isak-Muivah) and the National Socialist Council of Nagaland (Khaplang). The NSCN(I-M) and NSCN(K) themselves have had further splits, with splinter groups striking out on their own. The fighting, both between the groups and with the Indian and Burmese militaries, has waxed and waned over the years. Since 1997, the most powerful of the groups, the NSCN(I-M), has had a ceasefire and peace talks with the Indian government.

The decades of talks led, in 2015, to the signing of a 'Framework Agreement' between the Indian government and the NSCN(I-M). Indian Prime Minister Narendra Modi and Muivah shared the dais at the signing and spoke of an honourable end to the decades-old conflict. More than seven years have passed since then, but the framework remains an empty frame; at the time of writing, there is no final agreement yet.

Swu, one of the remaining stalwarts of the Naga underground, passed away from age-related ailments in 2016. His former colleague and rival Khaplang died a year later, in 2017. Muivah alone remains from the old guard. The Naga struggle for independence seems over in all but name. The assembly elections in Nagaland held in 2018 saw the unexpected spectacle of the Hindu nationalist Bharatiya Janata Party contesting twenty of the state's sixty assembly seats and—powered by its deep pockets—winning twelve. It ended up with one of its leaders holding the office of deputy chief minister. It repeated the feat in 2023. The final agreement to the Naga peace talks has proved elusive, but meanwhile life goes on, and a new generation, impatient for better roads, faster internet and the best of everything that money can buy, has come of age. Connectivity is the new buzzword.

The Indian Army began operations in the Naga Hills in 1954. They are still operating there. The Armed Forces (Special Powers) Act remains in force even now. In December 2021, soldiers shot dead six coal miners in Nagaland mistaking them for militants. Those responsible cannot be prosecuted without prior permission from the Government of India—which the government has denied. The place is largely peaceful. However, the declaration of the Naga Hills as a 'disturbed area' that perpetuates the state of exception justifying the need for the AFSPA is routinely renewed every six months.

4

MANIPUR'S PRINCES AND REBELS

ASSIMILATING AND SEPARATING THROUGH THE AGES

The road from Kohima to Imphal, the capital of neighbouring Manipur, winds south past forested hillsides dotted with Naga villages to the settlement of Mao at the border between the present states of Nagaland and Manipur. Here, if you are travelling by the shared, overcrowded vans that are a common means of public transport, your vehicle will halt. Passengers can stretch their cramped legs and buy some of the local produce from the roadside shops—items such as colourful Raja or king chillies, the hottest chillies in the world, which at over 1 million on the Scoville scale are at least twenty times hotter than the hottest Tabasco sauces. The driver, meanwhile, has a bit of work to do. He has to pay a toll in cash to a few men hanging around on the side of the road. They are not representatives of the government of Manipur, or Nagaland or India. They represent the parallel government of the NSCN(I-M). It so happens that the hills of this part of Manipur are the stronghold of the Tangkhul Naga tribe, the one to which NSCN chief Thuingaleng Muivah belongs. His native village, Somdal, lies 100 kilometres deeper into Manipur.

The Tangkhul are not the only Naga tribe living in the area. There are also Mao and Maram Nagas, and various other kinds, and members of a tribe that is not part of the greater Naga fold, the Kuki, with whom the Nagas have a history of clashes. Closer to Imphal, there is also a settlement of Gorkhas from the hills of Nepal whose ancestors were settled there by the British. The hills give way to an emerald-green valley of paddy fields, sparkling streams and rivers, including one that gives the capital its name, the Imphal river, and the largest freshwater lake in Northeast India, the Loktak. This is the Manipur valley, home of a community called the Meitei, who have historically dominated the state of Manipur, so much so that the word Manipuri in common usage generally means only them. Other inhabitants of Manipur, including the indigenous tribals, are known by the particular tribe or community to which they belong, such as Naga or Kuki. The capital city of Imphal at the centre of the valley that bears its name is the historic centre of Meitei power. To its south, the valley ends in other ranges of hills, inhabited mainly by other Naga or Kuki tribes. Beyond this is northern Myanmar on one side, and the Barak valley of Assam on another.

Meitei legends speak of an ancient kingdom and a king named Nongda Lairen Pakhangba, whose reign is dated to circa 33 CE. It is said that he could change his form into a giant snake; in iconography, he becomes a 'lai', or divinity, usually depicted as a serpentine dragon. The faith with which he is associated is the indigenous religion of the Meiteis, popularly known as Sanamahi after the supreme deity.

The legends are believed by historians to be based on a kernel of fact, clothed over the centuries with the colours of fancy. The story, according to Manipuri historian R. K. Jhalajit Singh, starts with a battle between Pakhangba and a Shan invader from Burma who had established himself in what is now Imphal. 'For some reason not yet known, the throne of the principality which came to be known as Ningthouja Principality from 33 A.D. onwards fell vacant in the spring of that year', writes Singh: 'A man named Pakhangba had distinguished himself as a warrior... Pakhangba fought for the throne with Poireiton and thoroughly defeated him in a decisive battle. He seized all his weapons and the women who came in his horde.'[1]

After ascending the throne of what became the Ningthouja principality, one of seven in the plains of Manipur, King Pakhangba set about consolidating his rule. He married the vanquished Poireiton's sister Laisna. The first territorial expansion of the Ningthouja principality began in the reign of Pakhangba's grandson, Taothing Mang, who conquered a few villages in the valley. It took another 500 years before the Ningthoujas were able to defeat the neighbouring principality of the Angoms and realise tributes from them. The process of consolidation through warfare and marriage continued for hundreds of years, according to Singh, who based his account mainly on the Manipur royal chronicles called Cheitharon Kumpapa.[2]

The Cheitharon Kumpapa is described by its translator, Saroj Nalini Arambam Parratt, as the only source on the history of Manipur for the pre-British period 'which is of any substantial historical value'.[3] Although Parratt translated it from the original Meitei Mayek into English, she held that 'the earlier part of the chronicle is problematic both as regards dating and historicity, though the information it contains is still useful in reconstructing Manipur's early history'.

Important administrative changes, with far-reaching social impacts, came during the reign of King Loiyamba, who ascended the throne in 1074. He divided the kingdom into six circles called 'pana', each of which had to send a team of workers under a system called 'lallup' to render free service to the state. Trades were specified by 'yumnak', or family line, so that there were particular families and villages assigned to each task. The geographical limits of the panas would vary over subsequent years, but the divisions themselves remained for centuries. So, too, did the concept of lallup, or compulsory free labour, as a form of tax paid in kind.[4]

Political unification of the seven clans that eventually made up the Meitei confederacy took another few centuries. As late as the thirteenth century, the Cheitharon Kumpapa records battles between the Ningthouja and other clans. 'Sakabda 1169 (1247 CE). Meetingu Puranthapa became king. They fought against the Khumans at Pairou in the eastern location and were victorious', the chronicle says.[5] There are also records of battles between the Meitei king and the people referred to then as Hao, meaning Tangkhul Nagas, although in common usage the term (now considered derogatory) was also a generic name for Naga tribes who inhabit the surrounding hills. For instance, 'Sakabda 1185 (1263 CE). Meetingo Khumompa became king. They fought in the centre of Thangkan village in the Hempa mountain range in the north and were victorious over the Hao village.'[6]

By the fifteenth century, the kingdom known as Kangleipak was beginning to assert itself over a wide area. King Kyamba, who ascended the throne in 1467, launched a combined attack with the Burmese kingdom of Pong on a smaller Shan principality called Kyang located around the Kabaw valley in what is now northern Myanmar. The attackers were victorious, and divided up the territory of Kyang between themselves.[7] The Kabaw valley was formally annexed to Manipur at this time, 'in virtue of an alliance which had taken place between a daughter of Kyamba of Munneepoor, and the king of Mogaung, the capital of the Pong dominions'.[8]

Contact with the outside world, with Burma and Yunnan in China to the east, and the Ahom and Mughal empires in the west, quickened thereafter. Vasco da Gama, the Portuguese explorer, had rounded the Cape of Good Hope to reach the Malabar coast of south India in 1498. New products started flowing in from across the seas—firearms, chillies, potatoes, dyes.

References to Mayangs, a word originally used for the people from Cachar and Sylhet, which lie west of Manipur, and now used generally for outsiders, becomes more frequent in the Chaitharon Kumpapa as the years roll on. The entry for the year 1504 in the royal chronicle says, 'The Mayangs revolted. Aangoupampa Loichangampa and others attacked the Mayangs. They lost the battle.'[9] Eventually the Meiteis regrouped and were victorious over the rebellious 'outsiders', after which they erected 'mounds both big and small over the heads' of their vanquished enemies. A hundred years later, in 1606, there was an attempted invasion by Mayangs. The Meiteis emerged victorious and 'captured thirty elephants, 1,000 guns, and a colony of 1,000 Pangans... All those Pangans who were captured alive were allowed to establish an institute.' There is now a sizeable community of Muslim Manipuris known as Pangan or Pangal. Parratt, the translator of the Cheitharon Kumpapa, notes that 'Bengal is sometimes known as Bangal. Pangan could be a corruption of Bangal.'[10]

Evidence of religious tensions begin to emerge around 1701. The entry for the month of Poinu, corresponding to November/ December, says that 'Panthoipi's shrine was set alight.'[11] Panthoibi is a popular goddess of the Sanamahi faith. The royal household did not escape attack. 'On the new moon Friday, the royal great palace was on fire', says the Cheitharon Kumpapa. There is also mention of a 'Kalika shrine' being set alight—Kalika being another name for the Hindu goddess Kali, who is much revered in Bengal.

The tension, it appears, was between the old Sanamahi faith and Hinduism, which had been making inroads into Manipur since the reign of King Kyamba.

In 1704, after a symbolic fast, King Charairongpa converted to Hinduism, thus becoming the first Meitei king to formally adopt Hinduism.[12] He was succeeded in 1709 by a celebrated king of controversial origins, known variously as Mayampa, Pamheiba or Garib Nawaz. 'From this period, we find the people assuming a position of peculiar interest', the colonial historian Boileau Pemberton wrote in his pioneering account published in 1835:

> Emerging from their mountain strongholds, they wage successful war in the fertile valley of the Irrawattee, attack and reduce the most important Burmese towns and villages ... and at last plant their standards in the capital itself. The truth of this portion of their historical annals receives most unexpected and satisfactory corroboration, from the records of Ava.[13]

Pamheiba, who later came to be known as Garib Nawaz, converted to Vaishnavism in 1717, being initiated into the faith by a Brahmin named Guru Gopal Das or Shanti Das.[14] He had a long reign, marked by several successful campaigns against the Burmese, and growing religious intolerance within his kingdom for followers of other faiths and even Hindu sects other than his favoured school of Vaishnavism. In 1732, the Cheitharon Kumpapa mentions the destruction of 'Lais' or divinities of the old faith. According to popular tradition, old Meitei chronicles known as 'puyas' written in the original Meitei script are also said to have been destroyed at this time at the instigation of the king's guru. The old script was replaced by the Eastern Nagari script used by Bengali and Assamese. Different accounts present different versions of the end of his rule. According to Pemberton, in 1749 Garib Nawaz again invaded Burma, but returned without fighting after his standard was blown down and, taking this to be a sinister omen, began a retreat. On the way back he was met by his son, Ugat Shah,

> who upbraided him with the unsuccessful termination of his expedition, and with having tendered homage to the king of Ava [Burma], by the presentation of his daughter: these remonstrances produced so strong a feeling of disaffection among the troops, that Gareeb Nuwaz was deserted by all but 500 men, with whom he again retired, for the avowed purpose of soliciting aid from the king of Ava against his rebellious son.[15]

This help did not materialise, and the king was murdered along with his supporters by his son's soldiers while trying to re-enter Manipur.

The death of the king and the guru was followed by a period of persecution of orthodox Hindus, according to Saroj Nalini Parratt. The murder of his father, and the unrest that followed, also cost Ugat Shah his throne. He was forced into exile to Cachar in the Barak valley of Assam. Another brother, Bharat Shah, took his place.

Even as the Manipur kingdom was descending into infighting and chaos, Burma was being unified under one of the most powerful rulers in its history, Alaungpaya. In 1755, a Burmese force attacked and invaded Manipur. The successful raid was followed by a larger invasion in 1758 led by Alaungpaya himself. This time, the Burmese devastated Manipur all the way to Imphal, and carried away a substantial population including horses and horsemen. They later formed the Cassay Horse cavalry of the Burmese Royal Army, which was instrumental in the successful Burmese attack on Siam (or Thailand).

A new power was rising on the other side of Manipur as well. In 1757, the Nawab of Bengal, Siraj ud Daulah, had been defeated—with the help of a traitorous general of his own army, Mir Jafar, and the financial backing of a very wealthy family of Jain bankers from what is now Rajasthan, known as the Jagat Seths—by the East India Company under Robert Clive at the Battle of Plassey. This made Clive the jagirdar, a kind of duke, of twenty-four revenue units of land called parganas. Even today, West Bengal has two districts called North 24 Parganas and South 24 Parganas. A few years later in 1764, another momentous victory in the Battle of Buxar made the East India Company rulers of all of Bengal, Bihar and coastal Orissa. The 'diwani', or taxation rights, to these territories were ceded to the East India Company by the Mughal emperor in Delhi, Shah Alam II. The Company Raj now reached the boundaries of what would become Northeast India.

The new king of Manipur, Jai Singh, seeking security against his Burmese foes, had already sent a representative named Hari Das Gossain to Chittagong to meet with the East India Company representative there, Harry Verelst, two years earlier. As Captain Pemberton wrote in his account:

> A treaty of alliance, offensive and defensive, was negotiated on the 14th of September, 1762, with Hurree Dosa Gossein, on behalf of his master Jaee Sing, by Mr. Verelst, in which the aid of a contingent of British troops is promised, whenever the Rajah may find it expedient to attempt the recovery of such portions of his territory, as had been wrested from him by the Burmahs... And he promises in return to make such grants of land to the English, as might suffice for the establishment of a factory and fort, and a distance of country round such factory and fort of eight thousand cubits, free of rent for ever.[16]

The kingdom was then not yet known as Manipur; the name used in the treaty was Meckley. Unfortunately for him, the treaty proved to be of no help to Jai Singh.

Verelst marched towards Cachar with a small force in 1763, but never got beyond the capital, Khaspur, due to heavy monsoon rains. He was still there when he received orders to return. 'Circumstances of a political nature rendering the recall of the force necessary, a letter was dispatched to Mr. Verelst, who returned with it to Chittagong', wrote Pemberton.[17] The next winter, the Burmese under King Hsinbyushin invaded and devastated Manipur again, carrying off thousands of its people into captivity. The Manipur king was forced to flee to Cachar.

The growing power of the Burmese brought them into conflict with a mighty force. The following year, Chinese imperial forces invaded Burma and years of war between the Chinese and Burmese armies followed. At last, in 1769, tired from the endless fighting, the generals of the two sides concluded a treaty and the Chinese withdrew. 'When he heard that the Chinese had been allowed to depart, the king was angry; he thought they should all have been killed', wrote G. E. Harvey in his *History of Burma*. 'So, the armies, afraid to return home, went off to Manipur in January 1770.'[18] The generals wanted to loot slaves and cattle with which to placate the king. The men of Manipur fought gallantly but were overwhelmed in a three-day battle near Langthabal. The raja fled again, to Assam. The Burmese raised their own nominee, the Moirang Raja, to the throne, and returned, taking with them such of the population as were not hiding in the woods.

Three years later, the Burmese were back in Manipur again. Once again Jai Singh was forced to flee, and once again he returned in a few months after the Burmese forces had left. After Jai Singh's rule, a fresh period of instability marked by repeated clashes between different claimants for the throne followed. In 1806, one of these, Marjit Singh, the brother of the then King, Chaurajit, rebelled. His first rebellion was put down with difficulty, upon which he fled to Burma via Cachar and Arakan. He returned in 1812 at the head of a large Burmese army obtained in exchange for a promise to give up Manipur's claims to the Kabaw valley and to acknowledge his dependence on Burma's king.[19]

After his successful invasion and ascent to the throne, Marjit fell foul of his Burmese allies. On the occasion of the coronation of the powerful Burmese monarch Bagyidaw, in 1819, all the tributary kings were summoned to attend and pay homage. Marjit declined to go. This was seen as a deliberate insult. The Burmese monarchs, who then believed they were the most powerful in the world, sent an army to invade Manipur and the neighbouring Ahom kingdom, whose ruler they had also helped to install. A period remembered as 'seven years of devastation' followed. Marjit was forced to flee and escaped to Cachar. There he reconciled with his brothers whom he had deposed, and a combined Manipuri army now invaded Manipur to recover the kingdom. The besieged Burmese forces, however, managed to cling on until support arrived from Burma, upon which the attackers fled again. Having run out of options, Marjit and one of his brothers, Gambhir Singh, now approached the British for help. While it was not yet forthcoming, the rise of Burmese power was pushing events in that direction.

In September 1823, the Burmese suddenly launched a midnight attack on a British outpost on the island of Shahpuri, near Teknaf, in what is now Bangladesh. Tensions between the two sides began to escalate. On 5 March 1824, the Viceroy of India declared war on Burma.[20] When the war ended two years later in the defeat of the Burmese king, a treaty was signed in the town of Yandabo in February 1826 between the Burmese and the British. It brought the former Ahom territories, Cachar and Jaintia, apart from Arakan and Tenasserim in Burma, under British rule.

Northeast India thus for the first time entered the political unit of British India. The Burmese had conquered the fertile river valleys of Assam and Manipur. The British soon inherited control of these. The hills, however, remained beyond their rule. It would take the better part of a hundred years for the new rulers to extend their administration into those hills, stretching from the Himalayan borderlands at the edge of Tibet to the Naga and Lushai Hills bordering Burma, and construct the new region.

* * *

During the Anglo-Burmese War, Gambhir Singh, one of the claimants for the Manipur throne, had successfully retaken Manipur leading a small force called the Manipur Levy, while the main Burmese army was busy battling the British forces. He went further, and even managed to drive away the Burmese garrison guarding the Kabaw valley, an area long disputed between Burma and Manipur. Manipur remained independent under the terms of the Treaty of Yandabo, and Gambhir Singh was recognised as the Rajah of Munnipore by both the Burmese and British. However, when he died in 1834, his son and heir Chandrakirti Singh was only one year old, and power went to a regent from the royal family, Nar Singh. At the same time, the British sent a political agent to the Manipur court. Chandrakirti's mother tried to poison Nar Singh but failed. She was able to escape with her child after this. In 1850, Chandrakirti, now a young man, successfully returned to take the throne of Manipur. He was quickly recognised as the rightful ruler by the East India Company government, which ensured his place on the throne by declaring that any attempt to dislodge him would be suppressed by force of arms if necessary.[21]

A long series of uprisings did indeed follow, and they were all put down. There was also some trouble at the state's border with Burma, where a Manipuri outpost at a place called Kongal near the disputed Kabaw valley (transferred to Burma from Manipur by the British in 1834)[22] was attacked in December 1877 by the forces of a local king described in colonial records as 'Rajah of Sumjok' in alliance with the Kuki chief of Chassad. The state's boundary with Burma had never been properly defined, although there was an old map and description left by Captain Pemberton from the 1830s, so the Government of India finally decided in 1881 to appoint a boundary commission led by the political agent there, James Johnstone, to settle the issue. This commission began its survey but the Burmese did not send a representative from their side, and the boundary commission was met with hostility on the ground. Despite this, the commission carried on with its work: pillars were erected and a line marked on the map. 'Manipur might, according to Pemberton's statement, have claimed a good deal of territory occupied by Burmese subjects, but this I refused to allow, as it would have been interfering with the status quo, which I desired to preserve', wrote Johnstone.[23]

In 1886, Chandrakirti died and his son Sura Chandra succeeded him. Another series of uprisings began, with his four half-brothers under the leadership of one of them, the Senapati or General Tikendrajit Singh, allied against the new king, while his three brothers remained loyal to him. Matters soon came to a head. 'During the year 1890–91 Manipur state was the scene of much anarchy', recorded Aitchison's *Treaties*:

> Matters reached a climax on 21st September 1890, when the palace walls were scaled by the two younger brothers, and a few shots in the air were sufficient to drive the timid Sura Chandra Singh to seek safety at the residency. The next day, contrary to the advice of the Political Agent, he declared his intention to abdicate and to proceed on a pilgrimage to Brindaban: and on the 23rd he left the State, accompanied by his three brothers and a few followers, and arrived at Cachar by the end of the month. Here he changed his tone, represented to the Chief Commissioner that he had no intention of abdicating, and solicited assistance to regain the 'gaddi' (throne). In the meanwhile, the Senapati, who was the real mover in the rebellion, had induced his elder brother, the Jubraj Kula Chandra Dhaja Singh, to occupy the gaddi, and application was made to the Government of India to ratify this accession. The whole question was considered by the Government of India and it was concluded that it would be to the advantage of the Manipur State to recognise the Jubraj in his new position rather than to restore Sura Chandra Singh. It was however decided to remove the Senapati from Manipur and punish him for his lawless conduct towards his eldest brother.[24]

This decision was to prove unfortunate for everyone concerned.

The Chief Commissioner of Assam, J. W. Quinton, was directed to carry out the government's order. He arrived with a force of 400 men of the Gurkha Rifles and announced a durbar, or assembly. Senapati Tikendrajit didn't attend on the grounds of ill health. The chief commissioner decided to arrest Tikendrajit in his house. In this, they were unsuccessful, and the residency in turn came under fierce attack.[25] After the fighting, an attempt at a negotiated solution at the Durbar Hall produced no result and the political agent Grimwood was speared to death in a melee on their way back. Chief Commissioner Quinton and Lieutenant Colonel Skene, the head of the military force accompanying him, were captured and later executed by beheading. This provoked a full-fledged invasion of Manipur by British Indian forces. Three columns from three directions—from Silchar, Kohima and Tamu—marched towards Imphal. The Tamu column faced a battle at a place called Khongjom, which they won decisively despite heroic resistance from a force of 400 warriors under the command of Major Paona Brajabashi. All three columns converged on Imphal on 27 April 1891. The Senapati and a senior member of the court who had assisted him, known as Thangal General, had gone into hiding. A month later they were found, and after a quick trial by a special tribunal were hanged for 'waging war against the Queen-Empress and abetment of murder of British officers'.[26] A Gurkha soldier, Subedar Niranjan Chhetri, who had earlier defected to the Manipuri side and joined Tikendrajit's bodyguard unit, also met the same fate.

Regent Kula Chandra Dhaja Singh, initially sentenced to death, received a reprieve and was sent into exile to the Andamans. A proclamation dated 19th April 1891 had already been issued by which the administration of the state was assumed by the officer commanding Her Majesty's forces in Manipur.[27] The British placed on the throne Chura Chand, the six-year-old grandson of Nar Singh, the former regent they had appointed after Gambhir Singh's death. A sanad was issued to the new king that provided for the complete subjection of Manipur state, payment of a war indemnity of Rs. 250,000 and of a yearly tribute of Rs. 50,000. Administration of the state during the minority of the king was vested in the British political agent. At the investiture of Chura Chand in 1892, slavery was abolished in Manipur and the practice of lallup, or free compulsory labour, was replaced with an annual house tax of Rs. 2 in the valley and Rs. 3 in the hills.[28]

Money became increasingly important for the population as a whole. Modern education, open to all classes and sections of society, followed. The *Annual Report on the Native States and Frontier Tribes of Assam* for 1897–98 records that 'At the close of the year there were 9 primary and 1 middle English school[s] operating in Manipur.'[29] Only two of these schools were in the hills. New roads were built soon after, including one upgrading the path that connected Imphal with Kohima and Dimapur, which remains the main artery of road communication for Manipur to this day. The demarcation of some of the state's boundaries also happened in this period. For instance, the same report also notes that

> The erection of stone prisms along the Chin–Manipur frontier, as fixed in March 1894, was carried out by an officer from the Chin Hills at the close of the year 1896–97... It had been intended that the settlement of the Manipur–Lushai boundary, from Lungle hill westwards to Tipaimukh, should be carried out during the cold season.[30]

The Chin–Manipur frontier lies between Manipur and Burma, while the Manipur–Lushai boundary is the one between Manipur and the state of Mizoram. The most important town on the Indian side of the border in that part of Manipur is Churachandpur, named after the Manipur king Chura Chand who was then still a student at Mayo College in Ajmer in Rajasthan, in the west of India. 'His Highness Chura Chand Raja and his half-brother Digendra Singh resided at the Mayo College, Ajmere, throughout the year', the *Annual Report* recorded: 'Both brothers are very favourably reported upon, and their education is progressing satisfactorily.'

The *Administration Report* for 1903–04 finds the brothers back in Manipur. 'His Highness Raja Chura Chand Singh was in residence in Manipur throughout the year', it says.[31] His imminent assumption of royal duties was preceded by clashes between two groups of Brahmins, arson, and an uprising led by women that is now remembered in Manipur as the First Nupi Lan or women's war. The *Administration Report* of 1903–04 makes no mention of this at all. The one for 1904–05 merely says:

> In September and October some discontent was exhibited by the residents of Imphal, who had been ordered to rebuild the Assistant to the Political Agent's bungalow which had been burnt to the ground some time previously. Assistance was obtained from the regiment stationed in Manipur; the crowds were dispersed and the ringleaders arrested and banished. Some other cases of incendiarism occurred during the year.[32]

The coyness may have been on account of one underlying cause for the unrest: the former king Sura Chandra's married daughter Sanatombi had eloped with the author of the report, British political agent Lt Col Henry Maxwell.[33] The Manipuri historian R. K. Jhalajit Singh mentioned the 'incendiarism' in greater detail in his account. He ascribed the acts to revolutionaries opposed to British rule: 'In March 1904 they burnt the bungalow of the Assistant Political Agent Mr J. J. Dunlop… In July they burnt all the sheds of Khwairamband Bazar which housed the stalls of 3,000 women. In August 1904, they burnt the bungalow to which Mr Dunlop had shifted.'[34] After Dunlop's bungalow was burnt for the second time, the political agent, Maxwell, ordered that the residents of Imphal, barring a privileged few, would have to rebuild it by contribution of free and compulsory labour—a throwback to the system of lallup that had been abolished at the time of Chura Chand's investiture in 1892. Immediately there were rumblings of discontent; Rajkumars, meaning princes, who were not immediate members of the ruling royal family, were not exempted from the free labour. Nor were Brahmins. This was viewed as an unacceptable insult. The protest took the form of 'gherao', or encirclement. Maxwell's bungalow was surrounded by a crowd of around 3,000 women.

In 1907, Chura Chand took charge of the administration with a durbar, or assembly. His durbar was comprised of himself as president, a British officer of the Indian Civil Services as vice president and six Manipuri members. The *Administration Report* for 1911–12 finds Chura Chand, now twenty-six years old, with three wives and five children. The report highlights celebrations in Manipur on the coronation in England 'of their Gracious Majesties King George V and Queen Mary'.[35] Further celebrations followed to mark the visit to India of 'Their Imperial Majesties the King-Emperor and Queen-Empress'. Chura Chand went to Delhi for the Imperial Durbar of 1911, where Indian rulers gathered in honour of their imperial majesties. He and his first wife were granted separate audiences with the British king and queen.

* * *

That old world of kings, queens and empires was about to start changing very abruptly.

In 1914 the First World War broke out. Manipur, in the far northeastern corner of India, felt the distant ripples of its effects. The raja and his durbar set about organising recruitment for the Labour Corps, whose services were required in the distant battlefields of Europe. Trouble started when sections of the Kuki tribe who inhabit the hills of Manipur objected to the recruitment of any members of their tribe. 'Labour Corps had been raised for France in 1916 among various clans of Nagas, Lushais, and others, who willingly came in, having done this sort of work for Government before in border expeditions, and knew the work and good pay', Leslie Shakespear wrote in his history of the Assam Rifles:

> Such had done extremely well wherever they were sent, but in 1917, more were needed, to supply which it was necessary to tap other sources, viz. the various Kuki clans inhabiting the hill regions of the native State of Manipur, a people who had never left their hills and knew but little of us and our ways.[36]

Unknown to the British, an influential Kuki chief, Chengjapao Doungel of Aisan, had passed a message to his brethren asking them to resist recruitment. Immediately these efforts ran into trouble:

> Optimism too strong with the higher authorities soon showed the fallacy of trying to induce these people to leave their country for the unknown, and the Chiefs, with whom the first attempt was made, declined to send men. A further effort on the part of the Political Agent only produced angry refusals. This Political Agent was then sent to France with Labour Corps and another officer took his place, who was directed to explain to the Chiefs the reasons why their men were wanted, the nature of the work required of them, pay to be received, etc., to which end he arranged for a Durbar and invited the Kuki Chiefs to attend.

The chiefs of the southern hills refused to attend and warned 'that if we used force to compel them to do what they had no intention of doing, they would also use force against us'. These messages of the chiefs of Mombi and Longya were considered insolent by the colonial rulers and 'the officiating Political Agent, with Captain Coote and 100 rifles, marched in September to visit Mombi, six days out from Imphal, where open hostility greeted them. A skirmish followed and the place was destroyed'.[37]

It was the start of what is remembered in Manipur as the Anglo-Kuki War, although there are discrepancies in the details about what happened right from the beginning, between Shakespear's account and those of Kuki historians such as Jangkhomang Guite. Guite wrote that there was a meeting between the Kuki chiefs and the British political agent at a place called Oktan near Imphal on 10–11 October 1917, at which the chiefs said their people feared to go so far from their homes and would rather die in their own country. As Guite wrote:

> On 14 October, barely two days after the Oktan meeting, the PA took 50 rifles to Mombi [Lonpi] to arrest its chief Ngulkhup… When the chief refused to give himself up, Higgins, before his party returned home, burnt down all the houses and properties of Mombi on the morning of 17 October 1917… The burning of Mombi was followed by a hectic phase of consultations, mobilisation and war preparation across the Kuki hills.[38]

After the consultation process, in November or December, a Kuki chief named Lhukhomang Haokip, more popularly known as Pache, convened the traditional Kuki war council, the grand chiefs-in-council, at his capital Chassad. The council was attended by 150 Kuki chiefs from Burma, Assam and Manipur who resolved to fight against the British government—a declaration of war. The war preparations began.[39]

Rumours of Kuki preparations soon went 'viral' all over the hills and valley of Manipur. This was followed by a few small attacks, described as Kuki raids in British accounts, although Guite argues that since the chiefs had decided on a defensive rather than offensive strategy, those attacks were in fact led or instigated by Manipuris—an identity of which the Kukis, at least in his definition, are clearly not a part. The British responded by sending detachments of eighty soldiers each of a then newly raised paramilitary force, the Assam Rifles, to the Kuki villages of Mombi and Ukah which they blamed for the troubles. The first detachment failed to reach Mombi and was beaten back with casualties. The second had only slightly better success. As Colonel Shakespear wrote:

> The first somewhat unfortunate occurrence and the first reverse (there were only two in the whole operations) sustained, served to put the Kuki rebels' tails well up; the whole southern and south-western hills were now in active rebellion, serious raids following, in which they closed the road to Burma, destroying the rest-houses, killing the chokidars, and damaging the telegraph line.[40]

The British now began their own preparations for this little war in a far corner of the empire on which the sun never set, then locked in the biggest war the world had ever seen: the First World War. Both Kuki and British accounts agree broadly on what ensued. The Kukis adopted guerrilla tactics, sniping at the advancing columns and vanishing into the woods. The British responded by simply marching on until they reached the villages, which they then proceeded to destroy, usually facing little resistance as the Kukis withdrew—a smart strategy, because the British Indian forces were better armed and had heavy weaponry, including mountain guns, while the Kuki village houses themselves, being lightly made from bamboo with thatch roofs, could be rebuilt without too much trouble or cost once the military withdrew.

Guite wrote:

> If the Kukis were difficult to get in person for war or arrest, what the 'flying' military columns did in the hills was, as Lt. Col. French-Mullen put down as their objectives: to overrun the rebel country with suitable columns, harrying the tribesmen, preventing them from cultivating and inflicting all the damage possible on them and their property, [and] giving them no rest whatever until the rains broke out.[41]

Nonetheless, the Kukis did not submit. With the coming of the rains, the military columns withdrew. By winter 1918 the First World War had ended. The few Kukis who had gone to Europe with the Labour Corps began to return home. The government now put them to work, sending forth a proposal for peace if the warring chiefs would surrender and subject themselves to trials in courts of law. This they refused to do. The British Indian forces had been bolstered by the return of officers and men from the war, and they now set out to capture the hostile chiefs and their followers. The entire 'hostile theatre of operation' was divided into six areas, each of which was to be enclosed by a chain of fifty-four outposts of fifty rifles each. These outposts would serve as bases and supply depots for mobile columns that would then go in search of the Kuki rebels.

'Once the operation started, all the schemes of "civilised barbarity" were carried out with impunity and the military occupation of the hills by "force of arms" was made', wrote Guite. He continued:

> The Kuki villages were systematically burned down to the ground, all their livestock and supplies were 'sequestrated or destroyed', and every effort at cultivation and new settlements [was] 'frustrated'... Besides this scorched-earth policy, the whole Kuki population was harried and hunted down from pillar to post, giving them no rest, inside the enclosed area. Those hapless Kukis such as women, children and aged, or even their fighters who were captured in the hunt, or who had surrendered, were put into the various 'concentration camps' close to military outposts. They were used as bait to the 'rebels' to submit and as human shield against their attack. While most of the leading men were incarcerated in the 'prison of war' annexed to Imphal Jail, hundreds of women, children and other men were kept in different 'concentration camps'.[42]

The net result of the military operations was that the hills of Manipur, which had previously not been under the direct administration of the British—they were indirectly administered after 1892 by the local headmen and state intermediaries known as 'Lambus'—now came to be directly administered. A formerly unadministered (i.e. independent) area, the Somra Tract of Burma, was also included in the administrative changes because its villagers had joined the war on the Kuki side. Roads were built using free labour by the locals as a form of war reparation paid in kind. Outposts had been set up. The structure for a permanent occupation was in place. A new administrative machinery now took charge. The traditional power structure that ran through village and clan chiefs, was replaced by a new power structure that flowed through the sub-divisional officer and the British political agent; the Manipur maharaja found no place in this structure. Other things accompanied this change: schools, offices and clinics came up, and Christian missionaries were better able to expand their activities among the hill tribes.

The Kukis were not the only tribe inhabiting those hills. A backlash against this ingress of a new world upon the old also came from the third major community inhabiting Manipur, the Nagas. There had long been a prophecy among them that a Naga king would arise, drive out the British, and rule over 'all who eat from the wooden platter'—that is, all Naga tribes. 'In 1929, a seer of Kambiron village, a man named Jadonang, proclaimed himself the promised Messiah', wrote the pioneering anthropologist and Second World War guerrilla, Ursula Graham Bower, in her account of the Nagas.[43] Jadonang launched a cult called Heraka, or 'pure', that mixed aspects of Hinduism and Christianity with the old Naga animist faith. It was a reform movement of the old Naga religion, doing away with several of the difficult rituals called 'gennas' expected of members of the community, but introducing in their stead something that had not previously existed in Naga animist worship: a temple. Information reached the government in 1930 that Jadonang had also proclaimed a Naga Raj; was demanding that the revenue from 1931 should be paid to him rather than to the government; and had begun collecting firearms, which made their old local rivals, the Kuki, nervous. Meanwhile, four Manipuri traders on their way to Silchar in the Barak valley of Assam had disappeared en route in March that year in Kambiron. A year passed without any trace of them, and then one day a drunk youth from Kambiron, in the course of a quarrel at a neighbouring village, let slip that the villagers had done away with the Manipuris. The locals had thought the traders had disrespected one of their 'gennas' or rituals by lighting a cooking fire on a day when it was forbidden. For this crime, the traders had paid with their lives.

Jadonang was arrested from Cachar in Assam. The British political agent and sub-divisional officer posted in Manipur came to Kambiron to investigate and found evidence against him. As Bower wrote:

> They found enough, in fact, to hang Jadonang for murder by human sacrifice, and to jail for several years the young bucks who had done the butchery for him. But, when all was done, when they had wrecked his temples and shot his sacred python, there still remained his disciple and priestess—a sixteen-year-old girl named Gaidiliu.[44]

They let Gaidiliu go, and proceeded to convict Jadonang for the murder of the four Manipuris, for which crime he was hanged in Imphal in August 1931. His followers believe, to this day, that Jadonang—who had been arrested once even before the murders came to light—was falsely implicated in the case and done away with for political reasons.

These were two wrong decisions. Immediately, Gaidiliu inherited his mantle, and raised the banner of revolt. 'A few days later the whole Kacha Naga country was alight. There then ensued something almost comparable to the hunt for Prince Charlie. Troops were sent out to all the three districts in which the Kacha Naga country fell—Manipur, Naga and North Cachar', wrote Bower.[45] It took months of searching before Gaidiliu was eventually caught by a detachment of the Assam Rifles from a village at the edge of the Angami Naga territory.

With Gaidiliu's arrest, the Naga rebellion in Manipur ended. Each of the three major communities that inhabited Manipur effectively came under British Indian administration. They had all fought their separate wars and rebellions, and each had been defeated in turn. The clashes in 1891, now remembered as the Anglo-Manipur War, that made the British political agent the most powerful figure in the princely state and the Imphal valley, was the first. The Kuki rebellion of 1917–19, which is remembered as the Anglo-Kuki War and resulted in the Manipur Hills coming under direct British administration, was the second. Sections of the Nagas of Manipur, who were distinct from the Nagas from the area that eventually became Nagaland, had their own little war with the British authorities after the hanging of Jadonang in 1931. The most powerful Naga tribe of Manipur, the Tangkhul, however, did not participate in this quasi-religious uprising. Christianity had made deep inroads among them by then, due to the pioneering efforts of the Scottish missionary William Pettigrew, who—at the same time that the British India authorities were facing rebellion from the Kukis over the issue of enlisting for the First World War Labour Corps—managed to recruit a predominantly Tangkhul Naga Labour Corps between 1917–19, and led it to work on the Western Front.

* * *

Life in the state, and the wider world outside, had been changing at breakneck speed during the First World War. With the end of the war, empires had begun to collapse. A relatively new fashion in world politics was catching on: the nation-state. Ideas of democracy were spreading, although no country in the world would qualify as a full democracy by today's standards. There were, in 1900, only two sovereign democratic republics—the USA and Switzerland—and neither gave women the right to vote. In the case of Switzerland, this right was not granted until 1971. The Indian freedom struggle had drawn its initial impetus from the desire for more democratic rights within the British empire. The agitations for democratic representation that began with a demand for seats in the councils of power of the British Indian empire trickled into the hundreds of princely states, including Manipur.

Its origins in the state had a rather unusual aspect. 'Movements for constitutional reform in the Indian States date from the 1930s and were actively encouraged towards the end of the decade', wrote Saroj N. Arambam Parratt and John Parratt in a 2001 paper. 'In Manipur, such organised protest may be said to have begun with the neo-traditional Sanamahi movement in the 1930s, which fiercely attacked the feudalism and Brahminism which Chura Chand used to exercise control.'[46] The Sanamahi movement itself traces its origins to a similar movement called Apokpa Marup (Association for Ancestor Worship) that was started by a retired teacher and police officer from Cachar's Meitei community named Naoria Phulo. Pictures show him clad in saffron, with a turban on his head, seated in the lotus pose, his appearance reminiscent of another celebrated religious icon and reformer a couple of decades older than him, Swami Vivekananda. Years later, one of the pioneering leaders of armed insurgency in Manipur, Nameirakpam Bisheswar, leader of a militant group called the People's Liberation Army, would write on his death-bed, 'Naoria Phulo is the pioneer of the Meetei nationalism and Meetei religion. He is the first legendary figure who openly challenged the viability of Hinduism and Hindu caste system accepted by the Meeteis.'[47] While Vivekananda had remained within the Hindu fold, pushing only against its rigid Brahminical taboos and superstitions, the faith Phulo founded morphed into a revival movement for the pre-Hindu Meitei faith that was dominant in the kingdom of Manipur before Hinduism was adopted as the state religion by King Garib Nawaz 200 years earlier.

King Chura Chand was by then well settled into his royal gaddi. The *Administration Report* for 1937–38 gives a full account of the rather long string of titles he had acquired in the intervening years. He is introduced in the report as 'Sreela Sree Astottara Satajukta Manipureswar His Highness Sir Chura Chand Singhjee K.C.S.I., C.B.E., Bhakta Rajarshi Sree Kunda Seva Binoda Dharma Palaka Beerchuramani Dampingamba Huyen Langsaiphaba Gora Bhakti Rasarnaba'.[48] By then he had added three more wives, now having a total of six. His eldest son, Bodhchandra, was already thirty years old. A second son, Priyabrata, was exiled to Benaras by his father in 1934, but was pardoned and returned to Manipur in 1937. The state had by then acquired a completely modern administrative structure and machinery, which continues to operate with relatively small changes to this day. The departments, with their familiar names ranging from public works to education and arts and crafts, were in operation in both the valley and the surrounding hills. The health and veterinary departments had sections on vaccination. There was a hydroelectric scheme and electricity, and motor vehicles and vehicle tax—a whole new world that was vastly different from that of the turn of the century, thirty-seven years earlier.

The already rapid social and political change was about to accelerate further. Major constitutional reform of the British Indian empire was coming. The Government of India Act was passed in 1935, opening the path for elected legislative assemblies and ministerial councils with considerable powers. Chura Chand and the British Raj, under whose rule the modern world was flooding into Manipur, were the old order, where the king and the British political agent were the lords and masters of the state and its subjects. Smaller chieftains lorded it over every department of government, each headed by a male member of the royal family. Hierarchies of caste were strictly observed. Prospects for commoners of all castes were limited—but the world was changing fast.

Public and social organisations were proliferating across India. In 1934, one such organisation, with Chura Chand himself as president, was launched, called the Nikhil Manipuri Hindu Mahasabha. The general secretary, who was the real leader and moving spirit of the effort, was a man named Hijam Irabot.

Irabot's was the classic rags to riches tale. As an orphan who had been brought up by his maternal aunt, who put him through school, he had accompanied his aunt's son to college in Dhaka in East Bengal.[49] After returning to Imphal on completing college, Irabot became a leading light of the town's cultural scene. He was a talented singer, actor, writer and poet. His activities somehow brought him to the attention of Rajkumari Khomdonsana, one of the daughters of King Chura Chand's elder brother. The penniless orphan, with the king's blessing, was married to the princess and given a respectable job as a member of the Sadar Panchayat court.

It did not take long for the fairy tale to sour.

The fourth session of the Nikhil Manipur Hindu Mahasabha was held in Imphal in 1938. At this meeting, under Irabot's leadership, the word 'Hindu' was dropped from the organisation's name, and it became the Nikhil Manipur Mahasabha. Irabot was elected president in place of the Maharaja. The organisation, which until then had been purely cultural, now set out an explicitly political agenda. The central planks of this were a proposal for a common administration of the valley and hills, and the establishment of a representative democratically elected government. The NMM demanded the setting up of a legislative council for the attainment of a fully representative form of government elected by adult franchise.[50] This was radical for the ancient princely state. Yet it was entirely in sync with what was happening in British India. Next door in Assam, the Legislative Assembly had been established in Shillong in 1937.

The uppity demand for democracy didn't please the Maharaja. His durbar declared that no employee of the state could be part of the Nikhil Manipur Mahasabha, forcing members to choose between their jobs and the organisation. All except two, of whom one was Irabot himself, chose to keep their jobs and resign from the Mahasabha. Irabot chose to resign from his job.

The simmering political tensions found expression the following year. In 1939, the normally bountiful rice crops of the Manipur valley were hit by unseasonal rains. The price of rice rose. The Manipur Durbar, aware of the problem, passed a resolution in September demanding that the export of rice be stopped. In November, this policy was reversed on the orders of the Maharaja.[51] The building of roads and the advent of motor vehicles had made it possible to export Manipur's rice swiftly and in bulk over long distances. The trade was run by immigrant businessmen from the traditional trading communities of Western India, who had developed close links with the king. Matters came to a head less than a month later. Arriving at the main market in Imphal, the Khwairamband Bazar, on the morning of 11 December 1939, people found there was no rice for sale.

The next day a crowd of thousands of women gathered around the durbar demanding an immediate halt to the export of rice. Other members of the durbar fled, but its president, T. A. Sharpe, remained and was surrounded by the agitated mob. He pleaded his inability to give effect to any order banning rice exports without the assent of the Maharaja, who was away on a pilgrimage to a Vaishnav site called Nabadwip in Bengal. At this, he was led to the telegraph office, and pressured to send a telegram to the Maharaja. The women refused to let him go until the king's reply was received. A platoon of the Assam Rifles arrived to rescue him.

The crowd did not disperse, and the soldiers used bayonets and blows from rifle butts to clear a path. They managed to get in to the telegraph office, but the crowd of women surrounded them again. It was not until midnight that they were able to leave. The incident left twenty-one women injured. The Maharaja replied two days later, giving his nod to the rice export ban.

Hijam Irabot was not in Manipur when these events happened. He returned four days later, on 16 December, and immediately called a meeting of the Nikhil Manipur Mahasabha, where sharp differences between Irabot and the other members, who were against the agitation, were revealed. Irabot now opted out of the Mahasabha, and on 24 December he formed a new political movement called Manipur Praja Sammilani.[52] He made a passionate speech on 7 January 1940, in which he said:

> We begged for rice and in return we received bayonet wounds and wounds from gun butts. For one handful of rice, we paid two handfuls of blood... The women's work is finished and now has come the time for the men. Let us take revenge for the spilt blood of the Brahmani.[53]

After this speech, Irabot was arrested and jailed for sedition. His presence even when he was imprisoned in Imphal proved troublesome for the government, and he was packed off to the jail in Sylhet. 'This proved a fruitful period for his political education, for his fellow detainees included a number of Indian Congress and Communist workers', John and Saroj Parratt wrote in their account, 'Irabot was able to gain a greater understanding of Marxist-Leninist ideology and his left-wing convictions were strengthened.'[54] He was still in jail when his erstwhile benefactor turned tormentor, Maharaja Chura Chand Singh, declared his intention to abdicate the throne in September 1941 on completing fifty years of his reign. He was ill, suffering from tuberculosis, and died a couple of months later.

It was again a time of fearsome global tumult. The Second World War was raging. When Japan entered the war in December 1941 with its attack on Pearl Harbor, there was no immediate concern in Manipur; the war was still far away. However, it got closer at pace as the Japanese invaded and swiftly overran Burma. 'In January and February 1942, refugees began to arrive in their hundreds from Burma and were housed on their way through in a camp five or six miles north of Imphal', the president of the Manipur Durbar, E. F. Lydall, wrote in the *Administration Report* for 1943–44: 'Foreign merchants started removing their families and then themselves departed in large numbers.'[55] Camps soon overflowed. Transport was in short supply. Prices of essentials rose. Then in May there were air raids, as a result of which 'the civil administration of the State ceased to function'. People escaped Imphal, fleeing to the surrounding hills. Even the police failed to report for duty, and convicts escaped from jail. 'In the centre of Imphal, almost the only civilians remaining were a few pilferers and looters', wrote Lydall.[56]

There were, however, no further air raids and gradually the panic dissipated. The king and the political agent, who were both away when the air raids struck, returned. The army began to prepare defences for which large numbers of labourers were hired at handsome salaries. Contractors made fortunes: 'Treasury transactions, which in peace-time had averaged about two lakh rupees a month, rose to between thirty and forty lakh rupees a month', wrote Lydall.[57] Next year, in April 1942, there were again Japanese air raids on Imphal. This time, hardly anyone fled the capital. Candidates writing their matriculation exams took shelter in trenches when the bombs were falling before returning to complete their exams.[58]

Through 1943, Imphal was prepared as a base for a coming Allied invasion of Burma. Major General Orde Wingate and his Chindits used it as the base for their raids. Another irregular unit called the V-Force was raised for intelligence gathering and guerrilla operations in the hills of Burma and Manipur. The Japanese finally attacked in March 1944. Three Japanese divisions mounted an invasion and laid siege to Imphal, arriving within less than 16 kilometres of the town. The Indian National Army, led by former Congress president Subhas Chandra Bose, accompanied them. Facing them were three divisions of the British Indian Army.

Bose's forces entered Moirang in Manipur and raised their flag, the leaping tiger, on 14 April 1944. In September 1943, they had declared the establishment of a provisional government of independent India, the Arzi Hukumat-e-Azad Hind, with Bose as head of state. This provisional government had Moirang and its surroundings in Manipur, and the Andaman and Nicobar Islands, under its rule. It also won formal recognition as the legitimate Indian government from the Axis powers. This was ultimately as far as the provisional government would go; its existence, and the fact that it had entered a corner of India, remained unknown to most Indians then and is still largely unknown now. The Japanese attacking India had very little armour or field artillery and negligible air support, and their supply lines were impossibly stretched, leaving troops suffering starvation and disease. They were eventually driven back after one of the bloodiest battles of the Second World War, which took place in Kohima. On 22 June 1944, the siege of Imphal was lifted.

* * *

The combination of social unrest, the Second World War and the impending departure of the British from India finally forced political changes in Manipur. King Chura Chand was an orthodox Hindu and observance of caste taboos known as 'mangba-sengba', or pollution-purification, was still common in his kingdom during his reign. The Brahma Sabha, a community organisation of the Brahmin caste that enjoyed the backing of the king, decided what constituted pollution, and had the powers to perform ritual purification rites for a fee. Being declared 'polluted' carried a cost. The 'polluted' could not eat a meal with caste Hindus, nor marry anyone other than an outcaste. Worse, the outcaste could not live in the same house or locality as upper castes. Naturally, this often led to extortion—and resentment. There were other grievances as well. A new educated class had emerged, but jobs in the state administration were generally given on the basis of birth, with all the higher positions reserved for those with some family connection to royalty. Even lower down the ladder, all appointments for jobs with salaries more than Rs. 15 a month were made by the king.[59]

King Chura Chand passed away in 1941. He was succeeded by his son Bodhchandra.

In 1946, the new ruler decided to allow Hijam Irabot, who was then out of jail and living in exile in Cachar, to return to Manipur. The Nikhil Manipur Mahasabha, sections of which he had developed differences with years before, had meanwhile grown closely aligned to the Indian National Congress in the intervening years. Irabot had developed communist sympathies.

'The political movements and labour strikes in British India had their repercussions in the State', wrote Captain M. K. Priyabrata Singh, King Bodhchandra's younger brother, in the *Administration Report* for 1946–47, in his capacity as chief minister of the Manipur state council:

> His Highness agreed to the setting up of a constitution-making committee composed of officials and non-officials to draft a constitution for the state; representatives for the Valley were returned by indirect elections held in the five Tahsils and those for the Hill were sent up by the President, Manipur State Darbar, in whose special responsibility lay the then administration of the Hill.[60]

The first meeting of the committee was held on 24 March 1947. 'The draft constitution was passed by the Committee on 8th May '47. It was a great credit to this Committee that they could in such a short time bring out an agreed constitution', wrote Singh.

The new constitution, hastily put together in little over a month, envisaged an elected assembly with powers to only debate and tender advice to the Maharaja's council of ministers. The Maharaja had the powers to veto debate on any issue and, of course, to withhold his assent to any bill passed by the assembly, in which case it would lapse. He would continue to rule with his council of ministers, consisting of a chief minister and six other ministers. The chief minister was bound to 'seek approval of the Maharaja in person or in writing' for any official measure—leaving him, in effect, with no decision-making power. However, the constitution did recognise certain fundamental rights of citizens for the first time, including the right to equality before the law and to individual liberty. The subsequent regulations for the elections—in advance of much of the world of that time—provided for full adult franchise.

It was too late. On 3 June 1947, Viceroy Lord Louis Mountbatten announced the plan to partition India into the dominions of India and Pakistan. He also arbitrarily brought forward the date for the transfer of power from June 1948 to August 1947, barely two months later. With the withdrawal of the British, paramountcy, meaning the recognition of the British Crown as the paramount power in undivided India, would lapse. This meant that the hundreds of princely states that had been brought under British suzerainty since the Battle of Plassey in 1757, including Manipur, would technically be free from the treaty obligations that had brought them under indirect British rule. As a result, the rulers of some of these states were also dreaming of ruling their own countries without an Indian or Pakistani prime minister replacing the departing British Viceroy as overlord—a return to political freedom of the sort that preceded the stitching together of the empire that was British India.

The immense task of signing agreements with the princely states to prevent them from all going their own ways began. It was a race against time. King Bodhchandra Singh was persuaded to sign the Instrument of Accession with India, the successor dominion of the British Indian empire, on 11 August, four days before India's independence. By the terms of this, Manipur would cede only the powers over defence, external affairs and communications to the Indian parliament.

In June and July 1948, the first democratic elections with adult franchise under the new Manipur constitution were held. Independents won a majority of the 53 seats, of which 18 were from the hill constituencies and three were reserved for Muslims. The Manipur State Congress emerged as the single largest party with 14 seats; a new royalist party, Praja Shanti, was second with 12. Irabot's party won six. Irabot was elected from a constituency called Utlou. He was never able to take his seat in the Manipur Assembly. His rivals found an opportunity to force him out of the political arena before the assembly session began. A proposal to create a new state called Purbanchal Pradesh incorporating Manipur, Tripura and Cachar was then doing the rounds. Irabot organised a protest meeting of the Manipur Krishak Sangha, representing farmers, and the Manipur Praja Sangha, of commoners, against this proposal, which would subsume Manipur's separate identity. The police cracked down on some of his supporters as they were on their way to attend the meeting, and in a scuffle that followed one policeman was killed, allegedly by the protesters. Immediately, Chief Minister M. K. Priyabrata Singh declared the peasant and worker organisations illegal, and announced a prize of Rs. 10,000 for Irabot's arrest.[61] Irabot went underground—the first of many who would do so over the following years.

The new assembly elected under the Manipur constitution lasted only a few months more. In September 1949, Maharaja Bodhchandra Singh, who had been chafing at the interference of the new Indian dewan of Manipur, Major General Rawal Amar Singh, went to Shillong to try and iron out the differences with the Governor of Assam, Sri Prakasa. His residence there, Red Woods, was soon surrounded by armed guards deployed by the Governor. The Maharaja's private secretary wrote a letter to the superintendent of police at Shillong, saying:

> I am directed to convey the grateful thanks of His Highness the Maharaja of Manipur for your sending guards for the protection of His Highness during his stay here in Shillong. Indeed, His Highness feels glad at the gestures. But since His Highness has brought adequate guards for himself, His Highness does not like to cause any trouble to you. Hence you can please arrange to withdraw your guards forthwith.[62]

The guards were not withdrawn, and instead the Maharaja was offered a privy purse of Rs. 225,000 per year for the rest of his life if he would sign an agreement merging his state with the dominion of India. He initially refused to do this without returning to Manipur and referring the matter to the elected state assembly, but was not permitted to leave. He then demanded that the purse be increased to Rs. 400,000 per annum and eventually a deal was struck for Rs. 300,000 per annum.[63] This was guaranteed in the Merger Agreement that was signed on 21 September 1949. The Merger Agreement also promised that 'His Highness the Maharaja shall continue to enjoy the same personal rights, privileges, dignities, titles, authority over religious observances, customs, usages, rites and ceremonies and institutions in charge of the same in the State, which he would have enjoyed had this agreement not been made.' He was also assured the 'full ownership, use and enjoyment of all private properties', with time until January 1950 to furnish the Indian government with an inventory of such properties.[64]

However, certain clauses from the draft agreement signed by Maharaja Bodhchandra Singh relating to administrative powers went missing from the final agreement.[65] From 15 October 1949, the ancient princely state of Manipur officially merged with India.

The merger was welcomed by the Manipur State Congress, which had actively agitated for union with India. The king and his court sullenly accepted it. The Praja Sangha opposed it, and was promptly labelled communist.[66] Irabot, under pressure from younger colleagues, now took an openly Marxist line. The Communist Party of Manipur began working on plans for village cells and the dissemination of communist literature. The military wing of the movement, the Red Guard, started training in guerrilla tactics some eighteen months later. After going underground, Irabot made his way to Burma and there established contact with the Burmese Communists. He set up headquarters in the Kabaw valley and initiated arrangements for the military training of his supporters, but died of typhoid in September 1951, before he could carry his plans into action.[67]

His rivals in the Manipur Congress and the royalists soon became dissatisfied with the political status of Manipur after the merger. The states and British presidencies of India, with the exception of the Andaman and Nicobar Islands, were classified into categories A, B and C by the constitution of India which came into force in 1950. Manipur was relegated to category C. This was the category of states that were to be ruled directly by a chief commissioner on behalf of the president of India. There was no elected assembly, and no political representation for the politicians of the Manipur

Congress who had campaigned for the merger with India. Nor did the terms of the Merger Agreement that he had negotiated for himself do much good to the Maharaja. He died in 1955, having enjoyed his privy purse for barely five years.

From 1953, the Manipur State Congress began demanding statehood for Manipur. 'The Political Resolutions of the first and second Manipur Political Conferences held on second July, 1953, and sixteenth August, 1954, urged upon our central leaders to grant statehood to Manipur', a pamphlet that was submitted years later by the State Congress unit to Prime Minister Indira Gandhi recalled.[68] The demands and entreaties fell on deaf ears. Manipur became a Union Territory in 1956, a notch up from its status as 'Part C' state, and that was where it remained. Meanwhile, its neighbouring Naga Hills made rapid political progress and emerged as a full-fledged state of the Indian Union in 1963. That same year, Manipur, where the demand for full statehood had been raised by all sections, was given a sop in the form of a Territorial Legislative Assembly with a council of ministers under a chief minister who would report to the chief commissioner of the Union Territory. Like Maharaja Bodhchandra Singh's constitution for Manipur in 1947, it was once again too little, too late.

* * *

A turn towards extremism was coming.

In November 1964, a revolutionary organisation called the United National Liberation Front of Manipur was formed under the leadership of a talented young playwright named Arambam Somorendra. Among the founding members of the UNLF were a Naga, Kalalung Kamei, and a Kuki, Thangkhopao Singsit. The stated aim was an independent, socialist republic of Manipur. In the initial years, the movement did not take up arms, working more in the cultural sphere. Until 1968, UNLF leaders including Somorendra were overground. The armed militancy began in December that year when a faction of the UNLF led by Oinam Sudhir Kumar with the help of his colleague N. Bisheswar, established a 'Revolutionary Government of Manipur' in exile with headquarters in Sylhet in East Pakistan.[69]

Barely three years later, East Pakistan became Bangladesh after the 1971 war. The Meitei rebel leaders, including Sudhir Kumar and Bisheswar, like their Naga counterparts wound up in Indian custody. The ensuing reorganisation of Northeast India saw Manipur elevated to the status of a full-fledged state with an elected assembly and a chief minister, thus meeting the political demands of a significant section of the population. A Constitutional amendment, Article 371C, was brought in with special provisions for the administration of the hill areas of the state. The first elections to the new assembly of sixty seats—a number that has remained the same to this day—were held in 1972. The Indian National Congress contested all sixty seats, and the Communist Party of India contested twenty-five. A local party of Congress dissidents, the Manipur People's Party, put up forty-two candidates. There were 103 Independent candidates, of whom nineteen, mainly from the hills of Manipur with their Naga and Kuki populations, emerged victorious. The Congress was the single largest party with seventeen seats, closely followed by the Manipur People's Party which won fifteen.[70] The first elected government of Manipur as a state of the Indian Union came to be formed by a coalition called the United Legislature Party, led by the MPP with a Manipuri Muslim leader, Mohammad Alimuddin, as chief minister.

It lasted only a year before being destabilised by defections. In March 1973, Alimuddin was forced to resign. Governor B. K. Nehru, a cousin of Prime Minister Indira Gandhi, dissolved the assembly and the new state came under president's rule. Fresh elections held in February 1974 saw the Manipur People's Party emerging as the single largest party, with twenty seats, while the Congress tally fell to thirteen. Two other parties, the Kuki National Assembly, representing the Kuki tribes, and the Manipur Hills Union representing the Nagas, contested the polls for the first time.[71] The Hills Union won a handsome twelve seats. Alimuddin returned as chief minister with support from the Hills Union, but his second tenure was even shorter than his first. Four months on, his ally Yangmasho Shaiza of the Manipur Hills Union, a Tangkhul Naga who had won the elections from Ukhrul in the Manipur

Hills, switched sides and became chief minister with Congress support. His tenure did not last much longer than Alimuddin's. Less than five months on, Shaiza himself was forced out of the chief ministership, and R. K. Dorendra Singh of the Congress took over.

In 1975, the year now chiefly remembered for the Emergency in India when democracy was temporarily suspended, Singh, as chief minister, offered a general amnesty and a rehabilitation package to the Meitei militants in various jails. Sudhir Kumar and his followers accepted this. Even Somorendra retired from his revolutionary activities and came overground to focus on his artistic work. Only N. Bisheswar, who had been jailed in neighbouring Tripura where he came in contact with Maoist inmates, refused to surrender. On getting out of jail, Bisheswar, with a band of sixteen men, set out for Lhasa in Tibet in search of Chinese assistance. Travelling via Nepal, the Manipuri rebels reached their destination in late 1975. They were given the training they sought, and much political indoctrination, but no weapons. On returning to Manipur the following year, they began the process of setting up bases and acquiring arms. In 1978, under Bisheswar's leadership, an underground leftist militant group called the People's Liberation Army (PLA)—also the name of China's military—was formed. The goal: the independence of Manipur by armed struggle.

Sudhir Kumar, the former UNLF leader who had given the organisation its radical turn by setting up a government in exile, was shot dead in January 1979 by PLA cadres. As militants began to make their presence felt, the state responded by clamping down. The Armed Forces (Special Powers) Act of 1958, which gave soldiers a literal licence to kill, was invoked in the entire state in 1980 by declaring it a 'disturbed area'. Bisheswar was arrested in 1981. Many cadres of the PLA and another militant group that emerged at the time, the People's Revolutionary Party of Kangleipak (PREPAK)—another name for the ancient kingdom of Manipur—were killed.

More than forty years have elapsed since, but the armed forces and the AFSPA which was first imposed on parts of Manipur in 1958 are still there. The ordinary citizens have suffered grievously through the decades of conflict. A case is now making its leisurely way through India's legal system. It relates to 1,528 instances of what are euphemistically termed 'fake encounters' or 'extrajudicial killings' by police and security forces between 1980 and 2012. The dead include all kinds of people. One of the cases being examined by the courts concerns the killing of an unarmed twelve-year-old boy. Protests by civil society for human rights after particularly egregious violations have had some impact. The rape and murder of a woman associated with the PLA, Thangjam Manorama, in 2004 led to a memorable protest by an organisation of elderly Manipuri mothers, the Meira Paibis, who protested naked in front of the Kangla Fort in the heart of Imphal, the symbolic centre of the first Meitei kingdom of Pakhangba, which had been taken over by the Assam Rifles. The Assam Rifles have since vacated the fort.

One Manipuri woman protester, Irom Sharmila Chanu, went on an epic hunger strike of sixteen years in protest against the AFSPA that enabled such atrocities. She was force-fed through a nasal tube in hospital through all those years. She survived, and eventually broke her fast, but the AFSPA that she fought so long and hard against remains. It has been withdrawn from Imphal and a few adjacent areas as a small concession to the protesters.

Of the storied militant leaders, only one, R. K. Meghen, the former chief of the UNLF, still survives. He is now retired like his predecessor Somorendra, who was shot dead by unidentified gunmen said to be from an outfit called Kanglei Yawol Kanna Lup in 2000. Meghen's three-decade-long run underground came to an end in 2010, when, following a change of government in neighbouring Bangladesh where he was based, he and several other leaders of Northeast militant groups were handed over informally to Indian intelligence agencies by their Bangladeshi counterparts. While others cut their prison time by agreeing to 'peace talks' with the Government of India, Meghen chose to stay in jail. He was finally set free by the Indian government in 2019, and returned to his home in Manipur to live with his family that he had left behind decades earlier.

The state to which he returned is one run by the Bharatiya Janata Party. The 'fake encounter' killings had peaked under the previous Congress government, and a kind of relative peace descended on the state. Instead of summary executions there are only summary arrests, with people being thrown into jail under charges including sedition for Facebook and Instagram posts criticising the state's BJP chief minister N. Biren Singh. Singh tried, unsuccessfully, to paper over tensions between the three major communities in the state—the Naga, Kuki and Meitei—but several crucial mutually interconnected issues are not really resolved either in the Imphal valley, the surrounding hills, or in Nagaland or northern Myanmar next door. Manipur remains suspended in an uneasy peace, prone to descending into fraternal conflict just as it was a thousand years ago, in the days when clan warred against clan and tribe against tribe.

5

TRIPURA'S SLOW JOURNEY TO THE PERIPHERY

FROM CONNECTEDNESS TO SPLIT PERSONALITY

At the time of India's independence, there was in what is now Northeast India only one significant princely state other than Manipur. This was the kingdom of Tripura, to the south of Manipur, from which it was separated by what were, until a few decades earlier, thickly forested hills inhabited by hostile Zo tribes quite distinct in language and culture from the dominant communities in the plains on either side. A large part of the Tripura population, however, was and still is settled along a thin strip of relatively flat land at the western edge of the state, where it meets Bangladesh. Here, in West Tripura district and the adjacent Sepahijala district, two of the eight districts that make up the state, live around 1.7 million of the state's 3.6 million people.[1] West Tripura is where the capital city of Agartala, with its handsome Ujjayanta Palace built by the Tripura kings, is located. The international border post of Akhaura in Bangladesh is less than 10 kilometres from the palace. Across on the other side of the Indo-Bangladesh border, barely 20 kilometres away, is the Bangladeshi town of Brahmanbaria. A second famous palace of the Tripura kings, the Neermahal Water Palace, sits in the middle of a lake in Sepahijala district. Barely 15 kilometres away along a highway that follows the Gomati river is the immigration check post of Sonamura on the Indian side. Going west from Sonamura, less than 10 kilometres away, is the Bangladeshi city of Cumilla, capital of a district also called Cumilla.

Until 1947 and the partition of India, these neighbouring places on either side of the border were closely connected by history, language, culture, trade and people. The Cumilla and Brahmanbaria districts were then marked in the maps of the British Raj as Tippera. The hilly state now in India was called Hill Tippera. They were distinguished from one another by more than topography. While the Tippera in the Bangladesh plains were technically royal estates, with the Tripura kings as zamindars paying taxes to the British Raj, Hill Tippera enjoyed the status of a princely state. It was a distinction born of a history of warfare and conquest going back centuries involving the Mughals, the East India Company and the rulers of Tripura—and it was to prove momentous when, in 1947, the country was divided into the domains of India and Pakistan. Tippera and the rest of the Tripura kings' zamindari estates in British India, collectively known as Chakla Roshanabad, went to East Pakistan. Hill Tippera remained in India. As a succession of riots between Hindus and Muslims broke out in the years preceding and following partition, a stream of Bengali Hindu refugees, mainly from Tippera, made their way into neighbouring Tripura. They were followed by Chakma Buddhist tribals, who in subsequent years were forced to leave their homelands in the neighbouring Chittagong Hill Tracts of Bangladesh. The issues of migration and identity have remained the cornerstones of Tripura politics from then until now, which primarily pits local tribal communities against the Bengalis. The general assumption is that the tribes are indigenous, while the Bengalis are later migrants—although the migration appears to have begun a few centuries before 1947.

The principal written record of the history of Tripura is a chronicle of the Tripura kings. Known as the Rajmala or 'garland of kings', it was written, according to most authorities, during the reign of a king named Dharma Manikya who ruled from 1431 to 1462. By its own account, it was the work of two Brahmins in collaboration with the royal priest. Further volumes were added to this over the centuries, until there were six volumes. The last two volumes however disappeared. The remaining four volumes were updated and a rewritten version in Bengali verse was produced in 1828 by a 'wazir', or minister of the royal court, named Durgamani Ujir.[2] It is a colourful tale, marked by much divine intervention, that traces the dynasty's origins to a king named Daitya,

> who was living in the Kirata city as if he was immortal. After long years a son was born to him. The king named his son Tripura... Tripura, from his very birth, never met any Brahman...or witnessed or practised any religious act... He had the nature and behavior of a Kirata.

Upon seeing his son's ways, King Daitya, according to the Rajmala, thought to himself, 'this is cent percent a land of the Kiratas... There is no better land in the whole world than Aryavarta.'[3] And he then proceeded to think longingly of all the wonderful Hindu pilgrimages in Aryavarta, while all he saw in Tripura was a land of Kiratas infested with ferocious wild beasts.

Who were these people called Kiratas, evidently considered lesser mortals by the people of 'Aryavarta' who called themselves Aryas, meaning Aryans? The linguist Suniti Kumar Chatterji, who authored a book on the history and culture of the Kirata people called *Kirata-Jana-Krti*, subtitled his work 'The Indo-Mongoloids'.[4] The Kiratas were people of East Asian appearance who were scattered along the eastern Himalayas from Nepal to India's Northeast and beyond. Along the borderlands where South Asia meets Southeast Asia, there is an enduring politics of racial difference, stretching from ancient times to the present, between the people of East Asian appearance and their neighbours from the plains to the west, who look different from them.

After King Daitya's death, his son Tripura became king:

> The king named Tripura, who was of the nature of a Kirata, cast to the winds all thoughts of Dharma (right conduct). He oppressed his people for long years... No other king was a match for him in battle, and so he conquered all by his power... Long years passed in this way.[5]

Eventually Lord Shiva, the destroyer in the Hindu trinity of creator, preserver and destroyer, arrived in person to meet King Tripura, according to the Rajmala. The arrogant king refused to recognise the god as a superior authority and so Shiva struck him dead with his trident, upon which the sinful king ascended to heaven—because he had died by Shiva's holy hand. The king's subjects, rather than rejoicing at this turn of events, were fearful, and fled to the 'Hedamba country', meaning Cachar in Assam, which borders Tripura in the north. There, as refugees, they were reduced to begging, and decided after years of suffering the indignity that they needed a new king, so began praying to Shiva to provide them with one. The god was propitiated by their ardent prayers and sacrifices and once again appeared, this time to grant the people a boon that a son would be born to the late King Tripura's wife, Queen Hiravati. A year after this, the queen conceived 'by the seed of S[h]iva' a child. A boy named Trilochana was born who soon after, while still a baby, was installed on the throne. Two new royal flags were drawn up for Trilochana: one with a crescent to indicate he was a Chandravanshi, or part of a lunar dynasty, and another with a trident to indicate his descent from Shiva. These symbols remained on the coat of arms of the Tripura kingdom until the end of its existence as a princely state.

The story proceeds thus, with several crucial appearances by the god Shiva and his divine consort Parvati, who apparently took a personal interest in the kingdom's affairs, until the advent of a king named Ratna Fa, who was the first to bear the title of 'Manikya' by which his dynasty was subsequently known. Ratna Fa, according to the Rajmala, when still a youth, left Tripura to live in the court of the king of Gaur in Bengal. He returned at the head of a large army supplied by the king of Gaur and easily overcame the armies of his father and brothers, thus becoming king of Tripura. In the Rajmala's tale, he is supposed to have been the 101st king of Tripura. He is, however, arguably the first who emerges as a historical rather than mythical figure. The historian Alexander Mackenzie, in his classic account on the Northeast frontier of India, writes that Ratna Fa was a younger son of the ruler—and therefore not first in line for succession—who 'obtained the throne with the aid of

4,000 Mahomedan troops lent him from Gaur'. He puts the date of this at around 1279. 'Ratna Fa received from the king of Gaur the title Manik by which all succeeding Rajahs have been known', wrote Mackenzie.[6]

After ascending the throne, Ratna Manikya presented the king of Gaur with elephants, in exchange for which he sought a collection of 'the nine essential castes' of people from Bengal. He was 'supplied' with 10,000 Bengalis from the various castes, who practised different professions in the hereditary manner prescribed by the Hindu caste system.[7] Dharma Manikya, in whose time the Rajmala was first composed, may have been the great grandson of Ratna Manikya—although there is controversy over both his origins and the chronology.[8] The Tripura kingdom enjoyed stability and prosperity during his time. It expanded greatly under the reign of his successor, his son Dhanya Manikya, who waged successful wars with his neighbours, such as the Hedamba kingdom of Cachar and the tribes in the adjoining hills that lay between Tripura and Manipur. He then turned his attentions towards the neighbouring plains of Bengal, and took the prized port of Chittagong. This brought him into conflict with the powerful ruler of Bengal, Sultan Hussain Shah, but Tripura in those days was a considerable power. Four expeditions by Hussain Shah's army were successfully driven back by Dhanya Manikya, who lost the plains of Cumilla but managed to hold the rest of his territories—except Chittagong. The port passed into the hands of the rulers of Arakan on the Burmese coast, who then became the principal targets of Hussain Shah's ire.[9] A war between the Bengal sultanate and the Arakan kingdom followed, at the end of which Chittagong was finally recaptured by the Sultan's forces in 1519.

The most important Hindu pilgrimage site in Tripura is the temple of goddess Tripura Sundari. It was established by King Dhanya Manikya in 1501 in his capital city of Udaipur, initially as a temple of Vishnu. The idol of the goddess is said to have been brought from Chittagong and installed there later, on Dhanya Manikya's orders. The Tripura Sundari temple thus changed from being a Vaishnava place of worship to a Shakti Peeth, a temple of the mother goddess—a change of sects that mattered in the politics of the time.

Dhanya Manika's son, who succeeded to the throne after him, took religion rather too seriously, and as a result was fooled by a Brahmin into offering up several of his generals as human sacrifices, before being done to death himself in a crematorium where he had been persuaded to go without his bodyguard for a ritual.[10] The next ruler, Vijay Manikya, was set on the throne by a general who effectively became the ruler of the kingdom. After having this general murdered by subterfuge, the king took charge and expanded his kingdom towards the Khasi and Jaintia hills of what is now Meghalaya, and the plains of Sylhet that lie between Tripura and those hills. In this he was successful. Then, like Dhanya Manikya, he launched an attack to try and capture Chittagong, where a rivalry between two aspirants for the position of Governor under the Bengal Sultan had spilled over into conflict, drawing in the neighbouring Arakanese under their powerful king Man Pa.[11] Man Pa died in 1553. Vijay Manikya's attack on Chittagong in the confused political situation that followed was successful, but brought him into conflict with the Sultan of Bengal. The Sultan sent a strong force under a general named Mamarak Khan to take Chittagong. The Tripura forces, bolstered by their own Pathan mercenary detachments, held on, and Mamarak Khan was taken captive and beheaded.[12]

Vijay Manikya, perhaps the most accomplished of the Tripura monarchs, died in 1572. A half-brother of his, Amara Manikya, became king. He attacked Sylhet and took it from its commander, and then successfully beat back an attack in 1587 by forces described by the Reverend James Long, in his analysis of the Rajmala, as 'Muhammadans', although the commander of the Tripura forces at the time was evidently also a Muhammadan named Issah Khan.[13] 'The Raja subsequently declared war against Arrakan, invaded it, and took many places. He was repulsed by a junction of the Mug troops with the Portuguese', wrote Long. A decisive battle for the control of Chittagong was 'gained by the Mugs in consequence of disagreement between two thousand Pathan cavalry. The Mugs marched on to Udaipur which they plundered, A.D. 1587, the Raja fled to the forests.'[14]

The Mugs, a term that was used by the British priest for the Arakanese now known as Rakhine, left Tripura of their own accord, but other more powerful forces were rising on Tripura's frontiers. The Mughal empire had expanded into Bengal next door. During the reign of Emperor Jahangir, a Mughal army attacked Tripura. 'Disaster befell the arms of Tripura, and Jasadhur Manik (the king) was sent captive to Delhi', writes Mackenzie. He died in exile at Brindaban, 'meditating on the excellency of Vishnu'.[15]

Tripura escaped becoming part of the Mughal empire because of a 'pestilence' that ran through the place after the Mughal occupation. People, including soldiers, began to die in large numbers and the Mughal forces, fleeing the epidemic, withdrew to Meharkul, near Cumilla. The Tripura nobles, now bereft of a king and any direct descendant, in 1625 installed a general from the royal family as king under the title of Kalyan Manikya. He proved a capable ruler, and put the kingdom back on its feet. He also saw off an attempted invasion by the Mughal governor of Bengal, who was 'ingloriously defeated and turned back'. After him, there was a struggle for succession between two of his sons, Govinda and Naksatra, in which the latter received military help from the Nawab of Murshidabad, and paid for it by becoming subject to the Nawab:

> and though they ever and again made fierce attempts to shake off the yoke, they never long succeeded. The Mahomedans were able to regulate the succession and exact tribute, and converted the raj into a simple zamindari. The very name of Tripura was changed to Roushanabad. One of the puppet kings set up by them, Bijai Manik, was allowed indeed only a monthly salary of Rs. 12,000, the whole remaining revenues of the country being sent to Dacca. For twelve years after him, a Mahomedan, Shumsher Khan, was the virtual ruler, but his oppressions became so great, and his remittances so uncertain, that the Nawab of Dacca, acting with strict impartiality, had him blown from the mouth of a gun.[16]

The Rajmala chronicles these later kings after Kalyan Manikya in its fourth and final part, which starts with the reign of Govinda Manikya. There is an account of Govinda Manikya who was dethroned by his half-brother Naksatra with Mughal help in 1661 living in exile in the court of the kingdom of 'Rasanga' of the Moghs—the people Reverend Long had called Mugs—in the Arakan, when the Mughal prince, Shah Shuja, arrived there fleeing from the forces of his brother Aurangzeb, who had prevailed in the battle for succession to the Mughal throne.[17] Aurangzeb however seemed to suspect that Shuja had found shelter in Tripura, because he had earlier sent a letter to Govinda Manikya asking him to capture and send Shuja to him. Prince Shuja, according to the Rajmala, married a Rasanga princess, but subsequently tried to assassinate the king by sending armed soldiers hidden in palanquins as a present for the royal harem. They were detected and killed. After this, Shuja himself disappeared from the scene, and from history, leaving behind tales of a lost Mughal treasure in the Arakan. Govinda Manikya was more fortunate; he returned from exile and regained his throne in 1667, thereafter becoming a tributary of the Mughal Emperor.

With the ascendancy of Aurangzeb, the great Mughal empire reached its last days. New forces from distant lands had entered the subcontinent. The harbingers of a new world that was coming into being far away, these people—merchants from Europe representing major trading companies –set up their outposts, called factories, in various places on the Indian coast. The Portuguese were there at Chittagong, which they called Porto Grande, or the big port, and at Satgaon in Hooghly district near Calcutta which they referred to as Porto Pequeno, or little port. Both names are mentioned in the account of an English traveller and 'gentleman merchant' named Ralph Fitch who passed through these areas in the 1580s.[18] He returned home safely to London in 1591. His accounts proved very useful for the East India Company, which was set up in 1600. The Company's first flagship was a pirate ship called the *Scourge of Malice* which made a voyage to what is now Indonesia in 1601.[19] The first East India Company ship to reach India, the *Hector*, under Captain William Hawkins, arrived in Surat on the Gujarat coast in 1608. The Company set up its first 'factory' to export goods from there in 1612. Other factories, in Masulipatanam on the Coromandel Coast of Tamil Nadu, and Kasimbazar in Bengal, followed. In the following decades, the Company continued to expand its network of factories across the subcontinent, from Dhaka and Hooghly in the east to the island of Bombay, which the Portuguese called Bom Bahia or 'good bay', in the west. Bombay had passed into British hands as part of the dowry of the Portuguese princess Catherine of Braganza following her marriage to King Charles II in 1662.

The first clash between the trading company and the Mughal empire took place during the reign of Aurangzeb over the issue of taxation, in what was then the richest province of the empire, Bengal. The Mughal Governor of the province, Shaista Khan, who had been transferred there after barely surviving an assassination attempt led by the Maratha king Shivaji, had imposed new taxes on import and export that the East India Company strongly objected to. It was facing stiff competition from a stronger rival: the far wealthier Dutch East India Company, the first joint stock company in the world to trade its shares in the open market. Having been driven out of the spice trade from the East Indies (which later became Indonesia) by the Dutch, its dependence on the India trade was great. The Bengal trade in textiles comprised the lion's share of this. The Company's leading light at the time, Sir Josiah Child, sent an expeditionary force of ten ships and six companies of infantry to force concessions from the Mughals in Bengal. Writing to the president of Fort St George in Madras on 9 June 1686, he underlined the imperative for the Company to transform itself from 'a parcel of mere trading merchants' into 'a formidable martial government in India'. The same tone filled his visionary call of 12 December 1687 for the president and council in Madras to 'establish such a politie of Civil and Military power, and create and secure such a large revenue to maintain both at that place as may be the foundation of a large, well-grounded sure English dominion in India for all time to come'.[20] The immediate result of all this was that the English got booted out of their factories in Bengal by the Mughals, who also laid siege to Bombay. The Company was forced to pay a fine of Rs. 150,000 for its impertinence, but was invited to return and continue its business, only losing its base in Hooghly, after which its Bengal chief, Job Charnock, was forced in 1690 to set up a new 'factory' in marshy land in the villages of

Kolikata, Sutanuti and Govindapur, which he acquired from a local zamindar. This became the city of Calcutta.

Aurangzeb died in 1707. The Mughal empire was riven by a war of succession from which no capable successor emerged. The centre could not hold; Hyderabad and Bengal emerged again as independent kingdoms. The Marathas overran Gujarat and central India. Then, in 1738, Nadir Shah, the ruler of Persia, invaded and struck the death blow, capturing Delhi and imprisoning the Mughal emperor Muhammad Shah and plundering treasure that included the fabled Kohinoor diamond and the Peacock Throne. He was followed by the Afghans under Ahmad Shah Abdali. In that milieu of chaos, the late Josiah Child's dream of the East India Company becoming a government in India began to translate into reality, with the unlikely victory of the Company's forces over the Nawab of Bengal, Siraj ud Daulah, at the Battle of Plassey in 1757. A sudden downpour wet the gunpowder of the Nawab's forces. The Company had brought tarpaulins to cover their artillery and ammunition.

In 1760, a British force from Chittagong invaded Tripura 'in support of the Mughals' and established Krishna Manikya on the throne.[21] In 1761, the plains ofTripura, which had fallen to Mughal rule during the reign of Emperor Jehangir, quietly came under British rule. On 20 January of that year, Governor HenryVansittart, representative of the Company now entering on its strange career of empire, wrote from Calcutta to Mr Verelst, the president of the factory at Islamabad (meaning Chittagong) as follows:

> With regard to the Tipperah Raja, as the Nawab's Foujdar has been obliged from his ill behaviour to take up arms against him, we desire that you will use your endeavours to reduce him to his due state of obedience to the Government of Islamabad, acquainting us then what advantages may accrue to the Company from the possession of that country, and we will answer any representations the Nawab may make on the subject.[22]

Following this order, a small force of 200 sepoys and 2 guns was despatched from Chittagong for Tripura. Having reached there they were told by the Dewan of the new Nawab of Bengal, Mir

Qasim, that 'he had obliged the Raja to take to the mountains and had got possession of every fort in his country'.[23]

Alexander Mackenzie wrote in his history of the Northeast frontier of Bengal:

> On arrival of our troops, the Rajah at once put himself in their hands. A collector of revenue was despatched from Chittagong with instructions to inquire into the resources of the country and demand payment of the expenses of the expedition... The revenue for the first year was fixed at one lakh and one sicca rupees.

No mention of the hills is found in connection with this arrangement, wrote Mackenzie. His explanation for this silence was that

> The officers of the Company had more regard to substantial advantages than to theoretical symmetry. The paying part of Tipperah lay on the plains, and appeared in the Mahomedan revenue roll as pergunnah Roushanbad. For this of course a settlement was made. We found it a zemindari, and as such we treated it. But of the barren hills that fenced it on the east, we took no cognizance... Accordingly the hills became Independent Tipperah and the Rajah who is an ordinary Bengali zemindar on the plains, reigns an independent prince over 3,000 square miles of upland, and was for many years a more absolute monarch than Scindia or Puttiala—owning no law but his sovereign will, bound by no treaty, safe in his obscurity from criticism or reform.[24]

After the British became the rulers of Bengal, disputes between contenders for the Tripura throne began to appear before the courts of the new administration they had set up. The first such case was fought between two claimants for the crown, Durgamani and Ramaganga, both of whom assumed the royal title of Manikya. The case, which was over the zamindari of Roshanabad in the plains, ran on from 1805 to 1809. On 24 March 1809, the Sadar Diwani Adalat gave a judgment in favour of Durgamani, confirming his succession as zamindar of Roshanabad, which it found to be an integral portion of an 'impartible' Tripura Raj. Durgamani ascended the throne of Tripura as Durga Manikya. After his death in 1813 the succession was again disputed, and went to court for the British judges of the Company Raj to decide. This time there were four claimants for the throne, including Ramaganga who had previously lost the first case. He was second-time lucky, and, after winning the case, became king of Tripura with the title Ramaganga Manikya.

Apart from the succession, matters of territorial disputes between Hill Tippera and at least two of its neighbours also went to court. The first was on the boundary between Tripura and Sylhet. A British survey led by a Lieutenant Thomas Fisher had delimited the territories of the two in 1822. The Tripura king disagreed with the line and was told he could take the case to court, which he did ten years later. Four lawsuits were filed in Sylhet District Court. The court ruled mainly in favour of the line drawn by the British authorities, and the king went in appeal to the Sadar Diwani Court. Here, issues of jurisdiction crept in, and eventually, in 1848, the court decided that 'questions affecting the boundary of two independent powers were not properly cognizable in municipal courts'.[25] After sixteen years of pursuing legal means, the Raja's cases were dismissed.

The boundary between Hill Tippera and the zamindari estate of Roshanabad, which included Noakhali and part of Sylhet, all areas the British had inherited from the Mughals, had not previously been delimited, and so a survey was started in 1848. As Mackenzie wrote:

> It was completed in December 1852, and arbitrators were immediately appointed to settle all disputed lines... In January 1855 the results were declared. It had been discovered that no definite boundary between the hills and plains had heretofore existed; but as the Government arbitrator liberally gave the Rajah the benefit of every doubt, no application to a referee was found necessary. Agurtolla, the Rajah's place of residence, was by the line now laid down included in the hill territory.[26]

The boundaries of the Tripura kingdom were thus fixed on two sides. On the third, the south towards Chittagong, the Feni river was recognised as the traditional boundary. There remained one direction in which the territory was yet to be demarcated: that of the hills that lay between Tripura and Manipur, inhabited by tribes related to the Kukis, of whom the dominant ones in the area were the Lushai. Kuki and Paite soldiers had, from time to time, fought on behalf of the kings of Tripura. There were also occasional raids by these groups on the Tripura king's lands. A major series of raids, which came to be known as the Kuki invasion, hit both Independent Tipperah and the estate of Chakla Roshanabad in 1860. The latter was technically British territory, and the British India government got involved. A military expedition was despatched against the person held responsible, a Lushai chief named Rothangpuia. Further raids by Lushai warriors on Cachar and Sylhet that passed through Tripura aggravated matters. In 1871, the British authorities mounted a campaign against them called the Lushai Expedition. At the same time, a British political agent was stationed in Agartala. An 'inner line' for the defence of Tripura from Lushai raids was fixed unilaterally by the British authorities in 1874. The Tripura Raj complained about 'the slicing off of huge strips of country' without reference to the Raja, but the line stayed where it was, and eventually became the boundary between Tripura and what is now Mizoram.[27]

* * *

The emergence of Tripura into modernity began in the 1870s, under British influence. Slavery in the state was abolished in 1878 'on the advice of the British government'. The practice of 'sati', the burning of widows at the funeral pyre, was discontinued by the king in 1888, 'in accordance with the advice given to him by the British authorities'.[28] However, the state of the administration was one that the British authorities remained unsatisfied with. 'In 1890, owing to Bir Chandra Manikya's maladministration, it was decided that, in consultation with the ex-officio Political Agent, he should select and appoint a minister with full powers of administration', according to the authoritative collection of documents popularly known as 'Aitchison's Treaties'.[29] The administration was reorganised after the British fashion, with laws being codified, a court established and new departments set up.[30] The assistant political agent who had been in office since 1878, Umakanta

Das, was appointed as minister heading the administration. He continued in office despite an order from the raja dismissing him. The raja protested and was 'permitted', in the words of Charles Aitchison, to resume his administrative role in 1892 on condition that he would submit an annual report of it and that he himself or his anointed successor, the Yubaraj, and the 'Bara Thakur' (who was next in line of succession after the Yubaraj), would visit Cumilla on the occasion of the visit of the commissioner of Chittagong.

The rules of succession to the Tripura kingdom having led to frequent disputes, the British authorities decided in 1904 to 'remove all doubts as to the rule of succession both to the State and to the ownership of the zamindaries and other properties in British India'. A 'sanad', or government charter, was issued by the Government of India which recognised the ruler's right to nominate any male member of his family, descended through him or any male ancestor of his, as successor. Every succession to the throne would require the recognition of the Government of India.[31] Radha Kishore Deb Barman, the recipient of this sanad, died in 1909, and was succeeded by his son Birendra Kishore Deb Barman, whose installation ceremony was, for the first time in the history of the state, carried out by the British Lieutenant-Governor of Bengal. The raja, meaning king, received a promotion from the government of British India in 1919, when he was given a sanad that bestowed on him and his descendants the title of Maharaja, or great king. When the Maharaja passed away in 1923, he was succeeded by his fifteen-year-old son, Bir Bikram Kishore Deb Barman.

The world outside changed drastically during the years of his reign, and Tripura could not remain isolated. When Bir Bikram Kishore became Maharaja, the kingdom was still an absolute monarchy and officially independent, although the British Raj was the indirect ruler. Politics, such as it was, had revolved for centuries around intrigues among members of the extended royal family for succession. Now, a very different kind of politics was gaining strength just outside the borders of the kingdom in neighbouring East Bengal. The first partition of Bengal in 1905 had sparked intense protests led by the Congress, one of whose leading lights at the time was the leader from Sylhet, Bipin Chandra Pal. At the extreme end of the politics of resistance that emerged as a response to the partition were two groups that believed in armed insurrection: the Anushilan Samiti with its headquarters in Dhaka, and the Jugantar with headquarters in Calcutta. These two groups embarked on a programme of assassinations, including an attempt in 1912 on the Viceroy, Lord Hardinge, during the ceremony to mark the transfer of the imperial capital from Calcutta to Delhi. The fire of extremism spread to Punjab. In response, the British government passed the Defence of India Act (1915), a wartime measure justified by the outbreak of the First World War that gave the police emergency powers of preventive detention for as long as they wanted. The act has lived on in one form or another beyond the end of British rule, and more than seventy-five years of the existence of independent India.

The extremists found allies and recruits in Chittagong and neighbouring Cumilla, in the Tripura king's zamindari estates. On occasion, they fled to his hill state for refuge. One such extremist, Nishikanta Ghosh, who was wanted by police in British India for a conspiracy case in Barishal in Bengal, was instrumental in starting a 'club' in Agartala that would train youth in fighting.[32] The Anushilan Samiti started two training camps in Hill Tripura disguised as farms, with the cadres working as farm labourers by day and training in revolution by night.[33] It also set up cells in Agartala.

The most daring of the attacks of this loosely connected network of extremists came in Chittagong in 1930, when a schoolteacher named Surya Sen, popularly known as 'Master da', led a raid on the local armoury. The plan had been to seize arms and ammunition and to launch an insurrection, but while the revolutionaries managed to get hold of the arms, they failed to locate the ammunition, and were thus unable to arm their supporters. Most of the revolutionaries were killed in subsequent police and military action. Some died fighting while others, including women such as the philosophy graduate Pritilata Waddedar, committed suicide. Surya Sen himself went underground, but was eventually found, arrested and hanged. The harsh crackdown that followed the immediate aftermath of the armoury raid angered more people. In 1931, two sixteen-year-old girls in Cumilla, Santi Ghose and Suniti Choudhury, inspired by Master da and his colleague Pritilata, shot dead the district magistrate Charles Stevens. They were arrested and jailed but emerged from prison after seven years.

The political situation in the Indian subcontinent had been transformed by then. A Federation of India, including the princely states, was being constructed by the office of the Governor General following the passage of the Government of India Act of 1935 in the British parliament. Assemblies had been set up and elections were being held and contested. Tripura, with its absolute monarchy, was ripe for the politics of popular representation. A new organisation called the Tripura Rajya Gana Parishad (Tripura Kingdom People's Council) came up to fill this void. It was the first declared political organisation in the state.[34] Among its early demands were the abolition of certain taxes and the system of 'taitung', by which villagers were compelled to act as porters for government officials on tour. More troublingly for the rulers, the group also demanded land for the tillers. Another organisation, with a more leftist bent, the Rajya Janamangal Samiti, followed in 1939. Among its founders was a former Anushilan revolutionary, Biren Dutta, who had turned Communist during his stint in jail. Their demand was for a responsible elected government under the Maharaja.

The young Maharaja, who had already constituted an unelected Mantri Parishad (council of ministers) and a Byabasthapak Sabha (corresponding to a legislative council), responded by initiating the process of drawing up a constitution for the state. The *Consolidated Administrative Report* of the state for 1940–43 declares:

> The development of the Constitutional Reforms inaugurated by His Highness the Maharaja Manikya Bahadur in 1349 TE [Tripura Era, corresponding to 1939 CE] continued under the control of Dewan B. K. Sen Bahadur, M.A., B.L., in cooperation with the Mantri Parishad, Manyabara Raja Rana Bodhjung Bahadur, F.R.G.S., Minister, holding the corresponding administrative portfolio... The Constitution of the Tripura Government deserves foremost mention... The Government of Tripura Act

> (or Act I of 1351 T.E.) embodying the Constitution received His Highness' assent on the 20th Asharh 1351 T.E. and came into effect from the 1st Sravan following.[35]

In other words, in July/August 1941, the first constitution of Tripura drawn up under the leadership of the Maharaja's Dewan and chief minister came into existence.

The constitution proposed the establishment of a unicameral legislature of forty-nine members, excluding the president of the assembly and the council of ministers who would automatically become members of the legislature. Of the total members, twenty would be nominated and twenty-nine would be elected by village councils, municipalities, tea planters, backward communities, and so on. Apart from legislative functions, the assembly would have 'recommendatory powers in respect of certain matters including the annual budget'. The executive authority of the government would rest in the Mantri Parishad, or council of ministers, 'to the extent of powers delegated by His Highness', with ministers holding office and exercising powers 'in respect of such Departments of the Government as His Highness may from time to time be pleased to direct'. Apart from these there would be a Raj Sabha, or privy council, of 'notable persons' appointed by the king to advise him on matters of state.[36] Direct elections would take place at the village level, where headmen would be elected.

However, no legislature was actually constituted, 'owing to practical difficulties consequent on the adverse situation'. The Second World War was then taking place, although in 1941 it was still far away from Tripura, but there were also other problems closer at hand. Communal riots had started to break out in Bengal in response to the heated jockeying for power between the Congress and the Muslim League. The dowager queen passed away and her funeral rites were completed on 1 April. As the *Administrative Report* records:

> Hardly had the ceremony concluded, when the State came in for a unique experience in the sudden influx of a large body of Hindu refugees in extreme distress from the Dacca district, as alleged, of serious communal disturbances. The total number soon came up

> to fifteen thousand with a preponderance of females and infants, who had to be promptly accommodated, given medical help and supplies with food and clothing.[37]

As the Second World War drew nearer, in 1942 the Maharaja 'personally raised and organised an Irregular Force of considerable strength from the hill tribes known as Tripura Rajya Rakhi Bahini (Tripura State Defence Force)'. However, one tribe, the Reang, rose up in revolt the following year, against their feudal overlords the Chaudharies (a title used in Tripura by village chiefs among some tribes) and Brahmins, under a charismatic god-man named Ratan Muni, and were eventually subdued by force. Members of the Tripura forces, including from the king's own bodyguard, were also placed at the disposal of the Government of India. A unit of these forces joined the V-Force, a guerrilla group that operated against the Japanese military in Burma and Northeast India. A good reason for Tripura forces to be included in the V-Force was geography. One route for the Japanese forces and the Indian National Army led by Subhas Chandra Bose was from Burma via Manipur towards Kohima and Dimapur. A second route—used by invading armies of the Arakan kings in the past—ran from Burma through the Arakan towards Tripura and Chittagong.

The close of the Second World War in 1945 saw a resumption of political activity in the state. Biren Dutta, the Communist leader who had been among the founders of the Rajya Janamangal Samiti in 1939, now initiated the formation of a new organisation called the Tripura Rajya Jana Siksha Samiti (Tripura State People's Education Forum). It was the first ethno-nationalist outfit in the state, with a mission of tribal emancipation.[38] Its founding members were educated tribal youths including future stalwarts of the state's politics Dasaratha Deb and Aghore Debbarma, writer and activist Sudhanwa Debbarma, the organisation's first General Secretary Hemanta Debbarma, and Nilmani Debbarma. The Samiti sought the help of the king's administration in opening schools in tribal areas, and received it. D. A. W. Brown, the then education minister of Tripura, was a patron of mass education. He helped the Samiti establish 400 schools, of which the state recognised 300, mainly established in secluded hilly areas.[39]

In 1948, when a section of the Communist Party of India decided to embark on the path of armed revolution to capture power, this organisation morphed into the Gana Mukti Parishad (People's Liberation Council), an underground Communist outfit that undertook armed action against the royalist administration to establish 'liberated zones'. The GMP filled a political void left by the ban of a more moderate political organisation with Jana Siksha Samiti links, the Tripura Rajya Praja Mandal, established in 1946 under the leadership of Jogesh Chandra Debbarma and Birchandra Debbarma. This group had called for the introduction of popular elected government in Tripura. By then, independence for India was a certainty. The question that remained was whether Pakistan would be created—and until the start of July 1946, the answer was that it would not. That month, Jawaharlal Nehru took over from Maulana Abul Kalam Azad as the Congress president, and immediately proceeded to make statements at a press conference in Bombay negating plans to prevent partition under the terms of the Cabinet Mission Plan that Jinnah and the Muslim League, as well as the Congress itself, apart from the British government, had all agreed to. Jinnah saw this as a betrayal and responded by calling for the marking of 16 August 1946 as 'Direct Action Day'. While this was meant to be a day of public protests and shutdowns, in Calcutta it rapidly turned into a massive communal riot, as the Muslim League, with the blessing of the premier, Husayn Shaheed Suhrawardy, tried to enforce a shutdown of the city, which the Congress and Hindu Mahasabha tried to prevent. At least 4,000 people were killed in the rioting, and no less than 40,000 were injured.

Further riots followed. The biggest was in Noakhali and adjacent Cumilla, both in the Tripura king's estate of Chakla Roshanabad. The population there was more than 80 per cent Muslim, but in the hierarchical society of the place, upper-caste Hindus constituted the local elite under the British and the Tripura king. Tensions between Hindus and Muslims had been running high since the Calcutta riots, and finally exploded in October. Private militias of local Muslim strongmen attacked and killed local Hindu leaders, looted their houses and, in many instances, abducted and raped the women.[40] The rioting continued sporadically for a month before Mahatma Gandhi arrived there. For the next four months, as India hurtled towards partition and independence, Gandhi remained in Noakhali. He was there until 3 March 1947, exactly three months to the day before Mountbatten announced his plan to partition India.

It was a crucial time in the history of India. Unfortunately for Tripura, its Maharaja, Bir Bikram Kishore Manikya, died a sudden and untimely death in May 1947, of a suspected massive heart attack. He was not even forty years old. His death paved the way for Hill Tripura's accession to India on terms quite different from those he had intended. The state had signed no treaty with British India. There was only the sanad of 1904, clarifying the matter of royal succession to the Tripura throne. Although the British authorities had done more or less as they pleased in deciding important matters, such as the state's borders and who would be king, technically, Hill Tripura (marked as 'Independent Tipperah' in British maps until 1866) was at least as independent as far larger princely states such as Jammu and Kashmir. When the Government of India Act was passed by the British parliament in 1935, Maharaja Bir Bikram Kishore Manikya had written a letter accepting an Instrument of Accession to a Federation of India under the British Crown. Dated 29 March 1937, and addressed to 'The Agent to the Governor General, Eastern States', the letter says:

> I have the honour to state that on consideration of all the facts and circumstances relating to the new constitution for India as embodied in the Government of India Act, 1935, I have come to the conclusion that Tripura State may accede to the proposed Federation of India, subject, however, to the safeguards and limitations indicated in this letter and its annexures.[41]

The Governor General's office had sent him, and rulers of other princely states, a standard template of the Instrument of Accession. The Maharaja sent back a 'revised draft of the standard form of the Instrument of Accession'. Among amendments in his revised draft, Point 8 begins: 'Nothing in this instrument affects the continuance of my sovereignty in and over this State.'[42] Point 9 states: 'Nothing in this Instrument shall be construed as authorising Parliament to legislate for or exercise jurisdiction over this State or its Ruler in any respect.'[43] The Maharaja proposed to accept the Instrument under certain other limitations, of which he provided a long list as an annexure. After his sudden death, his wife, Kanchan Prava Devi, princess of Panna in Central India, took charge of the administration. She signed an Instrument of Accession on 13 August 1947 that accepted the power of the dominion legislature to make laws relating to only three areas: defence, external affairs and communication. The document she signed also reiterated the point on sovereignty that the Maharaja had earlier insisted on, saying, 'Nothing in this Instrument affects the continuance of my sovereignty in and over this land.'[44]

Partition hit Tripura hard. Technically, the state was not divided in 1947, but Chakla Roshanabad and other estates of the Tripura state, comprising an area of over 1,100 square kilometres, lay in East Bengal in the districts of Tipperah, Noakhali and Sylhet. 'Most of the above properties are situated in an almost unbroken line contiguous to the western boundary of the Tripura State and having once been comprised in the kingdom of the ancient Rulers of Tripura. They form now an indivisible appanage of the State', the *Consolidated Administrative Report* for 1940–43 said. Roughly one third of the state's total annual income came from these zamindaris, although technically those territories were part of British India. At the moment of partition, along with the rest of East Bengal, they went, on the basis of their Muslim majority, to East Pakistan.

This sent a wave of mainly Hindu refugees into the state which had already seen a population explosion in the preceding decades. Tripura's first census was in 1872. The Census of 1931 found that the population had increased a staggering eleven-fold from the 1872 figure. 'In Tripura State and the Chittagong Hill Tracts the increase was more than 10 per cent in each decade, a rate not achieved in any other district of Bengal except Noakhali between 1911–21', the census report said.[45] In the preceding decade, however, this rate had been achieved by a dozen districts, a classification that included, apart from Tripura, the princely state of Sikkim. The increase of population between 1921 and 1931 in Tripura state was 25.6 per cent.[46] In absolute numbers, the population had gone up from 173,325 in 1901—the first census when enumerators were able to go to remote and far-flung areas—to 382,450 in 1931. The census commissioner, A. E. Porter, noted in his report that 'The increase in the state...appears to be due actually less to immigration than to increase of the native-born population and possibly also to increased accuracy of the enumeration on the present occasion.'[47]

The Tripura population in 1951 was 639,029. In the next decade up to 1961 the state's population again shot up by a staggering 78 per cent.[48] The reason was distress migration from East Pakistan, where the Hindus who had stayed back earlier faced increasing discrimination and violence. There had been those, including the Bengali Dalits led by Jogendranath Mandal, who had chosen Pakistan in 1947. Mandal, who was the first law minister of Pakistan, was forced to flee to India after raising his voice against horrific riots that broke out in Dhaka and other parts of East Bengal in 1950, in which the police and government machinery were, according to him, complicit. Thousands of men, women and children, most of them Hindu, were massacred, and the community's leaders, including elected members of the Legislative Assembly, were arrested. 'I would like to reiterate in this connection my firm conviction that the East Bengal Government is still following the well-planned policy of squeezing Hindus out of the province', Mandal wrote in his resignation letter.[49]

A further round of rioting followed in 1952, this time sparked by the efforts of the Pakistani state to impose Urdu as the sole official language—a mistake that would ultimately lead to the break-up of Pakistan and the emergence of East Pakistan as Bangladesh. For those who were squeezed out, especially from the areas in Cumilla, Noakhali and Sylhet that had been part of Chakla Roshanabad, the natural place of refuge was adjoining Tripura. By 1958, when the official registration of refugees in the state was stopped, the total number of displaced persons who had registered themselves as refugees there was 374,000, comprising 83,000 families.[50] It was against this backdrop of a huge refugee influx that democratic politics in Tripura developed. In 1941, tribals constituted 53 per cent of the population. In 1951, they had become a minority, at 37 per cent.

* * *

The Instrument of Accession had left Tripura with control of everything except defence, external affairs and communication. This last, communication, immediately became a huge problem for the state after partition. From being a strategically located outpost connected to the world through the port of Chittagong, it now found itself in a far corner of the new state of India, not connected to any other part of the country by land. In this situation, a local mahout-turned-businessman, Gedu Mian, who had floated a pro-Muslim League political party called the Anjuman-e-Islamia, began canvassing support for the merger of Tripura with East Pakistan.[51] To counter this, by mid-November 1947, several rival militia groups were set up across the state. The Congress and Communist Party—usually bitterly divided over everything—joined hands with an anti-Pakistan Muslim organisation, the Tripura Rajya Praja Majlish. A Kirit Bikram Rakshi Bahini 'resistance force' was formed to intimidate the Anjuman-e-Islamia and make sure Tripura didn't fall to Pakistan.[52] As the situation worsened, the Maharani dissolved the regency council, made herself sole regent and flew to New Delhi 'to secure Indian help to abort a possible Kashmir-type operation in Tripura'. Sardar Patel assured her of full military support from the Indian government, and soon after, the Governor of Assam, Akbar Hydari, arrived in the state. Finally, on 11 November 1947, the Maharani announced 'The Accession of this state to the Dominion of India', which had apparently been 'decided by the late ruler after due consideration and full consultation with all sections of the people'.[53] In September 1949, Maharani Kanchan Prabha Devi signed the Merger Agreement by which Tripura state merged into the dominion of India. As a result of this, from January 1950, along with Manipur, Tripura became a chief commissioner's province, administered by an officer of the Government of India.

There was only one significant flicker of rebellion against the merger that brought about the end of the ancient princely state. A member of the royal family and the dissolved regency council, Durjoy Kishore Dev Barman, led the formation of a militant tribal organisation called Sengkrak, or 'clenched fist', to oppose the merger of Tripura with India. It also spearheaded a movement called Bangal Kheda, which translates as 'drive out the Bangals'—meaning the Bengalis of East Bengal origin.[54] Sengkrak was the first open manifestation of the strong anti-refugee sentiment, overlapping with anti-Bengali or anti-Bangladeshi feelings, that still remains a potent force in the politics not just of Tripura but of all Northeast India.

The refugees themselves were hardly there by choice, and their situation in the refugee camps in Agartala was grim. 'One refugee committed suicide on the 10th July 1950 in Durgabari Camp near the Maharaja's Palace. It was learnt that the deceased could not secure food or money from the Relief Officer. Next day, another refugee was reported to have died of starvation at the Maharajganj Camp', historian Anindita Ghoshal wrote in a paper, citing an intelligence report from 1950.[55] According to Ghoshal, a number of organisations for the relief of refugees had begun work among them, including some with strong political affiliations. They spanned the political spectrum from left to right. The Bharatiya Jana Sangh leader, Syama Prasad Mukherjee, first talked about the amalgamation of these groups and advised them to fight through a common political platform. Accordingly, a Tripura Central Relief Organisation was formed, which set down a charter of eighteen demands including speedy resettlement and voting rights.[56]

It was, however, the Communists who managed to garner support across communities. They had abandoned the path of armed struggle by 1951, and entered electoral politics. The first elections to the Indian parliament were held in 1952. Tripura had two seats in the Lok Sabha, or lower house of parliament, for which direct elections were held. Biren Dutta of the Gana Mukti Parishad, who contested on a Communist Party of India ticket, won by a wide margin in the Tripura West constituency. Prince Durjoy Dev Barman, contesting as an independent candidate, finished a distant second, while the Congress and the Hindu right-wing Bharatiya Jana Sangh brought up the rear. Dutta's colleague Dasaratha Deb of the GMP, the leader of its armed wing, also on a CPI ticket, won the other seat, Tripura East, with similar ease. The Congress candidate, Sachindra Lal Singh, who as a student had been associated with the underground Jugantar movement, was second, and the Bharatiya Jana Sangh third. At the time he became member of the Indian parliament, Deb was wanted by the police, and was arrested in Agartala soon after. Although he was released on bail within hours, his arrest raised an issue of parliamentary privilege. Deb's written statement to the Privileges Committee explained the background of the case in which he had been held:

> Three men had allegedly been kidnapped—Rajani Bidyaratna, President of a society called Swasti Samiti, Dayananda Baidya and Nandalal Nath... The S.P. further told me that there was a conflict between the local tribal people and the said Swasti Samiti over some land disputes. The Samiti, it seems, had taken a lease from the Tripura Government and evicted about 500 tribals from their land.[57]

The kidnapped men, representing a cooperative society working for the welfare of displaced Bengali refugees, had been held in captivity for almost a month before being released. Deb was arrested in connection with their kidnapping. He denied knowledge of the case.

The story of the land dispute captures in microcosm something of the complex churn that was going on in Tripura as a result of the refugee influx. Only one man, Parakinkar Chakma, was convicted in the kidnapping case. According to the case papers:

> The facts of the case as alleged by the prosecution are that Rajani Mohan Bidyaratna P.W. 1 came to India after partition in the first part of 1948 and he migrated from Pakistan. He first came to Dharmanagar where he founded co-operative society named Swasti Samity... According to the prosecution the society got one thousand drones[58] of jungly and uncultivated land in Tripura in 1948 and this land is situated in Kailashahar. The society began to cultivate the land in 1949 but Chakmas and Reangs had

> jhum cultivation occasionally in that area and only hill people lived there.[59]

Under the leadership of Sachindra Lal Singh, the Tripura Congress, which had set up an organisation to help the refugees, was keen to get them land for resettlement. The government of Tripura had, in its wisdom, given the refugees cooperative land that the tribals saw as theirs, without bothering to consult with them. In the ensuing land dispute, the leaders of the Swasti Samiti had been assaulted and kidnapped.

The gathering ethnic conflict between the local tribal communities and the non-tribal Bengalis, of whom the majority by then were refugees rather than old residents, was postponed at the time by a combination of political factors. The ascendancy of the Communists, who had leaders and supporters among both tribals and Bengalis, was one. The fact that there were more immediate struggles for political representation was another. While Tripura after 1952 had two members in parliament, it had no state assembly. In 1951, India's Independence Day on 15 August was observed in Agartala as 'Legislative Assembly Demand Day'. In 1953, a committee was formed to campaign for the Assembly demand. In December the same year, a States Reorganisation Commission was appointed by the Nehru government to redraw the internal map of India. Hundreds of princely states including Tripura and Manipur that had, at least on the map, retained their separate existences throughout British rule, had been merged into India in the preceding years. New states with new names and borders were now about to be drawn onto the map.

A section of the Bengali intelligentsia in Tripura floated a proposal for the merger of Tripura, adjacent Cachar in Assam, Manipur and the Lushai Hills to form a state called Purbachal.[60] This had few takers. Another proposal was for the merger of Tripura and Cachar, which had ethnically similar majority populations, to form a smaller Purbachal state. This also did not find popular support. The States Reorganisation Commission for its part recommended the merger of Tripura with Assam. This was a proposal not acceptable to either the Communists or Congress supporters, and led to the formation in 1955 of a common platform called the Autonomous Tripura Committee, with Swarna Kamal Roy of the Praja Socialist Party as president and Dasaratha Deb of the Communist Party of India as general secretary.[61] Mass protests broke out across Tripura. The West Bengal Assembly, reviewing the case of Tripura along with the Goalpara and Dhubri districts of Assam—all of which had significant Bengali populations—debated the issue. In the face of the tumultuous protests, the States Reorganisation Act that was passed in August 1956 undid the merger proposal.[62] Instead, Tripura became a Union Territory, administered by the Centre.

The first step towards a democratically elected government for Tripura state came with the formation of a Tripura Territorial Council on 15 August 1957. It had thirty elected members, and the Congress leader Sachindra Lal Singh was the chairman. Its work was divided into four departments covering education, public health, engineering—primarily relating to construction and the upkeep of roads and government buildings—and animal husbandry. It was also responsible for the managing of markets, ferries and water tanks.[63] The limited powers of the Territorial Council did not satisfy the local political leaders for long. In December 1961, when a central government committee was formed to look into the administrative set-up of union territories including Tripura, all major political parties demanded the immediate introduction of a full-fledged legislature. The CPI presented a memorandum, dated 27 March 1962, denouncing the States Reorganisation Commission and the system of governance that it had left Tripura. 'The SRC recommended for a merger of Tripura with Assam. But the people of Tripura turned down that recommendation through innumerable mass demonstrations', it said. 'Finding Tripura Territorial Council inadequate to fulfil the democratic aspirations of the people both before and during the last General Elections our party made the demand for Bidhan Sabha (state assembly) its central political slogan.'[64]

The local Congress unit, after initial hesitations, was having similar thoughts. In a memorandum, the president of the Tripura State Congress said: 'The Union Territories cannot remain contented with the Territorial Councils in their present form. Creation of these local bodies which are...more or less like District Boards undoubtedly fell short of the demands for responsible government at the state level.' The Congress urged the Government of India to shape the administration in such a way that elected representatives could exercise control over 'as large a field as possible' without vital alteration in the constitutional relationship between the Centre and the Union Territory.[65] This was the path the government took. A Government of Union Territories Act was passed by parliament in 1963. Under the provisions of this new Act, an elected legislative assembly with a council of ministers headed by a chief minister was to be constituted to 'aid and advise the Chief Commissioner'.

In December 1963, an incident in Kashmir, more than 3,000 kilometres away from Tripura, came to have an impact on the state. A strand of hair went missing from a shrine near Srinagar named Hazratbal. It was believed to be a relic of the Prophet Muhammad. Immediately, there were angry reactions in Pakistan. In East Pakistan, politicians stoked public anger that sparked riots against the local Hindu minority. A fresh wave of ethnic cleansing started, and continued in waves. Through 1964, more than 100,000 fresh refugees, almost all Bengali Hindus, were forced to flee into Tripura. The existing tensions between the refugees and the local tribals increased.

That same year, the Communist Party of India suffered a split, and a faction became a new party, the Communist Party of India (Marxist). When the first elections for the new Tripura Legislative Assembly's thirty seats were held in February 1967, the Congress swept the polls, winning twenty-seven of the seats. The CPI won only a single seat with seven per cent of the popular vote. The CPI(M) won two seats, with a vote share of 21 per cent. The division among the Communists thus ensured that Sachindra Lal Singh of the Congress became the first chief minister of the Union Territory. The split also ensured the defeat of both Communist stalwarts, Biren Dutta and Dasaratha Deb, from their respective seats. The defeat of Deb, who was the unrivalled leader among the tribals, had come at the hands of a new Congress candidate who appealed to both tribals and

Bengali refugees: the last king of independent Tripura, Maharaja Kirit Bikram Kishore Deb Barman.

The political reaction began soon after.

An All-Party Tribal Leaders' Conference attended by leaders including Dasaratha Deb and his erstwhile colleague and rival Aghore Debbarma was organised in June 1967, at which an executive committee called the Tripura Upajati Juba Samiti (Tripura Tribal Youth Association) was formed.[66] Among its key demands was the restoration of traditionally tribal lands to tribals and the recognition of Kokborok, the most spoken tribal language of Tripura, as an official language of the state. Around the same time, the issue of resettlement of a thousand or so refugees in an area called Kanchanpur angered the local tribals there. When repeated requests by the local tribals to evict the refugees had no effect, the original militant group of Tripura, Sengkrak, resurfaced in a new avatar, under a new leader named Ananta Reang.[67] A fierce armed insurgency was then raging in the Mizo Hills that lay adjacent to Tripura in the direction of Manipur. Sengkrak established connections with the group leading the militancy there, the Mizo National Front. Their run of militancy was short-lived. They were crushed by the Tripura police which managed to infiltrate their ranks and engineer the assassination of Ananta Reang.[68] The remaining Sengkrak militants then gravitated towards the TUJS and formed the core of its new armed wing, the Tripura Sena, in 1969.

National general elections were held in March 1971. The Tripura Upajati Juba Samiti (TUJS) converted itself into a political party in these polls, and put up two candidates, Bijoy Kumar Hrangkhawl and Drau Kumar Reang, for Tripura's two parliamentary seats. Both candidates lost. The issue of festering internal tensions was soon overtaken by larger events in the neighbourhood. From 25 March, the Pakistan Army had launched a series of massacres in East Pakistan that escalated into a genocide. More refugees flowed into the state. Then India declared war, and East Pakistan turned into Bangladesh. Militancy in Northeast India suffered a crushing blow, as the bases in East Pakistan were overrun and the political reorganisation of Northeast India followed. Tripura was upgraded, finally, to the status of a full-fledged state on 21 January 1972. A new state assembly with sixty electoral seats was constituted. Tripura's first elections as a democratic state followed. The TUJS put up candidates in ten seats in tribal areas, but all of them lost miserably, forfeiting their deposits. The contest was entirely between the CPI(M) and the Congress, and the Congress won a clear majority with forty-one seats out of sixty. The CPI(M) won sixteen.[69] A Congress government under a Bengali leader, Sukhamoy Sengupta, took office. Among its main challenges at the time was the resettlement of recent wartime refugees. While most of those who fled to India from East Pakistan returned to their homes after the war, a section stayed back. Among these in Tripura, apart from Bengali Hindus, were tribal Chakmas. They had been forced to move since 1962, when their homelands in the Chittagong Hill Tracts were submerged by a dam built on the Karnaphuli river, causing the displacement of around 100,000 people, mostly Chakmas.

A similar hydroelectric scheme was nearing completion in Tripura. In 1974, the Gumti Hydroelectric Project was commissioned. It displaced thousands of tribal families from their lands. In a place, where contestation over land had sparked conflict between tribals and Bengali refugees from the time of independence, this displacement gave fresh cause for anger and anguish to the beleaguered tribal communities. The government of the day, adding to its insensitivity towards tribal concerns, also de-reserved over 3,000 square kilometres of lands that had been reserved for tribals by Maharaja Bir Bikram Kishore Manikya in 1943.[70] The resulting discontent could not find a voice through electoral politics. India went under Emergency in 1975. When the Emergency was lifted and elections followed in December 1977, the CPI(M) swept the Tripura Assembly polls, winning fifty-one out of sixty seats. The Congress, the ruling party until then, drew a blank. The TUJS, which contested twenty-eight seats, won four.[71] The Bengali leader Nripen Chakraborty of the CPI(M), was made chief minister by the party's Politburo, overlooking the claims of the veteran local tribal leader, Dasaratha Deb, whose candidacy was supported by his comrade Biren

Dutta. It was, Dutta would later comment, 'one big mistake by our party in Tripura'.[72]

The TUJS drew a blank in the Lok Sabha polls that were held simultaneously. In the tribal-dominated Tripura East seat, its candidate Bijoy Hrangkhawl was defeated by the Congress candidate, Maharaja Kirit Bikram Kishore Deb Barma. Disgruntled TUJS extremists, a section of whom had earlier formed the Tripura Sena under Hrangkhawl, now launched a new militant group called the Tripura National Volunteers. Their incipient movement received a fillip due to unrelated events elsewhere. The death of a member of parliament necessitated a by-poll in Mangaldoi in Assam in 1978. The ensuing revision of electoral rolls produced a controversy over the inclusion of the names of 47,658 alleged 'foreigners', code for illegal Bangladeshi immigrants. How many of those people were truly foreigners was never properly established, but the news sparked off a fierce agitation in Assam directed at evicting all suspected 'foreigners'. The agitation spread to other Northeast states. In Meghalaya, in 1979, there were riots targeting the local Bengali minority. In Tripura, where the Bengalis were the majority and held political power, extremists on both sides fanned the flames of ethnic conflict. A Tribal Areas Autonomous District Council Bill was passed by the state assembly but remained only on paper. The TUJS called 'bandhs', or shutdowns, to press for their demands; a Bengali chauvinist group called Amra Bangali took out protests and rallies against them. The situation was primed to explode, and it did, when an altercation between a Bengali man and a TUJS activist in a village called Lembucherra, not far from Agartala, blew up into violence. The Bengali man attacked the TUJS activist, Pradip Debbarma, with a machete. Debbarma escaped wounded but alive and narrated this to his friends. An atmosphere for reprisals against Bengalis in general built up. A tribal mob marched into Lembucherra and burnt down the Bengali houses. In retaliation, a Bengali mob attacked a tribal village and razed it to the ground.[73] Two days later, the tribal extremists took their revenge.

It happened in a village called Mandai, about 30 kilometres from Agartala, before dawn on 6 June 1980. In the words of an eyewitness, the block development officer of the area, B. K. Sharma:

> As I looked around, I could see only gutted houses, ashes and smoke billowing up. It was not the Mandai I had known. All the houses and huts were reduced to ashes—there was only one that was still standing at that time and it was the LAMPS building. Some tribal youths were still engaged in looting inside the building and as the armed security forces arrived, they fled. The RAC jawans (armed constables) opened fire at them and I believe at least three were killed in the firing... Suddenly I noticed a small boy trying to pull his mother out of a pit. She was full of blood and limp. It seemed she was dead. As we went to help the boy I noticed the first dead body—a school teacher, hacked to death. Then as we proceeded, we stumbled into bloody bodies, mostly hacked to death. I myself counted up to 212 dead bodies and then got confused. There were many more seriously injured people screaming and groaning.[74]

Other massacres followed over the next few days, with victims on both sides of the ethnic divide, as the state descended into widespread tribal-versus-Bengali communal rioting. Cadres of the militant group Tripura National Volunteers (TNV) were among those involved in the massacres, and its leader Bijoy Hrangkhawl was arrested within days. A police crackdown, remembered by tribal activists as indiscriminate and extreme, was unleashed by the state government. Talks between Hrangkhawl and the government led by Chief Minister Nripen Chakraborty followed, and in December 1980, Hrangkhawl agreed to disband the TNV in exchange for amnesty for himself and his cadres and financial packages. The surprise disbanding of the TNV, far from ending armed tribal militancy in the state, merely created a vacant space for a new formation. Within days, a new outfit called All Tripura People's Liberation Organisation, led by a primary school teacher named Binanda Jamatia, stepped into the gap. This organisation soon developed rifts after Jamatia fell out with his lieutenant, Chuni Koloy, who left with his supporters to form a rival militant group called the Tripura People's Liberation Army. The Koloy group also reached out to Hrangkhawl to return as leader. Jamatia's group then kidnapped Hrangkhawl and his wife Linda from their home and smuggled them out to their camps in the Chittagong Hill Tracts of Bangladesh—although there were suspicions that the kidnap had the secret approval of the state government. However, Koloy's men attacked the hideout and snatched the captives. The upshot of all this was that in November 1982, barely two years after it had been 'disbanded', a reunited TNV was revived with Hrangkhawl back as chief and Koloy as 'chief of army'.[75]

For the next year or so, the TNV carried out a number of attacks, but suffered a big setback when Koloy was apprehended by a routine patrol of the Central Reserve Police Force paramilitary. Then the Mizo National Front, the leading insurgent group from the neighbouring Mizo Hills, which had trained the TNV cadres, began negotiating a surrender with Indian agencies. The surrender came in 1986, and the MNF put down its weapons, with its chief Laldenga subsequently joining electoral politics and becoming chief minister of Mizoram, which was upgraded from Union Territory to a full-fledged state with an elected assembly in 1987. In these elections, the MNF candidates contested as independents and won, and Laldenga again became chief minister. The MNF's example evidently made an impression on Hrangkhawl and the TNV. He tried to reach out to the Government of India via his old friends in the MNF, but at this point, Indian intelligence agencies got involved. A message was passed to Hrangkhawl to open negotiations through the Congress' Mizoram chief Lalthanhawla.[76] Manas Paul, in his 2009 book *The Eyewitness*, cited intelligence reports confirming that Hrangkhawl contacted Lalthanhawla to negotiate a surrender:

> Lal Thanhawla indeed discussed Hrangkhawal's surrender issue with then Union Home minister Buta Singh. But Singh told Lal Thanhawla that such negotiation could only be held if a Congress government came to power in Tripura. The Mizoram chief minister in a letter told Hrangkhawl what the Union Home minister had said.[77]

Elections were due barely two months later, and for this the TUJS and Congress formed an alliance to defeat the CPI(M)-led government then in power. The TNV for its part unleashed a series of massacres against Bengalis in the run-up to voting day, with 102 men, women and children being slaughtered in just the week before the polls. This highlighted the inability of the Communist government to ensure security for the state's Bengali population.

The result was that the Congress-TUJS alliance won narrowly, securing thirty-two of the sixty seats. After this, the massacres ended. Soon after their government came to power, Nagendra Jamatia, the agriculture minister in the new government, got in touch with TNV commanders. An appeal for a peaceful settlement signed by Hrangkhawl went to the state's Governor, the former army general K. V. Krishna Rao. The entire leadership was flown to Delhi in a special flight and negotiations opened. In two months, an accord was hammered out and signed in August 1988, ending one bloody chapter in the state's history. It led to the reservation of 20 seats in the assembly for members of scheduled tribes and a redrawing of the boundaries of the autonomous district council which had started functioning in 1982. The accord, however, did not adequately satisfy tribal aspirations, with the Twipra Students' Federation sticking to its demand for reservation of at least half the 60 assembly seats. Nor did it bring armed militancy in the state to an end, because Hrangkhawl's deputy, TNV vice president, Dhananjay Reang, broke away to form a new outfit, the National Liberation Front of Tripura. Another ethnic militant organisation with a leftist bent, the All-Tripura Tribal Force, followed in 1990. A symbiotic relationship between 'overground' politicians and 'underground' militants had developed. The role of armed extremist groups in swaying election results had been established, and every part of the political mainstream wanted this powerful ally that could be both a sword and a shield.

6

MIZORAM'S CENTURY OF TRANSFORMATION

CHIEFS, COMMONERS, SLAVES AND CITIZENS

A roughly rectangular patch of land, covering 21,087 square kilometres of mostly hilly, forested terrain, lies adjacent to Tripura, Manipur and the Barak valley area of Assam. On two sides, this territory, inhabited by a number of tribes, is bordered by foreign countries: Bangladesh to the west and Myanmar to the east and south. This area is what is now the state of Mizoram, and its majority inhabitants are known as the Mizo. The identity it refers to is a confusing one: tribal communities similar to the Mizo are also variously called Zomi, Chin or Kuki in other places. There are also changes of names of the same communities over time. Now, in the Indian state of Mizoram, the word Mizo is commonly used. In the British colonial period, the word 'Lushai', which is the name of one particular sub-tribe of the larger umbrella grouping, was more commonly used, and the hills they inhabit were called the Lushai Hills. In Myanmar, the names Zo and Chin were and are more common, although even the Chin identity is a complex composite one. In Manipur and Tripura, the colonial records labelled tribes of this family as Kuki, and the name remains in use. Mizoram also has minorities such as the Lai and Mara, who have their own distinct identities.

Broadly speaking as the Mizo historian Lal Pudaite writes:

> All modern historians belonging to the various tribes...agree that all the tribal groups inhabiting the immediate neighbourhood of the present state of Mizoram—in such areas as Myanmar, Bangladesh, Tripura, Assam and Manipur—once belonged to the same proto-tribe. They often refer to themselves collectively as 'Zo Hnahthla', people of Zo ancestry, origin or progeny.[1]

These Zo people, according to a shared legend passed down orally through the generations, trace their origins to a place called Chhinlung or Sinlung. 'We, the Mizo, all agree that our origin was Chhinlung', according to another historian, B. Lalthangliana. 'However, the exact location of Chhinlung and the date and time of our origin remains a mystery.'[2] There are different variations of the tale, but the gist of it is that the progenitors of the Zo tribes emerged from a cave called Chhinlung whose location was probably somewhere in today's China, perhaps in or near Yunnan or eastern Tibet, from where the Zo people migrated to what is now Myanmar, reaching there, according to Lalthangliana, circa 800 CE. From northern Myanmar, they moved along the banks of the Chindwin river and settled down in the Kabaw valley near Manipur before being driven from there by Shan tribes around 1300. 'After leaving Kabaw valley to their enemies, most of the Mizo moved west to Than hills and the banks of the Run (or Manipur) River in the area which is now northern Chin state', writes Lalthangliana. They migrated from there in different stages into what is now Mizoram and adjacent areas, with the weaker clans being driven before the stronger ones. The earliest migrants, called the Old Kuki group, are believed to have arrived by the fifteenth century.

No written records of the Mizos exist from before the colonial period. There is one fascinating archaeological site, with about 170 carved menhirs and some rock art, in a place called Vangchhia in the Champhai district of Mizoram bordering Myanmar, but no details are known so far of who carved them, or even how long ago they were carved. A second, smaller site in Lunglei district called Lung Milem (meaning stone figures) has three carved figures on a rock wall that are thought to be related to Buddhism. No details are known about their origins. That leaves oral history, passed down as stories from generation to generation. The oldest major settlement about which there is a story is a large village of 3,000 houses called Dungtlang, which Lalthangliana asserts was established by 1670–80. The chiefs of this village and their followers were driven out by the powerful Sailo chiefs of the Lusei, or Lushai, clan, who arrived there circa 1700.[3] The second major settlement was Selesih, a village of 7,000 houses built by seven chiefs of the Sailo clan in the mid-1700s. This was a vast population by Mizo standards.

According to Lalthangliana, the claimed numbers of houses for Dungtlang and Selesih may both be exaggerations designed to dissuade prospective enemies from trying any attacks, 'but we can accept the fact that they had an immense population; and as for the exaggeration in the anecdotes we have written, we should regard them as the Mizo way of exaggerating things and it will relax our minds'. With minds thus relaxed, we can enjoy the tales remembered from songs. There is, for example, a song that is sung during a dance called Chailam—which has nothing to do with tea—where young men and women form circles and sing and dance while a brew more exciting than tea, rice beer, was traditionally passed around. According to the song, 'Zopui village extends far and wide, its chief in the centre resides.' This Zopui was a village established by a Lushai chief of the Sailo clan from Selesih, who found himself forced to pay tributes to his eastern neighbours from across the Tiau river, the Thlanrawn—the name of a powerful village of the Lai tribe in the Chin Hills—who wore their hair in topknots. 'Foes with topknots are hard to hold back, my mithun [a kind of native bison] follows the Tiau river track', goes the song.[4] Tired of losing their bison, elephant tusks and other treasures to the Thlanrawn, Lallula, the chief of Zopui, invited his extortionate neighbours over to collect a stash of booty, got them drunk and then massacred the lot, said to number 300, holding only their chief Thanchhuma and village elder Phunthanga captive. This was duly celebrated in the song, which went, 'Phungthang craved elephant tusks, so Thangchhum now wears handcuffs.'

Such songs could have serious consequences. 'In Mizo history', continues Lalthangliana, perhaps also with a touch of relaxed exaggeration, 'the best remembered event is the war between north and south, which took place between 1849 [and] 1856.' This war was between the descendants of the crafty chief of Zopui, Lallula, representing the north, and those of another chief named Lalrivunga from the south. The two main reasons for the outbreak of this war were a dispute over the possession of land and the composition of a mocking or scoffing song.[5] It eventually petered out inconclusively because of a natural calamity whose periodic recurrence has had a significant and lasting effect on Mizo history: the flowering of the bamboo, known to the Mizos as 'mautam'. Roughly every fifty years, the extensive groves of bamboo in Mizoram flower and die. At the time of their flowering, a type of beetle called 'thangnang' in Mizo multiplies until there are swarms of them. The beetles are joined by swarms of rats. Between them, they destroy crops and cause famine.

By the time this war and famine occurred, the tribe had come into contact with the British in the plains of Sylhet and Cachar. It was a process that began circa 1760, when Chittagong came into the possession of the East India Company. In a report in 1853, Colonel Frederick Lister of the Sylhet Light Infantry wrote:

> For many years back, and long before we obtained possession of the district, the inhabitants of the plains to the south were in constant alarm and dread of the tribes of Kookies who resided both within our boundaries and without... They used to come down and attack the villages in the plains, massacre the inhabitants, take their heads, loot and burn their houses. These aggressions used principally to be made after the death of one of the Kookie Rajahs, when the having human heads to bury with him is in the idea of the Kookie an idea of great consideration.[6]

Several Indian historians have disputed the attribution of all tribal raids to headhunting. They maintain that the encroachment of planters and settlers in traditional lands and hunting grounds of the tribes was the more common cause of the raids, during which heads were taken. This is also borne out by the writings of some of the British administrators. Many of the colonial writers were therefore probably mistaken about the principal cause of the raids—and they were certainly confused about the identities of the tribes they were describing. Early British colonial accounts tended to use the word 'Kookie' as a generic term, and applied it to several tribes that no longer identify as Kuki.

In 1842, there was a series of raids by the tribes into the British districts of Arakan and Sylhet. In the north, the Lushais had cut up some Sylhet wood-cutters on the grounds that they had withheld from them tribute due on timber extraction.[7] Towards the end of 1843 or beginning of 1844, a Paite chief named Laroo passed away following alleged mistreatment at the hands of two Manipuri princes near the Sylhet border, leaving his son Lal Chokla to head the tribe. Although the description of Paites as Kukis is now controversial (the term Zomi is generally preferred), old British accounts refer to them as Kookies. 'No Kookie Chief could go on his last journey unaccompanied by attendants to do his bidding in the unseen world', wrote Lister:

> The affection of his clansmen was not, however, put to too great a strain. They had not themselves to go away, so long as they could supply Bengali slaves, whose heads piled around the corpse of the Chief were earnest that their ghosts were keeping company with his. But slaves were scarce in the hills since the British government had discouraged this trade, so Lal Chokla and his cousin Botai hung their great relative's body in the smoke and set forth on the war path to slay the prescribed number of victims.[8]

The raiders attacked a Manipuri village and made off with twenty heads, which naturally had to be separated from their bodies before they could be carried away. The attackers had come from beyond the Tripura king's lands but he professed helplessness in the matter. He eventually agreed to allow a punitive expedition to pass through his territory that managed to force Lal Chokla's surrender. More headhunting raids in Sylhet and Cachar followed. In 1849, Lushais raided a Kuki village 16 kilometres from Silchar and killed 29 people, taking 42 captives. This time, a force under Colonel Lister was despatched from Silchar that attacked and burnt a Lushai village before returning. Lister reported that 'the fighting part of the Lushai population are composed, first, of Lushais, who appear to be a cross between the Kookies and Burmese, secondly, of a certain number of true Burmese, entertained for the purposes of warfare, and thirdly, of refugees and outlaws from Munipore and our own frontier'. He explained his remark about a Burmese element in the Lushai population further, saying 'this opinion is strengthened by a belief universally prevalent that a part of the Burmese army which occupied Telyne and its neighbourhood in 1824 never returned to Ava but settled in the jungles to the south of Cachar'.[9]

To get around their dependence on uncertain access through the Tripura king's lands, the British began work on opening up a road to the Mizo hills from Silchar. In October 1850, the Lushais made overtures of peace, and representatives of five chiefs came to Silchar to meet with Lister:

> They said they wished to become our ryots (tenant farmers) and pay tribute to get protection from the Pois, a tribe to the south, whose advance they dreaded, to whom they paid tribute, and through whom they got arms, and who were supposed to live in the province shown in old maps as Yo Pye, east of Arracan.[10]

According to the *Linguistic Survey of India*, 'the name Poi is a Lushei denomination of tribes who wear their hair in a knot upon the top of the head'. It probably corresponds to Pawi, the old name of the tribe now known as Lai, who still have their own autonomous area in the south of Mizoram.[11]

In December 1850, the Mizo chief Suakpuila known in British accounts as Sukpilal with another delegation reached Silchar to meet with Colonel Lister, who wrote:

> Their fighting population is composed almost entirely of men whom they call Chillings, belonging to the south end of their position, distant about seven days' march from their most southern village and extending, as they report, to the frontier of Burmah. The people of this country, which they call Poee (Poi) are described as a powerful tribe to whom they pay a yearly tribute and acknowledge a sort of allegiance. Two of these

> Chillings accompanied the Raja; they were stout, well-made men strongly resembling the Burmese and very unlike the Kookies. They were armed with good serviceable flint muskets, apparently of American manufacture, with the name of G. Alton on the locks. The Bengallee interpreter, Gobind Ram, states that there was one of these muskets in each house in the Raja's village. They procure them from the Poee people, giving them in exchange slaves, at the rate (as the Lushais themselves stated) of two muskets for a slave 4 ½ feet high.[12]

The abolition of slavery by the Company Raj in 1843, therefore, caused the Lushai chiefs some economic loss and inconvenience, with slaves escaping into British territory. It also disturbed a lucrative and long-running slave trade along the Arakan coast of Burma, where Portuguese and Arakanese pirates collaborated with Dutch and other merchants. The coast connected to hinterlands through inland routes and networks of exchange; an ancient 'Southwest Silk Route' connected Yunnan to Bengal. The Mizo Hills were linked to this network. When Lister carried out his first expedition into Mizo territory in 1850, he reported 429 slaves escaping to Company territory as a result of his attack on just one large village called Mullah.

There were major Kuki raids in 1860 on Tripura including the part of it in the Bengal plains which were British territory.

The tea industry in Assam was then expanding, and some gardens had by then opened up in Cachar. In 1869, Lushai raiders attacked two of these. The government, in response, despatched three columns of military forces into the Mizo Hills. They had timed their movement poorly. It was the rainy season, and the jungles were practically impassable. They returned without achieving anything. The Viceroy, Lord Mayo, opposed further military endeavours, and so the Cachar deputy commissioner, a Mr Edgar, instead went on a tour of the Mizo country to meet with the chiefs. He suggested measures such as giving 'sanads', or charters, to the chiefs and stationing a political agent in Hill Tippera. Only one sanad, in the name of the Lushai chief Sukpilal, was actually given. Dated 16 January 1871, it lays down a boundary between Cachar and the Lushai Hills. Apart from that, it merely states:

> The illustrious Government has further ordered that Sookpilall and all other Looshai Lalls, Muntrees and people shall not in any way injure or annoy any of the people of Sylhet or Cachar. If any Looshai suffers any injury or annoyance at the hands of Cachar or Sylhet people, and wishes to have his wrongs redressed, he must make a request to that effect to the Burra Sahib (Deputy Commissioner) of Cachar, who has been ordered by Government to do justice in such cases.[13]

It quickly became clear that the illustrious government's paperwork counted for little. Mr Edgar was still in Sukpilal's village when a series of Lushai raids started in Cachar. On 23 January 1871, only days after the sanad to Sukpilal had been given, a Cachar village was attacked and twenty-five persons killed, with thirty-seven more taken prisoner. 'On the same day the Alexandrapore tea garden was destroyed; Mr Winchester, a planter living there, being killed, and his child, a little girl, captured. A few hours later, Cutlicheerra, the adjoining garden, was attacked.'[14] More attacks on this garden followed and were repulsed with losses to both sides. Then another tea garden in the area, Monierkhal, was attacked. The police had deployed there and a sepoy was killed. Police reinforcements led by the district superintendent of police, a Mr Daly, arrived on the scene and beat back the raiders after a whole day of fighting. However, other nearby gardens were not so fortunate and one called Nudigram had eleven killed and three captured and taken away. More raids followed in Sylhet and along the borders of Hill Tippera.

The lengthening list of attacks and the kidnapping of five-year-old Mary Winchester finally compelled a government that had long been reluctant to mount a sufficiently large expedition into the hills—a costly proposition—to take the action that had been recommended by Colonel Lister two decades earlier. A column was sent from Cachar with half of the Peshawar Mountain Battery artillery, along with a company of sappers and miners, 500 men of the Punjab Native Infantry, 1,000 of the Assam Light Infantry—a force composed mainly of Gorkha troops—and 100 armed police. A telegraph party accompanied the troops and laid down a telegraph line from Silchar to Mynadhur, the furthest of the tea gardens towards the Mizo Hills. Then, setting up a series of camps, the column advanced into Lushai territory. The first skirmish occurred on the day before Christmas 1871, according to the eyewitness account of Lieutenant R. G. Woodthorpe, a member of the expedition. The officers sat down the next evening for Christmas dinner, with bullets flying in from the surrounding forest. 'Notwithstanding the excellent mark which the dinner-table and its lights presented to them, no shots were fired in that direction, though single sentries posted quite near to it were hit', wrote Woodthorpe. 'Another curious fact is that when some songs were sung after dinner, the Lushais stopped firing altogether while the singing lasted, commencing again when the song was over.'[15]

An attack in which a few elephants were injured and mahouts killed followed, but as the column pressed on ahead, destroying granaries and villages, eventually a chief named Pawibawia known to the British as Poiboi made peace. Another powerful chief, Sukpilal—the recipient of the government's sanad—was anyway sitting out the fight. This helped the invaders secure their lines of communication to their rear. With this 'armistice' in place, the invaders now began trying to win the confidence of the locals. 'Their sick were treated by our medical officers', wrote Woodthorpe, 'and we heard some of the wounded…were there. The villagers visited the camp daily, selling fowls and eggs.' The peace was, however, illusory, because as the column advanced further east, they were once more attacked, this time in an attempted ambush by a large force that included Poiboi's men, and the leader of the expedition, General Bourchier, took a bullet in his left arm. In the counterattack, the Lushais came off worse. Then, as they pushed further on, the British Indian forces finally began to use the artillery they had dragged all the way up and down the hills and jungles. The opposition crumbled. The column reached its objective of Chunfai (Champhai), the village of a famous—and dead—chief named Vanhnuailiana known to the British as Vonolel. After this the withdrawal commenced. The losses for both sides were greatest on account of cholera. Woodthorpe described it as 'a more dread enemy than any we had to encounter in Lushai land'. For the Lushais, it was worse. 'The seeds of the disease were left as a legacy among the Lushais, and, if we may believe reports, cholera has been busy among them since we left', he wrote.[16]

While the Cachar column was making its way towards Champhai, a second column had entered the southern part of the Lushai Hills from Chittagong with the objective of avenging the murder of Dr Winchester and rescuing his daughter Mary, now aged six, who was still in captivity. This column, which was led by General Brownlow, successfully made its way deep into the hills to the village of a chief named Vanhnuaia and established headquarters there. The Mizo chief named Rothangpuia, once a deadly foe and by then a friend of the British explorer of those hills, Lieutenant Colonel T. H. Lewin, was then sent to negotiate the release of Mary Winchester. 'In this he was successful. Legend has it that when Azim Subedar Sahib of the police held out his arms to her, she clung determinedly to her Lushai guardian's clothes till Azim, with considerable resource, offered her some sweets which proved irresistible', recounts Major Anthony Gilchrist McCall.[17] The child had been treated well and brought up like a member of the chief Bengkhuaia's extended family. Her captors had renamed her Zoluti, a name the girl continued to use, along with Mary, even after she grew up.

Each of the two columns had been accompanied by a survey party. They topographically delineated 10,460 square kilometres of new and difficult country.[18]

* * *

For the next several years, the Lushai raids on British Indian territory again stopped. Three new frontier bazaars were started. Ordinary relations of trade developed at border markets. An internal conflict between the eastern and western Lushai chiefs broke out in July 1877, during which the western chiefs led by Sukpilal sought assistance from the authorities in Cachar. The government refused to intervene. In 1881, Sukpilal died. The war between the eastern and western chiefs, like the earlier one between the north and south, petered out with the flowering of the bamboo and the ensuing famine. To ease the famine situation, rice was sent up into the Mizo Hills by traders under government supervision. A mutually profitable barter trade developed, with rice and salt going up, and rubber and bamboo coming down.

The peace was broken suddenly in February 1888. A survey party near the southern end of the Mizo Hills in the Chittagong Hill Tracts, led by a Lieutenant J. F. Stewart, was attacked by Pawi warriors—the tribe then known as Poi—and killed, with their heads being taken as trophies. A headhunting and slaving raid on a village attributed to people who were known then as 'Shendu' corresponding to the tribes now called Mara and Pawi, followed. The commissioner of Chittagong Division, D. R. Lyall, in a letter dated 4 March 1888, urged in the strongest terms that an expedition should be sent during the ensuing cold weather to exact punishment from the 'Shendus' in a thorough and unmistakable way. 'We are bound to protect the men living within our declared boundary, and not to avenge them would be a breach of faith', wrote Lyall, who continued: 'Lieutenant Stewart, too, was surveying ten miles from the boundary when attacked, and if these men be allowed to carry off from within our territory the heads of three white men with impunity, next year will doubtless be marked by even more savage raids.'[19]

He advised that three military columns be sent from three directions into the Mizo Hills: one each from Cachar and Chittagong, as before, with a third from Burma. In August, the government of Bengal endorsed Lyall's proposals. Assam had become a separate province in 1874, and now the proposal involved three governments—Assam, Bengal and Burma—apart from the 'Supreme Government' headed by the Viceroy of India. The chief commissioner of Assam wrote a letter in support of the proposal put forward by his Bengal colleague. The supreme government replied on behalf of Burma, saying the position in the Chindwin district there was not yet sufficiently consolidated to allow for such a joint expedition. Upper Burma had just been annexed in 1885, and the occupation there was still very new. Lyall, however, objected strongly to this position, and received the full support of his boss, the Lieutenant-Governor of Bengal, but once again the supreme government replied that they were unable to modify their earlier orders. The exchange of official letters between the two tiers of government in Calcutta was still carrying on when on 13 December 1888, a fresh raid occurred in British Indian territory only 6.5 kilometres from the settlement of Demagiri near the Chittagong Hill Tracts. The ruler of the village, Pakuma Rani, and twenty-one men were killed, thirteen heads taken and fifteen captives carried off.[20]

This incident decided the issue. The Government of India was now forced to agree that 'active measures should be immediately undertaken'. The government now ordered, among other things, that

> communications will be maintained by means of a road to be made from Demagiri as the force advances, and the officer in command will be instructed to select, if such can be found, a dominant central position suitable for the location of a sufficient force, and capable of being held throughout the coming rains and hot weather. A telegraph line will also be immediately constructed between Chittagong and Rangamati to Demagiri.[21]

The expedition set off in January 1889 under the command of Colonel F. V. W. Tregear, with a force of 1,150 men and two mountain guns for artillery. They faced no resistance the entire way to the village of Hausata, the chief who had been responsible for the headhunting raid the previous February, but who had meanwhile died and been buried. His grave was identified and the gun of Lieutenant Stewart was found buried with Hausata's body. A durbar was held after this that was attended by other chiefs, who pledged loyalty to the British. The new rulers established a permanent garrison called Fort Lunglei in the southern Lushai Hills. A road was constructed connecting this to the Chittagong Hill Tracts.

This was the start of the British occupation of the Mizo Hills, which would make it a part of the British Indian empire and eventually a part of modern India.

The success of Tregear's expedition did not end the raids, however. A large raiding party led by the sons of the Lushai chief Sukpilal, who had maintained friendly relations with the British government during his lifetime, descended on the Chengri valley on the Chittagong frontier in January 1889 and burnt 24 villages, killing 101 persons and carrying off 91 captives. The cause of the raids, according to the account of Lengpunga, one of the chiefs responsible for the attacks, was reported by the deputy commissioner of Cachar as having to do with a territorial dispute with Kuki villagers in the Chengri valley, and a matter of unpaid ransom. Seven women and a child had been released from captivity by Lengpunga on payment of Rs. 185 in cash, and a promise of a second instalment of Rs. 515. This second instalment was not paid.[22]

A further expedition was thus planned for the next season. The aim this time was to reduce the tribes to 'complete submission' and to establish, if necessary, semi-permanent posts in the region 'so as to ensure complete pacification and recognition of British power'. A Chittagong column under the command of Colonel Tregear and 3,400 men, mainly of the Bengal Infantry and the Gurkhas, left from Demagiri. A part of this force, of 800 men, broke off to head north. A smaller force of 400 men of the Surma Valley Battalion of Military Police left from Cachar. A third column, with a varied group of men from the Scottish Borderers, Gurkhas and the Madras Sappers, under the command of a General Symons, made its way up from Rangoon, entering the Chin Hills on the Burmese side in January 1890.

The columns were accompanied by engineers and opened up roads and laid telegraph lines as they went along. The Cachar column reached the vicinity of chief Lengpunga's village on 4 February, and identified a site described by the column leader, Surma Valley Police Commandant W. W. Daly, as 'a good one for a permanent post'. They were met a week later by the part of the Chittagong column that had headed north. Colonel Skinner, head of that force, visited the site recommended by Daly and built a stockade there. This was named Fort Aijal (or Aizawl).

Even before his force arrived, the captives had all been brought into Daly's camp and released without a shot being fired. Lengpunga, the chief responsible for the raid that had led to their capture, fled. None of the columns faced any real opposition. The result of the expedition was that permanent posts were established at Aizawl, and Lungleh (or Lunglei). These subsequently became the main towns of Mizoram, with Aizawl now the state capital. The main Chittagong column drove a road through the hills connecting Lunglei with Haka in the Chin Hills of Burma. The column that came up from Rangoon obtained oaths of loyalty and friendship from the Chins. Since the written word was unknown in these hills at the time, the treaties had to be concluded orally in the Chin style, by a ceremony that involved the sacrifice of a mithun—a kind of bison—and the drinking of rice beer, into which the burnt ashes of the paper on which the treaty had been written were mixed.[23]

In May 1890, the Mizo Hills began their journey towards administrative integration with India when a British officer, Captain H. R. Browne, arrived in Fort Aizawl as the first political officer there with orders from the chief commissioner of Assam to establish political influence among the chiefs. Captain John Shakespear, the field intelligence officer of the Chittagong column during the Lushai expedition earlier that year, was posted by the Lieutenant-Governor of Bengal with charge of Fort Lunglei and two other outposts in the southern Lushai Hills. Among the orders given to Browne were submitting a report on the chief Lengpunga (or Lianphunga), who had escaped arrest earlier. 'Captain Browne was charged with causing the capture of this evasive Sailo chief, who had managed to evade Colonel Skinner and Mr Daly', recorded the account of Major Anthony McCall:

> For this purpose, he soon summoned a conference of North Lushai Chiefs whom he met at a mound which was just north of Aijal, later the site of the District Jail. Captain Browne's efforts proved abortive and the meeting broke up but unfortunately not before the Chiefs scented that, as a result of the Political Officer's failure to obtain support of the Lushai chiefs to deliver Lianphunga, he might be embarking on a visit to the Chief Commissioner of Assam. There and then the Chiefs organised a plot to do Captain Browne to death. On his way down the Sairang road, when he was approaching Changsil, a Lushai ambush fell upon him and injured him so severely that he died shortly after he was able to reach Changsil.[24]

The post at Changsil and Fort Aizawl were both attacked and survived three weeks of siege before reinforcements, which were attacked and suffered casualties en route, finally arrived from Cachar up the Dhaleswari river. In the winter of 1890, under the leadership of the new political officer, Robert McCabe, a series of retaliatory raids was undertaken by the British Indian forces to capture hostile chiefs. Lengpunga and two other chiefs were arrested and deported to Hazaribagh jail in what is now the state of Jharkhand. There they committed suicide by hanging in the jail. That brought to an end the resistance of the western Lushais. The eastern chiefs, however, refused to pay house tax or supply porters and rice as demanded by the new rulers. When McCabe called for the chief Lalbura of Champhai to supply 100 'coolies' in February 1892, the chief flatly refused. In response, McCabe set off with a force towards Lalbura's village. This force was attacked repeatedly but managed to reach and hold the village. A Lushai raiding party also attacked two tea estates near the hills and killed forty-two people, taking thirteen others captive.

In the southern Lushai Hills, the assistant political officer Charles Murray—who was reputed to be in the habit of demanding local women for sex—nearly suffered the fate of his counterpart in the north, the late Captain Browne, when his convoy was attacked and he had to flee for his life. Murray was removed from office soon after this incident. Captain Shakespear, who was elevated to the position of superintendent of the South Lushai Hills in his place, was also put to the test with repeated ambushes and attacks on Fort Lunglei and on supply convoys heading there. His life was saved on more than one occasion by his Mizo staff, according to the account of Major McCall.[25] The advice of his interpreter Pu Dara Ralte, and the sharpshooting skills of his bugler Doluta are mentioned by McCall, who met Ralte decades later. A military column had to be sent up from Burma again in 1892, and it was once again forces from three directions—Aizawl in the north, Lunglei in the south, and a Burma column—that forced the recalcitrant chiefs into submission.

A major conference had meanwhile taken place at Fort William in Calcutta, attended by, among others, Chief Commissioner of

Assam William Ward, Lieutenant-Governor of Bengal Charles Elliott and Foreign Secretary Henry Mortimer Durand—after whom the Durand Line, the disputed border between Afghanistan and Pakistan, happens to be named. It was inconclusive on what ought to be done about bringing the North and South Lushai Hills and the adjoining Chin Hills area of Burma under a single administration. There followed a series of letters and telegrams between the main players, these being the Viceroy, Lord Lansdowne, Ward, Elliott and Durand. It took three years for the government to finally act on the matter.

On 5 and 6 September 1895, the Government of India issued two proclamations declaring that the North Lushai Hills would be included in Assam, and the South Lushai Hills would be included in the Lower Provinces of Bengal, a territorial unit that then included what are now Bangladesh, West Bengal, Bihar, Jharkhand and coastal Orissa. A year later, in December 1896, another conference to review the situation in the Lushai and Chin Hills was held, this time at the level of the local officers in charge of these tracts at Lunglei: 'As regards the amalgamation of the North and South Lushai Hills Districts, they were all agreed that on both political and financial grounds the transfer of the South Lushai Hills to Assam was eminently desirable, and that it might effect an annual saving of 2 lakhs of rupees [Rs. 200,000].'[26] Doing this took another two years. The North and South Lushai Hills Districts that now comprise Mizoram were finally amalgamated into a single administrative unit by a proclamation issued on 1 April 1898, and transferred to the management of the chief commissioner of Assam. The officer in charge of the Lushai Hills was given the designation of superintendent. Major John Shakespear, the field intelligence officer from the Lushai expedition of 1890, became the first superintendent of the Lushai Hills.

* * *

The intervening years from 1890 to 1898, during which the area was forcibly integrated into British India and took its modern political shape, had been momentous in more ways than one.

In 1891, a young Presbyterian missionary working in the Khasi and Jaintia Hills of what is now the state of Meghalaya, 'heard of the people who lived in the Lushai Hills and wondered if there would be a chance of preaching the gospel there'.[27] The Lushai raids of the previous year and the expedition that followed had made news. Lushai prisoners from the expedition were brought to Sylhet, near the Khasi Hills. In early 1891, just four months after the raids that killed Captain Browne and others, the missionary William Williams ventured into the Lushai Hills to see what the prospects of doing missionary work there might be. He stayed in Aizawl a little less than a month and wrote in a letter of passing the place where Browne's secretary and several of his porters were killed. 'Their bones and even the hair on their heads may be seen there to this day. They were bound to a tree and chopped to pieces with a hatchet. The marks of the hatchet still remain on the tree', he wrote.[28] Williams spent his time among the Lushais distributing pictures of Christ and trying, unsuccessfully, to persuade one or two of them to go back with him to the Khasi Hills. He returned to Shella in the foothills, near what is now Meghalaya's border with Bangladesh, and died soon after of typhoid at the young age of thirty-three.

Williams's failed pioneer effort was followed closely by that of two other missionaries, J. H. Lorrain and F. W. Savidge, who were then working in Brahmanbaria near Tripura, in what is now Bangladesh. These men, who were both members of the Highgate Road Baptist Church in London, tried to enter the South Lushai Hills but were denied permission by the local British authorities because of the risky security situation. They then made their way to Cachar in an attempt to enter the North Lushai Hills, and after a year of waiting in Silchar, were finally able to begin their journey on the day after Christmas in 1893.[29] A photograph from the time shows the duo, both sporting moustaches and turbans and dressed in the long Indian shirts known as kurtas. After a journey upriver by country boats on the Dhaleswari river, followed by a series of marches through forested, uninhabited country, they finally reached Fort Aizawl, which was occupied at the time by five British officers and two regiments, one of the Gurkhas and one of Bengal

Infantry. They set to work building their house, a bamboo structure with a thatch roof, for which they paid for the labour in salt.[30] After settling in, the duo prepared a grammar and dictionary of the Mizo language, building on the works of the explorer Captain T. H. Lewin and a Bengali scholar who had picked up the language while working as a medical officer, Babu Brojo Nath Shaha.

Savidge and Lorrain's stay in the Lushai Hills was cut short after only four years. They left Aizawl in December 1897. The reason, in their own words, was as follows:

> When we had got well started in our pioneering effort, we received a communication from the Welsh Calvinistic Methodist Mission, which had done such noble work in other parts of Assam, asking us whether we would object to their sending up men to work among the Lushais. We had already begun to feel that more men were needed to evangelize such a large tract of mountainous country, but Mr Arthington, who at the time was supporting us, would not send us any helpers, nor would he continue to support us in Lushai if another mission came up... We had been in the country four years before the first Welsh missionary arrived to carry on the work. During that time, we had reduced for the natives the hitherto unwritten language to writing, and had taught numbers of Lushais to read and write, besides translating into Lushei the Gospels of Luke, John, and the Acts of the Apostles, which were afterwards printed by the British and Foreign Bible Society.[31]

They had also converted the first Lushai to Christianity, a man named Taibunga.

Forced by circumstances to leave the Lushai Hills mission to a young Welsh missionary named D. E. Jones, who was later joined by another named Edwin Rowlands, Savidge and Lorrain returned to England, where they did a short course in basic surgery and medicine before returning once again to Northeast India to start a mission based in Sadiya, in Upper Assam, for the tribes then known as Abors (and now as Adis), in what is today the state of Arunachal Pradesh. Their work was once again cut short after only two years, this time by more fortuitous circumstances that saw them recalled to the South Lushai Hills which they had been unable to enter more than a decade earlier. This time, they were welcomed at Demagiri on the edge of the Lushai Hills by nineteen Christian Mizos who had come to receive them all the way from Fort Lunglei.[32] They reached Lunglei on 13 March 1903, after a very long journey that took them from Sadiya to Calcutta, Calcutta to Chittagong, Chittagong to Rangamati in the Chittagong Hill Tracts, and then by country boat up the Karnaphuli river to Demagiri, before finally trekking from there to Lunglei.

The number of Christian Mizos in the few years since they had first set foot in those hills in 1894 had risen to forty-five in 1901, from none barely five years earlier. By 1941 the number had shot up to 98,108, amounting to 64.2 per cent of the population.[33] Society was transformed by the advent of Christianity and the British administration. At the beginning of this period, it was a world of chiefs, commoners, shamans, slaves of different grades known as 'bawi' and 'sal', and raids that often involved the taking of heads. Trade was by barter and money was not commonly used, although the missionary Williams reported that copper halfpennies were valued (more than silver twopennies) because they could be used for making bullets.[34] The chief received the left foreleg of every animal killed in the hunt, and the village blacksmith received the spine and three ribs.[35] The written word was unknown. There were no roads, and going from any place to any other meant trekking or taking country boats in the less hilly sections.

By 1901, already the old political order had changed. The Mizo Hills, now part of British India, had been unified internally under a single 'chief' in the shape of the superintendent of the Lushai Hills. Telegraph lines and roads had been built, and the forts at Aizawl and Lunglei had become the nuclei for towns. The missionaries, fired by their zeal to spread the Bible, had standardised the Lushai language, set it to writing, and spread it via education. As Major Anthony McCall wrote in his account of life in the Lushai Hills in those early years:

> The missions had been placed, even before 1900, in the almost exceptional position of being the official educationists, while, in fact, being still inevitably wedded to their call of spreading

> the Holy Gospel. This combination of opportunities has resulted in their becoming most important employers, and education, itself the passport to material distinction, early became very nearly synonymous with the need for Christianity, if not with Christianity itself.[36]

In 1908, the venerable institution of slavery came under renewed pressure, thanks to the efforts of a missionary from Wales, a medical doctor named Peter Fraser, who thought the practice was incompatible with the Christian faith. The superintendent denied that the institution of 'bawi' amounted to slavery (the institution of 'sal' did), and for his pains, Fraser was asked to leave the Lushai Hills.

The tension between the government, which wanted to retain the old order and rule through the chiefs, and the missionaries who had come as agents of change, continued for years after, as is clear from the statements of McCall. Black-coated occupations became synonymous with progress, wrote McCall:

> Christianity led towards black-coatism. Blackcoatism involved monthly salaries which secured the beneficiary from subjection to the inevitability of traditional village life. Monthly salaries gave the beneficiaries a special, in fact, quite a new material power, while Christianity provoked a challenge to spiritual forces among the people...
>
> From the start it was the children and relations of the new rich for whom the new and novel experience of middle and higher education became possible. Among the new rich, in addition to the mission workers, can be included the salaried employees of Government.

Such employees were very few. McCall continues:

> An agricultural people numbering about one hundred and fifty thousand live in villages scattered over eight thousand square miles of territory subject to the jurisdiction of hereditary Chiefs. Within most villages is a school teacher paid by the missions and immediately responsible to the missions. In some villages, in addition, there are salaried Church Executives. In none of these villages does Government maintain any salaried worker. Contacts

> between Chiefs and Government Executives are necessarily very limited... The influence of Government, then, is chiefly represented by the ultimate force of power.[37]

It was in the service of that 'ultimate force of power' that a number of Mizos first saw the wider world. A Lushai Hills Military Police Battalion was raised and supplied 103 officers and men for the army at the start of the First World War in October 1914. Throughout the war it supplied 7 officers, 36 non-commissioned officers and 1,024 men. A Labour Corps of 2,100 men, raised through the efforts of the missionaries Lorrain and D. E. Jones, also served in France. While some men were traumatised by the strange war in strange lands, when the 2,029 of them who eventually returned home in 1918 received their accumulated salaries, in some cases of over Rs. 1,000, it was 'more money than had ever been seen before'.[38] The money economy had come to the Lushai Hills by then; shops had opened in Aizawl. With the money they had earned, the war veterans could afford a luxurious standard of living compared to the typical Lushai life. They also brought back new ideas and new fashions of hairstyle and dress. The whole tribe in the old days used to have the same hairstyle, with long hair and a middle parting. They now cut their hair short, and wore Western clothes. The Lushai Hills at the time only had schools for education up to middle-school level, with one middle school each in Aizawl and Lunglei. The war veterans, however, could afford to send their children for higher education outside the district, and some of them did.[39]

The place that became most popular for sending children to study was Shillong, the capital of Assam, located in the Khasi Hills. The first attempt at setting up a representative organisation for the Lushais, perhaps naturally, thus came in Shillong. A Lushai Students' Association was formed in October 1924 in Shillong, with branches in Calcutta and Guwahati.[40] The Calcutta branch had three members, while the Guwahati one had two. In Shillong there were fifteen members. They were, however, not the first to step into the field of political activism in the Lushai Hills. That initiative was taken in 1926 by a group of local shopkeepers in Aizawl who submitted a memorandum to the superintendent, N. E. Parry, protesting against compulsory labour for tasks such as construction of the chief's house and 'zawlbuk' (bachelor house for young men), village schools and the schoolmaster's house, and carrying the luggage of 'Circle Interpreters' and other officials on tour.[41] Parry responded to this petition by threatening them with imprisonment. The petitioners then sent their memorandum to the Governor, who sent it back to Parry, with the result that all the petitioners were arrested. They were subsequently released with a warning to desist from all such activities.[42] From the beginning of the British administration in the Lushai Hills, it had been established policy for the British to rule through the chiefs. Parry now set about trying to shore up the rapidly fading authority of this institution.

* * *

The old political order was by then changing rapidly across British India. An Indian Statutory Commission had been appointed in 1927 by the British government to report on the workings of the Indian constitution established by the Government of India Act of 1919. The following year, in 1928, the seven commission members led by its chairman Sir John Simon arrived in India to a storm of protests led by members of the Indian National Congress, who were angered that a body to determine India's future did not have a single Indian member. Among the many memoranda it received when it arrived in Assam was a note from the Lushai Hills district superintendent, Neville Parry. 'In origin the hill people have absolutely no connection with the Bengalis or Assamese', wrote Parry in his note dated 3 March 1928:

> The Lushais are of Mongolian origin and are allied to the Kukis and Chins. They are entirely untouched by Hinduism and Muhammadanism. They look down on and distrust the people of the plains, who, in their turn, despise the hillmen as untouchables... The natural tendency of the hillmen seems to be to develop on non-Indian lines.[43]

He highlighted the absence of caste in the hills, noting that 'A sweeper can associate on friendly terms with a chief or educated government official and in fact frequently does so.' Before the British occupation, the Lushais had been independent, said Parry, and the dwellers in the plains had 'never exercised even a shadow of suzerainty over them'.[44]

Parry also considered that the people of the 'backward tracts' were not yet fit for council rule. 'The Lushais are perhaps the most advanced educationally of the hill tribes. Such education as there is among them is however purely superficial... There is no politically minded class and no one fit to sit on a council, and if there were such a person, he would represent only himself', he wrote.[45] He summed up his views as follows:

> What is sauce for the goose is sauce for the gander and if it is good for the plainsman to manage his own affairs and to develop on his own lines under a camouflage of western democracy surely it is equally important that the hillman should be left to live his own life in his own way and should not be condemned while still unable to express his own opinions to succumb to the civilisation of the plains.[46]

Towards this end, he concluded by proposing two alternatives: either a hill division comprising all the backward tracts of Assam headed by a commissioner who would report to the Governor of the province, or a separate North-Eastern Frontier Hill Province including all the hills from the Chittagong Hill Tracts to Burma and the Tibetan frontier.

The colonial officer's ideas about the unsuitability of extending political reforms, in the shape of greater representation for the governed, found its counter in a note by the Khasi leader J. J. M. Nichols-Roy, who was then the minister for local self-government in Assam. 'I am very doubtful about the exclusion of the backward tracts from the Reforms', wrote Roy:

> They have for three terms of the Council been included in the Reforms. Now it is proposed to exclude them... I think if they are left with the Reforms in course of time a political consciousness will be aroused among those who are actually backward and they will take their place alongside their fellow citizens in the plains districts.[47]

Roy, however, focused his argument on the constituency he represented, the Khasi and Jaintia Hills, arguing that these were not 'backward'.

The Simon Commission submitted its report, a massive work of two volumes accompanied by another twelve volumes of memorandums it had received, in 1930. The details of the proposed 'Excluded and Partially Excluded Areas' were published in the *Assam Gazette* in 1933. While the Khasi, Jaintia, Garo Hills and Mikir Hills were given representation, the Lushai Hills were left out. This did not please the Mizos. In December 1933, a petition was submitted on behalf of the 'people of the Lushai Hills' seeking two representatives from the district in the Assam council.[48] A further petition on behalf of an organisation called the Aijal Association followed in 1934, this time directly to the Assam governor. The new superintendant, McCall, according to the historian J. Zorema in his book *Indirect Rule in Mizoram*, immediately called a public meeting, inviting the signatories to the petition, at which they were publicly forced to withdraw their names.

A parliamentary debate on the matter of 'Excluded and Partially Excluded Areas' took place in the House of Commons in London in May 1935. The new Government of India Act of 1935 was about to be passed, and a Sixth Schedule proposing special provisions for these areas had been framed. The eventual result, in line with the Assam government's proposals put forward by officers like Parry and J. H. Hutton in the Naga Hills, was that all the hill areas of the Northeast frontier were either wholly or partially excluded from the political reforms in the Government of India Act of 1935, which heralded the proper beginning of electoral democracy in India.

In June 1935, a Young Lushai Association was formed in Aizawl through the efforts of the Welsh Presbyterian Church, with Reverend Lewis Evans as president and Reverend Chhuahkhama, the first Mizo minister of the Presbyterian Church, as vice president.[49] Its objectives were non-political: to encourage the youth to use their leisure for beneficial activities; to serve for the welfare of the people; and to promote the Christian way of living. In the same year, the Lushai Students' Association, which had become almost defunct since being formed in 1924, was revived in Shillong. Its name was changed in 1946 to Mizo Zirlai Pawl (Mizo Students' Association).

McCall looked askance at these developments. The small new educated and salaried middle class was one he called an 'oligarchy'.[50] He organised three conferences of the traditional chiefs in 1936, continuing with his predecessor's policy of trying to shore up their fading authority. He followed this up by framing clear rules of succession for chiefs whose number had increased from about 60 at the start of British rule, to about 400. Then, in 1941, he created a 'District Chiefs' Durbar' of which he was the president. The Second World War had broken out by then, and it reached the borders of what is now Mizoram in March the following year, with the fall of Burma to the Japanese. McCall called two meetings of chiefs of the northern and southern parts of the Lushai Hills in April 1942, at which the chiefs decided to offer 'total resistance to any invader'.[51] Although the Japanese forces reached and occupied the Chin Hills bordering Mizoram, they delayed their invasion of British India until 1944, and eventually launched their attack through Manipur and the Naga Hills before being halted following the battles of Imphal and Kohima. The Lushai Hills escaped the war; the most lasting impact they felt was a positive one. Under threat of Japanese invasion, the road from Silchar to Aizawl was finally made a motorable one, and the first motor vehicle reached these hills.

On 7 February 1944, about a month before the Japanese invasion, Sir Robert Reid, who was the Governor of Assam from 1937 to 1942, addressed a meeting of the Royal Geographical Society in London. The Second World War was still far from over, but that evening, Reid's talk took little notice of it. His subject was the future of the 'Excluded Areas' of Assam, and his primary concern was not the impending Japanese invasion. 'A new constitution, in which we may be sure British control will be enormously diminished, is promised for India as a whole', said Reid, 'and it will be a question whether the hill tribes are to be included in it, or kept outside.' Reid's view was that they ought to be kept outside: 'We are responsible for the future welfare of a set of very loyal, primitive peoples who are habituated to look to us for protection and who will get it from no other source.' He continued:

> They are not, by a hundred years, ready to take their place in a democratic constitution, or to compete with the sophisticated Indian politician for place and power, and personally I have no doubt whatever that to allow them in any way to be involved in Indian politics, with no safeguards such as now exist, would spell disaster for them.[52]

He was not proposing stagnation as museum specimens or anthropological specimens, said Reid, 'Education is there and is in great demand... Contact with the outside world has been immensely widened by the war and will be more widened as time goes on, and the leaders of these peoples have no intention of being left in a state of savage contentment.' Reid's proposal, which he said was only repeating in a slightly different form what the government of Assam had said to the Simon Commission in 1928, was that the 'artificial union' between the backward tracts and the rest of the province of Assam should be ended. The political situation had changed tremendously since 1928, and what Reid now favoured was a 'civil administrative unit comprising the Hill Areas along the north and east frontiers of Assam and taking in as well the similar areas in Burma itself', an arrangement outlined in an influential report by Sir Reginald Coupland on the 'constitutional problem in India'.[53]

Coupland, it turned out, had got the idea from none other than Reid himself. In a confidential note on the future of the 'Excluded and Partially Excluded' areas of Assam, authored in November 1941, Reid had proposed a North East Province or Agency under a chief commissioner, separated from the Government of India and put under some appropriate department at Whitehall.[54] Naturally, that detail on the removal of the 'Excluded and Partially Excluded' areas from India was a delicate matter that Reid chose to avoid publicly mentioning in his talk at the Royal Geographical Society. However, the plan got the attention of Viceroy Lord Linlithgow, and Secretary of State for India L. S. Amery, who discussed it with

Lord Archibald Wavell shortly before the latter left England to take charge as Governor General.[55]

The end of the Second World War brought about a rush of political activity that had been suspended because of the war. In Britain, parliamentary elections saw the defeat of wartime leader Winston Churchill. Clement Attlee of the Labour Party became prime minister in July 1945. Assembly elections across an undivided India followed in early 1946, in which the Congress and Muslim League faced off, with the League—for the first time—emerging as the single largest party in the vitally important Muslim-majority provinces of Punjab and Bengal. In the Assam Assembly, the Congress won all the forty general seats and seven seats reserved for scheduled castes, while the Muslim League won thirty-one out of thirty-four Muhammedan seats, which were reserved for Muslims. The remaining three Muhammedan seats were won by a political front of the Jamiat-i-Ulema-e-Hind. Of the five seats reserved for Backward Areas (Hills), meaning the 'Partially Excluded' areas, independent candidates won three, and Congress two.[56]

The Lushai Hills, which were 'Excluded Areas', were yet to graduate to having their own political representation. On 14 January 1946, MacDonald convened a District Conference of chiefs and commoners to advise him on the administration and future political set-up of the hills. A plan was formulated involving adoption of a constitution for the Lushai Hills with legislature, ministry, judiciary and other useful organs of a full-fledged government.[57] Before any concrete discussion on its contents could be taken up, the plan hit a roadblock on the issue of representation. The conference had twenty representatives on behalf of the chiefs and an equal number representing the commoners. While the chiefs had only to elect twenty representatives from among themselves, the commoners had the more difficult task of first electing one person from every ten contiguous houses to make an electoral college that would then elect the twenty who were to represent them.[58]

Both the chiefs and the commoners—there were no more slaves as the system had been abolished in 1927—moved on separately.

The first political party in what is now the state of Mizoram was formed in April 1946, named the Mizo Common People's Union. The first meeting of the new party was held in Aizawl the following month, at which R. Vanlawma, who had taken the lead in founding the party, was elected general secretary, and a trader named Pachhunga briefly became president before handing over charge to his vice president, Lalhema. The chiefs, for their part, organised themselves into a Lushai Lal Council, or Lushai Chiefs' Council, and elected one of themselves, Lalsailova Sailo, as the chairman, with a large number of other chiefs from the traditionally powerful Sailo clan among its members.[59] The Mizo Common People's Union, renamed the Mizo Union, unfortunately developed factions between its more and less educated members within months of its formation, and in November both the president and general secretary found themselves deposed by the Union's leader in the South Lushai Hills, Saprawnga, and a master's degree holder, a man named Khawtinkhuma from Tripura. However, the deposed president and secretary refused to hand over their charges, as a result of which for a time the Mizo Union had two sets of office bearers. The power struggle remained unresolved. In January 1947, Khawtinkhuma was confirmed in his position of president of the Mizo Union, along with Reverend Zairema of the Presbyterian Church as his vice president and H. Vanthuama as general secretary.[60]

* * *

By then the Constituent Assembly of India had already started work on drafting a new constitution for the country. This body constituted an Advisory Committee on Minorities and Tribal Areas under Sardar Vallabhbhai Patel. A sub-committee of this advisory committee under Gopinath Bordoloi, the Assam premier, was tasked with looking into the issues of the 'Excluded and Partially Excluded' areas of Northeast India. The Bordoloi sub-committee visited the Lushai Hills in April 1947. The political situation it found was briefly described in its report. The District Conference established by the superintendent, with representation from the chiefs and commoners, had broken down and was virtually abandoned by October 1946, the report said. The Bordoloi Committee noted:

> Shortly before the visit of the Sub-Committee however fresh elections were held by the Superintendent. At this election a change was made in the franchise so that chiefs and commoners voted jointly. The ratio of chiefs and commoners was however maintained and on this account the Mizo Union decided to boycott the elections with considerable effect on it. In fact, it is claimed by the Mizo Union that only two or three hundred voters actually took part in the elections... The Superintendent being the President of the conference and the chiefs being largely under official control and influence, there was apparent justification for the suggestion that the District Conference was not representative of the views of the people.[61]

The Bordoloi Committee nonetheless met, first of all, five representatives of the District Conference, led by the Reverend Zairema, vice president of one faction of the Mizo Union. Vanlawma, the general secretary of the old guard in the Mizo Union, was also present at this meeting, which was held in Aizawl on 18 April 1947. After being subjected to some searching preliminary questions by Bordoloi and J. J. M. Nichols-Roy (a member of the committee from the Khasi Hills of Meghalaya), Zairema said, 'We want to ask certain questions.' They had been informed only on 23 March that the committee would be visiting, continued Zairema, and

> it is very difficult to form opinions on these big questions during this short period... You say that 'We want your views'. The thing is we have not discussed these things in the Conference. We have discussed some points only and it seems that you are taking it for granted that we would like to join the Indian Union.

Bordoloi replied, 'It is quite clear that if the British Government go away, India remains and you remain as part of India'. 'Whether we continue to be in the province of Assam?' asked Vanlawma. 'That is for you to say', replied A. V. Thakkar, one of the committee members, 'As at present you are and will remain a part of Assam'.[62]

Further meetings followed that afternoon with church representatives, ex-servicemen and chiefs. Unnamed representatives among the ex-servicemen spoke up in favour of independence. 'We have been in the army for 15 years mixing with the Indians and we are looked down upon', said one ex-serviceman. 'If such things happen, we do not like it.'

The Mizo Union, with three representatives from each faction, met the Bordoloi Committee members next. Vanlawma, the original general secretary of the Union was there again, as was Vanthuama, the general secretary of the faction that had overthrown him. So too was the Reverend Zairema, who had been there in the District Conference delegation, the church representatives' delegation, and was back again as part of the Mizo Union delegation. At this meeting, Vanthuama sought the right to secede from the Indian Union after ten years. 'You want to remain in the Union only to get money out of the Indian Union', Bordoloi retorted. 'We want to control immigration and land tenure; also, administration of justice', said Zairema.[63]

The gist of the discussion that day was that the Mizo Union representatives of both factions were agreed on joining the Indian Union for defence, external affairs and communications, but big questions remained about the other subjects. A series of further meetings and interviews followed. One of these was with Lal Biakthanga, one of the very few master's degree holders among the Mizos at the time, who would go on to launch the United Mizo Freedom Organisation (UMFO). 'We are now called Lushais which is only a part of the old Lushei tribes. We should be called Mizos and our district should also be called Mizoram District instead of Lushai Hills', he said.

The superintendent, A. R. H. MacDonald, also appeared before the commission in his capacity as president of the District Conference. 'This Conference strongly protests against the anti-democratic action of the advisory Sub-Committee in co-opting two members of the Mizo Union to be members of the Sub-Committee without consulting anyone in the district', he said. The co-opted members of the Mizo Union on the Bordoloi Committee were Khawtinkhuma and Saprawnga, the leaders who had split the Mizo Union.

At the time all these discussions were taking place, even Bordoloi himself did not know that independence was about to come in August 1947. The date he referred to during his discussions for the British leaving India, as recorded in the committee's report, was June 1948. This was the date Prime Minister Clement Attlee had announced on 10 February 1947 in the House of Commons, the lower house of Britain's parliament in London. He had also confirmed the appointment that day of Lord Louis Mountbatten as last Viceroy of India.

Mountbatten arrived in India and took the Viceregal Oath on 24 March 1947. He was a man in a tearing hurry. Barely two months later, on 3 June 1947, he made the fateful announcement on All India Radio that the country would be partitioned, and clarified in a press conference the next day that the date for India's independence would be advanced from June 1948 to 15 August 1947. A mad scramble followed to divide the country. A frenzy of violence resulted from the chaos as riots of a ferocity never seen before broke out. A million people across the subcontinent—this is the conservative estimate—mainly in Punjab and Bengal, are estimated to have died in those riots, for which Mountbatten's haste was at least partly to blame. Why he advanced the date remains a matter of conjecture and debate. By his own account, he had decided the precise date of 15 August 'out of the blue' in reply to a question at the press conference. It was a date that held personal appeal to him as the anniversary of Japan's surrender in the Second World War.

The unexpectedly early arrival of independence found people and communities across the subcontinent, from the borders of Afghanistan in the west to Burma in the east, unprepared. In the Lushai Hills, the new superintendent, L. L. Peters, called a meeting of the emerging political class on 14 August. Leaders of both factions of the Mizo Union were in attendance, as were church representatives and chiefs. At this meeting a resolution was adopted that began by saying that owing to the unexpected acceleration of the date of transfer of power, the Lushais had been left not knowing what was to be the 'proposed future constitution and form of administration of the district' where they lived. They sought to know whether they were, at that stage, allowed the option of joining Pakistan or Burma. A demand for joining Burma rather than India had been recently put forward by the

United Mizo Freedom Organisation. The final point in the short resolution was that 'the Lushais will be allowed to opt out of the Indian Union when they wish to do so subject to a minimum period of ten years'.[64]

The Bordoloi Committee's position, which was also the position of the new Government of India, was that the Lushai Hills were a district of Assam and would therefore enter India as a district of Assam. The committee in its report had promised the establishment of elected Autonomous District Councils and Regional Councils with certain executive, legislative and judicial powers at the local level over matters including education, healthcare, roads and so on. The Mizo Union, however, was in no mood to wait. It wanted the District Council established immediately. The old animosity between commoners and chiefs had resurfaced. The Mizo Union demanded an end to the ancient practices, still in vogue, of free labour to build houses of chiefs, of the payment of taxes to the chiefs in the form of paddy and a share of meat, and the bringing before them of disputes for trial.[65] The government of Assam, aware of the growing unrest, proposed a conference in Shillong which was attended by representatives of one faction of the Mizo Union, the UMFO and chiefs, who accompanied the superintendent. Here it was decided that an interim body called the Advisory Council would be established in the Lushai Hills pending the implementation of the Bordoloi Committee's recommendations. Of its thirty-seven members, ten were to be chiefs while twenty-five were to be commoners, and two seats were reserved for women.[66] Elections for this body were held separately for chiefs and commoners and the body met for the first time in August 1948. Apart from a couple of seats won by UMFO, the Mizo Union had swept the polls for commoners' seats.

From the start, there was conflict between the chiefs, aided by Superintendent Peters, and the Mizo Union, which had links with the Congress leaders in Assam. The situation escalated when the Union, which despite having a majority in the Advisory Council was unable to carry forward its agenda due to the opposition of Peters, issued an ultimatum for his dismissal. When there was no response to this, the unmet demand for abolition of the chiefs' privileges finally exploded in the form of a civil disobedience movement in December 1948 that in many places took the form of riotous assaults on the chiefs. On 18 January 1949, a mob surrounded the office of the superintendent, shouting slogans. Peters had to be rescued by police and the Assam Rifles. He responded by having all the Mizo Union leaders arrested and packed them off to jails in the plains of Assam. He also sent two armed columns into the interior to restore order. The Assam government had to despatch its adviser on tribal affairs, Nari Rustomjee, to mediate between the warring parties. A compromise was reached upon Rustomjee's intervention, following which Peters was replaced by the first Indian superintendent, Satyen Barkataki, and the arrested Mizo leaders were released.[67]

The Indian constitution came into force on 26 January 1950. The first elections under the new constitution took place in 1951. In Assam, which had been hit by a devastating earthquake in 1950, the 1951 polls actually took place in March 1952. There were three seats for the Mizo Hills in the Assam Assembly—two for Aizawl and one for Lunglei—and the Mizo Union won them all, defeating their UMFO rivals. The District Council elections followed on 4 April 1952. The total strength of the council was twenty-four, of which eighteen members were to be elected and six nominated. There were two parties, the Mizo Union and the UMFO, in the fray, and the Mizo Union won fifteen of the eighteen seats. The council was inaugurated by Assam chief minister Bishnuram Medhi on 25 April 1952.[68]

Abolishing the chieftainship had been the principal demand of the Mizo Union for a while, and the Union now went to work dismantling the institution. In October 1952, Prime Minister Jawaharlal Nehru visited Shillong. Members of the District Council presented him with a memorandum saying that for the peaceful and efficient administration of the district, 'it has now been tentatively agreed, with the sanction of the Assam government, that the Chief system in the Lushai Hills district shall be abolished and the existing Chiefs pensioned off'. The chiefs were also there to meet Nehru, and presented a memorandum asking for the preservation of their rights.[69]

The District Council passed a law called the Lushai Hills District (Reduction of Fathang) Act in 1953. 'Fathang' was the tax or rent that the household of every commoner had to pay to the local chief, in kind or cash. The act sought to reduce this tax to half, from an annual six tins of paddy (the standard tin was an empty 4-gallon tin of kerosene), or equivalent in cash reckoned at 2 rupees, to an annual three tins or 1 rupee. The chiefs went to court challenging this move, but the court ruled that 'the passing of the impugned legislation was within the legal competence of the District Council'.[70]

The institution of chiefship was finally abolished the following year when the Assam government passed the Lushai Hills (Acquisition of Chiefs' Rights) Act in June 1954. In place of the old chiefs and their assistants, known as upas, a new administrative mechanism of Village Councils was constituted. Elections for these councils were held in July and the Mizo Union swept the polls. From 16 August 1954, the rights and interests of 259 chiefs were taken over by the District Council and power in the villages shifted to the elected Village Councils. A separate Regional Council had been established for the Pawi and Lakher tribes in the far south of the district and the chiefs' powers there went to this Regional Council from 1956.[71] The name Pawi was later changed to Lai, and the Lakher to Mara. There are now three autonomous district councils in Mizoram, one each for the Lai, Mara and Chakma tribes.

* * *

Even before this historic social change in Mizo society had time to settle, other larger political events intruded. The Government of India had constituted a States Reorganisation Commission in December 1953, and the internal map of India was in the process of being redrawn. This sparked off major political activity in Assam. The idea of a separate hill state comprising the hills of Assam had been around well before independence, and found mention, for instance, in the note from Superintendent Parry to the Simon Commission in 1928. An Assam Hills Tribal Leaders' Conference was organised in Tura in October 1954, where delegates unanimously called for a separate hill state comprising the autonomous districts of Assam. The States Reorganisation Commission rejected this demand. A second conference of the hill leaders followed a year later, this time hosted by the Mizo Union in Aizawl, where a new platform to bring together the hill tribes, the Eastern India Tribal Union, was floated.[72] The United Mizo Freedom Organisation merged with the EITU.

The States Reorganisation Act by which the internal map of India was redrawn was passed in 1956. Major new states—such as Karnataka, Madhya Pradesh, Kerala—were created by merging into them the previously existing princely states in those places. Territory was transferred from the Nizam's state of Hyderabad to Andhra, and the state renamed Andhra Pradesh. The demand for a hill state in Assam was ignored. There was no major blowback, for the moment.

It was a contentious political move, made under political pressure by the chief minister of Assam, which united the divided hill tribes and galvanised them into action for the cause of the hill state. There had long been an idea of assimilation, as opposed to integration, prevalent at a national level in India and at a smaller scale in its constituent states. Adherents of this view sought to assimilate smaller communities into their own larger linguistic and religious folds. In 1960, the government of Chief Minister Bimala Prasad Chaliha, under pressure from the Asam Sahitya Sabha and Assamese student organisations, passed a law in the assembly making Assamese the sole official language of the state of Assam.

Immediately, protests broke out all over the state in areas where Assamese was not the language of the local majorities. Practically every tribe and sub-tribe of Northeast India has its own language and its own notional homeland where it is dominant; this is a place where the spoken dialect, if not the language, often changes from one hill to the next. Most of the languages spoken in these hills are not even from the same language family as Assamese, which is related to Bengali and Oriya and their common ancestors Sanskrit and Prakrit; they come from Tibeto-Burman roots. The imposition of Assamese therefore did not go down well with these peoples. The demand for a hill state that had been turned down by the States Reorganisation Commission was now resurrected. A new party, the All-Party Hill Leaders' Conference, was established to launch a movement for this, with R. Thanlira, vice president of the Mizo Union, as its first chairman.

The already rising differences between the Mizo Hills and the state government of Assam sharpened further over a natural calamity. In 1959 there was once again a 'mautam', the famine and plague of rats that follows the flowering of the bamboo once every few decades. The issue of organising relief became a bone of contention between the District Council and the government of Assam. The Mizo Union wanted the whole relief operation to be carried out through the District Council. The state government was reluctant. Chief Minister Chaliha said he had received charges of corruption against the District Council.[73] The dispute over who—the state government or the District Council—should lead the relief effort grew, with the state channelling a part of relief materials through its own machinery. Credible charges of delay and negligence in famine relief proliferated, with the blame laid squarely at the Assam government's door. In this milieu, a new organisation called the Mizo National Famine Front was born in September 1960 under the leadership of Pu Laldenga, a clerk in the District Council, to organise relief for the starving people. In October 1961, the organisation dropped the word 'famine' from its name and became the Mizo National Front, a political party.

The following year, there were again elections to the Assam Assembly. This time, the Mizo Union candidates contested as part of the All-Party Hill Leaders' Conference in support of a separate hill state to be carved out of Assam. The Congress, recently launched in the Mizo Hills, was their principal opposition. All three seats up for votes were won by the Hill Leaders' Conference. The movement for a hill state made no headway, however; the only hill state in formation was in the Naga Hills where a furious armed insurgency fighting for separation from India was taking place. A special assembly of the Mizo Union was held in June 1963 to decide the party's future course of action on the movement for a separate state. This meeting adopted a resolution that stated: 'The Indian Government has not conceded to our demand for a separate Hill State though we have been fighting so long. Therefore, this

Special Assembly of Mizo Union, after prolonged deliberations on the issue of party policy, unanimously resolved to adopt Mizoram State as party policy.'[74]

Nagaland achieved statehood in November 1963. The other demands for hill states went nowhere. The Mizo Union, miffed by the snub and facing political competition from the Mizo National Front, threatened 'Direct Action' unless their demand for a separate hill state was met by the end of 1964; but the threat fizzled out owing to internal rifts. It was the Mizo National Front that capitalised on the sentiment in favour of separation—by raising the demand, like the Nagas, for political unification of all Zo-inhabited areas and separation not only from Assam, but from India.

On 30 October 1965, the MNF, which had been contesting elections since its formation, submitted a memorandum signed by President Laldenga and General Secretary Lianzuala to the Indian prime minister Lal Bahadur Shastri, demanding independence from India. The Mizos, it pointed out, had never been under any Indian government, nor had any connection with the politics of India. It was political immaturity on the part of the Mizo leaders at the time of India's independence that had led to the integration of the Mizo Hills with India, the memorandum said: 'During the fifteen years of close contact and association with India, the Mizo people have not been able to feel that their joys and sorrows have really ever been shared by India. They do not, therefore, feel Indian.' They committed themselves to a peaceful freedom struggle and sought the right to self-determination for an independent Mizoram.

The Mizo National Front was, however, preparing secretly for an armed struggle.

At midnight on 28 February 1966, the MNF launched Operation Jericho, a blitzkrieg that led to the capture of eleven towns in the Mizo Hills at one stroke. Indian paramilitary troops barely managed to hold on to the capital, Aizawl. The next day the MNF declared independence.[75] The Indian government, in retaliation, promulgated the Armed Forces (Special Powers) Act in the Mizo Hills and sent in the army and the air force. Air force Hunter jets strafed rebel positions, including in the capital Aizawl, on 5 and 6 March. This and the use of helicopters to drop troops in key locations helped the government forces break the siege of Aizawl. The MNF, which had bases in the forested hills of the Chittagong Hill Tracts of what was then Pakistan, melted away to fall back on guerrilla warfare. A long war of attrition followed in which the civilians suffered the worst, as the Indian Army launched extensive cordon-and-search operations, followed by the uprooting of the entire rural population of the land in order to resettle them along highways where they could be monitored.

The kind of thing that happened in village after village was well documented, sometimes by the very officers compelled to carry out such tragic orders. 'Darzo [Mizoram] was one of the richest villages I have seen in this part of the world', one army officer recalled:

> My orders were to get the villagers to collect whatever moveable property they could, and set fire to their own village at seven in the evening. I also had orders to burn all the paddy and other grain that could not be carried away by the villagers to the new centre so as to keep food out of reach of the insurgents... Night fell and I had to persuade the villagers to come out and set fire to their homes. Nobody came out. Then I had to order my soldiers to enter every house and force the people out. Every man, woman and child who could came out with as much of his or her belongings and food as they could. But they wouldn't set their homes to fire. Ultimately, I lit a torch myself and set fire to one of the houses... My soldiers also started torching other buildings, and soon the whole place was ablaze.[76]

This period of suffering has passed into legend in Mizoram, where it is called the times of 'ram buai', meaning 'troubled land'.

The forcible and torturous resettlement of about 80 per cent of the Mizo population against its will continued for two years, from 1967 to 1969. There were accusations of many rapes by Indian soldiers. The human suffering this caused angered a great number of rural Mizo youths. Burnt out villages full of bitter Mizo families maintained a steady flow of recruits to the MNF in their bases in East Pakistan.[77] The general situation that resulted was that the Indian military dominated the towns and highways while the MNF ruled the rest.

It was the aftermath of an election in Pakistan in 1970 that turned the tide in India's favour. The Awami League, led by Sheikh Mujibur Rahman, with its base in what is now Bangladesh, won the elections. The West Pakistan political parties and leadership refused to accept the result. The dispute led to the Bangladesh genocide in which between 1–3 million people were killed, and to the war of 1971. India entered that war on the side of the Bengali rebels and, in the teeth of opposition from the US administration of Richard Nixon and Henry Kissinger—who in a memorable and well-remembered act of enmity sent an aircraft carrier group from Vietnam towards the Bay of Bengal to threaten India—emerged victorious. The creation of Bangladesh in December 1971 put an end to the bases and safe havens that all militant groups from Northeast India had enjoyed until then. Many years later, Zoramthanga, who was then MNF chief Laldenga's secretary, and later became chief minister of Mizoram, recalled:

> After the fall of Dhaka in the Bangladesh war, we escaped miraculously to Rangoon pretending to be refugees headed for Myanmar. In March 1972, we fled from Rangoon to Karachi on a Pakistani charter flight. Laldenga, his family, three others and I then moved to Islamabad for four years.[78]

Even before the Bangladesh War was formally over, Prime Minister Indira Gandhi had initiated the reorganisation of Northeast India. The entire map of the region was redrawn, and Bangladesh emerged as a new country. Internally within Northeast India, new states and union territories were created. Mizoram, which until then had been a district of Assam, became a Union Territory on 21 January 1972. The Mizoram Legislative Assembly was established with thirty seats. The first elections to this assembly took place in April, and the main contest was between the Mizo Union and the Congress. The Mizo Union led by C. Chhunga won twenty-one seats and Congress took six. The Union Territory also had one seat in each of the two houses of parliament, and the Mizo Union won these as well.[79]

The MNF rebels, however, were not finished. They stepped up their attacks, and a fresh series of assaults began on targets in the two main towns of Mizoram, Aizawl and Lunglei. Their comeback resulted in an unexpected political development: the Mizo Union, which the MNF saw as a foe, merged with the Congress, the ruling party of India, in January 1974. The politicians had hoped to unite their bases in favour of the status quo and against the MNF, but the effect the merger had was quite the opposite. Support for the MNF swelled.[80]

'The writ of the insurgents ran in Aizawl and Lunglei', Animesh Ray, a former Mizoram chief secretary—the top bureaucrat of the state—wrote: 'MNF's Aizawl town commander was Major Kapchhunga who levied and collected taxes from the residents including Government officials. He lived in Aizawl and had unfettered contact with Government officials, party leaders and newspaper editors. There was a parallel administration in Aizawl run by Kapchhunga.'[81] The reach of this parallel administration can be gauged from an incident that happened on 13 January 1975. MNF insurgents entered the office of the inspector general of police, shooting him, his deputy and the local superintendent of police of the special branch, meaning intelligence, dead. The attackers then walked out without facing any resistance.

The Indian government retaliated in kind. The security apparatus began killing MNF cadres in 'encounters', meaning shooting them dead. In parallel, a peace effort was launched through the good offices of the Church—a very influential body in Mizoram—with the veteran church leader and former Mizo Union vice president, Reverend Zairema, as chairman. The MNF leadership in Pakistan secretly opened a channel of communications with the Indian government via Kabul. In August 1975, Laldenga wrote to Prime Minister Indira Gandhi expressing his desire to come to a settlement which would ensure religious and cultural safeguards for the Mizos. The response was positive. In January 1976, with Indian assistance, the MNF leaders escaped the hospitality of their Pakistani hosts and made their way to Delhi. The phase of peace talks and negotiations began.[82]

* * *

The country was then under Emergency rule. In the first elections held after the Emergency, in 1977, Indira Gandhi was defeated. For the first time since India's independence, a government headed by opposition parties rather than by the Congress, the party that had won independence for the country, came to power. The new prime minister was the Gujarati leader, Morarji Desai, of the Janata Party, a formation that included the Hindu nationalist elements that would later go on to become the Bharatiya Janata Party. Desai wanted the MNF to surrender its arms. The MNF had initially agreed to this condition at the time of their return to India, but had subsequently gone back on it, saying they would only surrender arms after the successful conclusion of peace talks, and not before. The peace talks stalled.

May 1978 saw elections for the Mizoram Assembly. A new government led by retired brigadier Thenphunga Sailo at the head of a new party, the Mizoram People's Conference, came to power. Meanwhile, differences developed within the MNF over the issue of peace talks. A section headed by the MNF's army chief, Biakchhunga, was rebelling against Laldenga's leadership. The situation became more complicated as the Sailo government faced dissidence as well. President's rule was imposed on Mizoram in November.

Laldenga and the group that had accompanied him, including Zoramthanga, were then in Delhi. According to Zoramthanga, 'In 1979, Morarji Desai, then Prime Minister, told us to hand over arms. We said first negotiate, then we will surrender arms.' The Centre responded by detaining the MNF leaders at the Intelligence Bureau headquarters in New Delhi. But, as Zoramthanga recalled:

> we devised an audacious escape route and managed to board a flight to Calcutta. We then flew to Silchar in Assam (there being no airport in Mizoram at the time) and boarded a jeep to reach the Mizo jungles. I remember we walked for 27 days thereafter. Subsequently, I became the vice-president of MNF as Laldenga was in Delhi. Laldenga was incarcerated in Tihar jail, but was finally released and allowed to go to London.[83]

Their audacious escape had been made possible by the I.B. itself, which wanted Laldenga rather than his rivals in the MNF led by Biakchhunga to have control of the organisation.[84]

A fresh phase of insurgency followed, of which one of the characteristics was ethnic cleansing of people from the surrounding plains who are known as "vai" in Mizoram. The vais were issued a 'quit notice' warning of dire consequences if they did not immediately leave Mizoram. The threat was carried out in certain cases, including that of a school science teacher, R. C. Dutta, and a number of labourers working on road construction. The insurgents killed more people between January and March 1980 than in the previous ten years.[85]

General elections in January 1980 brought the Congress back to power in Delhi, and Indira Gandhi became prime minister once more. The failed peace talks with Laldenga and the MNF resumed. Laldenga met Indira Gandhi in April 1980, and both sides agreed to suspend operations from midnight on 31 July. Chief Minister Brigadier Sailo—whose removal from office Laldenga had consistently demanded—welcomed this, after having initially opposed the peace talks. In March 1981, Laldenga arrived in Aizawl and travelled onwards to the MNF headquarters in the Arakan area of Burma to meet his cadres. After returning to Delhi, he agreed to lay down arms and find a solution within the Indian constitution. His conditions were that Mizoram should become a state with special constitutional safeguards; that Mizo-inhabited areas of surrounding states should be included in it; and that an interim government should be formed, ousting the government of Chief Minister Sailo. The Government of India agreed to the demand for statehood, but the other two demands were more contentious. Talks stalled again, before finally breaking down in January 1982. Fighting resumed.[86] Laldenga, who was still in Delhi, was allowed to leave India and flew to New York.

Assembly elections for Mizoram came around again in April 1984. 'The Congress(I) has always been sympathetic to the MNF. Laldenga's elder son David, 29, in fact actively campaigned for the Congress(I) in the assembly elections. Besides, the Mizo patriarch's tape-recorded pro-Congress(I) speech was widely used by the party during the election', reported *India Today* magazine soon after the polls.[87] The combination of Congress(I) and MNF proved too much for Sailo; his Mizoram People's Conference was defeated. The Congress swept to power and its leader Lalthanhawla became the new chief minister. It so happened that Lalthanhawla was an old associate of Laldenga's. As the report in *India Today* added:

> Sailo, the thorn in Laldenga's flesh, is out of the way. He was voted out and the Congress(I) swept to power in the assembly elections in April this year. Even more heart-warming for Laldenga is the fact that Lalthanhawla, his former associate in the MNF, is now the chief minister.

Feelers for resumption of peace talks were sent via church leaders to Laldenga, who was then based in the UK. Laldenga announced from London that he was ready to order an immediate ceasefire as a first step for resumption of talks. Negotiations resumed. On 29 October 1984, Laldenga returned to New Delhi and announced, 'I have come back as an Indian to solve our problem and take my place as an Indian in Indian politics.'[88]

This resolution of the conflict in Mizoram was delayed by a conflict that had begun in Punjab. Two days after Laldenga's return, Prime Minister Indira Gandhi was assassinated by her Sikh bodyguards in retaliation for what was seen as a sacrilegious military operation by the Indian Army to clear armed militants from the holiest temple of the Sikh faith, the Golden Temple in Amritsar. Among her scheduled meetings later that day was one with Laldenga.

In the general elections that followed in December, the Congress won a massive majority. Indira Gandhi's son, Rajiv, became the new prime minister. Laldenga met him in February 1985, a couple of months after he had taken charge. On 30 June 1986, a historic peace accord was finally signed in New Delhi between Laldenga representing the MNF, Chief Secretary Lalkhama representing the Government of Mizoram and Home Secretary R. D. Pradhan on behalf of the Government of India. Under the terms of the accord, Mizoram would become a state—but the demand for integration of Zo-inhabited areas of neighbouring states into a Greater

Mizoram was dropped, to the disappointment of a section of the populations in those areas who had supported the MNF. The MNF went from being an armed insurgent group to a political party. Lalthanhawla, the elected chief minister of the Congress, made way for Laldenga, who became the interim chief minister of the Union Territory. On 2 February 1987, Mizoram formally became a full-fledged state. Fresh elections followed in the same month which were won by the MNF, defeating both the Congress and the Mizoram People's Conference. Brigadier Sailo himself lost his seat by twenty votes to the Congress candidate. Laldenga became the elected chief minister.[89]

Managing a cabinet proved harder for him than leading an insurgency. Barely weeks after his new government was sworn in, five of Laldenga's members of the Legislative Assembly threatened to join hands with the Congress if they were not made ministers. They helpfully mentioned the exact portfolios they wanted: public works, education, power, agriculture and revenue. The person orchestrating the moves, it turned out, was Laldenga's old associate, who had been forced to make way for him—Congress leader Lalthanhawla—who successfully engineered a split in the MNF. His aspiration of cobbling together a new government with himself as chief minister was shattered when the Governor, former Assam chief minister Hiteswar Saikia, and the authorities in Delhi, chose instead to put the state under president's rule.[90]

Laldenga never returned to office. He had cancer, and passed away two years later in July 1990 in London, on his way back to India after treatment in New York. The peace accord he signed has held, and Mizoram was an oasis of peace throughout the violent decade of the 1990s, when the rest of Northeast India was roiled by powerful armed insurgent movements. His one-time secretary Zoramthanga, who once literally waged war against the Indian state, is now in his third term as chief minister of Mizoram, perhaps the most ardently Christian state in India. His party, the MNF, which started life as a rebel army, is now a constituent of the North East Democratic Alliance, a grouping led by the Hindu nationalist Bharatiya Janata Party of Prime Minister Narendra Modi.

7

MEGHALAYA

MEGALITHIC, MYSTERIOUS, MATRILINEAL AND MODERN

The British administrators who drew and redrew maps and decided the future of the region lived and worked there. The leaders of modern Assam were there. Some of the earliest leaders of modern Mizoram were there as well. Several leaders of the Naga rebellion studied there. The last king of independent Manipur signed away his kingdom there. The king of Tripura had a palatial home there. What is now Arunachal Pradesh was administered from there. If there was one place where people from around the region and the world came together to midwife the birth of Northeast India, it was the erstwhile Assam capital of Shillong in the Khasi Hills in what is now the state of Meghalaya—the first modern city in the entire region.

Up until the early 1980s, Shillong was a charming little hill town of pine trees and crystal-clear streams, and pretty cottages with sloping tin roofs on which the frequent rain drummed a soporific beat. Before the partition of India in 1947, people from across the region and the world lived in or visited Shillong. There were the Khasis, of course—the local tribe—and Garos and Jaintias from the neighbouring hills. There were the British, from all parts of the British Isles. There were also Americans who came during the Second World War, and Chinese followers of Mao Tse-tung's arch-rival Chiang Kai-shek, and Assamese from every part of Assam, plus Bengalis, Mizos, Nagas, Manipuris, Tripuris, Nepalis, Marwaris, Punjabis...an unexpectedly diverse mix of the subcontinent's myriad peoples who, for one reason or another, had made this hill town in the far eastern corner home. After partition, some would leave, but others would come: Bengali refugees from Sylhet, Sindhi refugees from Sindh in Pakistan and, a few years later, Tibetan followers of the Dalai Lama who were fleeing the Chinese.

The streets of Shillong still bear the signs of its past. In the heart of the city is Quinton Road, named after the chief commissioner of Assam who lived there and was killed in Manipur by Bir Tikendrajit's men, thus sparking the invasion that effectively brought the state into the British Indian empire and India. There is Bivar Road, named after Major H. S. Bivar, who was deputy commissioner of the Khasi and Jaintia Hills when Shillong was being founded in 1864. There is Hopkinson Road, commemorating Bivar's boss, the commissioner of Assam, Colonel Henry Hopkinson, who had successfully overseen the acquisition of the land from the local Khasi chieftain, the Syiem of Mylliem, on which Shillong now stands.

It was the cool climate that first attracted the British to Shillong. The surrounding plains of East Bengal and Assam had become their territory, and they had their offices there, but the heat and humidity in those days, unrelieved by electric fans and air conditioning, were infernal. The Khasi Hills lay enticingly close, between the British Indian territories of Sylhet in Bengal on one side and the Brahmaputra valley of Assam on the other, and offered more salubrious climes along with riches in the form of a profitable trade in limestone. After a short-lived foray into Nongkhlaw, the British set up their first permanent base in the hills at the edge of the Sylhet plains in a place called Cherrapunjee. It turned out to be, literally, the rainiest place in the world. Forced to look again for a less rainy alternative, they hit upon a place the Khasis called Iewduh, meaning 'big bazaar', and set about acquiring the land for a sanatorium that would become the nucleus of a new town. The agreement was signed on 8 December 1863, and stated:

> I, Melay Sing, having, on behalf of myself and my Muntrees, and all others concerned, ceded the Raj rights and title in the land at Shillong known as the Shillong lands ... hereby renounce all right and title thereto, resigning the same to Her Majesty the Queen of England with the trees, water, and all things thereon or therein, and hereby acknowledge to having received, in full satisfaction therefor, the sum of Rupees 2000 (two thousand) from Lieutenant Colonel Haughton, Governor General's Agent, North-East Frontier.[1]

And so, for a princely sum of Rs. 2,000, the British Raj became owners of a patch of land in the middle of the Khasi Hills, and proceeded to build there a new capital for a new province, Assam, that would become the core of the new region they were inadvertently creating—Northeast India. It is a region of immense diversity, but a great majority of the 160-odd tribes that inhabit the area are speakers of Tibeto-Burman languages. There is one notable exception: the Khasis. They alone, in all the vast linguistic diversity of subcontinental India, speak a language from the Mon-Khmer branch of the Austro-Asiatic language family.[2] Mon-Khmer is dominant today in Cambodia and Vietnam.

How and when the remote ancestors of the Khasis first made their way into the hills that now bear the tribe's name is unknown. Linguistic and genetic studies suggest that they were there, in what is now Northeast India, before the earliest speakers of Tibeto-Burman languages, such as the Garo spoken by their neighbours, the Naga of the Naga Hills tribes, and the Mizo of the Mizo Hills, first arrived. 'The origin of the Khasis is a very vexed question', wrote Lieutenant Colonel P. R. T. Gurdon in his account, *The Khasis*: 'Although it is probable that the Khasis have inhabited their present abode for at any rate a considerable period, there seems to be a fairly general belief amongst them that they originally came from elsewhere.'[3]

No material evidence exists to enable a dating of their arrival or suggest where they came from, but there are mysterious megaliths, giant stones reminiscent of Stonehenge, dotted across the Khasi and Jaintia Hills. These megaliths were closely associated with funeral ceremonies, according to the Khasi historian Hamlet Bareh. The rites associated with their erection have been forgotten. There are menhirs that stand upright, associated with male progenitors of the tribe, and dolmens that lie horizontal, associated with females. The largest array of these megaliths is found near the market at a place called Nartiang in the Jaintia Hills, the erstwhile summer capital of the Jaintia kingdom. From their appearance, the megaliths give an impression of great age, but, confusingly, the colourful stories they are associated with—often the only source for these oral cultures from pre-colonial times—relate to the Jaintia kingdom which came into existence relatively recently, during or after the thirteenth century CE, at a place called Sutnga. The Jaintia capital moved westwards to Nartiang and then south into the Sylhet plains, in what is now Bangladesh, sometime around 1500. According to Bareh, 'The megalithic remains in the district belong definitely to different periods of history raised during different periods of people's settlement.'[4]

Apart from the legends and myths, there are a few tantalising archaeological remains. The Khasis call themselves the people of 'hynniew trep', or 'seven huts', representing the seven households who are believed to have been the founders of the Khasi and Jaintia tribes. These seven families themselves are said to have descended to earth from nine celestial huts, with which they were in contact until they sinned and the 'golden bridge', called U Sohpet Bneng, that connected them with the heavens collapsed. The site associated with the foundational seven huts is a peak called Lum Sohpetbneng, meaning the 'umbilical peak', about 25 kilometres from Shillong, not far from the town's airport. Recent archaeological excavations there have unearthed remnants of a Neolithic settlement, in the form of rough stone tools, shards of pottery and a few iron implements, dating from around 3,200 years ago.[5]

The oldest remaining sign of a continuous culture in the area from a hoary antiquity comes in the form of a living social practice: matriliny. The Khasi-Jaintia and Garo cultures are matrilineal, with descent traced through the mother and property inherited by the youngest daughter. In this, they are almost unique in this traditionally stoutly patriarchal part of the world. The most important site associated with the matrilineal culture of the ancient Khasis is the famous temple of Kamakhya in Guwahati, which is a very important Hindu place of worship. It is called a 'Shakti peeth' in Hinduism, a place associated with the worship of a mother goddess. Bareh wrote that the word 'Kamakhya' was a corruption of 'Ka Meikha', which means paternal grandmother in the Khasi language. This was a name for a 'revered mother exalted to the position of a deity', according to Bareh, who adds that 'It appears that both the Khasis and the Garos were associated with the legendary history of Ka Meikha.'[6]

While the Khasis and their kin, the Jaintia, both trace their descent from Austro-Asiatic ancestors and speak dialects of the Khasi language, the Garos speak a language from the Tibeto-Burman family and are one of a number of related Tibeto-Burman tribes, such as the Bodo and Dimasa in Assam and the Rabha who inhabit Assam and parts of Meghalaya. According to Garo tradition, their remote ancestors migrated from Tibet. 'The Garos remember that when they migrated to Assam from Tibet, they were met on the way by their enemies who challenged them, and the Garos escaped in time by floating across the Brahmaputra on trunks of plantain to the opposite bank', writes Bareh.[7] The story goes that they found shelter with the Khasis atop the Kamakhya hill and adopted the practice of worshipping the mother goddess, as well as the tradition of matriliny.

In what remote past such an event may have occurred can only be a matter of conjecture, because there is nothing in the rare remnants of the ancient past to substantiate any of this today. The oldest epigraphic evidence to have been found to date anywhere in that vicinity is the Umachal inscription, which was discovered on Nilachal Hill, atop which the Kamakhya temple stands. Written in the Gupta Brahmi script and the Sanskrit language, it says: 'this cave-temple of the illustrious Lord Balabhadra was constructed by Maharaja Sri Surendravarman'. It is usually dated to the fifth century CE, and Surendravarman is thought to be the same person as Mahendravarman of the Varman dynasty, who was king of Kamrup from 470 to 494 CE. The curious thing is that the temple was of Balabhadra, the brother of Lord Jagannath of Puri, a Vaishnav deity more popular in Odisha. Close connections between what are now Odisha and Assam seem to have existed in those times.

The cult of mother goddess worship seems to have been widespread in the broader area at one time. There is a Durga temple at Nartiang in the Jaintia Hills, believed to be around 500 years old, where a legend lives on of a subterranean connection with Kamakhya and rituals of blood sacrifice, including human sacrifice. There were several other such temples too; we know from the written records of the Ahom kings that during the course of a war with the Kachari kingdom in 1706, Ahom forces sacked a temple of the goddess Kamakhya in a village called Dharmapur.[8] The Kachari kingdom, ruled by kings of the Dimasa Kachari tribe, was the eastern neighbour of the Jaintia kingdom, and its capital of Maibong lay about 70 kilometres east of the original Jaintia capital of Sutnga.

In 1707, the Kachari king Tamradhwaj, who had been forced by the Ahom invasion to flee from his capital, sought the help of his Jaintia counterpart, Ram Singh, who raised an army. In the meantime the Ahoms withdrew, upon which Ram Singh seized Tamradhwaj and took him to Jaintiapur, hoping thus to become the master of the Kachari kingdom. Word of this reached the Ahom king Rudra Singha, who sent two columns of his army against the Jaintia king. Ram Singh surrendered without a fight and was taken captive. The Ahom army, returning with two captive kings—the rulers of the Kachari and Jaintia kingdoms—and the idol of the goddess Jainteswari, the form of the goddess Kamakhya worshipped at the Nartiang temple, now came under fierce attack from the Jaintias. The idol of the goddess was recovered by the attackers. Eight garrisons that the Ahom general had left in the hills were overrun. The defeated Ahom soldiers were all put to death, barring a few who managed to flee. The main Ahom column, however, managed to get away with their royal captives and return to their kingdom, where the Jaintia king died of illness.[9] After this, the Khasi, Jaintia and Garo Hills were left largely to themselves for the next few decades, following which their relatively isolated existence came to be disturbed by the rise of a new force in the plains of Sylhet to their south, where they had their capital of Jaintiapur.

* * *

Sylhet came under Mughal rule after 1612, when a Mughal force defeated the local Afghan ruler, Bayazid Karrani. In 1764, East India Company forces led by Major Hector Munro defeated the far larger combined forces of the Mughal emperor Shah Alam II, the Nawab of Bengal Mir Qasim, and the Nawab of Awadh (or Oudh) Shuja-ud-Daulah at the Battle of Buxar. The Mughal emperor was forced to confer on the Company the title of 'diwan', or revenue collector of Bengal, Bihar and coastal Odisha. The Company thus became the effective ruler of these rich provinces. As the scholar-administrator Charles J. Lyall wrote:

> The first contact between the British and the Khasis followed upon the acquisition by the East India Company, in consequence of the grant of the Diwani of Bengal in 1765, of the district of Sylhet. The Khasis were our neighbours on the north of that district, and to the north-east was the State of Jaintia, ruled over by a chief of Khasi lineage, whose capital, Jaintiapur, was situated in the plain between the Surma river and the hills. Along this frontier the Khasis, though not averse from trade, and in possession of the quarries which furnished the chief supply of lime to deltaic Bengal, were also known as troublesome marauders, whose raids were a terror to the inhabitants of the plains.[10]

In 1772, the Company Raj appointed its first official in Sylhet, William Makepeace Thackeray, grandfather of the novelist of the same name. Thackeray's job as the Company's tax collector for Sylhet also entailed protecting the areas under his charge from the depredations of rivals, of whom the main one was the neighbouring Jaintia king. Thackeray found the Jaintia king controlling both sides of a river that served as a highway for trade, which was mainly carried on by boats. He soon asked the Company's Court of Directors for permission to take military action to push the Jaintias to the far bank of the river. The court refused, but in the months between his letter and the reply's arrival, Thackeray's troops had already taken control of the Jaintia capital of Jaintiapur, forcing the raja to escape into the hills.[11] According to the earliest comprehensive report on the eastern frontier of British India, published in 1835:

> In 1774, Jynteeah is said to have been attacked by a force under a Major Henniker; but of the causes which led to this step, there appears to be no record in the archives of Government, though from its being one of the most considerable of the Cossya states, it is probable that some aggressions against the inhabitants of the adjacent plains of Sylhet had rendered the chastisement necessary.[12]

Thackeray did not remain long in Sylhet. He was removed after getting into a spat with his employers. His successors had brief and unremarkable stints, until the arrival in Dhaka in autumn 1776 of a young man from Scotland named Robert Lindsay. Lindsay had travelled to Cadiz to work with his mother's brother, William Dalrymple, as a fourteen-year-old before making his way, a few years later, to Calcutta. The enterprising Lindsay managed to supersede several of his seniors and wrangle the appointment of Sylhet Collector within two years. He found a place where collecting tax was easier said than done because the local currency was cowrie shells—and 5,120 of these cowries made one rupee. The equivalent of £1 was 40,960 cowries. 'You may imagine then how troublesome it was to manage this ponderous circulation, when received as the revenues of the country', wrote Lindsay. 'How they became the only circulating medium of a country three hundred miles distant from the sea, is a question neither I nor any other person has been able fully to explain.'[13]

Lindsay soon discovered that the 'only great and staple item of commerce' for export from the area was limestone, of the best quality, and this was sourced from the neighbouring Khasi Hills. The business of importing the limestone was dominated then by a handful of Armenian, Greek and 'low European' merchants, according to his account, and Lindsay decided to cut them out and corner the business for himself. For this, he needed to meet with the Khasi chieftains. 'A meeting was accordingly fixed at a place called Pondua, situated close under the hills, forming one of the most stupendous amphitheatres in the world', he wrote. He was greatly charmed by the appearance of the place and its cool climate, but of its inhabitants he initially had little good to say: 'The appearance of the inhabitants of this garden of Eden did not enable me to follow out the theory I could have wished to establish; it certainly deserved a different style of inhabitants from those wild-looking demons, then dancing on the banks before me.' Following a feast of 'six or eight large hogs barbecued whole', a deal was struck and Lindsay got exclusive rights to the limestone quarries, after which the inhabitants who had so recently looked like demons to him began to remind him of 'our native Highlanders when dressed in the Gaelic costume'.[14] He made a fortune from this trade in short order, buying his limestone using cowrie shells and transporting it to Bakerganj, a river port near the Bay of Bengal, by boats, where he sold it for rice or cash. Having survived a couple of assassination attempts and a minor uprising during the remainder of his long stay in the area, in 1787 Lindsay decided to return home to Scotland, finally reaching there in 1789 a very rich man.

* * *

The year Lindsay made up his mind to leave was one in which the geography of a vast tract of land adjoining the Garo and Khasi Hills changed drastically. There were floods of unusual severity that year, and the Teesta river, the last major tributary of the great river of rivers that is the Brahmaputra, changed course. The Brahmaputra itself shifted westwards away from Mymensingh and neighbouring Sylhet and began flowing into a river called the Jamuna, so that the Brahmaputra in that part of its course came to be called the Jamuna—the name by which it is known in Bangladesh even today. These massive changes in water flows were accompanied by larger changes in river systems that altered the landscape of the entire region.[15]

The political landscape was also shifting. Lindsay's successor as collector, a man named Willes, faced problems from a community of mixed Khasi and Bengali origins known as Bengali Khasis. A leader of this group, named Ganga Singh, captured both sides of a river carrying mountain trade with Sylhet. In April 1789, the Company launched a military operation against him and his associate, Aboo Singh, and their neighbours the hill Khasis, apart from Bengali dacoits. The Khasis burnt the 'thana', or police outpost, at Pandua and threatened Sylhet, forcing Willes to send for more troops. The Pandua fort also fell to an attack by Aboo Singh. Willes was forced to escalate matters, writing to the Viceroy, Lord Cornwallis, for a permanent force to guard Sylhet and the military force required to enforce a boundary between the Khasi and Jaintia Hills and the nearby plains. For the rebellion he was facing, he blamed the 'Cosseahs', or Khasis, but also the Bengalis, especially the Choudhurys (meaning landlords) and Armenian merchants.

Ganga Singh was captured and imprisoned in 1790 after the Company troops unleashed a reign of terror against civilian populations in the villages. The war led to the establishment of a boundary between Sylhet and the Khasi and Jaintia Hills, and between the Bengali and Khasi identities. In the words of the historian David Ludden:

> The English drew the boundary to restrict mobility and sever social bonds between people in mountains and lowlands. The boundary altered Sylhet's geography by crimping mobility in cowry country, defining northern mountains as alien Khasia territory, making northern Khasias aliens in Sylhet, and defining all the farmland below as Bengali... In the official culture of Company Raj, the new boundary separated 'races' of Khasias and Bengalis. It restricted 'intercourse and intermarriages' that produced the so-called 'degenerate Race called Bengalee Cosseahs'.[16]

The Khasi and Jaintia Hills were thus left outside British India for the time being. So too were their neighbours and comrades in matriliny, the Garos.

The Brahmaputra River, the oldest highway of Northeast India, curves around the western edge of the Garo Hills. There are intriguing signs in those areas of ancient and forgotten connections. Remains of an ancient Shiva temple and an even older Buddhist stupa have been unearthed in a place called Bhaitbari in West Garo

Hills district. Nothing is known with any certainty about how they came to be there—only speculations exist. During Mughal times, those same areas had contact with the passing Mughal armies as they made their way into and out of Assam. The Mughal general from Persia, Mir Jumla, who died on his way back from an invasion of the Ahom kingdom in 1663, lies buried about 50 km south of Bhaitbari in what is now the South West Garo Hills district. The earliest British report of a visit to the Garo Hills was that of John Eliot, the commissioner at Dhaka, who was sent there by Lord Cornwallis in the winter of 1788. He visited three Garo villages along the southern frontier of the Garo Hills after travelling there upriver on the Brahmaputra. The villages were ruled by chieftains holding a title he wrote as 'Booneah', probably a corruption of Bhuiyan. 'Their religion appears to approximate to that of the Hindus, they worship Mahadeva; and at Baunjaun, a pass in the hills, they worship the sun and moon', wrote Eliot. He also mentioned a caste of people called 'Hajins', referring to the tribe called Hajong, and wrote that 'their customs nearly resemble the Garrows; in religious matters they partake more of the Hindus'.[17]

According to the Garo historian Milton Sangma, Eliot was on the Mymensingh frontier of the Garo Hills in 1789, and got a Garo chieftain known as Renghta—a nickname derived from 'lengta', meaning 'naked'—released from the captivity of Mohendra Narayan, the powerful zamindar of an estate called Karaibari, who had taken him captive while he was on his way back from a bazaar in the plains:

> Mr Eliot got Renghta released, and he and all his people then offered to become government ryots (peasants) provided they were protected from the Karaibari zamindar. Mr Eliot, eager to avail himself of the great trade advantages promised by such an arrangement, strongly supported the proposal. The government in 1790 accordingly directed that Renghta should be made a zamindar under the Company, and that the Karaibari zamindar should be forbidden to molest him... This negotiation fell through owing to the unparalleled audacity of the Karaibari zamindar who simply arrested the messengers sent to Renghta to conclude the arrangements.[18]

The continuing troubles between the Garos and their neighbours eventually led to the intervention of Company Raj officials in Rangpur, in what is now northern Bangladesh, which lay across the Brahmaputra. David Scott, the magistrate of Rangpur, was informed about Garo raids on the frontier zamindaris. 'Scott's first measures against the Garos were military actions and installation of an economic blockade by closing the weekly markets', according to Sangma. The punitive measures produced more conflict: the number of raids increased from two in 1815 to 150 in 1816.[19]

Scott went on tour of the troubled areas and found that the zamindars had forced the Garos living on their estates to become ordinary ryots (peasants), and were extracting tributes from the ones on their borders in the form of cotton, which grew plentifully in the hills. He secured an agreement with nine of the Garo chiefs from the western Garo areas by which they swore 'upon a skull and upon earth and salt and our swords' that they would 'abjure the practice of keeping or of bringing and selling human heads', and would come unarmed to bazaars and pay the price required for buying goods. Scott proposed that the Garos be separated from the zamindars' control—an arrangement dating from Mughal times—and put under government management, with compensation to be paid to the zamindars. This was approved by the Company Raj government, and in 1817 the Garo Sardars of Tikri Duar executed an agreement in accordance with Scott's proposal.[20] In 1822, the area under British influence expanded as the Garos of the outlying hills bordering the plains came under the rule of the Company Raj. Regulation X of 1822, in the language common in those days, proposed to 'promote the desirable object of reclaiming these races to the habits of civilized life'. Towards this end, the thanas or police station areas of Goalpara, Dhubri and Karaibari, all now in Lower Assam, were separated from the jurisdiction of Rangpur in Bengal. Administration of these areas now fell upon a newly created office, that of the Civil Commissioner for the northeastern parts of Rangpur. Scott, the natural choice for this position, took charge as the first civil commissioner.

The Garos of these areas, who now became British subjects and were assessed for revenue, did not all welcome the new regime with open arms. The branch of the tribe from the western part of the hills, known as Ambengs, refused to pay up, so Scott sent a force under a Garo Muslim official in the Company's employment, Mirza Bundally Beg, to force the tax out of them. The extension of administration into these areas was still a work in progress when larger forces interfered, with historic consequences.

* * *

By 1819, the Burmese had already conquered and occupied the territories of the Ahom kingdom in Upper Assam and overrun Manipur. In 1824, Burmese forces invaded Cachar. As Captain R. Boileau Pemberton's report on the eastern frontier of British India stated:

> The invasion of Kachar, by the forces of Ava (Burma), in 1824, and the information that they were likely to march through Jynteeah to Assam, rendered some precautionary measures immediately necessary, to prevent such an intention being carried into effect, which, if successful, must have seriously compromised the security of Sylhet... Mr. Scott, the Governor General's Agent, opened a negotiation with the Rajah of Jynteeah, proposing that he should enter into a treaty of alliance with the British Government; but this, with the usual procrastinating policy of all natives, he declined doing, until the necessity for such a measure became more apparent.[21]

Scott sent a letter to the commander of the Burmese forces prohibiting his entry into the Jaintia king's territory, which lay immediately west of Cachar, on the grounds that the Jaintia king had sought the East India Company government's protection. The Burmese for their part sent a letter to the Jaintia king demanding his presence at their camp, on the grounds that his kingdom was tributary to the Ahoms, who themselves were now tributaries to the Burmese. This forced the Jaintia raja, Ram Singh, to conclude a treaty with Scott in March 1824, by which he swore 'allegiance to the Honourable Company' and placed his 'country of Jynteeah under their protection'. He also promised to use his forces to launch an attack on the Burmese to the east of Guwahati, in exchange for which he was promised a part of the territory of Assam upon its conquest by the Company Raj.[22]

The Company officials alleged that he did not fulfil any of these conditions with sincerity. 'It was notorious, that during the war, he permitted a Burmese detachment from Assam to occupy his territory, in direct violation of the treaty which had preserved his country from the calamities that overwhelmed the less fortunate states of Kachar and Muneepoor', wrote Pemberton in his report. He also tried to use the situation for a bit of land grab, setting up a toll gate at a place called Chaparmukh in the Brahmaputra valley, deep inside what is now Assam, and 'in 1830, he was repeatedly, but fruitlessly' ordered by Scott to remove it. By then, the war between the British and Burmese had ended, with the British having emerged victors—at the cost of roughly 15,000 lives of the mostly Indian sepoys who had fought for them. By the Treaty of Yandabo, concluded in 1826, Assam had come under British control. Cachar and Jaintia were listed in the treaty as 'dependencies' of Assam, which was exactly what the Burmese had said in pressing their claim on these territories.

The British found a pretext for exerting their control over Jaintia six years later in 1832. Four British subjects were allegedly kidnapped by a Jaintia chieftain and taken to a temple of the goddess Kali, where three of them were sacrificed. The fourth managed to escape and narrate his tale to the Company Raj authorities, upon which they immediately demanded the handing over of the culprits. But the Jaintia king Ram Singh did not comply. He died in November 1832 before the issue could be resolved, and was succeeded by his young nephew Rajender Singh. The British moved in:

> On the 15th of March 1835, Captain Lister, with two companies of the Sylhet Light Infantry, took formal possession of Jynteeahpoor, the capital of the country; and the determination of Government, to annex the plains to the British territory, was made known by proclamation ... and in the following month of April, the district of Goba, in which the sacrifice had been perpetrated, was taken possession of by a detachment of the Assam Light Infantry.[23]

With that, the process of drawing a border between the hills and plains, and between the Khasi and Bengali identities, which had been started by the Company Raj under its first officer in Sylhet, William Makepeace Thackeray, in the 1780s, was significantly advanced. David Scott, the agent to the Governor General for the Northeast frontier of Bengal, who had played a crucial role in extending the Company Raj into the area at the critical moment of the Anglo-Burmese War, did not live to see the fruits of his labours. He passed away in 1831 at the young age of forty-five. Among his unfinished projects was the opening up of two roads connecting the East India Company's possessions of Sylhet in the south with the Brahmaputra valley to the north.

Between these two lands, separating them, lay the Khasi and Jaintia Hills. A few years earlier, when the king of the most powerful among the twenty-five Khasi states, Nongkhlaw, U Tirot Singh, sought to rent some lands in the plains of Assam as they had done earlier during Ahom rule, Scott had seized the opportunity to ask for free passage. The Khasis had an ancient indigenous democratic culture; Tirot Singh replied that he would convene an assembly of his people and put the proposal before them, and invited Scott to witness the proceedings—an invitation that he accepted with alacrity. 'On the 1st of November, 1826, we started for the hills. There being no regular road at that period, we experienced considerable difficulty in making our way across the woody hills, which lie between Goahattee and Nunkhlow, a distance of 60 miles', wrote Major Adam White, one of Scott's group on that first journey by a Company Raj official deep into the Khasi Hills.[24] White, Scott and their British companions were immediately enchanted by the scenery and weather, which reminded them of southern Scotland, and impressed by the democratic deliberations of the Khasi assembly, which concluded in favour of granting the right of way for a road. White continued: 'Delighted with the climate, Mr. Scott immediately commenced another negotiation for permission to rent a piece of land upon which a house was to be built, to "eat the Europe air" as it was phrased. This, after considerable opposition, was granted.' [25]A treaty was signed between Scott and Tirot Singh at the conclusion of the deliberations, on 30 November 1826. Article 1 of that treaty says: 'Rajah Teerut Sing, the Ruler of Nungklow and its dependencies, with the advice and consent of his relations, dependent Lushkurs and Sirdars in council assembled, voluntarily agrees to become subject to the Honorable Company, and places his country under their protection'.[26]

The road construction work started and a bungalow was built at Nongkhlaw. A small military force was brought up to guard these. Scott introduced the cultivation of potatoes, pears, cabbages and beets in the area, 'a permanent gift to the Khasis'.[27] For a year and a half, all went well. Yet, beneath a surface of apparent peace and bonhomie, resentments were stirring. As Khasi historian Bareh explained:

> According to local traditions, the soldiers took away the articles and foodstuffs from the poor sellers in the market without paying for them. Wood-cutters and peasants were oppressed. They ill-treated the Khasi labourers employed in the service of the Company. Such attitude came from the lower ranks of soldiers. The country became infuriated with the arrogant and disgraceful behaviour of the soldiers.[28]

The lower ranks of the Company's soldiers in the Bengal Army, the sepoys, were largely drawn from upper castes in what are now Bihar and Uttar Pradesh, places where ancient hierarchies of caste and taboos of food were then very strictly observed. In their societies, they were entitled to be arrogant towards lower castes and tribes in much the same way as white populations in those days were entitled to be arrogant towards brown and black native people.

The brewing resentment exploded suddenly. On 4 April 1829, the Khasis rose in revolt and massacred the Company's staff that were stationed in Nongkhlaw, including fifty to sixty Indians and two British officers. Scott was fortunate to escape the massacre; he happened to be on his way from Nongkhlaw to Cherrapunjee. The British struck back, sending forces from Sylhet and Assam, and hostilities commenced. Bur Manick, king of the Khasi kingdom of Khyriem, was forced to surrender in January 1830 after his lands were occupied by the Company Raj forces. The chiefs of Cherrapunjee similarly had to cede land to the Company.

A prolonged guerrilla resistance between the Khasis, armed mainly with bows and arrows, and the Company Raj forces, equipped with guns and muskets, now developed. 'A harassing warfare commenced, in which the lives of many most valuable officers were sacrificed, and which continued to be waged up to a very recent period', wrote Captain Pemberton in his report of 1835.[29] In Major White's account, published while the conflict between the British and Khasis was still ongoing, he wrote:

> The principal obstacle to the pacification of the country has been the heroic conduct of a Cassya leader named Monbot. Born in the ignoble condition of a slave to the Rajah Teeruth Singh, he has risen, by his undaunted spirit, to the chief command. Foremost in every fight, although often discomfited, and once severely wounded, he has ever breathed the same spirit of defiance, and has proudly expressed his determination never to submit to the British Government with his dying breath.[30]

Monbot, or Mon Bhut, who is said to have had his origins in the Jaintia region, is remembered in Khasi accounts as a 'giant' far above the average height and build of the Khasis. His name, Mon Bhut, is not a typical Khasi name and has no meaning in that language. Sometimes written as Mun Bhut, the word may be a corruption of 'Maan bhut' which is 'Burmese ghost' in Assamese. He eventually fell foul of a close follower of Tirot Singh, and fled after killing the man. Bereft of support, he was forced to surrender in October 1832, shortly after Tirot Singh had opened negotiations for his own surrender through Singh Manik, the new British-approved king of the Khasi state of Khyriem.[31] Tirot Singh was finally taken captive in January 1833, in a surrender negotiated via Henry 'Harry' Inglis of the Sylhet Light Infantry, and deported to Dhaka, where he died a political prisoner. The British appointed in his place a boy named Rujjum Singh, who was forced to sign a treaty by which he declared 'That I have no objection to land being taken up by the Honorable Company for the purpose of making a road in any direction', and 'That I have no objection to bridges, bungalows of sorts, storerooms, fortifications, and stockades for sepoys being built for the Honorable Company wherever it may be deemed expedient to select sites for them.'[32] The East India Company thus became the paramount power in the Khasi Hills. Only five Khasi states which had remained neutral during the war remained nominally independent; the rest were brought under the overlordship of the Company Raj. 'All opposition having been at length overcome...Captain Lister was shortly afterwards appointed Political Agent for Cossyah affairs, over which he exercises a general control', Captain Pemberton wrote in his 1835 account, soon after the formation of a political agency for the area in February with its headquarters in Cherrapunjee.[33]

The nearby Garo Hills followed. In 1835, a British officer of the Company Raj, John Strong, was placed in charge of the Garo enclaves in the plains. He went on an expedition with a military escort into the neighbouring hills in 1837 to extract pending taxes out of villages, a task he accomplished without bloodshed. British paramountcy was thus clearly established over what is today's Meghalaya. The chief debate that followed this development among the Company's ranking officers—a white and male British cadre—was over where in the Khasi Hills a sanatorium and military base ought to be located. The first 'station', including the first sanatorium and a base to replace the one in Nongkhlaw, was established in Cherrapunjee, the place where David Scott lay buried.

* * *

On 22 June 1841, a missionary couple from distant Wales arrived in Cherrapunjee. Their names were Thomas and Ann Jones, and they had come to 'raise up the banner of the cross' in the Khasi Hills. They initially found shelter in the house of a devout invalid soldier named Lieutenant William Lewin and his wife Jane. Two months after their arrival, Jones managed to buy a house in the military station at Cherrapunjee and there set up the Welsh Missionary Society Mission House.[34] So impactful was his work in the Khasi and Jaintia Hills that 22 June is now a public holiday there and celebrated as Thomas Jones Day.

Soon after their arrival, Jones embarked on what historian and encyclopaedist Andrew May calls 'a complicated daily ritual':

> He ... enjoined two Khasi men—U Doowan Rai and U Juncha—to teach him the rudiments of their language. The trio faced off in a curious spectacle of posture, motion and utterance, their bodies moving to communicate particular meanings as in turn the everyday objects of the material world were enacted in physical display...
>
> On the basis of this theatrical interchange, Jones was progressively able to compile an alphabetical list of Khasi words, as well as longer sentences with literal translations.[35]

Khasi has various dialects that differ from one another in speech. Jones's efforts ensured that the dialect of Sohra, the Khasi name for the Cherrapunjee area, became standard Khasi. He fixed the script for Khasi which is used to this day. Earlier efforts by earlier missionaries to render the Bible in Khasi had used the Bengali script. According to May, with no knowledge of Bengali, Jones employed the Roman script when using Khasi words. This was in most respects simply a pragmatic decision, but it turned out to be a fortuitous one. As Jones wrote:

> The Khasians generally avoid the Bengali script with a superstitious dread, and they fervently believe that if they try to write letters, they will immediately be struck down with blindness or a deadly disease. In several places people have told me that so and so tried to write and they were struck blind![36]

No such superstition attached to the Roman script, with happy results for the cause of education in the Khasi Hills. Jones, who had fathered those efforts, was, however, not entirely pleased. The missionary had hoped to gain converts to his faith. He reported that parents would send their boys to his school to learn English only in the hope that they might secure government jobs, and that girls would court his wife's attentions in the hope of receiving gifts.[37]

In January 1843, two more missionaries, William Lewis and Owen Richards, from the Welsh Calvinist Church, joined Jones in Cherrapunjee. They ran three mission schools in the area, whose pupils included children of the leading families and the chiefs—but drew a blank when it came to winning converts. It took five years for the mission to win its first converts. Two Khasi men, Amor and Rujon, were baptised on 8 March 1846. 'This event marks the formal establishment of the Nongsawlia Presbyterian Church, the "mother church" of all subsequent Presbyterian churches in North East India', according to Reverend Lyndan Syiem. 'The honour of conducting these first baptisms belonged to the slow and steady William Lewis, rather than the brilliant but temperamental Thomas Jones', he adds.[38]

Jones's wife Ann passed away in 1845. The following year he married Emma Cattell, a girl of fifteen, in Cherrapunjee. His subsequent conduct came in for serious examination at the mission's headquarters in Wales, and in November 1847 he was dismissed as an agent of the mission and ordered to hand over all mission property to Lewis. Richards, the third missionary there, had already left earlier following an alleged sex scandal. Jones left with the mission he had established in disarray. He was unable to make his way back home. Embroiled in a legal battle with Harry Inglis, the soldier who had obtained Tirot Singh's surrender years before, he found himself in trouble. Inglis had become a wealthy merchant and the personal assistant to the man who had been political agent from the start of British rule in the Khasi and Jaintia territories, Colonel Lister. Jones was forced to leave Cherrapunjee. He passed away from malaria in Calcutta in 1849, and is buried there. In a short and eventful life of thirty-eight years, he had laid the foundations of both education and Christianity in the Khasi and Jaintia Hills.

Inglis, his powerful antagonist, was also Colonel Lister's son-in-law—and in 1851 he got into another legal dispute, this time with a Mr Cattell (evidently a relative of Emma Cattell) of the firm of Duncan and Gibson, over rights to quarry limestone. Matters got messy as two separate cases were filed in Sylhet and Cherrapunjee. While the Sylhet court ruled against Inglis, the one in Cherrapunjee ruled in his favour. The dispute escalated and attracted the attention of higher authorities. A judge, A. J. M. Mills, was despatched from Calcutta to inquire into the matter. He filed a report in 1853 in which he noted that the colonel would naturally have a bias in favour of his son-in-law, and recommended that 'As the time is not far distant when Colonel Lister will obtain promotion, I would suggest that the opportunity be taken to place the Cherrapunjee courts in regard to appeals in all civil and criminal matters under the control of the Civil and Sessions Judge of Sylhet.' He also suggested that the language of the court be changed from Bengali to English, 'as Bengali is a language quite foreign to the people, and the language of the Khasias is not a written language'.[39]

Colonel Lister as political agent had continued to hold charge of the Sylhet Light Infantry battalion posted at Cherrapunjee up until then. The following year, in 1854, the Governor of Bengal passed an order separating the civil and military functions, and transferring the civil powers to an assistant attached to the Assam Commission, a body that looked after the administration of Assam. Lister went back to England on sick leave, and charge of the administration passed to a Mr C. K. Hudson. Inglis, however, remained—and so did his power, exercised through a large retinue of local Khasi underlings. He maintained his monopoly on the lucrative limestone trade of the area by keeping out competition, often through physical violence. The new administrator, Hudson, passed an order in 1856, with a view to keeping the peace, that prohibited the entry of 'any European or Bengali aliens' in groups without first obtaining the permission of the local Khasi chieftains, known as Wahdadars, several of whom had business ties with Inglis.

A second officer, W. J. Allen, was deputed from Calcutta in 1857 to prepare a report on the administration of the Khasi and Jaintia Hills. In the report, published in 1858, Allen stated that 'the present Wahdadars are notoriously the creatures of Mr Inglis, and if no person be allowed to enter the district without their permission, it is very clear that the trade of Cheyla will be virtually closed to every trader except Mr Inglis and his dependents'. He also noted that the revenue of the district had risen sharply from Rs. 1,047 in the year 1853–54 to Rs. 23,023 in 1857–58, and that this was done by declaring the lime quarries state property. An order had been passed on 25 August 1855 by which the government took over the quarries and gave them on lease. A house tax of Rs.

2 per house had also been levied on 'certain families of the Meekir tribe' who had fled from North Cachar and settled in the Jaintia Hills. Among Allen's recommendations was the demarcation of a boundary between Sylhet and the Khasi Hills, and of the Jaintia Hills territory. The boundaries had been established but had not yet been demarcated on the ground, and a copy of the map could not be found in 'any of the public offices in this frontier'.[40]

Allen also thought that 'a light and judicious taxation would contribute to the preservation of tranquillity and good order in the Jaintia Hills'. It would, he suggested, make the Jaintias 'less turbulent and aggressive' and 'more thrifty, diligent and submissive to the authorities'.[41] In 1860, accordingly, house tax was imposed by the British authorities across the Jaintia Hills. It turned out that Allen had been mistaken, however: the so far peaceful Jaintias, who until then had been paying an annual tribute in the form of one he-goat per village, immediately rose in revolt. The rebellion was put down by force in a couple of months, but the peace that resulted was the calm before the next storm. 'Scarcely had the agitation of this disturbance had time to settle, when the necessities of Imperial Finance imposed the income tax throughout British India', wrote Alexander Mackenzie in his account.[42] The government ruled that house tax would remain, and the income tax would be in addition to this. A total of 310 persons in the Jaintia Hills turned out to have taxable incomes and were assessed for a total of Rs. 1,259 in income tax.[43]

In December 1861 revolt broke out. The immediate cause, according to Hamlet Bareh, was police interference in a local festival at which weapons such as swords and shields, which formed part of the traditional ceremony, were confiscated. There had been tensions related to local customs already; a Jaintia convert to Christianity named Solomon had managed to offend his unconverted brethren by hunting in a sacred grove, where this was prohibited. The rebellion found its leader in a commoner, U Kiang Nangbah, who sought the overthrow of British rule from the Jaintia Hills. It was serious enough for the British Indian Army under Brigadier-General G. D. Showers to be called in to handle the situation. A war of attrition began that spread through the Jaintia

Hills. A year later, on 27 December 1862, Nangbah, who had a bounty of Rs. 1,000 on his head, was arrested after being betrayed by a compatriot who gave away his location.[44] He was executed three days later. The last embers of the rebellion continued to burn even after his death, and were finally extinguished by November 1863.

The end of the fighting brought about the consolidation of British rule. Indirect rule gave way to direct rule. A British officer was posted to the Jaintia Hills. Elections were instituted for the positions of 'dolois', or chiefs, whose appointments would have to be approved by the British officer. Education was to be 'liberally encouraged', with the Welsh Mission being made the instrument. The country was to be opened up by eight roads. And last, but not least, the income tax whose imposition had contributed to sparking the rebellion was virtually abolished by raising the exemption limit to Rs. 500 a year—a princely sum in those days.[45]

In the same year of 1863, the land on which the capital city of Shillong was built was acquired by the British administration for Rs. 2,000. Shillong became the headquarters and seat of the district officer. The tasks of surveying the land and drafting rules for its allotment began. Roads suitable for carriages connecting the new settlement with Sylhet were built. In 1874, when Assam was separated from Bengal to become a province headed by its own Chief Commissioner, the new town became its capital. Its growth thereafter was rapid. Municipal administration was inaugurated in 1878. The town was already spilling over beyond the lands the British had acquired, and an agreement was signed to extend municipal administration to adjacent areas that fell in the territory of the Syiem of Mylliem—a process that would be repeated in subsequent years, as the town grew into a cosmopolitan city.

* * *

By then, the Garo Hills had been brought under direct British rule. Starting in December 1867, a British officer, Captain W.J. Williamson, had been posted to the new settlement of Tura in the Garo Hills in the role of deputy commissioner. Up until 1872, there remained about sixty independent villages occupying the centre of the hills which held out. That year, a raid by these independent villages on a village under British rule sealed their fate. The government, in retaliation, decided to send an expeditionary military force into the Garo Hills to subdue the last of the independent villages. Three columns were despatched, from Goalpara, Mymensingh and Tura.

'One of the last portions of the interior to submit was Rongrenggiri in 1872', writes Milton Sangma, quoting from the account of an Italian priest named Father Pianazzi:

> Rumour had reached those independent chiefs that government soldiers had hollow spears that spat fire at a great distance, and Gwal, the bravest of them, who acted as a sort of Commander-in-Chief, was impressed by the news. He determined to counter-act and so, while the other chiefs and warriors were down-hearted at the unwelcome news, he busied himself in heating up his spear and thrusting it, red hot, into a banana stem. To his great joy, the iron cooled down at once.[46]

The Garo warriors immediately bound up layers of banana stems on their shields and charged into battle. The heroism of one of them, Pa Togan Sangma, who fell in that unequal battle is remembered to this day. It was swords and spears against guns, with predictable results.

The demarcation of boundaries, and the separation of the hills from the surrounding plains—which had been done throughout the region wherever the British Raj extended its rule—followed. So did roads and surveys, and the establishment of markets and government offices and schools. Here, too, Christian missionaries followed the British administrators. Miles Bronson, the American Baptist missionary who played a significant role in the history of Assam had baptised the first two Garos, Omed and Ramke Momin, in Guwahati in 1863. He bought a house in Goalpara at the foot of the Garo Hills in 1867. By the end of the year, a missionary named Dr Ira J. Stoddard and his wife were posted there. From his base in Goalpara, Stoddard began visiting the nearby Garo villages, with some success in winning converts. In 1871, Stoddard, along with Bronson and a third missionary named M. B. Comfort, visited

Tura, chose a site for a compound and left a teacher there along with two other boys from their school who were employed as vaccinators and preachers. 'At first the people sought to turn them back, but when it was discovered that they were vaccinators, they were welcomed', writes Sangma.[47]

The missionaries, who had received encouragement from British administrators to enter the Garo Hills for years, finally established themselves in Tura in 1876. They immediately set about doing what they had done elsewhere across Northeast India. The local language was reduced to writing and standardised for print. The fluidity of dialects gave way to the fixities of grammar books and dictionaries. Education commenced. The missionary William Carey wrote in his account, first published in 1919:

> Soon Mr Bronson had in process a Garo primer and reading-book of some sixty pages, and the first catechism. The missionaries in reducing the Garo language to writing were free to choose between Bengali, already familiar to the Christian leaders as it was used by both the Bengalis and the Assamese, and the Roman characters which would introduce them to the English vocabulary... The Bengali unfortunately was chosen and retained for years, but has recently been discarded in favour of the Roman.[48]

In the Khasi Hills, by this time, a small crop of educated elites had emerged. One of them was a man from Cherrapunjee named Jeebon Roy, whose father, Ram Sing, had been educated by the missionaries in Serampore near Calcutta. Roy himself found work for the government as an interpreter for Brigadier-General Showers during the war with the Jaintias in the early 1860s. He remained in government service thereafter, rising through the ranks to become an important officer in the district administration of those days—an Extra Assistant Commissioner. Pictures of the time show him as a turbaned man sporting a thick upturned moustache, a look very different from that of later Khasi men who adopted Western attire and styles.

Roy was a pioneer and a visionary. In 1878 he successfully established a school in Shillong, the first set up by a native Khasi.

He then went on to establish, in 1896, the first printing press in the region outside of missionary or government hands, called Ri Khasi, and began to publish from this press the first Khasi newspaper, the monthly *U Khasi Mynta*, meaning *The Khasi Today* edited by Hormu Rai Diengdoh. Apart from Khasi and English, Roy was well versed in Bengali and also knew Sanskrit. His press also published books, including Khasi translations of Hindu religious texts such as the Ramayana and the Bhagavad Gita.[49] All that he had built came crumbling down in barely a minute on 12 June 1897. An earthquake that struck Assam with its epicentre near the edge of the Shillong Plateau reduced to rubble every single masonry structure in Shillong. The earth opened up in places. There were landslides in the hills. Rivers shifted and riverbeds rose. The dam holding the Shillong Lake in the heart of the city burst. There were around 1,500 casualties—a low number considering the intensity of the quake.

Roy survived the quake, rebuilt, and continued his work. He was in touch with members of a prominent reform movement in Hindu society from Bengal, the Brahmo Samaj, and was instrumental in the establishment of an organisation called Seng Khasi in 1899. This organisation, which initially had only sixteen members, sought to preserve the indigenous Khasi religion, the Niam Khasi, and its associated culture. It is still around, and so is the indigenous faith.

The vast majority of the Khasi population now, though, is Christian. The Welsh Presbyterian Church's pioneering efforts were followed by those of Anglicans, Catholics and others, including the Church of God, a Pentecostal church from America. One convert to this denomination, also with the surname Roy, has had a lasting impact on the Khasi Hills and the wider region.

Joy Mohan Roy, born in 1884 to Khagendra Mohan Roy and Rimai Syiemlieh in the village of Shella, where the Khasi Hills meets Bangladesh, became a member of the Welsh Presbyterian Church in 1899. After completing his school education in Shillong, he went to Calcutta for higher studies at what was then called Duff College and later became part of the Scottish Church College. There he came in contact with a Muslim convert to the Church of God from Mymensingh, in what is now Bangladesh, named John Allauddin Khan. It so happened that after some time Khan was invited to visit America by a member of the church there, and returned in 1904 with a small group of missionaries. One of them was a woman named Nora Evelyn Nichols.[50] Joy Mohan Roy married her in 1907 and changed his name to James Joy Mohan Nichols-Roy.

Those were times of tumultuous change. Bengal had been partitioned for the first time in 1905 into east and west on the basis of religion, and the resulting agitation, whose nerve-centre was Calcutta, had shaken the British Raj in India. Reforms designed to greatly expand the Indian presence in the Imperial Legislative Council for India and in the Provincial Councils, on the basis of limited franchise, followed with a new Indian Councils Act in 1909. Two years later, in 1913, the Assam Legislative Council was established in Shillong. Nichols-Roy and his wife Nora were at this time busy with their evangelical work for the Church of God in various parts of India. In 1913, the couple left on a visit to Nora's home country, the US. They were there for the next three years. By the time they returned in 1916, the First World War was well underway.

The war changed the world. Indians in their hundreds of thousands were recruited for the war effort, with the support of Indian leaders. The support of the Indian nationalists came at a price: they wanted greater political representation at every level. Indian soldiers fought and died for Britain on foreign battlefields in Europe, North Africa, Turkey and Mesopotamia in a bargain that enabled Indian political leaders to have more seats in the councils of imperial power in British India, but fell short of satisfying their demands.

In December 1916, the Congress and the Muslim League concluded the Lucknow Pact, jointly demanding complete self-government. The first step to that goal was to have an elected majority in the central and provincial legislatures, control of all of India's internal affairs through these legislatures, and half of the positions on the Viceroy's and Governor's executive councils for Indians drawn from the legislatures.[51] The following August, as the war dragged on and war loans as well as manpower from India remained crucial, Secretary of State for India Edwin Montagu announced in the House of Commons that 'the policy of His Majesty's Government...is that of the...gradual development of self-development institutions with a view to the progressive realization of responsible government in India as an integral part of the British Empire'.[52] A year later, Montagu was in parliament again, presenting before the House a 'Report on Indian Constitutional Reforms' on which he had worked with the Viceroy, Lord Chelmsford. This formed the basis of the Government of India Act of 1919 by which electoral politics took a major step forward in India, as the sizes of provincial legislative councils and the proportion of elected members in them were significantly increased. Control of certain departments, such as education and agriculture, were handed over to a council of ministers to be appointed from among the elected members of the legislative councils.

Nichols-Roy, meanwhile, had come back from America with new ideas. He was now a man as interested in this world as in the next. In 1918, he set up a company with a name already familiar across Central America: the United Fruit Company. It was the name of the corporation whose dominance of politics in parts of Central America gave the world the expression 'banana republic'. Nichols-Roy's venture, which was unrelated to the American company whose name it shared, was one whose purpose he would subsequently express in terms of economic freedom. 'When we consider our situation from all angles, excluding the spiritual aspect, the one thing extremely important for our land is to strengthen its economy, if it is to free itself from the inevitability of slavery', he wrote.[53]

Assam was now a full-fledged province. With the coming into force of the new Government of India Act, it had been elevated from a province headed by a chief commissioner to one headed by its own governor. The promotion in its status came with an elevation in political activity as the number of elected members in the Assam Legislative Council nearly doubled from twenty-one to forty-one. Elections with a franchise limited to those paying above a certain amount in taxes—which restricted the vote to 9.5 per cent of the urban and 3.7 per cent of the rural population—were held in 1921.[54] Among the winning candidates was the evangelist and businessman Nichols-Roy, from the only urban constituency in Assam in those days, the Shillong general urban constituency. He was appointed to the Governor's Council. He was the first tribal in Northeast India to attain high office through elections. Apart from him, the Garo member Jangin Sangma Laskar was nominated to the Assam Legislative Council to represent 'Backward Tracts'. Legislative Council polls followed again in 1923, and Nichols-Roy once again won his seat.

On 27 July 1923, a notice was circulated to the chiefs of the Khasi states by a group including two chiefs—the Syiems of Mylliem and Nongkhlaw—and Nichols-Roy, stating that a Khasi durbar called the Khasi National Durbar would be convened from 4–6 September 1923 at Nichols-Roy's residence in Shillong. The Syiem of Sohra, Join Manik, was appointed the first president of this body, while Nichols-Roy became the first secretary.[55] 'In 1927, Nichols-Roy became a minister in the Assam government, and gave up the secretaryship of the durbar in favour of a personal follower, Joab Solomon', according to S. K. Chaube in his book *Hill Politics in Northeast India.*[56]

The political pulse of India had by then quickened; great changes were afoot.

The key demand of most Indian nationalists even then was 'dominion status' within the British empire that would put it on a par with other, whiter parts of the British empire such as Canada, Australia and New Zealand. An Indian Statutory Commission appointed by the British government, commonly referred to as the Simon Commission after its chairman, Sir John Simon, arrived in India in 1928 to report on constitutional changes for the country. Among the places the Simon Commission visited in 1928 was Shillong. The Khasi National Durbar under the Syiem of Khyriem decided against submitting a memorandum before the body. 'But Joab Solomon along with two other Khasi gentlemen, Rai Saheb Hormu Rai Diengdoh and Rai Mohan Diengdoh, made a representation to the Statutory Commission in which Solomon signed as the Secretary, Khasi National Durbar', writes Chaube.[57] The memorandum, among other things, demanded that 'a central Durbar should be established as a federation of all the (Khasi) states'. It further suggested that the Khasi National Durbar 'which is now in its formative stage may be legalized and made representative as much as possible', and went on to present a draft constitution for such a reformed durbar.

'The reaction', Chaube writes, 'was immediate. Another representation, signed by Babu Sib Charan Roy [Jeebon Roy's son], a landlord of Mawkhar and others was sent to the Statutory Commission denouncing the representative character of Solomon's memorandum'. A stormy meeting at the Seng Khasi Hall followed at which Macdonald Kharkongor, a lawyer, opposed Solomon, not because 'in the Memorandum a proposal had been made that there should be a Federation of the Khasi States', but because the authors of the memorandum wanted 'the present body constituting the Khasi National Durbar [to] be legalized'. The difference, according to Chaube, 'thus centred on the question whether democracy would mean, in the Khasi society, the creation of a centralized organization like the Durbar where the new oligarchy—the followers of Nichols-Roy—were in considerable strength or maintenance of the islands of autonomy that were the siemships'.[58]

The proposed federation eventually took shape a few years later in 1933, when the Viceroy, Lord Willingdon, visited Shillong. The ruling chiefs of the Khasi Hills urged upon the Viceroy, that, with the impending constitutional changes in the whole of India, 'the position of the Khasi States which are in Subsidiary Alliance with the British Government may also be defined and that they also find a place among the units of the Indian States which may be members of the Federal Legislature'. In his reply, the Viceroy wrote:

> for some time past, you have been considering the feasibility of closer association amongst yourselves with a view to constituting a federation of the Khasi States. I would commend this idea of your most earnest attention and this is obviously the first and most useful step which should pave the way towards your entry into the greater federation.[59]

The Viceroy's advice was followed with alacrity, and the Federation of Khasi States came into existence in 1933.

A series of three Round Table Conferences, attended by representatives of the Congress, the Muslim League and princely states, had been held between 1930 and 1932 in London to decide a future constitution for India. These, and the earlier work of the Simon Commission, led to the Government of India Act of 1935, and electoral politics heated up everywhere. The Assam Legislative Assembly came into existence in 1937. Elections threw up a hung verdict; the Congress was the single largest party, but short of a majority. A ministry had to be formed by 1 April 1937. The leader of the Assam valley Muslims, Sir Muhammad Saadulla, managed to cobble together a coalition and took his first cabinet of four to see Sir Robert Reid, the Governor of Assam. Reid recalled the meeting in his memoirs. They were, he wrote:

> a motley lot: Rohini Chaudhury, an Assam valley Hindu; Nichols-Roy, a Khasi; Ali Haider, a Sylhet Muslim; and an aged Muslim called Shamsul Ulema Wahid. He (Saadulla) himself was to be chief minister and politically stood head and shoulders above them. They took the oaths of office next day and we had made a start. The Congress party was not then participating, nor did its M.L.A.s attend the first meeting of the Assembly. They avoided social contacts, too, not attending a garden-party we gave on the 8th.[60]

In 1939, the Second World War began. The destruction of the old world that the First World War had started was completed. Before the First World War, it was still an age of empires and horse-drawn carriages and gas lamps. Queen Victoria had passed away in 1901, but the world of imperial Britain was still Victorian. By the time the Second World War ended, the reign of the old empires of Western Europe was effectively over, destroyed in the titanic struggle with the aspiring empires of Germany and Japan. Countries across Asia and Africa began to emerge into freedom.

In Assam, a ministry led by the Congress's Gopinath Bordoloi came to power. It did not last much longer than Saadulla's. 'Towards the end of October, the All-India Congress Committee ordained that Congress Governments must resign, in protest against the way India had been involved in the war', wrote Reid, 'so on 15 November he and his Cabinet came to Government House to say farewell. They had been in office just over a year.'[61] A second Saadulla ministry followed, this time with a larger cabinet, among whose ministers was the first woman in Assam to hold the job—a lady of mixed Khasi and British descent from Shillong, Mavis Dunn Lyngdoh. The war was then still far from Northeast India, and the routines of daily life continued largely undisturbed until the fall of Burma in 1942.

* * *

Ever since it was built in the 1860s and 1870s, Shillong had been a British-ruled enclave surrounded by twenty-five native Khasi states. When the war ended and the independence of India became imminent, the political situation of the Khasi Hills presented a complicated picture. Shillong—along with thirty-one 'British' villages in the Khasi Hills—would automatically become a part of newly independent India when the British withdrew. The status of its surroundings, though, was similar to that of the hundreds of princely states, small and big, across British India. Wars followed by treaties that they had signed with the British Raj had brought them under indirect British rule—but technically they were not part of British India. What would become of them once the British withdrew was thus a question in search of an answer.

Under the leadership of Nichols-Roy, a public meeting was held on 2 August 1946 in Shillong to highlight the unfolding changes. This meeting passed the following resolution:

> Whereas the Khasis of the Khasi Hills are of one Khasi stock and we recognise among ourselves that we are one stock, and whereas, though there are different local dialects, all speak and understand Khasi language and whereas in the impending political changes in India, it is the passionate desire of all our people dwelling in the Khasi and Jaintia Hills which are at present divided into two kinds of administration—the Khasi States and the British Areas—to be united into one administration... Be it resolved that this unprecedented and great gathering, where thousands of

> representatives from the Khasi States and the British Areas are present from all parts of the district expressed their ardent desire and demand that they should be united into one administration and be formed into one Khasi Jaintia Federated State on the line planned by the Reverend J. J. M. Nichols Roy and to be connected with the province of Assam in certain subjects only.[62]

Nichols-Roy's leadership in the situation did not go unchallenged. The following day, there was another public meeting, organised under the banner of an outfit called the Khasi Jaintia Political Association.[63] This body, which had the backing of the syiems, or chiefs, reacted sharply against the resolution adopted by the Khasi Jaintia Federated State National Conference, and adopted a resolution saying the Khasi states would speak for themselves, and not have Nichols-Roy speaking on their behalf. Meanwhile, the Cabinet Mission Plan with its vision of an undivided federal India had been circulated to the chiefs, along with a circular suggesting that they should all meet. The Khasi rulers and Nichols-Roy met at the residence of the Syiem of Nongkhlaw, Kedro Manick, in Shillong twice in July 1946. They met for a third time in August and revived the defunct Federation of Khasi States which had been founded in 1933, with the Syiem of Khyriem as chairman, and other chiefs as office bearers. Nichols-Roy, a man of the new order, found no place in this body representing the old, traditional power structure.

In February 1947, the British announced that they would finally be quitting India by June 1948. Partition had not yet been announced, and the contours of the future country were still very fluid. The Federation of Khasi States set about drafting their own constitution. This was quickly done and presented to the Government. On 9 August 1947, the Khasi states signed the 'Standstill Agreement', with the new India agreeing that the status quo on administrative arrangements was to be maintained. Barely a week later, on 14 August, the British Indian empire was partitioned and Pakistan officially came into existence as an independent country. India celebrated its independence the following day. The Khasi states were then not yet a part of India. It was only in

December 1947 that nearly all of them signed the Instrument of Accession, thus joining the Indian Union.

Three of the states, however, tarried. One of them was Hima Nongstoin, a state whose deputy chief, Wickliffe Syiem, was determined that it would be independent. The state broke off from the Federation of Khasi States and, after holding a public meeting on the issue, declared independence on 14 January 1948. The Government of India, naturally, was having none of this. It leaned on the chief Sib Singh, who was finally forced to sign the Instrument of Accession two months later. Wickliffe Syiem, who stayed resolute, went into exile in neighbouring Bangladesh and remained there until his death in 1988.[64]

The birth-pangs of independent India in the form of partition overshadowed the jubilation of freedom in those parts of the country that experienced its chaos and horrors. Sylhet, which had been taken out of Bengal and appended to Assam during a reorganisation of the colonial administration in 1874, was one of the unfortunate areas. It went to East Pakistan in a tight referendum held in July 1947. The Hindus of Sylhet, close to half the population, turned refugees overnight. Most were Sylheti Bengalis, who went to Silchar in the Barak valley of Assam. For many, Shillong—the capital of Assam, of which province they had until a day earlier been a part—was the natural place of refuge. It was less than 100 kilometres from the Sylhet border, and it was a place where families often had someone working. A large population of Hindu Sylheti Bengali refugees thus made their way into the town.

The Bordoloi Committee, meanwhile, had submitted its report in which it recommended the extension of universal adult franchise to the Garo, Mikir, Naga, Lushai and North Cachar Hills. The Khasi and Jaintia Hills already had electoral politics and representation in the Assam Assembly, but only in the British-administered areas—which technically did not include even Shillong in its entirety at the time. The Bordoloi Committee proposed continuing with a seat each from the Khasi and Jaintia Hills, including Shillong. It also suggested a rule banning people from the plains from contesting elections in the hill constituencies. Shillong was to be the exception to that rule. A new institution, the District Council, was to be set up in the hill districts with considerable powers over the occupation and use of land. There could also be autonomous regions with their own Regional Councils. The administration of justice, except in cases for which punishment exceeded imprisonment for five or more years, was to be left to District Council courts or tribal councils, unless non-tribals were involved. The councils would have powers to impose and collect certain taxes and no non-tribal would be allowed to carry on any business without a licence from the District Council.

Most of these recommendations found their way into the Sixth Schedule of the Indian constitution, which came into force on 26 January 1950, and they continue to govern many aspects of life in Meghalaya, Mizoram and the tribal areas of Assam and Tripura. Among the District Councils they envisaged, the one for the Khasi and Jaintia Hills was inaugurated in June 1952. On the day of its inauguration, there was a big demonstration led by Hoover Hynniewta, a Khasi graduate, against the District Council that was in the control of Nichols-Roy.[65] Hynniewta and his senior, Wilson Reade, managed, in September, to take over control of the Khasi National Durbar, evicting Joab Solomon and others from the Nichols-Roy camp. When Prime Minister Jawaharlal Nehru visited Shillong in October 1952, they presented a memorandum demanding, among other things, the unification of all the Assam Hills under a single administration, and expressing opposition to the primacy of the Assamese language. Their position found immediate support from the man who had been appointed chief executive of the new Garo Hills District Council, Captain Williamson Sangma.

The following year, the Government of India constituted the States Reorganisation Commission to examine the issue of redrawing the internal map of India. Immediately the campaign for the creation of a hill state to be carved out of Assam began in earnest. Captain Sangma convened a meeting of the chief executive members of all District Councils 'to discuss things of mutual interest'. This was held in Shillong on 16–17 June 1954, and attended by the chief executive members of the Lushai, North

Cachar, Garo and the United Khasi-Jaintia Hills District Councils. B. M. Roy, who had become the Chief Executive Member (CEM) of the Khasi-Jaintia Hills District Council, took the chair in the conference and opened the proceedings, saying:

> From the number of points for discussion proposed and submitted separately by you and by us, I find—wrongly or rightly—that they can conveniently be reduced to and covered by two common points of supreme importance and those points are: (1) Formation of a separate Hills State and (2) Amendment of the Sixth Schedule, which, evidently, you all have found out by experience does not fully satisfy us because it confers no real autonomy.[66]

Captain Sangma spoke first. The Sixth Schedule, he held, had many loop-holes and did not safeguard the interests of the Hills peoples adequately. The attitude of the plainsmen was also not conducive to unity. He cited a resolution of the Asom Jatiya Mahasobha (or Assam National Assembly), an Assamese nationalist political outfit, taken shortly before, to the effect that the areas opposed to Assamese as the state language should be severed from Assam. If this was the attitude of the plainsmen there was no alternative to demanding a hill state, he said. Lalsawia of the Mizo District Council (controlled by the Mizo Union), on the other hand, stressed that the demand for a separate state could be advanced only after the demand for greater autonomy of the District Councils had been put up and declined. He was supported by Khotlang, CEM of the North Cachar District Council. In the end, a somewhat vague memorandum was drafted, which stressed that

> in the working of the provisions of the Sixth Schedule, the people have felt that this autonomy is very defective... The younger generation especially are feeling very unhappy and they see that they will, in time, be extinct. The fear of their future destiny naturally makes them feel that it will be far better for them to have a Hill State of their own.[67]

The next step was a conference in Tura in the Garo Hills, convened by Captain Sangma. There, a decision was taken to submit a memorandum demanding a hill state to the States Reorganisation

Commission. This was duly done—and buttressed by a secret note, supporting the hill state demand, submitted by a minister of the Assam cabinet, Nichols-Roy. The States Reorganisation Commission, however, rejected the demand out of hand. Nor was the rejection made sweeter by a compensatory increase in the powers of the District Councils. The SRC report bluntly stated that 'the formation of a hill state in this region is neither feasible nor in the interests of the tribal people themselves'. It added that 'no proposal for the amendment of the Sixth Schedule, which would have the effect of encouraging disruptive tendencies, should be entertained'. It was more sympathetic to a demand put forth by the government of Assam: 'Assam...would welcome the merger, if possible, of Cooch-Behar, Manipur and Tripura, and closer connection with the administration of the North-East Frontier Agency, which is now constitutionally part of Assam.' The SRC noted that

> As a small Part C State, Tripura cannot obviously stand by itself. The West Bengal Government, moreover, has not claimed this area; and its merger in Assam, in our opinion, can be supported among other reasons on the ground that it will be desirable to bring the entire border between India and Pakistan in this region under one single control, namely, that of the Assam Government.[68]

A political platform called the Eastern India Tribal Union was formed in 1955 to press for the demand for a hill state. Assembly and parliamentary elections came around in 1957. The Congress, which was opposed to the hill state, was practically wiped out from the hill constituencies of Northeast India. The defeat of the Congress in the 1957 election gave an impetus to the Hill State Movement. The Congress leadership attempted to work out a power-sharing arrangement, appointing Captain Sangma Minister for Tribal Areas in the Assam cabinet, but it came unstuck over a demand raised by the Asam Sahitya Sabha (Assam Literary Society) that Assamese should be the sole official language of the state. The Assam Pradesh Congress Committee backed the demand. This set off a chain of protests and counter-protests, as supporters and opponents of the proposal mobilised to organise rallies and public meetings.

The state government of B. P. Chaliha, politically caught in a cleft—it could not afford to alienate its Assamese base—barrelled on with preparing the Assamese Official Language Bill. A meeting of hill leaders was called by Captain Sangma to discuss this and other issues. In July 1960, a new political platform called the All-Party Hill Leaders' Conference was born. Even the District Congress Committees of the Hills Districts joined it. There the demand was made not for a hill state but for the dropping of the Language Bill which, according to the resolution, anticipated the imposition of Assamese on the hill communities. The APHLC set up a Council of Action which made representations to the prime minister and president of India against the Language Bill. When that failed to elicit the desired response, a second meeting of the APHLC was held in Shillong that authorised its Council of Action to 'prepare a plan or pattern of separation'. The APHLC then issued an ultimatum to the chief minister of Assam, which went unheeded. On 24 October 1960, the Assam Assembly in a special session adopted the Assamese Language Bill. The APHLC now declared that the immediate creation of a separate hill state was the only solution.[69]

The then general secretary of the APHLC, P. Ripple Kyndiah, recalled years later that

> the decision by the Government of Assam to declare Assamese the sole official language was looked upon by the hill people as an attempt to assimilate them into the Assamese community. The hill people rose up against this as one man—under the APHLC. The Hill State as proposed by the APHLC was basically to include areas of all the autonomous hill districts of Assam and also the areas geographically contiguous to the hill districts if the people inhabiting in these areas so desired.

Prime Minister Nehru offered the APHLC a plan which was popularly known as the Scottish Pattern of Administration, wrote Kyndiah, 'as it embodied certain provisions similar to the case of Scotland in the British parliament'.[70] The APHLC, after initially agreeing to give it a try, eventually rejected this plan. Nehru's Congress Party, however, accepted it, and thus parted company from the All-Party Conference. Elections came around in 1962, and the APHLC joined the fray. The issue before the hill people was either to accept the plan of the 'Scottish Pattern of Administration' or to continue struggling for a full state, according to Kyndiah. The APHLC swept the polls in the Garo and Khasi Hills. They then decided to launch a non-violent 'direct action' movement. The newly elected APHLC members of the Legislative Assembly resigned in October 1962, and the direct action was planned for not later than March 1963.

Their plans were disrupted by something neither they nor the governments of Assam and India had foreseen: direct action on the part of Mao Tse-tung's China. The People's Liberation Army invaded areas of India bordering Tibet in 1962. As war broke out and the Chinese military advanced into Northeast India, the APHLC suspended its agitation. After the disastrous war, Nehru made one final effort at solving the hill state imbroglio, but passed away in 1964 before it could come to fruition. The next prime minister, Lal Bahadur Shastri, appointed a 'Commission on the Hill Areas of Assam' in 1965—called the H. V. Pataskar Commission after its chairman—to examine the issue. It was tasked with recommending 'a detailed scheme for the reorganization of the administrative set-up of the hill areas having regard to the main objectives of conferring a full measure of autonomy on the hill areas, subject to the preservation of the unity of the State of Assam'.[71] It eventually recommended no basic change, and the APHLC rejected its report. A subsequent offer by a cabinet committee headed by the then home minister of India, Gulzarilal Nanda, for what Kyndiah called 'a sort of sub-state', with a legislature and a council of ministers subordinate to the Assam government, was also rejected. The APHLC began to revive its plan of direct action.[72]

Finally, on 27 December 1966, the new prime minister, Indira Gandhi, visited Shillong. 'Then, on 13 January 1967 a historic announcement was made by the Government of India to reorganise the state of Assam in appreciation of the political aspirations of the people of the hill areas', wrote Kyndiah. Immediately opposition to the plan began in the Brahmaputra valley of Assam, and Indira Gandhi appointed a commission, headed by her cabinet minister

Ashok Mehta, to find a solution. This commission recommended greater autonomy for the hills but stopped short of even the 'sub-state' idea of a federal Assam that the APHLC had already rejected. Naturally, the APHLC rejected the Mehta Commission plan, and resigned all the assembly seats it held in the Khasi and the Garo Hills. In Assam, resistance to the planned 'Balkanisation' of the state—the term used by the Assam Congress—had meanwhile hardened with the appearance of an organisation called Lachit Sena that served notices to industrialists from outside Assam to quit the state.[73] The APHLC started a non-violent satyagraha on 10 September 1968. That very day, the Congress Working Committee led by Prime Minister Indira Gandhi gave its endorsement to the Assam reorganisation plan, having overcome internal opposition from a section led by her deputy, Morarji Desai.[74] The next day, the Government of India produced an Autonomous State plan for the Garo Hills and the United Khasi-Jaintia Hills Districts.[75]

Explaining the plan, the *Amrita Bazar Patrika*, then a leading Indian newspaper, said:

> the hill areas will constitute a state within a state enjoying full autonomy over the subjects transferred. It will be separate from Assam in the sense that it will have a separate legislature and a separate council of ministers with a chief minister of its own, yet it will remain an integral part of Assam participating in the legislature, the Government and administration of the parent state in respect of the common subjects.[76]

The autonomous sub-state was tentatively named Meghalaya, meaning 'abode of clouds' in Sanskrit.

'The decision of the APHLC to accept the Autonomous State plan was not easy. A few leaders refused to associate with the decision', wrote Kyndiah. J. J. M. Nichols-Roy's son, Stanley Nichols-Roy, who had by then entered politics and become secretary of the APHLC, was one of the dissenting leaders. Nonetheless, on Captain Sangma's urging, the APHLC decided to give the scheme a try. The government introduced the Assam Reorganisation (Meghalaya) Bill in parliament. 'The Bill was passed in both Houses of Parliament on the evening of 24th December

1969… it was indeed a Christmas gift for the hill people', wrote Kyndiah. 'The Autonomous State of Meghalaya was born on the 2nd of April 1970 when the Prime Minister Mrs Indira Gandhi inaugurated it in Shillong.'[77] The experiment proved unsuccessful. Within months, the APHLC had returned to its demand for a full-fledged state. Finally, in November 1970, Indira Gandhi announced in parliament that Meghalaya would be raised to full statehood. This was ultimately done during the reorganisation of Northeast India that followed India's victory in the Bangladesh War in December 1971. Indira Gandhi inaugurated the new state at a mammoth public meeting at Shillong's Polo Ground on 21 January 1972.

Statehood for Meghalaya meant, for Assam, the loss of its capital: Shillong became the capital of the new state. There was an exodus of the Assamese population from the town as state government offices relocated to Guwahati. The sense of Shillong as a cosmopolitan space gave way to a new understanding of the town as the capital of the hill state, a place where the local Khasi tribe was meant to dominate. The presence of a large number of Bengalis, most of them refugees and their descendants from the district of Sylhet which had gone to East Pakistan during partition in 1947, began to become an issue within a few short years. The flames of the 'Assam Agitation' next door, aimed at driving out 'foreigners'—code for alleged illegal immigrants from Bangladesh, although to marauding mobs it often meant anyone of East Bengali descent—spread to Meghalaya in 1979. There were riots against the local Bengali minority that year, and then in successive waves against all non-tribal minorities living in Shillong, but especially Bengali and Nepali speakers (who were most likely to be viewed as migrants from Bangladesh or Nepal), in 1987, 1991 and 1992. Thousands of people were internally displaced. The escalating ethnic violence also saw the rise of extreme factions in both the Khasi and Garo Hills that favoured independence from India. Insurgent outfits proliferated, with the leaders and camps of the armed groups operating, somewhat ironically given their anti-Bengali politics, from bases in Bangladesh. The inevitable crackdown by police and security agencies followed. The insurgencies finally petered out after a change of government in Bangladesh in 2009 robbed the militants of safe havens across the border. Meghalaya since then has been peaceful and increasingly attractive to tourists.

8

ARUNACHAL PRADESH BETWEEN CHINA AND INDIA

QUICK TRIP TO MAPS AND MODERNITY

Among the states that now make up the new region called Northeast India, Arunachal Pradesh is the largest by land area. It stretches over 83,743 square kilometres of mostly hilly and mountainous tracts with Bhutan to the west, Tibet to the north and Myanmar to the south. The Indian states it borders are Assam and Nagaland. A long history of human mobility through its difficult terrain, marked by thickly forested hills to the south and Himalayan snow peaks to the north, connects it with its neighbours. It is through a pass in the Patkai range now on the Arunachal–Myanmar border, the Pangsau Pass, that the band of followers under Chaolung (meaning Great Lord) Siu Ka Pha, or Sukapha, who established the Ahom dynasty had made their way into what is now Assam from their ancestral home somewhere in the Myanmar–China borderlands. After fighting their way down into the fertile plains of the Brahmaputra valley beyond the hills they settled there and gradually over the centuries built an empire in the valley.

The surrounding hills remained the territories of the numerous tribes that inhabited them. There were—and still are—the Naga tribes such as Ao and Lotha in the hills closest to the old Ahom capitals near the town of Sivasagar. Other Naga tribes such as the Nocte, Wancho, Tutsa and Tangsa occupied, and still occupy, the adjacent Patkai hills of Arunachal further east. They share the space with tribes outside the broader Naga fold, such as the Singpho, a tribe akin to the Kachin of nearby Myanmar and Jingpo of Yunnan in China. Then there are the Khamptis, Mishmis, Misings, Adis, Nyishis, Akas, Apatanis, Galos, Monpas and Sherdukpens... In Arunachal Pradesh, a traveller going from one hill to the adjacent valley and on to the next hill, may find that the dominant tribe, language and culture have all changed.

The land is criss-crossed by numerous powerful rivers and streams that ultimately combine to become the mighty Brahmaputra. Of the Brahmaputra's tributaries, the three that are considered formative—the Siang, Lohit and Dibang—all flow through Arunachal Pradesh. The area where they meet to become the Brahmaputra, at the foothills of Arunachal, is a place with intriguing, near-forgotten remnants of kingdoms whose histories have become clothed in the colours of mythology.

About 12 kilometres from the Assam–Arunachal Pradesh border inside Arunachal is a nondescript little settlement of a few huts and some decrepit old houses built in the Assam style, with sloping tin roofs and walls of plastered reeds. A short distance from this on a dirt track is a raised plinth made of small, flat bricks. The walls that must have stood on the plinth are long gone. Only the stories remain, of a fortress of the kings of a local tribe called the Chutiya, who at one time were rivals of the Ahoms. It is said to have been built in the twelfth century CE. The name of the town that may have existed around this little fort, Bhismaknagar, is drawn from Hindu mythology. It was, according to myth, the town of King Bhismak, father of Rukmini, the wife of Lord Krishna—one of the principal gods in the Hindu pantheon. A more plausible location for King Bhismak's kingdom of Vidarbha exists in western India in the state of Maharashtra, but many stories being the norm in Hinduism, it is common to find the same myth associated with different locales.

A few kilometres from there, heading towards the Brahmaputra river—and Assam—the smooth new highway runs past a little-visited Hindu temple called Tamreswari Mai. This is identified with an ancient temple called Dikkarvasini which marked the eastern extremity of the Kamrup kingdom. Early accounts of British colonial officers speak of it as a place known for its human sacrifices. The author and historian Colonel Leslie Shakespear, in a book published in 1914, wrote that the temple

> was dedicated to Kamakhya and the Yoni; but Shiva and the Lingam were also worshipped with all barbarous rites, including human sacrifices, which latter obtained it is known in the early part of the nineteenth century. In 1850 Hannay knew of certain families living near Sadiya who for generations past had been specially set aside to provide the doubtful honour of becoming victims to the dread Goddess.[1]

The ruins of a second temple of ancient origins, the Bura-Buri Than, lie further west, not far from where the Dibang meets the Lohit and Siang to form the Brahmaputra. Now there are only a few stone blocks, the figures carved on them worn with age, lying scattered behind a couple of small new concrete structures. Around these is an avenue of very old trees. The deities worshipped here were Bura, meaning Shiva, and Buri, meaning his wife Parvati, and the goddess worshipped in Tamreswari Mai—Kechai Khaiti, the eater of raw flesh.

A more complete set of remains of a temple called Malinithan including idols of the god Ganesha and a Shiva linga from the medieval period can be found in Likabali, some kilometres downriver along the Brahmaputra. The idol of the goddess known as Malini who was worshipped there is believed to have been of Durga astride a lion, slaying the demon Mahishasura—an image familiar to anyone who has seen the Durga Puja, which is still celebrated annually by millions of people in Assam and West Bengal. A number of very old images of the goddess Durga have been found across the Brahmaputra valley. Opinions differ over the age of those statues. On the basis of their carving styles, the images are bracketed between the ninth and fourteenth centuries.[2]

The area came under Ahom rule after the collapse of the Chutiya kingdom circa 1523. An inscription in Tai script found in the bed of the Deopani river near Roing—not far from Bhismaknagar—dated to the seventeenth century, declares: 'I, the Dihingia Borgohain, do engrave on the stone pillar and copper this writing on the strength of which the Mishmis are to dwell on the hills near the Dibang river with their females, children, attendants and followers. They will occupy all the hills.'[3] The Ahom kingdom is long gone, but the surrounding hills, true to the Borgohain's promise, are still inhabited mainly by the Mishmi tribe.

The decline of the Ahom kingdom from the late 1700s brought British and Burmese forces into Assam. When war broke out between the British and Burmese in March 1824, detailed information about the lands that lay between the British territory of Bengal and the Burmese kingdom, and their inhabitants, became a matter of urgent military importance. In October 1824, officers of the East India Company employed for revenue surveys were placed under the superintendence of a Major Schalch to explore these newly accessible territories. The aim, in the words of one of those officers, Lieutenant R. Wilcox, was that

> they might derive advantage to the utmost practicable extent of the opportunities so suddenly and unexpectedly opened of pushing our investigations beyond those barriers which the well or ill-founded jealousy of our eastern neighbours had hitherto opposed to us, all which we had till then no immediate hope of surmounting.[4]

Wilcox was assigned, along with a senior of his, Captain Bedford, to survey Assam. The immediate focus of their attentions, it turned out, was not the lands towards Burma, but the principal waterway that ran through Assam. As Wilcox wrote:

> Captain Bedford was verbally directed to consider the Brahmaputra as the chief object to which his attention should be directed. He was to endeavour to unravel the mystery in which was enveloped each notice or tradition respecting its fountain head by proceeding up its streams as far as the influence of the neighbouring force, or the safeguard of a detached escort, might permit.[5]

Bedford and Wilcox did not proceed directly to attempt tracing the source of the Brahmaputra. Instead, they began by separately surveying several of the tributaries that feed into the river—a task of great practical importance in a place where there were barely any roads and the rivers and streams provided the best, and often the only, means of communication.

Another of their colleagues, Lieutenant J. B. Neufville, meanwhile headed further upriver along the Lohit, which was then considered synonymous with the Brahmaputra. Neufville correctly identified the Siang, then more popularly known by its alternative name, Dihang (and spelled in old British accounts as Dihong), as the point of keenest interest in the extension of geographical knowledge. 'The post of Sadiya is nearly encircled, at a distance of thirty to fifty miles, by lines of mountains, behind which are more lofty ranges covered with eternal snow—from which the Dihong and Dibong [Dibang] Rivers flow from the North, the Lohit East', wrote Neufville. He continued:

> The portion of the hills of the lower ranges, between the heads of the Dihong and Dibong, I have already described as the territory of the Abors; more to the eastward of them, on the line of hills including the opening of the Brahmakund, is the district of Mishmis, another numerous hill tribe, differing only in name from the others... Beyond this mountainous region extends the grand field of inquiry and interest, if any credit be due to the opinion universally prevalent here respecting the nations inhabiting those tracts.[6]

These nations, of course, were Tibet and China. The land Neufville mentioned as lying beyond the Mishmi hills was 'the country of the Lama'.

It was the post of Sadiya that became the first major settlement of the British East India Company Raj in eastern Assam. After the defeat of the Burmese in the war in 1826, western Assam became part of British India, being annexed to Bengal. The eastern areas, after a few years, were given over to a former Ahom king, Purandar Singha, on condition that he pay an annual tribute of Rs. 50,000. A strong military post with a force of two companies of the Assam

Light Infantry and a couple of gunboats was retained in Sadiya, which was a frontier settlement at the eastern extremity of the Ahom king's territory. This area was then dominated by a tribe called the Khampti. In his account published in 1835, Captain R. Boileau Pemberton wrote:

> The Khamptis of Suddya, who originally emigrated from the hills on the east, and obtained permission from the Rajah of Assam to settle in the plains, established themselves on the banks of the Thenga Panee [Tengapani river], from whence they made a successful irruption into Suddya, during the troubled reign of Rajah Gaurinath in 1794, and reducing the Assamese inhabitants to slavery, their chief assumed the title of Suddya Khawa Gohain, which he has ever since retained.[7]

They were allies of the Company Raj at the time, and provided a militia of 200 men who were supplied with arms by the British.

Two other groups from the general area were in a similar relationship of alliance with the Company Raj: the Moamarias, whose rebellion had brought about the downfall of the Ahom kingdom, and the Singphos. 'Of the three chieftains, who with their tribes occupy all the eastern borders of the Assam plain, the one known to us by the name of Burra Senaputtee, the head of the Mooamareea tribe, is the most considerable and important', Pemberton wrote in his near-contemporaneous account. This community had, Pemberton admiringly wrote, 'succeeded in preserving its independence, when the Burmese had effected the entire subjugation of every other portion of the Assam valley'. The Burra Senaputtee, he added, had been furnished with 300 muskets by the British government for the protection of the frontier, and promised to furnish the same number of fighting men when called upon to do so by the political agent.[8]

A similar arrangement existed with a number of Singpho chiefs. There was no single king or chief who ruled over the entire tribe, but in May 1826, David Scott, as agent of the Governor General, had signed an agreement with thirty-six of these chiefs, including one of the most powerful, the Bessa Gam. According to the agreement:

> Assam being now under the sway of the British Government, we and our dependent Singphoes, who were subjects of the Assam State, acknowledge subjection to that Government. We agree not to side with the Burmese or any other King to commit any aggression whatever, but we will obey the orders of the British Government.

Among its clauses, however, were a couple that led to certain anxieties among the Singphos. The third clause, for instance, required Assamese 'paiks', or commoners, residing voluntarily in Singpho villages, to pay taxes to the British government, although the Singphos themselves were exempted from this burden. The fourth clause of the agreement said: 'We will set at large or cause to be liberated any Assam people who we may seize, and they shall have the option to reside wherever they please.'[9]

The Singphos, during the years of chaos and war following the decline of the Ahom kingdom and the Burmese invasion, had acquired a large number of slaves from Assam. A British officer, G. T. Bayfield, who travelled to the Assam frontier from the Burmese side a decade after the end of the war, reported finding large numbers of slaves in their villages. In his journal entry for 2 February 1837, he wrote:

> Wa-lo-bhoom is a Mirip Singpho village, and the first of any kind we have seen since leaving Mogoung. It contains thirty barracks, like houses, built of mat and bamboo... There are from 160 to 200 Assamese slaves here, and probably not more than a third of that number of their Singpho masters.[10]

There was at the time no clear boundary between Burma and British India; the Arakan Hills at one end and the Patkai range at the other were understood to be the border. In 1838, a 'Map of the Eastern Frontier of British India, with the Adjacent Countries', drawn by Captain Pemberton, was published. It shows a dotted line, whose exact location is not clear, with the words 'Singpho tribes' written either side of the line. The map marks spots where tea plants and salt mines were located and names the major tribe inhabiting each area, but the precise location of the boundary is not clear.[11]

In 1830, a couple of Singpho chiefs who had not been among the signatories of the treaty with Scott attempted to mount an invasion of Sadiya. Their plan was discovered before the attack could commence, and thwarted by the Assam Light Infantry and the Khampti militia. A second clash followed in 1836, when the Duffa Gam, a Singpho chieftain from the Burmese side, attempted an incursion against the Bessa Gam who had allied with the British. This too was defeated.

Disaffection against British rule had, however, grown among the Khamptis as well, for much the same reasons: fears of taxation and curbs on slavery topping a curtailment of local authority. Until 1833, there was no British officer stationed in or near Sadiya, leaving the Khampti chief holding the title of Sadiya-khowa Gohain—with whom Scott had concluded an agreement in 1826 by which he agreed to 'perform all the duties of the Company'– in charge.[12] According to John Butler, a British officer posted in Assam, whose account was published in 1847, in 1834–35, Captain Charlton of the Assam Light Infantry was

> placed in charge of the Khamtee chiefs, and the Suddeah and Saikwah districts; and by the measures he adopted to check the traffic in slaves, and protect the Assam population from the oppressive exactions of the Khamtees, he created the utmost dissatisfaction among the latter, and caused them to be highly incensed... Moreover, in December 1834, instructions were issued requiring a census of the population to be taken; with the view of levying a capitation tax, to be renewed every five years, in lieu of military service to the state.[13]

The Assamese residing in the area were taxed at one rupee each. The Khamptis were exempted from this tax, but nonetheless suspicions about its impending imposition created tensions. Fearing attack, the British authorities decided to take away the firearms that had been given to the Khampti militia and remove Chow Rang Pha, the Sadiya-khowa Gohain, from his office of governor. In a further affront, they also charged him with slave-dealing. According to Butler:

> Thus passed the years 1836, 37 and 38: rumours of an insurrection being about to break out were occasionally prevalent, but it was supposed that the Khamtees had too much good sense to league with other lawless and disaffected tribes and hazard a rebellion, unless supported by a large Burmese army. In the following year, however, the deceitful calm was suddenly disturbed. About half past 2 o'clock on the morning of the 28 January 1839, the clouds that had long been gathering, burst on the doomed post of Suddeah.[14]

About 600 Khampti warriors attacked the Assam Light Infantry lines and the houses of officers. Eighty men, women and children—mainly Indian sepoys and their families—were killed. The sole European who died in the attack was the new political agent, Lieutenant Colonel Adam White, who had only arrived in Sadiya a few days earlier.

The Khampti attack came at a time of major political change in Upper Assam. In October 1838, the Ahom king Purandar Singha, who had been ruling Upper Assam as a British tributary, was removed from his throne. His territories, comprising the two districts of Sibsagar (Sivasagar) and Lakhimpur, were now annexed formally to British India. The Assam Light Infantry, in retaliation for the attack on Sadiya, was sent with reinforcements into the surrounding Khampti areas with the aim of carrying out what in today's terms would be called ethnic cleansing. The entire tribe with a few exceptions was 'driven beyond the frontier' into Burma.[15] In 1842, the tea-growing Moamaria areas ruled by the chief known to the British as Burra Senaputee (meaning big general) and the territories of their Khampti neighbours were finally annexed and added to Lakhimpur district, whose headquarters became the town of Dibrugarh, downriver from Sadiya.[16] With this, the territory of British India reached the foothills of what is now Arunachal Pradesh.

The hills beyond were the territory of other tribes, of whom the most powerful was the tribe then known as the Abor, and now as the Adi. They occupied the lands on either bank of the Siang. The Abors claimed absolute sovereignty over a tribe then called Miri, and now known as Mising, and a right to all the fish and gold found in the Dihang river.[17] A lot of the panning for gold dust in the rivers of that area used to be done by members of a caste of the largely Hindu Bodo-Cachari tribe, the Sonowals. Trouble began in 1848, when the Abors carried off a number of these gold-washers into their strongholds. A British officer, Captain Vetch, went into the hills with a small party of troops to get them back. 'The captives were restored, but his camp was attacked by night, and the Abors were only beaten off after hard fighting', according to the account of the colonial official and historian, Alexander Mackenzie. 'To punish this treachery, Captain Vetch burnt their village'.[18]

It was the beginning of hostilities that would last intermittently for decades.

Ten years later, on 31 January 1858, a village of gold-washers across the river Brahmaputra from Dibrugarh was sacked by Abors from the hills for refusing to pay tributes to them. A retaliatory force of 104 soldiers, armed with guns and howitzers, was sent in pursuit of the suspected culprits in March, but failed to reach its target, a village called Kebang, and was chased out of the hills with losses. A second expedition was then planned, and a force of more than 300 men, armed with weapons including howitzers and mortars, advanced into the hills the following year. The battle between bows and arrows and firearms was on this occasion won by firearms; the invading force, after halting in the area a few days, burnt the surrounding Abor villages, and 'retired leisurely to their boats'.[19]

This, however, did not end the fighting. In 1861, a different clan of Abors, known then as Meyong and now as Minyong, attacked a village of gold-washers on the same side of the river as Dibrugarh, only 24 kilometres from the town. A lot of land in the surrounding areas had then been made over to tea planters, and the threat to its tea interests roused the administration into action. Work had started on building a chain of forts along the foothills after the previous attack, but construction had been suspended owing to the cost. Now funds flowed and the work resumed. The renewed activity brought about overtures for talks from the Abors. In 1862, after discussions lasting a week, an agreement was concluded with thirty-five chiefs. 'The limit of the British Territory which extends to the foot of the hills is recognized by the Meyong Abors, who hereby engage to respect it', it said. The Abors also promised to recognise all persons residing in British territory as British subjects, and to leave them unmolested. In exchange for keeping the peace, they would receive annually '100 iron hoes, 30 maunds of salt, 80 bottles of rum, 2 seers of Abkaree opium, [and] 2 maunds of tobacco'.[20]

This system of certain tribes on the Arunachal frontier being paid to keep the peace, called posa, had existed since the days of Ahom rule. Similar agreements were concluded with other such groups over the next five years. It was a process that drew neat lines dividing hills from adjacent plains, and hill-peoples from plains-dwellers. The new lines between the two hardened further with the first law introduced by the government of British India for the region that later became Northeast India. Tea plantations had boomed in Assam after initial difficulties. The encroachment of these plantations into the foothills was becoming a cause of conflict with the tribes, who also claimed rights over these lands. It was not the only globally traded cash crop found in the area. Rubber trees, which grew wild in some of the hills, also attracted tappers from the plains. For the local tribes who considered the forest produce of the hills to be theirs by right, their extraction by outsiders amounted to theft—and they often made their annoyance at it known by kidnapping the offenders and holding them hostage. Such incidents inevitably became a headache for government officials who would then be tasked with recovering the hostages. The administration therefore came up with a policy measure to curb the problem. Called the Bengal Eastern Frontier Regulation of 1873, it laid down an 'Inner Line' along the foothills, beyond which British subjects were not allowed to go without a pass. The line acted as a border for tribals wishing to enter British India as well. They were not allowed to settle in British India without government permission and payment of taxes. Moreover, no member of a tribe would be allowed to cross the Inner Line whenever blockades were imposed on their tribe—which was each time there was heightened tension between that tribe and the administration.

Relations with each tribe beyond the Inner Line which marked the border of areas under British administration had to be maintained separately, a task then carried out via influential locals. 'The only civil official who has any influence at Sadiya or any knowledge of the tribes beyond the border, is Rai Lahmon Bahadur, a native gentleman of a fine presence and of much natural intelligence who [sic] and his brother, the political sheristidar, are heads of the important Muttak tribe', wrote the Assam chief commissioner, Charles Elliott, in a letter to his bosses in 1882. He continued:

> He has been employed for many years on the border, first as Inspector of Police, then as Honorary Extra Assistant Commissioner, a post he now holds, and he is very widely known to the Abors, Mishmis, Singphos and Khamptis, and has great weight among them. But he is beginning to grow old and it is dangerous that he should be the sole repository of so much experience, lest it should die with him, and he is believed by some to be mixed up in trading, and elephant hunting operations, in the debatable land across the Inner Line;[21] and he has a deep distrust and dislike of the Abors—feelings which are known to them and which they reciprocate.[22]

To remedy this situation, the authorities appointed an assistant superintendent of police in Sadiya, a Mr Livesay, 'with the intention that he should have all the knowledge that Lahmon has acquired, and should gradually become fit to take his place as Political Officer on the Frontier'. Livesay, however, proved unequal to the task, and so was removed from his position not long after. The search began afresh for a replacement. This time, Elliott picked an Irishman named J. F. Needham of the Bengal Police. In October 1882, the commissioner wrote to the deputy commissioner at Dibrugarh:

> You should ordinarily issue through him orders upon all matters relating to affairs on the Abor, Mishmi, and Singpho-Khampti frontiers, and the arrangements regarding the location of the frontier outposts, their supplies, the patrolling between them, etc. as well as the political relations with the Abors and Mishmis will be carried on through him as soon as he has acquired sufficient local knowledge.[23]

Needham would go on to spend twenty-three eventful years in the area. In 1884, he became the first British officer to enter Abor territory in about thirty years. More remarkably, he went there with only one companion rather than the customary retinue of a large number of armed guards. 'He was received by the villagers of Membu in a relaxed, if not entirely friendly, manner. Having learned the Abor tongue fluently he was able to communicate on a very informal level with his hosts', wrote Charles Allen in *A Mountain in Tibet*. The curious tribespeople, unused to seeing white people, gathered around and subjected Needham to a public examination of his clothes and body, during which he was compelled to shed his coat, shirt, shoes and socks.[24]

He returned safely, and the next year made a historic journey up the Lohit river valley, again unaccompanied by any armed escort, to within a mile of the Tibetan village of Rima. In his report he wrote:

> I am in the proud position of being able satisfactorily to settle a great geographical question. Having followed the course of the Brahmaputra from Sadiya to a spot within a mile or so of the Tibetan frontier village, or town, of Rima I can confidently assert that no river in any degree corresponding to the Sanpo in size joins it between Sadiya and Rima, and consequently the Sanpo must pass into the Brahmaputra west of Sadiya, and in my opinion, it can be no other than the Dihong.[25]

Needham married a local Miri[26] woman, settled down in Sadiya and undertook a number of other expeditions, but his hopes of leading a peaceful expedition through Abor country had come no nearer to fruition when, in December 1893, there was an Abor raid on a Miri village in which they made off with a number of captives. Negotiations for their release were taking place when three sepoys from the military police were killed in an ambush. On Needham's advice a punitive force of 500 infantrymen and police was assembled under the command of a Captain Maxwell, with Needham as its political officer.[27] This force advanced towards the village from where the attackers had apparently come, Bomjur, but found it deserted. They then moved against a strongly fortified village, Dambuk, 'having a double palisade with 2 or 3 feet thickness of stone in between, which was quite impervious to shellfire'. This was successfully rushed with a loss of three killed and twenty-two wounded on the British side.[28]

However, Needham had by then become convinced that a village called Damroh, deep in the Abor territory, was the headquarters and stronghold of the raiders, and that the expedition would fail in its object unless it was punished. Needham and Maxwell decided to leave the bulk of their food and supplies behind, taking only enough food to last them eight days, and headed towards this village. These supplies, together with a small force of sixty sepoys and camp followers, were left behind in Bordak, an Abor village not far from Pasighat where the Siang river—then known as the Dihong—enters the plains. Their column spent a week hacking through the jungle under fire from poisoned arrows in pouring rain, but failed to reach Damroh. With food running out, they were forced to turn back. They returned to Bordak, only to find bodies lying scattered all over the place. The force that had been left behind had been massacred, with thirty-five killed and more missing.[29]

The massacre effectively destroyed Needham's career. He left the area in 1907, and retired to Shillong in the Khasi Hills. His dream of travelling through Abor country into Tibet found a new home in the head of his successor, Noel Williamson. In 1909, Williamson, following Needham's example, went into the Abor territory without an armed escort. As an insurance policy, he took with him two marvels unseen in that part of the world: a gramophone and a magic lantern. His visit went well, and two years later, in March 1911, Williamson returned to the area with forty-seven porters bearing medicines and gifts and accompanied by a tea-garden doctor named J. D. Gregorson. Some of the party's rations and liquor were unfortunately stolen at an Abor village a short distance into the hills. Williamson left the village after reprimanding the villagers, and went on further into Abor country. He sent back from his camp three letters with a mail-runner for Sadiya. The Abors, who could not read, saw the letters, interpreted them as a sign of imminent punishment for the earlier theft, and proceeded to kill the mail-runner and three sick porters who were being sent back with him. Then, having gone down that path, they proceeded to massacre Gregorson, Williamson and forty-four members of their party.[30] Only three survivors managed to make their way to an Abor village near the mouth of the Siang river where it meets the Brahmaputra.

News of the massacre reached the British authorities in Dibrugarh. Immediately telegrams flew around the world. It turned out that the Government of India had no idea that Williamson was going into territory that lay beyond what was called the 'Outer Line', an imaginary line that marked the outer perimeter of the frontier of British India. The Inner Line marked the inner perimeter; within the Inner Line, which ran largely along the foothills, was the territory under British administration. Beyond this was an un-demarcated area where the political officer exercised 'a very loose jurisdiction' up to the imaginary Outer Line.[31] The place where Williamson was murdered, Komsing, is barely 75 kilometres from Pasighat at the foothills near Assam—but it lay beyond even the Outer Line. From there to Tibet stood row upon row of forested hills, a terra incognita for the most part, unadministered by any power other than the tribes that inhabited the lands.

Their days of isolated independence were about to end. Larger powers were entering their remote mountain fastnesses. A great game between faraway powers was afoot.

* * *

Around May 1910, two Tibetans had arrived in Pangum, a small Mishmi village high up in the Lohit Valley. They brought word that Chinese troops had occupied the TIbetan town of Rima, a few days' march away. The astonished villagers were informed that Dzayul's new rulers expected them to carve them a track all the way from Tibet to the plains of Assam.[32] In April 1911, a party of Chinese appeared in what is described in an intelligence report of the time as 'Akha country', meaning the Kameng river valley, close to the frontiers of Assam and Bhutan. The Chinese officials at Rima in Tibet in the upper reaches of the Lohit river valley sent summons to Mishmi tribal chiefs to appear before them, 'with a view to annexation of their country', and there were unconfirmed reports that the Chinese government had approved the despatch of a force down the Dihang (now called Siang) river towards the Abor country. One anonymous report stated:

> So long as the tribal territory lay between us and a peacefully dormant Tibet, an undefined frontier presented neither inconvenience nor danger. With the recent changes in that country, however, the question of a boundary, well defined and at a safe distance from our administrative border, became one of imperative importance and admitted of no delay.[33]

The 'recent changes' mentioned in this report were an invasion of Tibet by Chinese forces which reached Lhasa in the spring of 1910. The Dalai Lama had fled to British India and arrived in Darjeeling. The Chinese attack had come a few years after a somewhat similar one by the British. In 1903–04, a British military expedition, the Younghusband mission, had fought its way into Lhasa in 'peacefully dormant Tibet' because the Viceroy, Lord Curzon, suspected it was slipping into Russian hands. The 'Great Game' was then on between the British and Russian empires, and the presence in Tibet of a curious and influential Buddhist monk of Russian origin, Agvan Dorjieff, who was close to both the Dalai Lama and the Russian Tsar, had aroused Curzon's suspicion that Tibet was slipping into the Russian orbit. The Russians did not react violently to the British invasion of Lhasa, and differences between the British and Russian empires regarding their imperial spheres of influence in Tibet, Afghanistan and Persia (Iran) were settled by an agreement signed in 1907. Both sides essentially agreed to leave Tibet to the Chinese. The Chinese emperor, who considered Tibet a tributary state, found his path clear after this, and sent in his troops. Tibet thus came under more direct Chinese control. The Chinese began to swiftly expand the definition of Tibet all along the Himalayan frontier.

Meanwhile, in India, the government had decided that the Abor massacre of Noel Williamson and his team in 1911 could not go unpunished—and that it afforded an opportunity to 'carry out such surveys and exploration as may be possible, in order that we may obtain knowledge requisite for the determination of a suitable boundary between India and China in this locality, as to which at present we know practically nothing'.[34] Major General Hamilton Bower was given full charge of the expedition. His objects were 'to exact severe punishment and reparation for the murder of Mr Williamson, Dr Gregorson and their party'; to visit as many villages as possible on the way and impress upon the tribespeople that 'for the future, they would be under our control'; to explore and survey as much of the country as possible; and to 'submit proposals for a suitable frontier line between India and Tibet'.[35]

Proceeding with steady caution by first constructing a road along which the main column of the force could advance, General Bower's men, having started out in October 1911, took a month and a half to reach their target of Kebang, the powerful Abor village in the upper reaches of the Siang valley where Williamson and his party had been killed. The Abor resistance was worn down by the slow, patient but inexorable advance of the force, comprising mainly Gurkha and Sikh soldiers under British officers, armed with rifles, machine guns and mortars. Their enemies had spears, bows and arrows, and a few muzzle-loading rifles, and never stood a chance. As a result of this expedition, the objective of pushing the Outer Line outwards towards Tibet, up to the limits of tribal territory, which had been discussed in letters between the Government of India and the secretary of state in London in September, just before the launch of the expedition, was achieved in the case of the Siang river valley.[36]

Around the same time, two other expeditions, the Mishmi Mission and the Miri Mission, fanned out into the areas inhabited by those tribes to explore the country. The boundary between Tibet and British India east of Bhutan was yet to be delimited. It was an opportune time, from a British Indian perspective, to try and settle this boundary, because in 1911 the 300-year rule of the Qing empire in China had been ended by a revolution. The new Republic of China was born in 1912, but the chaos of civil war had given Tibet a new lease of freedom. The Chinese garrison at Lhasa surrendered to Tibetan forces and the Dalai Lama returned from exile. In February 1913, he declared independence from Chinese overlordship—a declaration not recognised by China either then or now. The British authorities, taking advantage of the situation, moved quickly to settle the question of the boundary between India and Tibet at this time.

In the winter of 1912–13, a British expedition went up into the higher reaches of the Dibang river valley in what is now Arunachal Pradesh. The ostensible purpose of the small party, led by F. M. 'Eric' Bailey of Military Intelligence—who had been on the Mishmi Mission the previous year—and Henry Morshead of the Survey of India, was to explore the Tsangpo river that eventually becomes the Brahmaputra in Assam. The real purpose of the journey, however, was to map the Himalayan watershed along its entire stretch east of Bhutan. Their journey had been facilitated by the foreign secretary for India at the time, Henry McMahon. Bailey and Morshead made an epic journey through Tibet and the Arunachal borderlands, returning eventually via Tawang and eastern Bhutan to Assam. They were in Calcutta after the long rigours of their travels when Bailey received a telegram from McMahon, addressed to him care of Thomas Cook & Sons Calcutta, which said: 'Delighted to hear of your safe return hope you are well I would like you to come up to Simla as quickly as possible.'[37]

A conference to decide the future boundary between India and Tibet was taking place in Simla 'after months of delay in which the Tibetan and Chinese representatives had bashfully waited in the wings, each for the other to come on to the stage', wrote Bailey. 'The Indian Government had finally notified the Chinese that if their representative did not turn up, the Indian Government would negotiate with the Tibetans alone. Mr Ivan Chen, thereupon, arrived from China post-haste.' Negotiations, however, were very slow, as noted by Bailey:

> The Chinese and the Tibetans had to refer back to their governments at every stage, a very long process with the Tibetans who had no telegraphic communication with Lhasa. There was in consequence plenty of time for Morshead to prepare his map and for me to go pig-sticking when I was not wanted for consultation.[38]

The map that Morshead prepared, delineating a border between India and Tibet following—but not everywhere—the Himalayan watershed, became the basis for the line now known as the McMahon Line. The British and Tibetan representatives at the conference, McMahon and the Dalai Lama's prime minister, Lonchen Shatra Paljor Dorje, proceeded to sign what came to be known as the Simla Convention, but the Chinese representative, Ivan Chen, left without signing the final document after having initialled an earlier draft. His superiors in the Republic of China government, unhappy with the terms, had denied him permission to sign. Then the First World War began, barely weeks later, and the remote borderlands between India and Tibet were forgotten in the distant capitals. The matter of Chinese objection to the McMahon Line remained unresolved; the Simla Convention, signed in 1914, was not published then nor in the 1931 edition of the collection of treaties signed by the Government of India, popularly known as 'Aitchison's Treaties', which contained all treaties, engagements and sanads concluded up to 1929. Aitchison's *Treaties* only mentioned that a conference had been held on the matter in 1913 between the British, Tibetan and Chinese plenipotentiaries and that a convention was drawn up and initialled in 1914.[39]

On the ground, the situation began to change as the British Indian government began to bring areas beyond the Inner Line, and the erstwhile Outer Line, under its administration. As a Gazetteer of India states:

> The history of administration of the territory now known as Arunachal Pradesh may be taken as beginning from the Government of India, Foreign and Political Department, Notification of 1914, which promulgated that the Assam Frontier Tracts Regulation, 1880 would extend to the hills inhabited or frequented by the Adis, Miris, Mishmis, Singphos, Nagas, Khamptis, Bhutias, Akas and Nishis. These hill areas were separated from the then Darrang and Lakhimpur Districts of Assam. As a result, the North-East Frontier Tract was constituted.[40]

Following Major General Bower's successful expedition in 1911, the Government of India had in 1912 divided the area into three sections—eastern, central and western—and sanctioned the appointment of officials for each of them. In 1914, at the time of the formation of the North-East Frontier Tract, there was a slight rejig; the central and eastern sections were clubbed together, and a new frontier tract, the Lakhimpur Frontier Tract was carved out from Lakhimpur district of Assam. W. C. M. Dundas, who had led the 1911 expedition into the Mishmi Hills, was appointed deputy commissioner for the central and eastern sections with his headquarters at Sadiya. In his report for 1917–18, Dundas wrote:

> During the year the remaining few Abor and Singpho villages and all Khamtis were brought under administration and assessed for poll-tax... The plains as far as the foot of the hills have always been claimed as British territory. It was not however expedient to enforce the claim until recent years, and several Abor villages, all the Khamtis and half the Singphos enjoyed immunity from taxation.[41]

The land was surveyed, roads were built, telegraph lines erected, trading marts established and the process of integrating these places into the British Indian empire and the modern capitalist economy began. Posa payments had already been changed from payments in kind to cash by 1877. The arrival of the market economy brought more of a very basic commodity. Salt was then rare and precious in the hills of Arunachal. Bower had reported that 'Their condition owing to their inability to obtain salt is pitiable. They will do almost anything to obtain it. They are also anxious to obtain cloth, cooking pots, etc.'[42]

In 1919, the central and eastern section of the North-East Frontier Tract was renamed Sadiya Frontier Tract. The western section was renamed the Balipara Frontier Tract. The *Census of India* published in 1921 noted that while the enumeration exercise was carried out in the new Sadiya and Balipara Frontier Tracts, in 'the old settled parts transferred from the districts of Lakhimpur and Darrang, and certain other parts regularly administered by the Political Officers', there was 'no defined outer boundary to these tracts, and no attempt was made to extend the census to the hills inhabited by tribes which are only under loose political control'.[43]

The *Annual Report on the Frontier Tribes of Assam* for 1921–22 shows a peaceful acceptance of the new rulers. 'The year on the whole was uneventful', it begins:

> In the Abor country an outpost at Amili was opened during the year and the track thereto graded and improved. Memorials to the late Mr Williamson and Dr Gregorson, who were murdered at Komsong and Panggi in 1911, were also constructed during the year at the sites of the tragedies.[44]

The quiet acceptance of British administration was a sea change from the past. It came at a time when in the Indian mainland, the country's freedom struggle was in full cry. The adjacent plains of Assam felt the effects of the freedom struggle, but the hills of Arunachal evidently remained untouched by it. The section of the report on the Balipara Frontier Tract, which lies not far from the town of Tezpur in Assam, says:

> During the troubled times of the past cold weather there were many disaffected persons who were anxious to stir up trouble in order to embarrass the Government, quite regardless of the results that might have occurred. Certain persons I believe did approach various Akas and Daflas, but they were not in the least interested and took no notice of these people.[45]

* * *

A decade later, the remote hills of Arunachal Pradesh were still a place for explorers in search of discoveries. In 1933, the celebrated botanist Frank Kingdon-Ward led an expedition from Sadiya via Rima into Tibet through the Mishmi country, following the route earlier traversed by Bailey and Morshead. He was accompanied by a surveyor, Ronald Kaulback, and a filmmaker armed with a cinematograph, Bertram Brooks-Carrington. Their journey was made without hostile opposition; on the contrary, they were able to hire sixty-five porters from the local Mishmi tribe. 'The tribesmen were very willing to earn the several thousands of rupees which the expedition brought into the country', the Assam Governor, Robert Reid, wrote in his account published some years later.[46]

The peace was, however, fragile. Later that same year, 1933, there was a raid by Mishmis from beyond the British-administered territories on a village not far from Nizamghat in the Lohit valley where the river enters the plains. This sent a 'military promenade' of one platoon of the Assam Rifles into the hills in 1934. The platoon returned without bloodshed. Another expedition followed later in the year, with similar results. In his report for 1936–37, the political officer W. H. Calvert wrote:

> With an escort of one British officer and 25 rifles, the Political Officer carried out a three weeks' tour in unadministered territory of the Abor Hills. The column crossed the Dihang River at Yembung, inspected the memorial to Dr Gregorson at Pangi and that to Mr Williamson at Komsing, and proceeded north... This is the first occasion villages north of Komsing and Pangin have been visited since the Abor Survey of 1913.[47]

From Komsing to the McMahon Line is a road distance of more than 300 kilometres. It was the quickening rush of political change in the faraway centres of power that finally brought these areas under Indian administration.

In 1935, the Simon Commission's proposals for constitutional reform led to the framing of a new Government of India Bill. The tribal areas at the frontiers were then still outside the official definition of India. This was quietly changed in the new bill. Olaf Caroe, then deputy secretary in the Foreign and Political Department, wrote on 13 February 1935, in a file marked 'Secret':

> Clause 289(1). It seems likely that the frontier between India and Burma will pass through tribal areas and therefore a definition of Burma as lying to the east of Assam would not be formally correct... An interesting point to which attention may be drawn is that the definition of India as now drafted in clause 289(1) of the Bill definitely includes tribal areas and thus sets at rest the difficulty which had previously been felt in respect of non-inclusion of these areas in the old definition in the General Clauses and Interpretation Acts. Similarly, the definition of 'tribal areas', as it appears in the same clause, will include such areas as Agency territories in Baluchistan and unadministered tracts on the borders of Assam.[48]

Caroe received a reply, dated 3 April 1935, from the official then heading the Reforms Office branch in the Assam capital of Shillong—the former census commissioner C. S. Mullan, author of a memorable note on migration into Assam. 'Dear Caroe', he wrote:

> His Excellency the Governor sees no objection to the treatment of the Assam unadministered areas as 'tribal areas' as defined in clause 289(1) of the Government of India Bill. It would, however, appear from the definition of Burma given in the same clause that the unadministered areas at present dealt with by Assam as within the sphere of influence of this province (all of which will become tribal areas) will be included in 'Burma' unless action is taken under clause 433 to define the boundaries of Burma.[49]

The Government of India Act, 1935, eventually came up with the following definitions: 'India means British India together with all territories of any Indian Ruler under the suzerainty of His Majesty, all territories under the suzerainty of such an Indian Ruler, the tribal areas, and any other territories which His Majesty in Council may, from time to time, after ascertaining the views of the Federal Government and the Federal Legislature, declare to be part of India'. Burma and its boundaries were also duly defined. The Act explained the meaning of 'tribal areas' as 'areas along the frontiers of India or in Baluchistan which are not part of British India or of Burma or of any Indian State or of any foreign State'. In 1937, Burma, which had been reduced to a province of the British Indian empire fifty-one years before, was formally separated from India. The unadministered areas (meaning areas that were then independent) that lay between India and Burma were absorbed into one country or the other. The frontier, as Caroe had observed, passed through the tribal areas, dividing the communities that lived on both sides of this new border, although it was not until 1967 that an agreement would be signed between India and Burma to formally delimit and demarcate it along its entire length. As was still normal at this period, the lines were drawn on maps by sahibs in distant capitals without anyone bothering to ask the people whose lives would be affected by them. The officials also moved to bring back to life a line that had by then been almost consigned to the dustbin of history: the McMahon Line.

After the new Government of India Act 1935 came into force in 1937, the North-East Frontier Tracts became 'Excluded Areas' of the province of Assam, under the direct rule of the Governor. The Government of India, in January 1938, sanctioned the formation of a 'Control Area' to the north of Pasighat, ostensibly as a measure to abolish slavery in the unadministered areas—but there were other reasons:

> In 1938, the Political Officer, Mr Godfrey, reported to Government on the subject of annual incursion by Tibetan officials into the villages along the Tsangpo as far as Karko which had been going on for the last 20 years, and which was stated to be getting yearly more of a burden.[50]

Tibet, emerging from Chinese overlordship, had begun expanding, and had already run into conflict with its neighbours.

A key area in the emerging dispute was Tawang.

In April 1935, Kingdon-Ward had returned for another expedition into Tibet. Starting his journey from Tezpur in Assam, he reached Senge Dzong en route to Tawang on 28 May. 'I was now on the Se La range, which separates Assam from Monyul, and still awaiting a permit to enter Tibet. At last, permission having been granted, on June 3, I was able to cross the Se La, a pass about 14,000 feet high', Kingdon-Ward told a meeting of the Royal Geographical Society the following year on 20 April 1936.[51] However, that evening he left out a detail in his story: he had been arrested in Tibet for unauthorised entry. The matter had come to official notice when an angry letter from Lhasa reached Delhi. A certain 'King da', a British subject, had entered Tibet without authorisation.[52]

Olaf Caroe, in the foreign ministry, was perplexed. Upon enquiry the man turned out to be Frank Kingdon-Ward. The Indian authorities were furious. Kingdon-Ward's wanderlust had not only caused tensions with Lhasa; his travels had also unveiled a disturbing situation in Assam's Frontier Tracts. Far from respecting the McMahon Line, Tibet controlled Tawang. There was more.

Prompted to confirm where the McMahon Line lay so that Delhi could raise the issue with Lhasa, Assam replied that they did not know anything about a boundary, and had anyhow no influence beyond the foothills.[53] Caroe called for the papers on the boundary alignment and 'with considerable difficulty and almost by chance unearthed the true position'. His discovery was the red line drawn in Simla in 1914. On 6 February 1936, Caroe wrote to J. A. Dawson, the chief secretary of Assam, saying 'It is now clear that the whole of the hill country up to the McMahon Line is within the frontier of India', and asking whether

> any measure of political control has been extended up to that line in the last twenty years, and in particular whether the Tibetan Government honour the frontier by refraining from administrative measures such as the collection of revenue on the Indian side of the frontier, more especially in the Tawang area.[54]

The Sikkim Agency Office, which had a camp office in Shillong, got involved; it transpired that the boundary between the Balipara Frontier Tract and Bhutan, which adjoins Sikkim to the east, was also unclear. Letters and telegrams flew between the political agent for Sikkim, B. J. Gould, the Assam chief secretary Dawson, and Caroe in the Foreign Office. Captain Lightfoot, the political agent for the Balipara Frontier Tract, was sent off on an expedition to examine the boundary between this area and Bhutan up to Tawang. He was accompanied by a man from Kalimpong, the agent to the Maharaja of Bhutan, Raja S. T. Dorji. Dawson replied to Caroe's letter after Lightfoot's return. There were, he replied, four officials appointed by the Tawang monasterial council—under the Dalai Lama's administration—who collected revenue from an undefined area between Dirang, far south of the McMahon Line, and the Inner Line of the Balipara Frontier Tract. This was apart from the revenue collected for the maintenance of the monks in the Tawang monastery, he added. It was revenue meant for Lhasa. Two other officials of the Tibetan administration, known locally as Tsona Dzongpons, collected revenue from around Tawang itself and the neighbouring Tibetan district of Tsona. 'The Political Officer in his report sums up the result of his inquiry as follows', wrote Dawson, in his confidential letter to Caroe dated 29 May 1936:

> The people around the Tawangdzong especially definitely consider themselves as being under the Tibetan Government and there is no doubt whatever that the Tibetan Government definitely rule the Tawang area and collect revenue from as far south as Dirangdzong... As to the question whether the Assam government has exercised any measure of political control in the Balipara tribal areas up to the McMahon line, the policy of the Government in the tribal areas has always been to interfere as little as possible in internal administration.[55]

The matter was also referred to the British embassy in Peking. The reply from there, dated 25 June 1936, was not encouraging, and the issue escalated. 'The latest Chinese atlases show almost the whole of the tribal area south of the McMahon line up to the administered border of British India in Assam, together with a portion of northern Burma, as included in China', Foreign Secretary Henry Metcalfe noted in a letter to the India Office in London in August. Metcalfe strongly urged that advantage should be taken of a mission to Lhasa by the Sikkim political officer to obtain from the Tibetan government a reaffirmation acknowledging the McMahon Line as the frontier between India and Tibet.[56]

Caroe now began a flurry of official correspondence to have the 1914 Simla Convention, with the McMahon Line as the border between India and Tibet in the east, published in a fresh edition of Aitchison's *Treaties*. This revised edition, which still bore the imprint of 1929, was produced in August 1938.[57]

Tibet, meanwhile, was recalcitrant. In the winter of 1942, with the Second World War raging, two Tibetan generals arrived in Tawang on an 'enquiry commission' to put a stop to migration between Tawang, Tsona and Bhutan. Caroe was dismayed. Tibet's actions not only breached India's protectorate over Bhutan, but they also indicated its continuing disregard for the McMahon Line.[58] A formal protest was lodged with Lhasa on their 'boundary violation'. The matter ended with a change in policy. Advocates of a forward policy in the eastern Himalayas won the day.

On 16 April 1943, the Secretary of State for India sanctioned the policy—and accepted that it would shoulder its costs. For the first time, authorities at every echelon of the colonial hierarchy had agreed to assert 'effective control' over the eastern Himalayas.[59]

The Second World War made immediate implementation of the forward policy difficult. With Burma then already under Japanese rule and an invasion of India imminent, the focus shifted to shoring up defences on that side. Lightfoot, the political agent for the Balipara Tract, was sent to the Naga Hills as part of the irregular commando unit called V-Force. After the war ended, India's independence and partition soon followed. Meanwhile, there was a civil war in China between the Communists led by Mao Tse-tung and the nationalists led by Chiang Kai-shek in which, in October 1949, the Maoists finally emerged victorious. They wasted little time in asserting their sovereignty over Tibet. Negotiations between the Tibetans and Chinese held in Kalimpong in West Bengal, India, in March 1950, produced no results. In October 1950, the Chinese military invaded Tibet and swiftly overran the country. By May 1951, it was all over. Tibet had agreed, at gunpoint, to 'return to the family of the motherland of the People's Republic of China', with the signing of the Seventeen-Point Agreement between the representatives of the Dalai Lama and the new Chinese government.

'The Chinese invasion, in 1950, of eastern Tibet was the signal that NEFA [North-East Frontier Agency] could no longer remain as a forgotten frontier', the officer who handled the job of extending Indian administration up to the McMahon Line, Nari Rustomji, later wrote in his memoirs. Rustomji was then in Shillong working as adviser to the Assam Governor, Jairamdas Daulatram. He continues: 'With a Chinese presence in Tibet, it became necessary to strengthen further our ties with the hill-people of NEFA and to make known our own presence, in unmistakeable terms, up to the international frontier.'[60] According to Rustomji, two unfortunate events of recent years had made this feasible: the Second World War, which vastly improved communications to and through Assam, and the great earthquake of 1950, one of the most powerful ever recorded anywhere, which had led to relief flights operating into the hills between Assam and Tibet, because the floods that followed the quake made road and ferry communications difficult.

Rustomji recced positions for the establishment of administrative posts in the hills towards the McMahon Line by air, using small aircraft owned by European tea planters in Assam. The post of Ziro in the Subansiri river valley was the first. Others followed. 'The region that caused us special anxiety was the region of Tawang in the extreme north-west of the Kameng Frontier Division and across the 14,000-foot Se La pass', wrote Rustomji. With the Tibetans still unrelenting, 'we decided the time had come to take a firm stand and establish a permanent administrative centre in the region. We selected Bob Khathing for the task—and could not have made a better choice.'[61] Khathing was a Tangkhul Naga from the Manipur Hills who had been part of the V-Force during the Second World War, and served with distinction. He was made a Member of the Most Excellent Order of the British Empire (MBE) and won a Military Cross for his wartime exploits.

In February 1951, Khathing marched into Tawang with a force of 100 soldiers of the Assam Rifles and a large number of porters and support staff, including a handful of civilian officials, to set up a permanent Indian administration there. He raised the Indian flag, and cowed the local Tibetan officials into submission with a show of force—but no actual violence. 'They promptly reported to their higher authorities, who reported to India's Consul-General in Lhasa, who reported to the Political Officer in Sikkim, who reported to the External Affairs Ministry in Delhi, who reported to the Adviser to the Governor in Shillong, who reported back to Bob in Tawang', wrote Rustomji. 'After a round or two of this futile exercise in musical chairs, Bob very understandably shot us a wireless message that, unless he received clear instructions by return, he proposed packing his bags and would we please send someone at once to relieve him.'[62] He was persuaded to stay on, and eventually returned after establishing the proposed administrative centre in Tawang.

The relatively peaceful advance of Indian forces and administrators into the Arunachal Hills was interrupted two years later by an incident of the sort that had shaken the British more than forty years earlier. Rustomji was to recall the event in his memoirs:

> It was a delightfully sunny October afternoon in Shillong and I was making the most of the Puja holidays blissfully sipping beer, when I was rudely shaken by a message that an Assam Riles column moving in the Achingmori region of the Siang Frontier Division had been massacred by Tagin tribals.[63]

Only one person had managed to escape alive, which was how news of the incident got out. Forty-seven others had been massacred and some taken hostage. The mention of hostages was left out of Rustomji's account. 'The Assam Rifles', wrote Rustomji, 'were out for blood.' A strong punitive expedition was sent to encircle the area from three directions and bring to book the culprits. It took them three weeks to march up to the place, and another two months of scouring the jungles, before they were able to apprehend a few suspects and release the hostages.[64] The task of integrating the area into India went ahead with some urgency, prodded by the expanding Chinese presence in Tibet. A full-scale administration of the area was inaugurated in 1954 with the promulgation of the North-East Frontier Areas (Administration) Regulation.[65] The North-East Frontier Tract, including the Tuensang area which was later made part of the Naga Hills in 1957, had by then been renamed the North-East Frontier Agency. A special cadre, the Indian Frontier Administrative Service, was constituted, with its first batch of officers drawn mainly from the armed forces. It was these officers who oversaw the task of setting up government offices in the hitherto unadministered hills.

Life for them was not easy. Prem Nath Kaul, one of the officers from that first batch, recalled in his memoirs that the selected officers assembled in Delhi's South Block in December 1953 for a briefing from Prime Minister Jawaharlal Nehru. From there they headed to Shillong and met Nari Rustomji: 'During our brief stay in Shillong we were given talks by eminent speakers conversant with tribal affairs. One of our senior colleagues was the late Dr Verrier Elwin who had just been appointed adviser for tribal affairs in the NEFA secretariat.'[66] They had to battle, first of all, the very bureaucracy of which they had now become a part; salaries did not come on time, or at all. Kaul did not receive his arrears for the first two years of his service in the IFAS. Getting to the place he was posted to in 1954 also proved to be a bit of a task. 'I found myself enduring the heavy August rains from Pasighat to Along, most of the way fighting the leeches', recalled Kaul:

> The tracks were only foot-tracks and the gradients extremely steep. Each day's journey, though a distance of only ten to twelve miles, involved a march of six to eight hours... The two assistant political officers, since redesignated assistant commissioner, Kishan Chand Johorey (at that time acting political officer) and U. Chakma, had taken pains to receive me on entry to the so-called town of Along which was the newly-established district headquarters. I was led into what was my residence, a basha [bamboo hut] on a mound.

The village of Achingmori, where the massacre had taken place, fell in Kaul's area. The ringleaders of the massacre were still free in 1955, two years after the incident, and one of these, named Agi Radap, told Kaul how the massacre was planned and executed—and why. 'It was due to rumours spread amongst themselves that the government party was coming to emancipate slaves from their area. This was unfortunately confirmed by the village priest on the ominous examination of a chicken's liver or egg yolk', recorded Kaul.[67]

Indian policy on how to deal with such matters in NEFA was clarified in a contemporaneous and influential book called *A Philosophy for NEFA* (1957) by the anthropologist Verrier Elwin. In a section titled 'The Prime Minister's Policy', Elwin wrote:

> We are agreed that the people of NEFA cannot be left in their age-long isolation. We are equally agreed that we can leave no political vacuum along our frontier; that we must bring to an end the destructive practices of inter-tribal war and head-hunting and the morally repugnant practices of slavery, kidnapping of children, imposition of cruel punishments and opium-addiction, none of which are fundamental to tribal culture... Above all, we hope to see as a result of our efforts a spirit of love and loyalty for India.[68]

Since the foreword of the book was a ringing endorsement of it written by Nehru himself, there was little doubt that this was the prime minister's position. So far as NEFA was concerned, the administration was not isolating the tribal people at all, Elwin noted:

> Indeed, if it is to be criticised, it might rather be on the ground that it is bringing them a little too quickly into the mainstream of modern life. It is pressing forward everywhere with roads which will make the plains easier of access; it is encouraging both the national language and Assamese to help the people communicate more readily with the outside world... Its officers are penetrating into the wildest regions with the message that beyond the hills there is a friendly world with a desire to help and serve.[69]

The rapid advance of Indian administration towards the McMahon Line gained further urgency after the Dalai Lama fled from Lhasa in March 1959. He arrived in Tawang in NEFA a fortnight later, and was received by the assistant political officer there. The border dispute between India and China was already occupying the minds of the leaderships in both countries. This added further to the tensions between the two sides. In February 1960, Nehru invited the Chinese premier Chou En-lai to Delhi for discussions. He was immediately attacked for this in parliament by the opposition, and clarified that the move did not represent any reversal of his government's policy, which consisted of 'firm refusal to negotiate concerning India's entire 2,500-mile border with China'.[70]

Chou En-lai duly arrived in April, and offered a deal. His position, recorded in a file marked 'Top Secret', was that 'There are disputes about the boundary because it was never delimited and therefore, we must conduct negotiations but neither side should ask the other side to withdraw.'[71] Translated, this meant that China would accept the McMahon Line in the east if India were to accept the Chinese occupation of Aksai Chin bordering Ladakh in the west. Nehru, under pressure from the opposition and fearful of the political cost, refused this offer of a settlement. This was interpreted by China as India making a territorial claim on Chinese territory. Relations between the two countries soured further.

In early September 1962, trouble between the two countries began at a place called the Thagla Ridge near the tri-junction of India, Bhutan and Tibet north of Tawang. A Chinese patrol came to an Assam Rifles post in the area and asked them to withdraw. According to the Chinese, the post was on their side of the border. The Indian post commander held his ground. A few days later, a bigger Chinese patrol of sixty soldiers returned with the same demand. Thinking that the Chinese had returned with intent, the junior commissioned officer panicked and radioed that a force of 600 soldiers was closing in on his position. The junior officer's exaggerated reaction set in motion events that would eventually culminate in a full-scale attack by the Chinese.[72]

The Indian side sent more soldiers up towards the post, but getting there was no easy task. They had to march carrying heavy loads on mountain tracks in high altitudes. They eventually reached their destination and dug in. The Chinese responded in kind, and soon the two forces were facing one another. A decision was taken by the Indian side to 'evict the Chinese as soon as the Brigade has concentrated… the Army should prepare and throw the Chinese out as soon as possible'.[73] The fighting started in earnest in late October, and it was the Chinese who attacked. Their advance down the Tawang tract was rapid. In less than a month, despite gallant resistance from the men on the ground in certain pockets, the war was essentially over; the Chinese had taken Bomdila and were less than 100 kilometres from the foothills of Arunachal. The Brahmaputra valley lay open before them only a short distance ahead. Preparations were begun to evacuate the important town of Tezpur in Assam—but the Chinese forces then withdrew of their own accord before the onset of winter for logistical reasons. The Arunachal Hills remained Indian territory.

***

After the war, in 1964, a committee was constituted to examine the issue of extension of local self-government in NEFA. The chairman of the committee was a man from Pasighat named Daying Ering, one of the first educated members of the tribe earlier known as Abor (and now called Adi) and a member of the

Indian Frontier Administrative Service, who had been nominated as a member of parliament by the Government of India in 1961. In 1965, the Ering Committee recommended a four-tier system of village, circle, and District Councils, atop which would sit an Agency Council for all of NEFA. The final steps in the political and administrative integration of the area into India happened that year. Control of NEFA finally passed from the Ministry of External Affairs of the Indian government to the Ministry of Home Affairs. The frontier divisions were redesignated as districts, and the rule of political officers finally gave way to administration by deputy commissioners. The recommendations of the Ering Committee were accepted by the Government of India and put into effect over the next few years. In December 1969, this led to the inauguration of democratic politics in the area in the form of 'panchayati raj', a Hindi expression signifying village administration. Voting for assembly and parliamentary seats was still some way in the future; voting rights under the Indian constitution had not yet been extended to NEFA.

That process began after the Bangladesh War of 1971, which was followed by the redrawing of the map of Northeast India. NEFA, too, was affected. From being an acronym, it became a territory with a name—Arunachal Pradesh—and in 1974 acquired a capital of its own, a town called Itanagar. It was now a Union Territory, one of several such administrative units under the central government. The Agency Council acquired a new name, the Pradesh Council, but it was still only an advisory body. In 1975, this was again upgraded into a provisional Legislative Assembly, and a council of ministers was constituted from among its members. Voting rights were finally extended to the citizens of Arunachal Pradesh in 1977. In the Indian general elections held in March 1977 after the national Emergency, voting took place in the new Union Territory of Arunachal Pradesh for the first time. There were two constituencies, Arunachal West and Arunachal East. Only one candidate, Rinchen Khrime of the Indian National Congress, filed his nomination for the Arunachal West seat, and therefore no voting took place there. The more advanced Arunachal East constituency saw three candidates in the fray. The winner there was an independent candidate named Bagin Pertin who polled 28,557 votes to defeat his nearest rival of the Congress Party.

The assembly elections held a few months later were more hotly contested. By then, Indira Gandhi and the Congress had lost power in Delhi, and the Janata Party was ruling. The Union Territory of Arunachal Pradesh had been divided into thirty assembly constituencies. The electoral battle for these seats was entirely between the Janata Party, a local party called People's Party of Arunachal, newly formed by Pertin, and independents.[74] The Congress could not find candidates and contested only one seat; practically all its leaders had switched to the Janata Party, which duly won the largest number of seats and a narrow majority when the results were declared in March 1978.

Many politicians who would go on to dominate the state's politics for decades after were among the winners in those first assembly polls. They included Prem Khandu Thungon, who won as Janata Party candidate from Dirang and became the first chief minister of Arunachal Pradesh, and the long-serving future chief minister, Gegong Apang, who won from the Yinkiong-Pangin constituency, also on a Janata Party ticket. Daying Ering, the pioneering leader whose recommendations had paved the path to those elections, was unfortunately no longer around to participate in the polls. He had passed away in 1970 aged only forty.

Arunachal Pradesh's journey towards becoming a state of the Indian Union was completed in 1986 when the parliament of India passed the State of Arunachal Pradesh Act. The number of assembly seats was simultaneously increased to forty. The state of Arunachal Pradesh was inaugurated on 20 February 1987, with Gegong Apang, who had switched to the Congress Party, as chief minister. He ruled the state as chief minister until 1999, and then again from 2003 to 2007.

Arunachal Pradesh is now the only state in Northeast India where Hindi is the link language among the many tribes, who speak different and mutually unintelligible languages and dialects. Fear of Chinese incursions has helped make good Indians of them. Alone among the hill states of Northeast India, Arunachal Pradesh has had no notable separatist insurgency seeking freedom from

India—although insurgents from neighbouring states such as Nagaland and Assam have used Arunachal for hideouts and bases.

The state's politics, which was grafted on from above by successive rulers in Delhi, still continue to follow the trend set in the first assembly elections. MLAs switch sides back and forth, often en masse, to align with the powers that be. Whatever the party is in power in Delhi, is almost inevitably the party that rules Arunachal Pradesh.

9

SIKKIM AND THE COMPLETION OF REGION-MAKING

THE NORTHEAST IN MODERN INDIA

The integration of the hills of Arunachal Pradesh into India, although fairly recent, did not complete the current political map of the country, or of the region into which it was integrated—Northeast India. That honour belongs to another territory that lies between India and the Tibetan Autonomous Region of China, namely Sikkim. The erstwhile Himalayan kingdom, which sits wedged between Tibet in the north, Bhutan in the east, Nepal in the west and the Indian state of West Bengal in the south, merged with India in 1975.

Sikkim's origin story as a kingdom begins with the ascent to the throne of a man of Tibetan roots named Phuntsog Namgyal in 1641/42. Three venerable Tibetan Buddhist monks of the Red Hat sect, who were then fleeing a sectarian conflict with the followers of the Yellow Hat sect, had divined that he was a descendant of a prince of Kham in eastern Tibet named Khye Bumsa. Namgyal's rise to power, they said, had been prophesied centuries earlier by a venerable elder of the indigenous Lepcha tribe of Sikkim, a chief named Thekong Tek, who himself was said to be blessed with magical powers.[1] According to oral tradition, sometime in the thirteenth century, at a place called Kabi Lungchok, this great Lepcha chief concluded an alliance of 'blood brotherhood' with Khye Bumsa, who, being childless, had gone to him seeking a boon of progeny.[2]

The kingdom from its inception had close ties with Tibet, and as the hostility between the warring Buddhist sects abated, 'the religious and political bonds linking Sikkim with Tibet came to be drawn tighter'.[3] The Dalai Lama became the final appellate authority for the Sikkim Buddhists. Tibetan became the court language. Kings married Tibetan wives.

Their ties were deepened further by the rise of a common threat: the Gorkha kingdom of Nepal.

In 1769, the Gorkhas under King Prithvi Narayan Sah conquered Kathmandu, thus unifying most of Nepal. Sah died in 1775, but his successors continued the task. In 1787, a Gorkha force attacked Sikkim. It was successfully repulsed by the Sikkimese who pursued the attackers into Nepali territory before being beaten back. In 1788–89, the Gorkhas attacked again. A lightning advance saw them sacking the Sikkimese capital. The king and queen were forced to flee with their infant son.[4] A second Gorkha army then followed the first and conquered all Sikkimese territory west of the Teesta river including the tract of land that would later become Darjeeling. The Gorkha army also invaded Tibet and occupied several strategic and commercial centres. This led to escalation, as the Chinese emperor, who saw the Tibetans as tributaries, became involved. A Chinese force came to the rescue of the Tibetans, and a negotiated settlement was arrived at by which Tibet agreed to pay some yearly tribute to Nepal, while Nepal in turn would send a yearly tribute to China.[5]

The arrangement, however, did not hold, because the Tibetans refused to pay subsequent installments of the promised annual tribute of 300 silver ingots. In 1791, Gorkha forces once again attacked Tibet and looted Tashilhunpo, the seat of a famous and rich monastery. The Chinese emperor now took personal notice of this affront and despatched a strong army to punish the 'bandits'. After marching across China and Tibet, the Chinese Army of some 8,000 soldiers entered Nepal and fought its way to Nawakot on the outskirts of Kathmandu in August 1792. Their final assault on

Kathmandu itself was thwarted by the Gorkhas, who successfully defended their capital.[6]

A few years later the Gorkha kingdom was at war again, this time with the power then building an empire in the plains of India: the East India Company government. Trouble started over a territorial dispute near Gorakhpur in what is now Uttar Pradesh in northern India. In 1814, after a few border skirmishes, both sides declared war. The British sent in four columns of division strength, each under a major-general. The action commenced with a British attack on Dehra Dun in northern India, which was then Gorkha territory. It was a disaster: the much smaller Gorkha force repulsed the attack and General Gillespie, who was leading the British assault on a fort called Nalapani, was killed. Subsequent attacks and bombardments also failed to dislodge the Gorkhas. Finally, a siege in which their water supply was cut off forced the survivors to evacuate.[7]

For the first year or so, the war went badly for the British. The operations of three of the four British divisions were total failures. Time and again, the Gorkhas prevailed. However, the situation began to change when the British successfully took Kumaon in what is now the state of Uttarakhand in India. After that, peace negotiations began. The British demanded Kumaon, Garhwal and the parts of Sikkim under Gorkha rule as terms for peace. A treaty called the Treaty of Sugauli was signed, but the Gorkha court's reluctance to ratify it on those terms led to a resumption of hostilities in which the British Indian forces, despite stiff resistance, eventually prevailed. The treaty was ratified in 1816 and brought into British Indian hands tracts of hill country including those on which its future summer capital, Simla, and the tea plantations of Darjeeling would come to be located.[8]

The Sikkim king, who had allied with the British during the Gorkha war, was rewarded for his services with the return of the lands, including the Darjeeling tract, that had been taken from him by the Gorkhas. However, ten years later, fresh disputes arose between Sikkim and Nepal. The British officers who were sent up into the hills from the sweaty heat of the Bengal plains to investigate chanced upon a largely uninhabited place then known as Dorje-ling, a Tibetan name meaning land of the thunderbolt. The desire to have a sanatorium there and a retreat from the heat of the Indian summer, along with the benefit of an outpost in a strategic location, was immediately communicated up and down the bureaucracy. In 1835, after some negotiations, the Raja of Sikkim by a deed 'gifted' the lands of Darjeeling to the East India Company out of 'friendship to the Governor General'.[9]

Darjeeling developed rapidly, 'chiefly by immigration from the neighbouring States of Nepal, Sikkim and Bhutan, in all of which slavery was prevalent'.[10] The East India Company Raj abolished slavery in its territories in 1843. Escaping slaves rushed to Darjeeling. This soon became a bone of contention between Sikkim and Darjeeling. As the authoritative collection known as Aitchison's *Treaties* says:

> There had always been an arrangement for a mutual exchange of escaped slaves between Sikkim and Bhutan, and Dr Campbell, the Superintendent of Darjeeling, was constantly importuned by the Maharaja and his Diwan to persuade the British Government to make a similar arrangement with Sikkim: a request which was, of course, steadily refused.[11]

This led to some discontent in the Sikkimese court. In 1849, Campbell and a Dr Hooker, while visiting Sikkim with the permission of the Maharaja, were suddenly seized and taken prisoner. The Governor General responded by informing the Maharaja that he would 'answer with his own head for any injury done to them'.[12] The threat had the desired effect: the prisoners were released unharmed. However, the incident led to a small British force entering Sikkim and conveniently occupying a part of its territory suitable for growing tea, which was added to Darjeeling district.

A few years later, trouble again cropped up between the two sides. Another British force entered Sikkim. This time the king fled to Tibet, and remained there until his death. In 1888, one of his successors tried to return to his kingdom with Tibetan help. This brought the British and Tibetan forces into direct conflict. The Tibetans were routed—but matters threatened to escalate further. Tibet being under Chinese suzerainty, the Chinese now got involved. Parleys began between the two sides, and in 1890 a convention was signed at Calcutta between representatives of 'Her Brittanic Majesty' and 'His Majesty the Emperor of China' which fixed the boundary between Sikkim and Tibet as the crest of the mountain ranges separating the waters flowing into the Teesta to the south, from those flowing northwards into Tibet.[13] No map accompanied this convention. No Sikkimese or Tibetan representative signed the convention, which was an Anglo-Chinese one.

Sikkim thus became a British protectorate, and a political officer named John Claude White was posted there. He began a restructuring of the administration and encouraged immigration from Nepal. Sikkim was still a princely state under British Indian suzerainty when India became independent in 1947. The then maharaja of Sikkim, Tashi Namgyal, signed a 'standstill agreement' with the country's new rulers that essentially meant continuation of the status quo. Under this agreement, India assumed control of Sikkim's external affairs, communications and defence.[14]

By then, other changes were afoot. A political party, the Sikkim State Congress, had been established in December 1947. Its immediate demands were the establishment of a popular government, formation of an interim ministry and immediate accession to India. The king responded by engineering the formation of his own National Party, with support mainly from the Lepcha and Bhutia communities, to oppose the Sikkim Congress and its demands. In April 1948, the National Party adopted a resolution stating that 'Sikkim shall not under any circumstances accede to the dominion of India'. For good measure, it also pointed out that 'historically, socially, culturally, and linguistically, Sikkim has closer affinities with Bhutan and Tibet'.[15]

The Sikkim Congress, which was friendly towards India and drew its support mainly from the Nepali-speaking majority, adopted the path of agitation. In May 1949, a crowd besieged the royal palace demanding the formation of a popular government. The Indian Army had to be called in to rescue the maharaja. A popular ministry led by the Sikkim Congress chief, Tashi Tsering, was inaugurated within days of this, but it lasted less than a month before being dismissed by the king. India decided against direct intervention at this juncture, and an India-Sikkim Friendship Treaty was signed in 1950. The agitation for popular government, however, continued and gathered momentum. In 1953, the maharaja created a legislature called the Sikkim State Council to address the pro-democracy demands, with a mix of elected and nominated members. Although this failed to satisfy the Sikkim Congress, four elections were held to this legislature between 1957 and 1970.

The situation began to change with the redrawing of the wider map of the region following the 1971 war between India and Pakistan that led to the creation of Bangladesh. The reorganisation of Northeast India followed. Sikkim, meanwhile, separated by geography—it does not border any other state of the region—continued its existence as an Indian protectorate...but the new maharaja had begun to chafe at the influence of his protectors. He sought an amendment to the India-Sikkim Friendship Treaty. Negotiations followed, but the maharaja was inflexible in his demands; he hoped his kingdom would attain the kind of independent protectorate status enjoyed by his neighbour Bhutan, which had then recently become a member of the United Nations. He had misjudged his position. In 1973, the then prime minister of India, Indira Gandhi, fresh from leading the country to a famous victory in war, tasked India's external intelligence agency chief, R. N. Kao, with '[doing] something about Sikkim'.[16]

Agitations against the monarch soon gained momentum, and the palace was once again besieged by protesters demanding reforms. A new agreement was concluded between India and Sikkim by which the Indian government took control of law and order. The maharaja conceded a demand for fresh elections to be conducted by the Indian Election Commission, in which his foes won a landslide. His days as monarch were soon over. On 14 April 1975, a referendum was held on abolishing the monarchy and merging with India. When the results came in two days later, there were 59,467 votes in favour and 1,496 against joining India.[17]

* * *

The integration of Sikkim into India completed a process of map-making in the region that is now the Northeast which had begun roughly 150 years earlier with the Anglo-Burmese War of 1824–26. For the next twenty-seven years after its entry into the Indian Union, the Himalayan state remained in a bubble of splendid isolation within the Union. Geographically and culturally, its nearest neighbours were the same as they had always been—Darjeeling and the plains of West Bengal in India on one side, and Tibet, Bhutan and Nepal on the other three. In 2002, it was made a member of the Government of India's North Eastern Council, a body for the states of that region that has been in existence since 1971. The awkward, belated inclusion of Sikkim—which has no geographical contiguity with any other state of the region—into the NEC completed the creation of Northeast India.

It is a region that is bounded almost entirely by foreign countries. Only a tiny sliver of land, the Siliguri Corridor, barely 21 kilometres wide at its narrowest point, connects the region with the rest of India, or what people in Northeast India often call the 'Indian mainland'. The sense of space it occupies is that of an island—but it is an island surrounded entirely by dry land, created by the drawing of borders that cut it off from all its neighbours. It has been birthed by lines drawn on maps that created new realities on the ground—lines such as the Pemberton-Johnstone-Maxwell line separating Burma from British India, the McMahon Line between India and Tibet drawn in 1914, and the Radcliffe Line separating what is now Bangladesh from India that appeared in 1947.

India's longest international border is the 4,096-kilometre border with Bangladesh which apparated in a matter of weeks with partition. It is a boundary that separates Bangladesh from West Bengal, Assam, Meghalaya, Tripura and Mizoram. The word, worn to cliché, that is usually used to describe it is 'porous'. India's security agencies have long been concerned about this unruly porosity that defies the authority of the map, with its neat lines separating countries, and the powers of bureaucracies to control the destinies of billions of humans and animals, especially cattle, with pieces of paper. Attempts to run a high, barbed-wire fence along its entire length, thus creating an illusion of security mainly for the satisfaction of those who live far from the borders, have proceeded fitfully since 1989. Despite persistent efforts under successive governments in Delhi of various political dispositions, the project remains incomplete. It is a project whose immensity is perhaps lost on those championing it.

The geographic region that includes Northeast India is one defined by the Himalayas in the north and the Bay of Bengal in the south. Between the mountains and the sea, the land—hills and valleys—is connected by a dense network of arteries in the form of rivers and streams. There is no natural boundary within this geographical region. It is all one interconnected whole. The greatest of the arteries that run through it, the central one, along which the forces that shaped its history have flowed, is the Brahmaputra river. In the longue durée of history, life in this region, for its human and non-human inhabitants, has been shaped by the ways of water. Long before there were any roads, or countries, or kings and kingdoms, the rivers were there.

The earliest kingdoms of which there are memories in this region are from the valley of the Brahmaputra river. They concern the kingdom of Pragjyotish, mentioned in the Mahabharata, whose king, Bhagadatta, was referred to in that account as the chief of Mlecchas and accompanied by Yavanas.[18] The dynasty to which Bhagadatta belonged was one that according to Hindu myths had replaced the dynasty of the Danava kings founded by Mahiranga Danava. Bhagadatta was described as son of a mighty king named Narak-Asura, who had earlier been vanquished in an epic battle with Lord Krishna, one of the main Hindu deities. Lord Krishna is also said to have battled the king of the place where the town of Tezpur by the Brahmaputra in Assam now stands, a king named Ban-Asura.

The words 'danava' and 'asura' have interesting connotations. Danava in common usage means demon. Asuras are typically characterised in Hindu lore, starting with the Puranas, as powerful but villainous beings who are defeated by Hindu gods and heroes in war.[19] The imagery is one that is seen every year, even now, during the annual Durga Puja celebrations which are popular in West Bengal, Odisha and Assam. They depict the goddess Durga, armed with a trident, slaying an asura named Mahish-Asura, who is the villain of the piece. Curiously, the same word, 'asura' or 'ahura', refers to the god Ahura Mazda in the ancient pre-Islamic Zoroastrian faith of Persia (Iran), a land with which the Indo-Aryans who established the Vedic faith in India evidently had close ties. The moral order is reversed in the Persian stories, where the 'deva' (also spelled as daeva), the word for gods in Sanskrit, are the demons.

The replacement of the letter 's' with 'h' also occurs in a word of considerably more contemporary relevance. The word 'Hindu' is derived via the Persian term 'Hindu' and the Arabic term 'Hind' from the word 'Sindhu', meaning the river Indus. The 'Sapta Sindhu' or seven holy rivers mentioned in the Rig Veda, the oldest of the four Vedas, were the Indus and five of its tributaries, and a lost river, the Saraswati. The name by which the dominant group of people who inhabited the lands east of the Indus called themselves from early Vedic times, more than 3,000 years ago, was 'Arya' or Aryan. This was, incidentally, also the name by which the old Persians called themselves: Iran literally means 'land of the Aryans'. The Aryas who lived in India and followed the religious practices that came, many centuries later, to be called Hinduism, also called the territory they inhabited 'Aryavarta' or 'abode of the Aryans'. This formed the core of a larger entity known as Bharat, the territorial extent of which is a matter of regular debate in today's India. Hindu nationalists allied to the Bharatiya Janata Party led by Prime Minister Narendra Modi assert that the entire landmass between the Himalayas in the north, the Indian Ocean in the south, Iran in the west and Indonesia in the east was Bharat. They dream of someday recreating an 'Akhand Bharat' or 'undivided Bharat', which would include Afghanistan, Pakistan, Nepal, Bhutan, Bangladesh, Myanmar, Sri Lanka and the Tibetan Autonomous Region of China.[20]

It is not clear, though, that the peoples of all these areas would fit comfortably into Bharat. According to the anthropologist Catherine Clémentin-Ojha:

> In the *Purāṇas* and other Sanskrit texts of the first centuries of the Christian era, it [Bharat] refers to the supraregional and subcontinental territory where the Brahmanical system of society prevails. It seems to have absorbed the older and spatially narrower toponym *Āryāvarta* (the land of the *Āryas*) described in the Laws of Manu.

A key feature of the Brahminical system of society was the observance of caste. According to Clémentin-Ojha, 'Bhārata then refers to a spatially delimited social order, but not to a politically organized entity.'[21] This is a position borne out by the author of the *History of Dharmasastra*, Pandit Pandurang V. Kane, who wrote:

> Bharatavarṣa itself has comprised numerous countries from the most ancient times... There was no doubt a great emotional regard for Bharatavarṣa or Āryāvarta as a unity for many centuries among all writers from a religious point of view, though not from a political standpoint. Therefore, one element of modern nationhood viz. being under the same government was wanting.[22]

It is clear from the early Hindu myths and texts that the kingdoms of what is now Northeast India, ruled by mighty asura kings such as Narak-Asura and Ban-Asura, lay outside the Brahminical order. The common word for hell in several Indian languages, including Hindi, is 'Narak'. 'Ban' signifies jungle. The description of the king Bhagadatta in the Mahabharata was 'king of Mlecchas'. Mleccha was the word for barbarians outside the Aryan social order who were considered unclean because they did not observe the rules of caste. This clearly placed the lands they inhabited outside the definition of Bharat.

The existence of many kingdoms throughout the imagined territory of Bharat, whatever its extent, is beyond dispute. Indeed, it is a situation that existed as late as 1947, when the 562-odd princely states across the country were famously integrated into modern India. This is a reality that seems to have been all but forgotten. The political imagination of the present views Bharat as the ancient name for a pristine and fully formed Hindu India that stretched from Iran to Indonesia, or at minimum, Afghanistan to Myanmar. Hindu nationalism's oft-repeated goals of making India, that is Bharat, a 'Hindu Rashtra' and of eventually creating an 'Akhand Bharat' seek to 'restore' the country to that imagined past.

What the preceding chapters have made clear is that, at least in the case of Northeast India, this imagination cannot be supported by facts. In state after state, the tale is one of different communities and kingdoms being brought into British India following wars with British forces, meaning mainly Indian sepoys under British officers. Thus, for example, in the first two chapters, we saw how Assam became part of the British Indian empire following the Anglo-Burmese War of 1824–26. The chapters on Manipur and Tripura traced how they came under British Indian indirect rule. The chapter on Nagaland traced the process by which the Naga Hills entered British India in the late 1800s and early 1900s. The chapter on Meghalaya found the Khasi and Jaintia kingdoms entering British India in a process that began with trade wars in the late 1700s and ended after the independence of India in 1947. The chapter on Mizoram found that area coming into British India following wars in the late 1800s. The chapter on Arunachal Pradesh found that area starting to come into British India only in the early 1900s.

The idea of the nation is a modern notion. There were hardly any to be found before 1800—the world then was still one of empires and kingdoms. It is a notion that became predominant, as Benedict Anderson wrote in his masterpiece *Imagined Communities*, with revolutions, the Enlightenment, and the spread of the printing press, the map and capitalism.[23] The standardisation of vernacular languages and their elevation to national languages is a recent event in historical terms. The maps of the world we see now are drawn according to the Mercator projection, invented by Gerardus Mercator in 1569. In the case of Northeast India, the oldest existing maps are all from the colonial period.

The idea of India as a nation-state first appears only during colonial rule—and rather late in the day at that. None other than the original Hindu nationalist, Bankim Chandra Chattopadhyay, lamented this fact, in an 1879 essay titled 'The Shame of Bharat', in which he writes: 'Only twice, in recorded history, did Hindus rise as a nation.'[24] The two instances he cites are of the Marathas under

Chhatrapati Shivaji and the Sikhs under Maharaja Ranjit Singh—the latter being an inclusion that stretches the definition of Hindu, because the Sikhs view themselves as a religious community distinct from Hindu. 'The British are our beneficiaries', he says, 'Many of the things they are teaching us are priceless. I have referred in this essay to two priceless jewels we have acquired in this manner: a love for freedom and the establishment of a nation. The Hindus did not know what these meant.'[25]

The amorphousness of the idea of India was reflected in the view from outside as well. As historian Sanjay Subrahmanyam pointed out in an essay on Indian civilisation, 'several centuries after the arrival of Vasco da Gama on Indian shores, there was no single dominant idea of India in writings by Westerners: several contradictory views existed, depending on whether one wrote from Madurai or Agra, whether one was Protestant or Catholic, whether one knew Persian or Sanskrit'.[26] A new homogeneity can be found in views of what India was by the late eighteenth and early nineteenth centuries, wrote Subrahmanyam.

The notion that the world is made up of contiguous nation-states, and that each of these states has a border with its neighbours marked by neat lines on the map that correspond to neat lines on the ground—this is an idea that was absurd in India even in the early 1800s. In the preceding chapters, there are many mentions of the drawing of border lines along the northeastern frontier of British India. Every single one of those was drawn after 1826, and the most significant ones were drawn after 1900. The struggles of the British Indian empire and its successor state of India to translate those lines, which bear the names of colonial officers, into realities on the ground is testimony to both their newness and strangeness. The McMahon Line of 1914 that separates India from China, and the Radcliffe Line of 1947 that separates India from Pakistan and Bangladesh, have been enduring problems for every government. The border between India and Myanmar makes less news, but movement across it has also been a worry for security agencies in both countries for decades.

The old political order in much of the Indian subcontinent was made up of pyramids of chiefs and kings ordered by suzerainty rather than sovereignty. At the apex, for intermittent and relatively brief periods often centuries apart, a distant 'great emperor' would rise to whom the nearest regional power paid a grudging tribute. The replacement of that hierarchy of shifting suzerainties with a unitary sovereignty, and of the concept of a fluid and amorphous frontier zone with border lines, has been problematic for India and its neighbours. Northeast India, which is bounded almost entirely by foreign countries, has been particularly affected, as communities have found their traditional homelands divided by new lines and administrative borders that in the ambitions of officialdom are often viewed as incipient versions of the Great Wall of China.

The loss of the old world has been a complicated thing.

The old world was one where all of nature was imbued with gods and spirits. There was a god for rain and thunder, a god for love and one for war. River spirits inhabited the waterways. A forest pool might have a nymph. A large cast of other non-human characters of various kinds and proclivities—from fairies to werewolves, were-tigers and vampires—completed this world for its human inhabitants. Local names varied, along with local specificities of character, but the world was then a place where the gods reigned supreme. The king—queens were rare—generally derived his authority from god. By his side, legitimising his rule, was the religious intermediary between him and whatever god ruled the lives of his people. Priests coronated kings; they also 'discovered' genealogies. For many centuries, one of the crucial tasks of priests was to discover, or invent, how a certain king was descended from the gods.

That world started dying when the old pagan gods began to die. The death of the old gods de-sacralised the earth and sent divinity into the unknown heavens. This opened up the path for the growth of a more mechanistic worldview. Nature was transformed into natural resources. A notion of one single, linear path of 'development and progress' for all societies around the world followed.

Both development and progress are measured primarily in economic and technological terms. It was the profit motive that birthed the East India Company in 1600. Some technologies—such as superior firearms and the advent of modern communications—apart from the abundant collaboration of Indians across classes and communities helped it to establish its rule over 'mainland' India. Similar pressures and avarices, and the same technological superiority, brought Northeast India into British India. The key event was the Anglo-Burmese war of 1824–26, but as mentioned in the chapter on Assam, the East India Company did not immediately annex Upper Assam to its domains after its victory over Burma. That happened only after 1838 by when it was established that tea could be grown there—a discovery that coincided with the first Opium War between Britain and China, which obstructed the supply of tea from what had, until then, been the only source of the brew. The British love of tea thus contributed to the annexation of Upper Assam to British India.

The further expansion of the British Raj from there into the adjacent hills of Northeast India has been traced in the preceding pages. They show a pattern, repeated across the region over a span of decades through the second half of the nineteenth and the early twentieth centuries, of British India's encroachment into lands the tribal groups claimed rights over. This often triggered raids by tribal groups from the hills into villages and tea plantations in the plains where the British ruled—which were inevitably followed by punitive counter-attacks and expeditions by Indian sepoys under British officers into the hills. The unequal contests between guns on the one hand and spears and bows and arrows on the other, would typically end in victory for the British, after which some form of treaty, drawing boundary lines between plains and their adjoining hills, along with a recognition of British overlordship, would result. Following this, in several states of Northeast India, the history is one of intrepid missionaries, compelled by their enthusiasm to gain converts to their faith, making their way in. Driven by the need to translate the Bible into the local language, they drew up the first dictionaries and grammars of these cultures—with vocabularies built by pointing at things and writing down their names as they sounded to their ears—and fixed a dialect of the local language into the standard vernacular, thus laying the ground for the emergence of a linguistic identity. The spread of education followed.

Both the missionaries and the colonial administrators were able to reduce the resistance to their entry into new territories by dispensing basic medical care and bringing in useful commodities. In most places, the first hospitals and the first shops opened during colonial rule. Exposure to Western education and the ideas that came with it accelerated the desires for material progress and development. Native elites across India, where generation after generation had long followed the life-pattern of the one before, woke up to the shocking realisation that we were 'backward'; we had to catch up. We might still consider our society morally superior to that of the West, but the arena of our backwardness that could not be denied was material. The West had better things—and people wanted many of those same things. Education and jobs became the paths to relative prosperity. A new educated middle class emerged, and connected with the political ideas then swirling through India. The ideas of national self-determination, and of rebellion against local feudal overlords, were two of these.

Throughout history, to reach what is now Northeast India had been a long and very difficult journey from the Indian heartland. Its history, recounted in the preceding chapters, shows closer and more frequent political interactions with immediate neighbours such as Burma, Tibet or what is now Bangladesh than with Indian states further away such as Gujarat, Madhya Pradesh or Karnataka. Until the end of Mughal rule, thanks in part to an Ahom victory in the Battle of Saraighat in 1671, practically all of what is now Northeast India had remained outside the territory of Hindustan, the Perso-Arabic name by which the region of North India had popularly been known since the days of the Delhi sultanate. This can be seen in the 1782 Rennell map of Hindustan in the opening pages of this book.

Distance, terrain and climate all played their parts. Getting there in those days was no simple matter. Every monsoon, even today, the rivers flood, tracks turn to mud and many areas become almost impossible to reach except by elephant or helicopter. The safe season for travel is winter.

When the pioneering American missionaries first entered Northeast India, they started their journey from Calcutta by boat on 20 November 1835 and reached their destination, Sadiya in Upper Assam, on 23 March 1836—a good four months later. They were fortunate to arrive safely. One of the two missionaries who brought the first printing press into the region the following year, with historic consequences, died en route.[27] Ancient connections existed between places far and wide, but the connections were relatively thin and sporadic. It was only with the creation of British India that Northeast India came to be linked with the regions of Hindustan, Bengal and the Deccan by regular communications networks.

It was the Industrial Revolution that changed everything. Writing in the closing years of the nineteenth century, Alfred Brame, a historian of the India General Steam Navigation Company Ltd, which ran steamer services from Calcutta to Dibrugarh and Allahabad, reflected that 'The India of the early years of the present century is so far removed from the India of today as to make one marvel how our predecessors of but a generation or two back managed to make life worth living.' The Ganges, he continued,

> was then the great highway from Calcutta into the interior; for although the Grand Trunk Road was in existence, it was used in cases of great emergency only and involved the utmost discomfort. The civilian, the soldier, the planter and trader all journeyed to Patna, Allahabad, or Delhi by water, in pinnaces, bauliahs, or budgerows, according to their means and station in life.[28]

These different kinds of wooden boats, all powered by oars and sails, differed from one another in size.

'The boats were generally tracked along the bank by ropes when ascending the river, unless the wind was favourable, when sail was set and the weary crew had a welcome rest', wrote Brame. There was a standard scale of time for travel between different points: 'Calcutta to Monghyr [Munger in Bihar] 1 month 8 days, Calcutta to Buxar 2 months, Calcutta to Allahabad 3 months... Calcutta to Dacca took 1 month in those days, and such far-away places as Assam or Sylhet were beyond the range of any fixed timing.' Basically, until the early 1800s, if you were going to Assam or

Sylhet from Calcutta, or vice versa, you set sail hoping you would eventually reach there alive some day, a few months hence. The advent of steamers changed that. It revolutionised travel. 'It was only in 1828 that it took 3 months to make a journey that is now traversed in 18 hours', wrote Brame in 1899. The specific route he was referring to was the journey from Calcutta to Allahabad.[29]

Railways followed steamers. The revolution in communication technologies including the telegraph enabled central authorities to impose their dominion over greater distances in less time than had ever previously been possible. What James Scott calls the 'friction of terrain' which had kept much of the highlands of Northeast India and Southeast Asia as non-state spaces until the advent of British rule, was finally overcome, at least in the dry seasons.[30] This enabled the construction of Northeast India in its present form. The framework of political and economic structures and systems within which modern identities were imagined and ordinary lives are lived developed. Ways of life and the relationship with land changed. Several communities had traditionally been migratory; they now became permanently settled. Necessities of colonial administration created new territorial units. Maps froze these into territorial identities.

The extension of the reach of states into formerly non-state spaces led to other frictions, though. The friction between India and China along their Himalayan frontier, mentioned in preceding chapters, is a case in point.

The 1947 border between India and East Pakistan, which became Bangladesh in 1971, has been problematic in a different way. The issue of migration from there has dominated the internal politics of Northeast India for decades. It is an issue intimately linked to the idea of the nation, and to two features of the modern state that came with British rule and India's struggle for independence: the census, and the vote.

Censuses force-fitted identities, which could previously be amorphous, or fluid, or quite local, into the rigid, unchanging and unitary big boxes of caste, tribe, religion and language. Then the vote came, and the matter of choosing one's primary identity became a political issue. Suddenly, who was in a numerical majority and who was in a minority was a determinant of power. The English, Scots, Irish and Welsh in India, an infinitesimal minority numbering only in thousands, had ruled the whole subcontinent of teeming millions without requiring any great numbers, thanks largely to the collaboration from the very beginning of Indian sepoys (soldiers), seths (bankers), nawabs and maharajas, and babus (clerks). The concept of majority rule obviously put paid to the legitimacy of that.

India as a whole has been haunted by the calculation of majorities and minorities since the advent of electoral politics in the 1920s. It sparked Muslim fears that they would become a permanent minority in a Hindu-dominated India. The issue eventually led to the partition of India on the basis of the two-nation theory, according to which Hindus and Muslims are two distinct nations; but the trouble for South Asia is that the pattern of majorities and minorities repeats like a fractal throughout the region. The politics of majority and minority is thus still very much with us.

Minorities have fared rather badly across South Asia since 1947. Naturally, no group wants to be a minority in a big state if it has the chance of being a ruling majority in a smaller state. This combination of fear and desire has been the driver of politics in the Northeast for well over a century. At first it energised the politics in Assam against Bengali domination, giving rise to the anti-migrant, specifically anti-Bangladeshi, politics that is still very much around. Later it gave shape to the current political geography of Northeast India, where different local majorities—in the Naga, Mizo, Khasi, Garo and Jaintia Hills—carved out their own areas of dominance from Assam, which was dominated by Assamese upper castes and Ahoms.

The most extreme assertion of the separate identities, each claiming to be a nation and drawing legitimacy from the right to self-determination, was through the armed insurgencies across Northeast India seeking independence from India. Beginning with the Naga insurgency in 1947, these had their best chances before the Bangladesh War of 1971. After the war, the map of the region was redrawn and its politics recast with the formation of new states, as recounted in the preceding chapters. Nonetheless, the insurgents retained striking power until the late 2000s, when a change of government in Bangladesh finally robbed them of their bases and safe houses there. The years of peace that have followed have transformed the region, and mindsets in the region.

Back in the 1980s when I was growing up in Shillong, the erstwhile capital of undivided Assam, a slogan was emblazoned in big letters on the outer walls of the state assembly, the oldest in the Northeast. 'Khasi by blood, Indian by accident', the graffiti said. No one removed it for months. The sense of separateness was stronger in some of the other states of the region. It was common in those days for friends travelling from Nagaland or Manipur to cities in the mainland to casually say they were 'going to India'.

Those declarations of separateness have now been replaced by cries for inclusion. There are, for instance, frequent demands for inclusion of the history of Northeast India as a part of the history of India. The fact that India's national anthem, 'Jana Gana Mana', which mentions territories such as Punjab, Gujarat, Maharashtra, Bengal and the Dravida lands of the south, does not mention any place in Northeast India, is often brought up with a sense of grievance at the exclusion. However, when it was written in 1911, Assam and East Bengal were still one province, most of the present states of the region did not exist in anything like their present shapes on the political map, and the hills of Arunachal Pradesh and eastern Nagaland lay outside British India.

These demands for inclusion signify that the process of political integration of the Northeast into India that started with the 1826 Treaty of Yandabo between the East India Company and the Burmese king, is substantially complete—not only administratively but mentally. The big questions—about the external and internal boundaries of the territory, and the form of government—are largely settled, as far as India is concerned. Thus there is, for instance, an existing territorial dispute with China over the McMahon Line, but Arunachal Pradesh is the only state in Northeast India that has *not* seen a popular separatist insurgency to leave India. The territorial boundaries of Northeast India, both internal and external, are essentially colonial inheritances—and they are by and large accepted by the people, although there are some remaining territorial disputes not just externally between India and China, but also internally, between neighbouring states. Assam, for example, has boundary disputes with Mizoram, Nagaland and Meghalaya.

The structure of administration in the states of Northeast India now is much the same as the one that was put in place during colonial rule. We still have district administrations headed by district collectors, the police still operate using the Indian Penal Code of 1860, and the Inner Line Permit—the first law instituted for what is now Northeast India in 1873—is still in force. The Governors sent from Delhi still occupy, in several state capitals, the same bungalows from where their colonial predecessors ruled. Their powers are less than in colonial times, but the tradition of local leaders acting as tributaries of the ruler in Delhi is unchanged. Whenever a powerful prime minister is in office in the national capital, it has become established custom for chief ministers across Northeast India to align with that ruler. So long as the Congress Party ruled India, Northeast India was a Congress bastion. Since 2014, when the Bharatiya Janata Party led by Narendra Modi came to power, the entire region has come to have BJP governments or governments in alliance with the BJP. The success of the Hindu nationalist party in a region whose population in large part is neither Hindu nor historically Indian nationalist may seem odd, until one considers the simple question of what people want.

The aspirations of people in Northeast India now are largely the same as those of people everywhere else. No political party or leader in any state of the region can hope to win an election without promising 'development', a word of immense flexibility that accommodates myriad aspirations. In some places, this might mean a tarred, all-weather road or a bridge across a local river or stream. In many places, it means mobile towers and the Internet. Everywhere, people want education, jobs, access to healthcare and more money in their wallets to buy the shiny things that stare alluringly out of advertisements. Identity politics of every kind inevitably invokes nostalgia for tradition, but no party, leader or pressure group advocates going back to the traditional ways of life of the pre-modern world that existed well into the nineteenth century in many of these hills—the world before schools, offices, hospitals, roads, electricity, piped water, concrete houses with bathrooms and toilets, motor cars, mobile phones, the Internet … and money.

The force that animates both politics and society is money.

Within the sameness of the developmentalist paradigm in which nature has become 'natural resources', the internal politics across Northeast India now is animated by clashes for shares of the pie between groups that acquired their current political identities in the colonial period. The Hindu nationalists who rule India and Assam are now in ascendancy in the region, and a complicated accommodation is currently underway between the little nationalisms with their histories of separatism, and the big nationalism of Hindutva that seeks to integrate them all by swallowing them whole. Beneath these big political contests, underlying it all, is the force that in actual practice drives electoral politics at the ground level in every state of the region—hard cash. How it all plays out will arguably depend not so much on political ideologies of secularism, liberalism, Hindu nationalism or local linguistic and ethnic nationalisms, about which politicians and parties across the region have records of yogic flexibility, but on the system that has the most to offer in material terms: capitalism, the original force that, operating through a corporation called the East India Company, first brought the Northeast, kicking and screaming, into the political map of India.

NOTES

PREFACE

1. Stephanie Kramer, 'Religious Demography of Indian States and Territories', in Pew Research Centre, *Religious Composition of India*, 21 September 2021. https://www.pewresearch.org/religion/2021/09/21/religious-demography-of-indian-states-and-territories/

1. TEA, CHRISTIANITY AND MODERNITY

1. The Sanskrit shloka is 'Pragjyotishadhipah suro mlecchanamadhipo, Yavanaih sahito raja Bhagadatta maharathah', in the Sabha Parva of Mahabharata, cited in Dimbeswar Neog, *Introduction to Assam* (Bombay: Vora Publishers, 1947).
2. Suniti Kumar Chatterji, *Kirata-Jana-Krti* (1951; Calcutta: Asiatic Society, 1998).
3. Ibid.
4. E. A. Gait, *A History of Assam* (1906; Guwahati: EBH Publishers, 2008).
5. Suniti Kumar Chatterji, *The Origin and Development of the Bengali Language* (Calcutta: Calcutta University Press, 1926).
6. Gait, *A History of Assam*.
7. Worshippers who consider the god Vishnu the supreme deity.
8. Gait, *A History of Assam*.
9. S. K. Bhuyan, ed. and trans., *Tungkhungia Buranji, or A History of Assam, 1681–1826 A.D.* (London: Oxford University Press, 1933).
10. Peter Auber, *Rise and Progress of the British Power in India*, Vol. II (London: Wm. H. Allen & Co. and Calkin & Budd, Pall-Mall, 1837).
11. Gordon P. Means, *Tribal Transformation: The Early History of the Naga Hills*, ed. Achilla Imlong Erdican (New Delhi: Prestige Books International, 2013).
12. Auber, *Rise and Progress of the British Power in India*, Vol. II.
13. Ibid.

14. H. K. Barpujari, *Assam in the Days of the Company, 1826–1858* (Gauhati: Lawyer's Book Stall, 1963).
15. Ibid.
16. A. Burrell, 'Indian Tea Cultivation: Its Origin, Progress, and Prospects', *Journal of the Society of Arts* 25:1264 (9 February 1877).
17. W. Nassau Lees, *Tea Cultivation, Cotton, and Other Agricultural Experiments in India: A Review* (London: Thacker, Spink & Co., 1863).
18. *Asiatic Journal and Monthly Register for British and Foreign India, China, and Australasia* 30 (London: Wm. H. Allen & Co., September–December 1839).
19. Burrell, 'Indian Tea Cultivation'.
20. C. A. Bruce, *An Account of the Manufacture of the Black Tea as Now Practised at Suddeya in Upper Assam by the Chinamen Sent Thither for That Purpose. With Some Observations of the Culture of the Plant in China, and its Growth in Assam* (Calcutta: G. H. Huttmann, Bengal Military Orphan Press, 1838).
21. Ibid.
22. Ibid.
23. Barpujari, *Assam in the Days of the Company*.
24. Lees, *Tea Cultivation, Cotton, and Other Agricultural Experiments in India*.
25. Ibid.
26. Ibid.
27. E. W. Brown, *The Whole World Kin: A Pioneer Experience Among Remote Tribes, and Other Labors of Nathan Brown* (Philadelphia: Hubbard Brothers Publishers, 1890).
28. Ibid.
29. Ibid.
30. Ibid.
31. American Baptist Missionary Union, *The Baptist Missionary Magazine* 24:7 (July 1844).
32. N. Brown, *Grammatical Notices of the Asamese Language* (Sibsagor: American Baptist Mission Press, 1848).
33. A. J. M. Mills, *Report on the Province of Assam* (Calcutta: Thos. Jones, 'Calcutta Gazette' Office, 1854).
34. *Selections from the Records of the Bengal Government*, Published by Authority, No. 22 (Calcutta: Thos. Jones, 'Calcutta Gazette' Office, 1855).
35. Ibid.
36. William Robinson, *A Grammar of the Assamese Language* (Serampore: Serampore Press, 1839).
37. *Selections from the Records of the Bengal Government*, Published by Authority, No. 22.
38. Ibid.
39. Ibid.
40. H. K. Barpujari, S. K. Barpujari and A. C. Bhuyan, eds., *Political History of Assam*, Vol. I: *1826–1919* (Gauhati: Government of Assam, 1977).

41. Ibid.
42. Ibid.
43. Cecil Merne Putnam Cross, *The Development of Self-Government in India, 1858–1914* (Chicago: University of Chicago Press, 1922).
44. Barpujari, Barpujari and Bhuyan, eds., *Political History of Assam*, Vol. I.
45. *Report on the Administration of Bengal, 1872–73, With a Statistical Summary* (Calcutta: Bengal Secretariat Press, 1873).
46. J. B. Bhattacharjee, 'The First Partition of Bengal (1874)', *Proceedings of the Indian History Congress* 66 (2005–06), 1022–29. http://www.jstor.org/stable/44145915
47. Barpujari, Barpujari and Bhuyan, eds., *Political History of Assam*, Vol. I.
48. Sanjib Baruah, *India Against Itself: Assam and the Politics of Nationality* (Oxford: Oxford University Press, 2001).
49. For details, see ibid.

2. THE POLITICS OF REPRESENTATION

1. Sir Verney Lovett, *A History of the Indian Nationalist Movement* (London: Frank Cass & Co. Ltd, 1968).
2. Sanjib Baruah, *India Against Itself: Assam and the Politics of Nationality* (Oxford: Oxford University Press, 2001).
3. Large landowners were called zamindars.
4. H. K. Barpujari, S. K. Barpujari and A. C. Bhuyan, eds., *Political History of Assam*, Vol. I: *1826–1919* (Gauhati: Government of Assam, 1977).
5. *Report on the Administration of Bengal, 1872–73, With a Statistical Summary* (Calcutta: Bengal Secretariat Press, 1873).
6. E. A. Gait, *Census of India, 1891: Assam*, Vol. I: *Report* (Shillong: Assam Secretariat Printing Office, 1892).
7. J. McSwiney, *Census of India, 1911*, Vol III: *Assam*, Part I: *Report* (Shillong: Assam Secretariat Printing Office, 1912).
8. Ibid. The term 'coolie', the use of which is now deemed offensive, was and still is the word for a porter in Hindi and several other Indian languages.
9. Barpujari, Barpujari and Bhuyan, eds., *Political History of Assam*, Vol. I.
10. G. T. Lloyd, *Census of India, 1921*, Vol. III: *Assam*, Part I: *Report* (Shillong: Government Press Assam, 1923).
11. Ibid.
12. Ibid.
13. Ibid.
14. Sanjib Baruah, *India Against Itself: Assam and the Politics of Nationality* (Oxford: Oxford University Press, 2001).
15. C. S. Mullan, *Census of India, 1931*, Vol. III: *Assam*, Part I: *Report* (Shillong: Government of India Central Publication Branch, 1932).
16. Ibid.
17. Ibid.

18. See *Memorandum Submitted by the Government of Assam to the Indian Statutory Commission* (Indian Statutory Commission, Vol. XIV) (London: His Majesty's Stationery Office, 1930).
19. Ibid.
20. Ibid.
21. Ibid.
22. Penderel Moon, *Divide and Quit* (London: Chatto & Windus, 1961).
23. R. Coupland, *Indian Politics, 1936–42* (London: Oxford University Press, 1944).
24. Robert Reid, *Years of Change in Bengal and Assam* (London: Ernest Benn Ltd, 1966).
25. Amalendu Guha, *Planter-Raj to Swaraj: Freedom Struggle and Electoral Politics in Assam, 1826–1947* (New Delhi: Indian Council of Historical Research, 1977).
26. Ibid.
27. V. P. Menon, *The Transfer of Power in India* (Princeton: Princeton University Press, 1957).
28. S. K. Sharma and Usha Sharma, eds., *Documents on North East India: An Exhaustive Survey*, Vol. IV: *Assam (1936–1957)* (Delhi: Mittal Publications, 2006).
29. Ibid.
30. Letter from M. A. Jinnah to Lord Wavell, 8 June 1946, reproduced in Anil Chandra Banerjee, *The Making of the Indian Constitution, 1939–1947* (Calcutta: A. Mukherjee & Co., 1948).
31. Details in 'Extracts from Proceedings of All-India Congress Committee, Bombay, 6–7 July 1946', reproduced in Banerjee, *The Making of the Indian Constitution*.
32. 'Gandhi Stops British Plan; Riots Kill 5', *The Washington Post*, 26 June 1946.
33. Extracts from Pandit Nehru's Statement at Press Conference, Bombay, 10 July 1946, reproduced in Banerjee, *The Making of the Indian Constitution*.
34. Ibid.
35. Ibid.
36. Maulana Abul Kalam Azad, *India Wins Freedom* (1958; Hyderabad: Orient Blackswan, 1988).
37. Sharma and Sharma, eds., *Documents on North-East India*, Vol. IV.
38. Satish C. Kakati, 'The Man Who Saved India from Disaster', reproduced in *Lokpriya Gopinath Bordoloi: An Architect of Modern India*, ed. Lily Mazinder Baruah (New Delhi: Gyan Publishing House, 1992).
39. Ibid.
40. From C. H. Philips and M. D. Wainwright, eds., *The Partition of India: Policies and Perspectives, 1935–1947* (London: Allen & Unwin, 1970), cited in Rajmohan Gandhi, *India After 1947: Reflections and Recollections* (New Delhi: Aleph Book Co., 2022).
41. Moon, *Divide and Quit*.

42. Details can be found in Gary J. Bass, *The Blood Telegram: Nixon, Kissinger, and a Forgotten Genocide* (New York: Alfred A. Knopf, 2013).
43. Seymour M. Hersh, *The Price of Power: Kissinger in the Nixon White House* (New York: Summit Books, 1983).
44. Details in Ramachandra Guha, *India After Gandhi: The History of the World's Largest Democracy* (Delhi: Picador India, 2007).
45. Sangeeta Barooah Pisharoty, *Assam: The Accord, the Discord* (Gurgaon: Penguin Random House India, 2019).
46. Ibid.
47. Ibid.
48. Ibid.
49. 'Problem of Foreigners in Assam: Memorandum of Settlement' (1985). https://assamaccord.assam.gov.in/portlets/assam-accord-and-its-clauses
50. Hiren Gohain, 'Chronicles of Violence and Terror: Rise of United Liberation Front of Asom', *Economic and Political Weekly* 42:12 (2007), 1012–18. http://www.jstor.org/stable/4419382
51. Ibid.
52. Ibid.
53. Details in Samrat Choudhury, *The Braided River: A Journey Along the Brahmaputra* (Haryana: HarperCollins India, 2021).
54. Ibid.
55. Special Correspondent, 'Assam NRC Final List: Students' Body AASU to Challenge NRC Findings in SC', *The Hindu*, 31 August 2019. A lakh means 100,000 and is the term commonly used in South Asia: 19 lakh is 1.9 million.

3. THE NAGA REBELLION

1. Difficult Decolonization: Debates, Divisions, and Deaths Within the Naga Uprising, 1944–1963, Jelle J.P. Wouters, *Journal of North East India Studies*, Vol. 9(1), Jan.–Jun. 2019.
2. Christoph von Fürer-Haimendorf, *The Naked Nagas: Head-Hunters of Assam in Peace and War*, revised ed. (1946; London: Spectrum Publications, 2004).
3. Details in ibid.
4. Hokishe Sema, *Emergence of Nagaland: Socio-Economic and Political Transformation and the Future* (New Delhi: Vikas Publishing House Pvt Ltd, 1986).
5. Ibid.
6. Charles Chasie, 'Nagaland', in *Sub-Regional Relations in the Eastern South Asia: With Special Focus on India's North Eastern Region*, ed. Mayumi Murayama, Kyoko Inoue and Sanjoy Hazarika (Chiba: Institute of Developing Economies, Japan External Trade Organization, 2005).
7. Details in Marion Wettstein, 'Origin and Migration Myths in the Rhetoric of Naga Independence and Collective Identity', in *Origins and Migrations in the*

Extended Eastern Himalayas, ed. Toni Huber and Stuart Blackburn (Leiden: Brill, 2012).

8. Ibid.
9. Details in E. A. Gait, *A History of Assam* (1906; Guwahati: EBH Publishers, 2008).
10. Sanjib Baruah, *India Against Itself: Assam and the Politics of Nationality* (Oxford: Oxford University Press, 2001).
11. Details in Saroj Nalini Arambam Parratt, *The Court Chronicle of the Kings of Manipur: The Cheitharon Kumpapa* (London and New Delhi: Routledge, 2005).
12. Wettstein, 'Origin and Migration Myths'.
13. W. Robinson, 'Descriptive Account of Assam' (1841), reprinted in *India's North-East Frontier in the Nineteenth Century*, ed. Verrier Elwin (New Delhi: Gyan Books, 2019).
14. Chasie, 'Nagaland'.
15. Alexander Mackenzie, *The North-East Frontier of India* (Delhi: Mittal Publications, 1979). Originally published as *History of the Relations of the Government with the Hill Tribes of the North-East Frontier of Bengal* in 1884.
16. Ibid.
17. Ibid.
18. Gordon P. Means, *Tribal Transformation: The Early History of the Naga Hills*, ed. Achilla Imlong Erdican (New Delhi: Prestige Books International, 2013).
19. Ibid.
20. Ibid.
21. C. U. Aitchison, *A Collection of Treaties, Engagements and Sanads Relating to India and Neighbouring Countries*, Vol. XII: *The Treaties, &c, Relating to Jammu and Kashmir, Sikkim, Assam and Burma*, revised ed. (Calcutta: Government of India Central Publication Branch, 1931).
22. For more on this, see Means, *Tribal Transformation*.
23. Ibid.
24. Ibid.
25. Major-General Sir James Johnstone, *My Experiences in Manipur and the Naga Hills* (London: Sampson Low, Marston & Co., 1896).
26. Means, *Tribal Transformation*.
27. Mackenzie, *The North-East Frontier of India*.
28. Means, *Tribal Transformation*.
29. Mary Mead Clark, *A Corner in India* (Philadelphia: American Baptist Publication Society, 1907).
30. Details in ibid.
31. Ibid.
32. Ibid.
33. Quoted in Robert Reid, *History of the Frontier Areas Bordering on Assam from 1883–1941* (1942; Guwahati: Bhabani Books, 2013).

34. Quoted in ibid.
35. Ibid.
36. Thepfulhouvi Solo, 'Corrected Story of Naga Club and Simon Commission Petition', *The Morung Express*, 6 July 2017.
37. Ibid.
38. Ibid.
39. Ibid.
40. Ibid.
41. Details of this are in Chapter 4 of this volume, on Manipur.
42. [G. N. Bordoloi], *Constituent Assembly of India: North-East Frontier (Assam) Tribal and Excluded Areas Sub-Committee*, Vol. I: *(Report)* (New Delhi: Government of India Press, 1947).
43. Ibid.
44. Durga Das, ed., *Sardar Patel's Correspondence*, Vol. V: *1945–50* (Ahmedabad: Navajivan Publishing House, 1973).
45. Nirmal Nibedon, *Nagaland: The Night of the Guerrillas* (Delhi: Lancer, 1978).
46. Nari K. Rustomji, *Enchanted Frontiers: Sikkim, Bhutan and India's North-Eastern Borderlands* (Oxford: Oxford University Press, 1971).
47. File No. 78-GG/79, Office of the Secretary to the Governor General, Government of India, 1949, National Archives of India.
48. Ibid.
49. Nandita Haksar and Sebastian M. Hongray, *Kuknalim: Naga Armed Resistance: Testimonies of Leaders, Pastors, Healers and Soldiers* (New Delhi: Speaking Tiger, 2019).
50. Hokishe Sema, *Emergence of Nagaland: Socio-Economic and Political Transformation and the Future* (New Delhi: Vikas Publishing House Pvt Ltd, 1986).
51. Haksar and Hongray, *Kuknalim: Naga Armed Resistance*.
52. Robert Trumbull, 'Booing Tribesmen Walk Out on Nehru; Naga Headhunters Quit Rally in Bid for Independence—Burma Chief Sees Snub', *The New York Times*, 31 March 1953.
53. Haksar and Hongray, *Kuknalim: Naga Armed Resistance*.
54. Charles Chasie and Sanjoy Hazarika, *The State Strikes Back: India and the Naga Insurgency* (Washington: East-West Center, 2009).
55. 'The Assam Maintenance of Public Order (Autonomous Districts) Act, 1953', *Assam Gazette*, 3 June 1953.
56. Haksar and Hongray, *Kuknalim: Naga Armed Resistance*.
57. Ihezhe Zhimomi, 'The Beginning of the Indo-Naga War', *Nagaland Post*, 21 August 2019.
58. Ibid.
59. Ibid.
60. Jawaharlal Nehru, Statement Re. North-East Frontier Agency, *Parliamentary Debates: House of the People, Official Report*, 18 August 1955 (New Delhi: Parliament Secretariat).

61. Ram Narayan Kumar and Laxmi Murthy, *Four Years of the Ceasefire Agreement Between the Government of India and the National Socialist Council of Nagalim: Promises and Pitfalls* (New Delhi: Other Media Communications, 2002).
62. Lt General H. S. Panag, 'The Turning Point in Naga Insurgency', *The Times of India*, 15 September 2018.
63. Motion Re. Situation in Naga Hills, in *Lok Sabha Debates*, Vol. VI: *1956 (13th August to 8th September)*, Thirteenth Session (New Delhi: Lok Sabha Secretariat), No. 27, 23 August 1956.
64. Ibid.
65. Ibid.
66. Ibid.
67. Ibid.
68. Ibid.
69. Ibid.
70. Ibid.
71. Haksar and Hongray, *Kuknalim: Naga Armed Resistance*.
72. The Armed Forces (Special Powers) Act, 1958. https://legislative.gov.in/actsofparliamentfromtheyear/armed-forces-special-powers-act-1958
73. Ibid.
74. Armed Forces (Assam and Manipur) Special Powers Bill, in *Lok Sabha Debates*, Vol. XVII, Fifth Session (New Delhi: Lok Sabha Secretariat), No. 6, Monday, 18 August 1958.
75. Ibid.
76. Ibid.
77. Ibid.
78. Ibid.
79. Ibid.
80. Ibid.
81. The 16 Point Agreement between the Government of India and the Naga People's Convention, 26 July 1960. https://peacemaker.un.org/files/IN_600726_The%20sixteen%20point%20Agreement_0.pdf
82. Letter dated 7 February 1962 from K. L. Mehta, M.E.A. to A. S. Mehta, Consul-General of India in Geneva, File No. CG/133/61, Ministry of External Affairs, National Archives of India.
83. Constitution (Thirteenth Amendment) Bill and State of Nagaland Bill, in *Lok Sabha Debates*, Third Series, Vol. VII: *1962*, Second Session (New Delhi: Lok Sabha Secretariat), No. 17, 28 August 1962.
84. Ibid.
85. Ibid.
86. Sema, *Emergence of Nagaland*.
87. Haksar and Hongray, *Kuknalim: Naga Armed Resistance*.
88. Ibid.
89. Ibid.

4. MANIPUR'S PRINCES AND REBELS

1. R. K. Jhalajit Singh, *A Short History of Manipur*, 2nd ed. (Imphal: R. K. Jhalajit Singh, 1992).
2. Ibid.
3. Saroj Nalini Arambam Parratt, *The Court Chronicle of the Kings of Manipur: The Cheitharon Kumpapa* (London and New Delhi: Routledge, 2005).
4. Singh, *A Short History of Manipur*.
5. Parratt, *The Court Chronicle of the Kings of Manipur*.
6. Ibid.
7. This is mentioned in Parratt, *The Court Chronicle of the Kings of Manipur*.
8. Captain R. Boileau Pemberton, *Report on the Eastern Frontier of British India* (Calcutta: Government of India, 1835).
9. Parratt, *The Court Chronicle of the Kings of Manipur*.
10. Ibid.
11. Ibid.
12. Ibid.
13. Pemberton, *Report on the Eastern Frontier of British India*.
14. Saroj Nalini Parratt, *The Religion of Manipur: Beliefs, Rituals and Historical Development* (Calcutta: Firma KLM Pvt Ltd, 1980).
15. Pemberton, *Report on the Eastern Frontier of British India*.
16. Ibid.
17. Ibid.
18. G. E. Harvey, *History of Burma* (London: Longmans, Green & Co., 1925).
19. Pemberton, *Report on the Eastern Frontier of British India*.
20. Harvey, *History of Burma*.
21. C. U. Aitchison, *A Collection of Treaties, Engagements and Sanads Relating to India and Neighbouring Countries*, Vol. II: *The Treaties, &c, Relating to Burma, Nepal, Eastern Bengal and Assam, Bhutan, Sikkim, Tibet, Siam and the Eastern Archipelago* (Calcutta: Superintendent Government Printing India, 1909).
22. Details in M. McCulloch, *Valley of Manipur* (Delhi: Gian Publications, 1980).
23. Major-General Sir James Johnstone, *My Experiences in Manipur and the Naga Hills* (London: Sampson Low, Marston & Co., 1896).
24. Aitchison, *A Collection of Treaties, Engagements and Sanads*, Vol. II.
25. An eyewitness account can be found in Ethel St Clair Grimwood, *My Three Years in Manipur and Escape from the Recent Mutiny* (London: Richard Bentley & Son, 1892).
26. Aitchison, *A Collection of Treaties, Engagements and Sanads*, Vol. II.
27. Copies of all the relevant documents can be found in Manipur: *Treaties and Documents (1110–1971) (Volume One)*, edited by Naorem Sanajaoba (Delhi: Mittal Publications, 1993)
28. Ibid.
29. *Annual Report on the Native States and Frontier Tribes of Assam, for the Year 1897–98* (Shillong: Assam Secretariat Printing Office [n.d.]).

30. Ibid.
31. Lieut. Col. H. St P. Maxwell, *Administration Report of the Political Agency, Manipur, for the Year 1903–1904* (Shillong: Assam Secretariat Printing Office, 1904).
32. Major J. Shakespear, *Administration Report of the Political Agency, Manipur, for the Year 1904–05* (Shillong: Assam Secretariat Printing Press, 1905).
33. Khomdon Singh Lisam, *Encyclopedia of Manipur*, Vol. II (Delhi: Kalpaz Publications, 2011)
34. Singh, *A Short History of Manipur*.
35. J. C. Higgins, *Administration Report of the Manipur State for the Year 1911–1912* (Shillong: Assam Secretariat Printing Press, 1912).
36. Colonel L. W. Shakespear, *History of the Assam Rifles* (London: Macmillan & Co., 1929).
37. Ibid.
38. Jangkhomang Guite, '"Fighting the White Men Until the Last Bullet": The General Course of the Anglo-Kuki War', in *The Anglo-Kuki War, 1917–1919*, ed. Jangkhomang Guite and Thongkholal Haokip (London: Routledge India, 2018).
39. Ibid.
40. L. W. Shakespear, *History of the Assam Rifles*.
41. Guite, 'Fighting the White Men Until the Last Bullet'.
42. Ibid.
43. Ursula Graham Bower, *Naga Path* (London: John Murray, 1950).
44. Ibid.
45. Ibid.
46. Saroj N. Arambam Parratt and J. Parratt, 'The Second "Women's War" and the Emergence of Democratic Government in Manipur', *Modern Asian Studies* 35:4 (2001), 905–19. http://www.jstor.org/stable/313195
47. N. Bisheswar, *The Last Expression on My Death Bed* (Imphal: Pax Publications, 1986).
48. *Administration Report of the Manipur State for the Year 1937–38* (Imphal: State Printing Press, 1942).
49. John Parratt and Saroj Arambam Parratt, 'Hijam Irabot and the Radical Socialist Democratic Movement in Manipur', *Internationales Asienforum* 31:3–4 (2000). https://doi.org/10.11588/iaf.2000.31.988
50. Ibid.
51. Sanamani Yambem, 'Nupi Lan: Manipur Women's Agitation, 1939', *Economic and Political Weekly* 11:8 (1976), 325–31. http://www.jstor.org/stable/4364388
52. Ibid.
53. MSA Civil Case of 1940, cited in J. Parratt and S. A. Parratt, 'Hijam Irabot'.
54. Parratt and Parratt, 'Hijam Irabot'.
55. E. F. Lydall, *Administration Report of the Manipur State for the Year 1943–44* (Imphal: State Printing Press, 1945).

56. Ibid.
57. Ibid. This converts to a rise from a monthly average of Rs. 300,000 to Rs. 3–4 million a month.
58. Recounted in Singh, *A Short History of Manipur*.
59. Ibid.
60. Capt. M. K. Priyabrata Singh, *Administrative Report of the Manipur State for the Year 1946–47* (Imphal: State Printing Press, 1948).
61. Parratt and Parratt, *Hijam Irabot*.
62. Sajal Nag, *India and North-East India: Mind, Politics and the Process of Integration, 1946–1950* (New Delhi: Regency Publications, 1998).
63. Ibid.
64. Manipur Merger Agreement, 21 September 1949, available at United Nations Human Rights Office of the High Commissioner. https://www.ohchr.org/sites/default/files/lib-docs/HRBodies/UPR/Documents/Session1/IN/COHR_IND_UPR_S1_2008anx_Annex_V_ManipurMergerAgreement.pdf
65. For more on this see Wounded Land: Politics and Identity in Modern Manipur, John Parratt, Mittal Publications, New Delhi, 2005)
66. Parratt and Parratt, *Hijam Irabot*.
67. Ibid.
68. Manipur Territorial Congress Committee, 'Memorandum Submitted to Smt. Indira Gandhi, Prime Minister of India, and Shri S. Nijalingappa, President, A.I.C.C.', in *Case of Manipur: Manipur Demands Statehood* (Imphal: Manipur Territorial Congress Committee, 1968).
69. John Parratt, *Wounded Land: Politics and Identity in Modern Manipur* (New Delhi: Mittal Publications, 2005).
70. *Statistical Report on the General Election, 1972 to the Legislative Assembly of Tripura* (New Delhi: Election Commission of India).
71. *Statistical Report on the General Election, 1974 to the Legislative Assembly of Tripura* (New Delhi: Election Commission of India).

5. TRIPURA'S SLOW JOURNEY TO THE PERIPHERY

1. Census of India, 2011. https://www.census2011.co.in/
2. Deepayan Chakraborty, 'Situating the Historical Chronicles of Tripura in Traditional Indian Historiography', *Karatoya: North Bengal University Journal of History* 10 (March 2017).
3. Dr N. C. Nath, trans., *Sri Rajmala, Vol. I to IV* (Agartala: Tribal Research and Cultural Institute, Government of Tripura, 1999).
4. Suniti Kumar Chatterji, *Kirata-Jana-Krti: The Indo-Mongoloids: Their Contribution to the History and Culture of India* (Calcutta: Asiatic Society, 1951).
5. Nath, trans., *Sri Rajmala*.

6. Alexander Mackenzie, *The North-East Frontier of India* (Delhi: Mittal Publications, 1979). Originally published as *History of the Relations of the Government with the Hill Tribes of the North-East Frontier of Bengal* in 1884.
7. Nath, trans., *Sri Rajmala.*
8. Certain accounts assert that Ratna Manikya was the son of Dharma Manikya, and the first king of the dynasty was Maha Manikya. See, e.g., Nalini Ranjan Roy Chaudhuri, 'The Historical Past', in *Tripura: The Land and Its People*, ed. Jagadis Gan-Chaudhuri (Delhi: Leeladevi Publications, 1980).
9. Nitish Sengupta, *Land of Two Rivers: A History of Bengal from the Mahabharata to Mujib* (London: Penguin Books, 2011).
10. Details in Nath, trans., *Sri Rajmala.*
11. Details in Jacques Leider, 'On Arakanese Territorial Expansion: Origins, Context, Means and Practice', in *The Maritime Frontier of Burma*, ed. Jos Gommans and Jacques Leider (Leiden: KITLV Press, 2002).
12. Details in Nath, trans., *Sri Rajmala.*
13. Rev. James Long, *Analysis of the Rajmala or Chronicles of Tripura* [*Journal of the Asiatic Society of Bengal* (1850)] (Agartala: Tribal Research and Cultural Institute, Government of Tripura, 2008).
14. Ibid.
15. Mackenzie, *The North-East Frontier of India.*
16. Ibid.
17. Nath, trans., *Sri Rajmala.*
18. See William Foster, ed., *Early Travels in India: 1583–1619* (London: Oxford University Press, 1921).
19. You can hear more about this on the Empire podcast by William Dalrymple and Anita Anand.
20. Nick Robins, *The Corporation that Changed the World* (London: Pluto Press, 2012).
21. J. E. Webster, *East Bengal District Gazetteers: Tippera* (Allahabad: Pioneer Press, 1910).
22. Mackenzie, *The North-East Frontier of India.*
23. Ibid.
24. Ibid.
25. Ibid.
26. Ibid.
27. K. D. Menon, ed., *Tripura District Gazetteers: Tripura* (Agartala: Department of Education, 1975).]
28. Ibid.
29. C. U. Aitchison, *A Collection of Treaties, Engagements and Sanads Relating to India and Neighbouring Countries*, Vol. II: *The Treaties, &c, Relating to Burma, Nepal, Eastern Bengal and Assam, Bhutan, Sikkim, Tibet, Siam and the Eastern Archipelago* (Calcutta: Superintendent Government Printing India, 1909).
30. Menon, ed., *Tripura Gazetteer.*

31. Aitchison, *A Collection of Treaties, Engagements and Sanads*, Vol. II.
32. Satyaranjan Bose, *Tripurar Biplobider Smriti*, cited in Menon, ed., *Tripura Gazetteer.*
33. The state was called Hill Tippera until 1920, when at the request of the maharaja the name was changed to Hill Tripura.
34. From Anindita Ghoshal, 'Tripura: A Chronicle of Politicisation of the Refugees and Ethnic Tribals', *Development and Change* 14:2 (July 2017).
35. *Tripura State Consolidated Administration Report for 1350, 1351 and 1352 T.E. (1940–1943 AD)* (Agartala: Political Department, 1943).
36. Ibid.
37. Ibid.
38. Ghoshal, 'Tripura'.
39. Ibid.
40. B. Ghosh, 'Religion and Politics in Bengal: The Noakhali Carnage, 1946–47', *Proceedings of the Indian History Congress* 72 (2011), 936–946. http://www.jstor.org/stable/44146785
41. Letter from His Highness Maharaja Manikya Sir Bir Bikram Kishore Deb Barman Bahadur. K.C.S.I, Maharaja of Tripura, to the Agent to the Governor General, Eastern States, Ranchi, dated the 29th March 1937, on the subject of the accession of Tripura State to the Federation of India (Tripura State Press).
42. Ibid.
43. Ibid.
44. Instrument of Accession, 1947. Available at https://www.satp.org/document/paper-acts-and-oridinances/instrument-of-accession-1947
45. A. E. Porter, *Census of India, 1931*, Vol. V: *Bengal States and Sikkim* (Calcutta: Central Publications Branch).
46. Ibid.
47. Ibid.
48. Menon, ed., *Tripura Gazetteer.*
49. See 'Lone Hindu Quits Pakistan Cabinet; Mandal, Law Minister, Said to Protest Policy Directed at his Co-religionists', *The New York Times*, 9 October 1950.
50. Menon, ed., *Tripura Gazetteer.*
51. Sam Dalrymple, 'Gedu Mian and the Partition of Tripura', *Partition Studies Quarterly* 5 (Jan. 2022).
52. Ibid.
53. Ibid.
54. B. Ghosh, 'Ethnicity and Insurgency in Tripura', *Sociological Bulletin*, 52:2 (2003), 221–243. http://www.jstor.org/stable/23620336
55. Report of the Assistant Central Intelligence Officer, Tripura State, to the Joint Secretary, Rehabilitation Department, Government of India. File No. 20-R/50 II (Secret), Rehabilitation Branch, Ministry of States, NAI, cited in Ghoshal, 'Tripura'.
56. Ghoshal, 'Tripura'.

57. House of the People, Committee of Privileges (The Dasaratha Deb Case) (New Delhi: Parliament Secretariat, July 1952).
58. A drone is a unit of land used in Tripura. One drone is about 6.4 acres.
59. Parakinkar Chakma vs State of Tripura, 16 December 1954, Gauhati High Court.
60. Mahadev Chakravarti, 'Reorganization Question of Tripura (1949–62): Reactions of Different Political Parties', in *Reorganization of North-East India Since 1947*, ed. B. Datta Ray and S. P. Agrawal (New Delhi: Concept Publishing, 1996).
61. Ibid.
62. Ibid.
63. *Annual Administration Report for 1959–60* (Agartala: Government of Tripura).
64. Chakravarti, 'Reorganization Question of Tripura (1949–62)'.
65. Ibid.
66. Jagadis Gan-Chaudhuri, 'Tripuri Political Consciousness', in *Tripura: The Land and Its People*, ed. Gan-Chaudhuri (Delhi: Leeladevi Publications, 1980).
67. See ibid.
68. Subir Bhaumik, 'Tripura: Ethnic Conflict, Militancy and Counterinsurgency', *Policies and Practices* 52 (Mahanirban Calcutta Research Group, 2012).
69. *Statistical Report on the General Election, 1972 to the Legislative Assembly of Tripura*, Election Commission of India.
70. Details in Gan-Chaudhuri, 'Tripuri Political Consciousness'.
71. 'Statistical Report on the General Election, 1977 to the Legislative Assembly of Tripura', Election Commission of India.
72. Bhaumik, 'Tripura: Ethnic Conflict, Militancy and Insurgency'.
73. Recounted in Manas Paul, *The Eyewitness: Tales from Tripura's Ethnic Conflict* (New Delhi: Lancer, 2009).
74. Ibid.
75. Ibid.
76. Subir Bhaumik, *Insurgent Crossfire: North-East India* (Delhi: Lancer Publishers, 2008)
77. Ibid.

6. MIZORAM'S CENTURY OF TRANSFORMATION

1. Lal Pudaite 'Mizoram', in *Sub-Regional Relations in the Eastern South Asia: With Special Focus on India's North Eastern Region*, ed. Mayumi Murayama, Kyoko Inoue and Sanjoy Hazarika (Chiba: Institute of Developing Economies, 2005).
2. B. Lalthangliana, *Culture and Folklore of Mizoram* (New Delhi: Publications Division, Ministry of Information and Broadcasting, Government of India, 2005).
3. Ibid.
4. Ibid.

5. Ibid.
6. Alexander Mackenzie, *The North-East Frontier of India* (Delhi: Mittal Publications, 1979). Originally published as *History of the Relations of the Government with the Hill Tribes of the North-East Frontier of Bengal* in 1884.
7. Maj. Anthony Gilchrist McCall, *Lushai Chrysalis* (London: Luzac & Co., 1949).
8. Mackenzie, *The North-East Frontier of India*.
9. Ibid.
10. Ibid.
11. George Abraham Grierson, *Linguistic Survey of India*, Vol. III, Part III (Calcutta: Government of India, 1904).
12. Mackenzie, *The North-East Frontier of India*.
13. C. U. Aitchison, *A Collection of Treaties, Engagements and Sanads Relating to India and Neighbouring Countries*, Vol II: *The Treaties, &c, Relating to Burma, Nepal, Eastern Bengal and Assam, Bhutan, Sikkim, Tibet, Siam and the Eastern Archipelago* (Calcutta: Superintendent Government Printing India, 1909).
14. Mackenzie, *The North-East Frontier of India*.
15. R. G. Woodthorpe, *The Lushai Expedition, 1871–1872* (London: Hurst & Blackett, 1873).
16. Ibid.
17. McCall, *Lushai Chrysalis*.
18. Mackenzie, *The North-East Frontier of India*.
19. Robert Reid, *History of the Frontier Areas Bordering on Assam from 1883–1941* (1942; Guwahati: Bhabani Books, 2013).
20. Ibid.
21. Ibid.
22. Ibid.
23. A. Scott Reid, *Chin-Lushai Land* (Calcutta: Thacker, Spink & Co., 1893).
24. McCall, *Lushai Chrysalis*.
25. See ibid.
26. Reid, *History of the Frontier Areas Bordering on Assam*.
27. Rev. J. Meirion Lloyd, *On Every High Hill* (Liverpool: Foreign Mission Office, 1952).
28. Ibid.
29. Grace R. Lewis, *The Lushai Hills: A Story of the Lushai Pioneer Mission* (London: Baptist Missionary Society, 1907).
30. Ibid.
31. Ibid.
32. Ibid.
33. J. V. Hluna, *Church and Political Upheaval in Mizoram: A Study of Impact of Christianity on the Political Development in Mizoram* (Aizawl: Mizo History Association, 1985).
34. Rev. W. Williams, 'A Visit to the Lushai Hills', *The Monthly Tidings* (August 1891).

35. McCall, *Lushai Chrysalis*.
36. Ibid.
37. Ibid.
38. Baptist Missionary Society Report for 1918, cited in J. Zorema, *Indirect Rule in Mizoram, 1890–1954* (New Delhi: Mittal Publications, 2007).
39. Lalhmuaka, *Zoram History (1800–1950)* (1992), cited in Zorema, *Indirect Rule in Mizoram*.
40. Zorema, *Indirect Rule in Mizoram*.
41. The whole territory of Lushai Hills district was divided into sixteen circles with one circle officer and one interpreter posted in each circle.
42. Zorema, *Indirect Rule in Mizoram*.
43. N. E. Parry, 'Extract from a Note…dated 3rd March 1928', in *Memorandum Submitted by the Government of Assam to the Indian Statutory Commission* (Indian Statutory Commission, Vol. XIV) (London: His Majesty's Stationery Office, 1930).
44. Ibid.
45. Ibid.
46. Ibid.
47. J. J. M. Nichols-Roy, 'Note on the Khasi and Jaintia Hills', in *Memorandum Submitted by the Government of Assam to the Indian Statutory Commission* (Indian Statutory Commission, Vol. XIV) (London: His Majesty's Stationery Office, 1930).
48. Zorema, *Indirect Rule in Mizoram*.
49. Ibid.
50. McCall, *Lushai Chrysalis*.
51. Ibid.
52. Robert Reid, 'The Excluded Areas of Assam', *The Geographical Journal* 103:1–2 (1944), 18–29. https://doi.org/10.2307/1789063
53. R. Coupland, *The Future of India: Report on the Constitutional Problem in India* (Oxford: Oxford University Press, 1943).
54. D. R. Syiemlieh, 'The Crown Colony Plans: The British and the Hill Areas of North-East India, 1945–46', *Proceedings of the Indian History Congress* 59 (1998), 691–8. http://www.jstor.org/stable/44147039
55. Ibid.
56. 'Provincial Elections (1945–46) Assam Legislative Assembly: Analysis and Full Results' (Government of India Information Services, 1946).
57. Animesh Ray, *Mizoram* (New Delhi: National Book Trust India, 1993).
58. Zorema, *Indirect Rule in Mizoram*.
59. Ibid.
60. Ibid.
61. [G. N. Bordoloi], *Constituent Assembly of India: North-East Frontier (Assam) Tribal and Excluded Areas Sub-Committee*, Vol. I: *(Report)* (New Delhi: Government of India Press, 1947).
62. Ibid.

63. Ibid.
64. See C. Chawngkunga, *Important Documents of Mizoram* (Aizawl: Art & Culture Department, Government of Mizoram, 1998).
65. S. K. Chaube, *Hill Politics in Northeast India* (1968; Hyderabad: Orient Blackswan, 2012).
66. Zorema, *Indirect Rule in Mizoram*.
67. Ibid.
68. Ray, *Mizoram*.
69. Zorema, *Indirect Rule in Mizoram*.
70. Lalthaw Venga v. Lushai Hills District Council and Anr., High Court of Gauhati, Civil Rule No. 61 of 1954.
71. Ray, *Mizoram*.
72. Benjamin Ralte, 'The Formation and Role of Eastern India Tribal Union in Hill Politics of North East India', in *Politics of Regionalism in North-East India*, ed. Malsawmliana and Lalsangzela Pachuau (Delhi: Mittal Publications, 2015).
73. See Chaube, *Hill Politics in Northeast India*.
74. Malsawmliana, 'From Greater Autonomy to the Hill State With Reference to Mizoram', in *Politics of Regionalism in North-East India*, ed. Malsawmliana and Lalsangzela Pachuau (Delhi: Mittal Publications, 2015).
75. Subir Bhaumik, *Insurgencies in India's Northeast: Conflict, Co-option and Change* (Washington: East-West Center, 2007).
76. N. Sundar, 'Interning Insurgent Populations: The Buried Histories of Indian Democracy', *Economic and Political Weekly* 46:6 (2011), 47–57. http://www.jstor.org/stable/27918119
77. Bhaumik, *Insurgencies in India's Northeast*.
78. Sudipta Bhattacharjee, 'We Orchestrated Daring Escapes from Indian Custody, Including One from IB Headquarters in James Bond Style', *The Telegraph*, 27 June 2021.
79. Ray, *Mizoram*.
80. Ibid.
81. Ibid.
82. Ibid.
83. Bhattacharjee, 'We Orchestrated Daring Escapes from Indian Custody'.
84. Subir Bhaumik, *Insurgent Crossfire: North-East India* (Delhi: Lancer Publishers, 2008)
85. Ray, *Mizoram*.
86. Ibid.
87. S. Venkatnarayan, 'Laldenga's Visit Signals Hope for Troubled Union Territory of Mizoram', *India Today*, 31 October 1984.
88. Ray, *Mizoram*.
89. Ibid.
90. Ramesh Menon, 'Mizoram Comes Under President's Rule', *India Today*, 30 September 1988.

7. MEGHALAYA

1. C. U. Aitchison, *A Collection of Treaties, Engagements and Sanads Relating to India and Neighbouring Countries*, Vol. XII: *The Treaties, &c, Relating to Jammu and Kashmir, Sikkim, Assam and Burma*, revised ed. (Calcutta: Government of India Central Publication Branch, 1931).
2. There is one other Mon Khmer language in India, spoken by some tribes of the Nicobar Islands.
3. Lt Col P. R. T. Gurdon, *The Khasis* (London: Macmillan & Co., 1914).
4. Hamlet Bareh, *Meghalaya* (Shillong: North-East India News & Feature Service, 1974).
5. Marco Mitri and Dhiraj Neog, 'Preliminary Report on the Excavation of Neolithic Sites from Khasi Hills Meghalaya', *Ancient Asia: Journal of the Society of South Asian Archaeology* 7 (2016). http://doi.org/10.5334/aa.119
6. Hamlet Bareh, 'The History and Culture of the Khasi People', published PhD thesis, University of Gauhati, 1964.
7. Ibid.
8. E. A. Gait, *A History of Assam* (1906; Guwahati: EBH Publishers, 2008).
9. Ibid.
10. Lt Col P. R. T. Gurdon, *The Khasis*, with an introduction by Sir Charles Lyall (London: Macmillan & Co., 1914).
11. Gunnel Cederlöf, *Founding an Empire on India's North-Eastern Frontiers, 1790–1840: Climate, Commerce, Polity* (Oxford: Oxford University Press, 2013).
12. Captain R. Boileau Pemberton, *Report on the Eastern Frontier of British India* (Calcutta: Baptist Mission Press, 1835).
13. Robert Lindsay, 'Anecdotes of an Indian Life', in *Lives of the Lindsays; or, A Memoir of the Houses of Crawford and Balcarres*, Vol. IV (Wigan: C. S. Simms, 1840).
14. Ibid.
15. Cederlöf, *Founding an Empire on India's North-Eastern Frontiers*.
16. David Ludden, 'The First Boundary of Bangladesh on Sylhet's Northern Frontiers', *Journal of the Asiatic Society of Bangladesh* 48:1 (June 2003).
17. John Eliot, 'Observations of the Inhabitants of the Garrow Hills Made During a Public Deputation in the Years 1788 and 1789', *Asiatick Researches* 3 (1794).
18. Milton S. Sangma, *History and Culture of the Garos* (New Delhi: Books Today, 1981).
19. Ibid.
20. Aitchison, *A Collection of Treaties, Engagements and Sanads*, Vol. XII.
21. Pemberton, *Report on the Eastern Frontier of British India*.
22. Aitchison, *A Collection of Treaties, Engagements and Sanads*, Vol. XII.
23. Pemberton, *Report on the Eastern Frontier of British India*.
24. Major A. White, ed., *Memoir of the Late David Scott* (Calcutta: Baptist Mission Press, 1832).
25. Ibid.

26. C. U. Aitchison, *A Collection of Treaties, Engagements, and Sunnuds Relating to India and Neighbouring Countries*, Vol. I: *The Treaties &c., Relating to Bengal, Assam, Burmah, and the Eastern Archipelago*, revised by Lieutenant A. C. Talbot (Calcutta: Foreign Office Press, 1876).
27. Bareh, 'The History and Culture of the Khasi People'.
28. Ibid.
29. Pemberton, *Report on the Eastern Frontier of British India*.
30. White, ed., *Memoir of the Late David Scott*.
31. Pemberton, *Report on the Eastern Frontier of British India*.
32. Aitchison, *A Collection of Treaties, Engagements and Sunnuds*, rev. Talbot, Vol. II.
33. Pemberton, *Report on the Eastern Frontier of British India*.
34. Andrew May, *Welsh Missionaries and British Imperialism: The Empire of Clouds in North-East India* (Manchester: Manchester University Press, 2012).
35. Ibid.
36. Ibid.
37. Ibid.
38. Rev. Lyndan Syiem, 'The successors to Thomas Jones', *The Shillong Times*, 22 June 2020. https://theshillongtimes.com/2020/06/22/the-successors-to-thomas-jones/
39. A. J. M. Mills, *Report on the Khasi and Jaintia Hills, 1853* (1854; Shillong: North-Eastern Hill University Publications, c.1985).
40. W. J. Allen, *Report on the Administration of the Cossyah and Jynteah Hill Territory* (Calcutta: Bengal Hurkaru Press, 1858).
41. Ibid.
42. Alexander Mackenzie, *The North-East Frontier of India* (Delhi: Mittal Publications, 1979). Originally published as *History of the Relations of the Government with the Hill Tribes of the North-East Frontier of Bengal* in 1884.
43. Ibid.
44. Helen Giri, *The Khasis Under British Rule, 1824–1947* (New Delhi: Regency Publications, 1998).
45. Mackenzie, *The North-East Frontier of India*.
46. Sangma, *History and Culture of the Garos*.
47. Ibid.
48. Rev. William Carey, *A Garo Jungle Book; or, The Mission to the Garos of Assam* (Philadelphia: Judson Press, 1919).
49. 'A Society in Transition', *The Shillong Times*, 16 May 2021. https://theshillongtimes.com/2021/05/16/a-society-in-transition/
50. Bakyrmen Nongpluh, *Pioneering Indigenous Leadership: A Study of the Contribution of John Alla-ud-din Khan and James Joy Mohan Nichols-Roy in Establishing the Church of God in India, with Special Reference to Meghalaya* (Delhi: ISPCK, 2012).
51. Hugh F. Owen, 'Negotiating the Lucknow Pact', *Journal of Asian Studies*, 31:3 (1972), 561–87. https://doi.org/10.2307/2052234

52. E. A. Benians, J. Butler and C. E. Carrington, eds., *The Cambridge History of the British Empire*, Vol. III: *The Empire-Commonwealth, 1870–1919* (New York: Cambridge University Press, 1959).
53. J. J. M. Nichols-Roy, 'Ka jingdonkam bakongsan jong ja Ri', in *Ka jingshai ka Gospel* 26:1 (January 1930), reproduced in translation in Nongpluh, *Pioneering Indigenous Leadership*.
54. Indian Franchise Committee, Vol. I: *Report of the Indian Franchise Committee, 1932* (London: His Majesty's Stationery Office, 1932).
55. Giri, *The Khasis Under British Rule*.
56. S. K. Chaube, *Hill Politics in Northeast India* (1968; Hyderabad: Orient Blackswan, 2012).
57. Ibid.
58. Ibid.
59. Giri, *The Khasis Under British Rule*.
60. Robert Reid, *Years of Change in Bengal and Assam* (London: Ernest Benn Ltd, 1966).
61. Ibid.
62. Giri, *The Khasis Under British Rule*.
63. Ibid.
64. For details, see P. Gracefulness Bonney, '*Syiemship* in Khasi Society: The *Syiemship* of Nongstoin', in *Revisiting Traditional Institutions in the Khasi-Jaintia Hills*, ed. Charles Reuben Lyngdoh (Newcastle upon Tyne: Cambridge Scholars Publishing, 2016).
65. Chaube, *Hill Politics in Northeast India*.
66. Ibid.
67. Ibid.
68. *Report of the States Reorganisation Commission* (New Delhi: Government of India Press, 1955).
69. For details, see Chaube, *Hill Politics in Northeast India*.
70. *APHLC, 1960–74, The Souvenir* (APHLC, July 1974).
71. H. V. Pataskar, *Report of the Commission on the Hill Areas of Assam 1965–66* (Delhi: Government of India, Ministry of Home Affairs, 1966).
72. *APHLC, 1960–74, The Souvenir* (APHLC, July 1974).
73. Dilip Mukerjee, 'Assam Reorganization' Asian Survey 9, no. 4 (1969). https://doi.org/10.2307/2642547
74. Ibid.
75. Chaube, *Hill Politics in Northeast India*.
76. A. N. Das, 'New Constitutional Experiment in Assam', *Amrita Bazar Patrika*, 16 September 1968.
77. *APHLC 1960–74, The Souvenir*.

8. ARUNACHAL PRADESH BETWEEN CHINA AND INDIA

1. L. W. Shakespear, *History of Upper Assam, Upper Burmah and North-Eastern Frontier* (1914; Memphis: General Books, 2010).
2. J. C. Dutta, *Malinithan: A Study on Iconography* (Itanagar: Government of Arunachal Pradesh, 1997).
3. Basudeb Malik, 'The Sources for Reconstruction of the History of Arunachal Pradesh', *Journal of Ancient Indian History* 23 (2005–06).
4. Lt R. Wilcox, 'Memoir of a Survey of Assam and the Neighbouring Countries, Executed in 1825–6–7–8' (1832), reprinted in *Hill Tracts Between Assam and Burma: Selection of Papers* (Delhi: Vivek Publishing Co., 1978). Originally published as *Selection of Papers Regarding the Hill Tracts between Assam and Burmah and on the Upper Brahmaputra* (1873).
5. Ibid.
6. J. B. Neufville, 'On the Geography and Population of Assam' (1828), reprinted in *India's North-East Frontier in the Nineteenth Century*, ed. Verrier Elwin (New Delhi: Gyan Books, 2019).
7. Captain R. Boileau Pemberton, *Report on the Eastern Frontier of British India* (Calcutta: Baptist Mission Press, 1835).
8. Ibid.
9. C. U. Aitchison, *A Collection of Treaties, Engagements and Sanads Relating to India and Neighbouring Countries*, Vol. XII: *The Treaties, &c, Relating to Jammu and Kashmir, Sikkim, Assam and Burma*, revised ed. (Calcutta: Government of India Central Publication Branch, 1931).
10. G. T. Bayfield, of the Medical Establishment of Fort St George, 'Narrative of a Journey from Ava to the Frontiers of Assam and Back, Performed between December 1836 and May 1837, under the orders of Lieutenant-Colonel Burney, Resident at Ava' (1873), reprinted in *Hill Tracts Between Assam and Burma: Selection of Papers* (Delhi: Vivek Publishing Company, 1978).
11. A digitised copy of Pemberton's map is available in Yale University Library: https://collections.library.yale.edu/catalog/15512910
12. Aitchison, *A Collection of Treaties, Engagements and Sanads*, Vol. XII.
13. John Butler, *A Sketch of Assam with some Account of the Hill Tribes* (London: Smith, Elder & Co., 1847).
14. Ibid.
15. Ibid.
16. *Report on the Administration of Eastern Bengal and Assam, 1905–1906* (Shillong: Eastern Bengal and Assam Secretariat Press, 1907).
17. Alexander Mackenzie, *The North-East Frontier of India* (Delhi: Mittal Publications, 1979). Originally published as *History of the Relations of the Government with the Hill Tribes of the North-East Frontier of Bengal* in 1884.
18. Ibid.
19. Ibid.

20. Ibid.
21. The land beyond the Inner Line was 'debatable' because private companies operated beyond this line by striking deals with local tribal chiefs.
22. Robert Reid, *History of the Frontier Areas Bordering on Assam from 1883–1941* (1942; Guwahati: Bhabani Books, 2013).
23. Ibid.
24. Charles Allen, *A Mountain in Tibet: The Search for Mount Kailas and the Sources of the Great Rivers of India* (London: Andre Deutsch, 1982).
25. Reid, *History of the Frontier Areas Bordering on Assam.*
26. The tribe is now known as Mising.
27. Allen, *A Mountain in Tibet.*
28. Reid, *History of the Frontier Areas Bordering on Assam.*
29. Ibid.
30. Allen, *A Mountain in Tibet.*
31. Reid, *History of the Frontier Areas Bordering on Assam.*
32. Bérénice Guyot-Réchard, *Shadow States: India, China and the Himalayas, 1910–1962* (Cambridge: Cambridge University Press, 2017).
33. Intelligence Branch, Army Headquarters, India, comp., *Frontier and Overseas Expeditions from India*, Vol. VII: *Official Account of the Abor Expedition, 1911–1912* (1913; Delhi: Mittal Publications, 1983).
34. Reid, *History of the Frontier Areas Bordering on Assam.*
35. Intelligence Branch, Army Headquarters, India, *Frontier and Overseas Expeditions from India*, Vol. VII.
36. Details can be found in Reid, *History of the Frontier Areas Bordering on Assam.*
37. Lt Col F. M. Bailey, *No Passport to Tibet* (London: Rupert Hart-Davis, 1957).
38. Ibid.
39. K. Gupta, 'Distortions in the History of Sino-Indian Frontiers', Economic and Political Weekly 15, no. 30 (1980): 1265–70. http://www.jstor.org/stable/4368898
40. S. Dutta Choudhury, ed., *Arunachal Pradesh District Gazetteers: Lohit District* (Shillong: Government of Arunachal Pradesh, 1978).
41. Reid, *History of the Frontier Areas Bordering on Assam.*
42. Ibid.
43. G. T. Lloyd, *Census of India 1921*, Vol. III: *Assam*: Part I: *Report* (Shillong: Government Press Assam, 1923).
44. *Annual Report on the Frontier Tribes of Assam for the Year 1921–1922* (Foreign and Political Department, Government of India, 1922), in collection of National Archives of India.
45. Ibid.
46. Reid, *History of the Frontier Areas Bordering on Assam.*
47. Ibid.
48. Treatment of the Assam Unadministered Areas as Tribal Areas and the Discharge of Functions by the Governor as the Agent of the Governor General in Respect of these Areas, File No. 113 X/35, Government of India.

49. Ibid.
50. Reid, *History of the Frontier Areas Bordering on Assam*.
51. F. Kingdon Ward, 'Botanical and Geographical Explorations in Tibet, 1935', *The Geographical Journal* 88:5 (1936), 385–410. https://doi.org/10.2307/1785960
52. Bérénice Guyot-Réchard, *Shadow States: India, China and the Himalayas, 1910–1962* (Cambridge: Cambridge University Press, 2017).
53. Ibid.
54. International Frontier Between Bhutan and Assam vis-à-vis Tibet Status of Tawang, Political Branch, File No. 6-P, Sikkim Agency Office, 1936, National Archives of India.
55. Ibid.
56. Ibid.
57. K. Gupta, 'Distortions in the History of Sino-Indian Frontiers', Economic and Political Weekly 15, no. 30 (1980): 1265 -70. http://www.jstor.org/stable/4368898
58. Guyot-Réchard, *Shadow States*.
59. Ibid.
60. Nari Rustomji, *Enchanted Frontiers: Sikkim, Bhutan and India's North-Eastern Borderlands* (Oxford: Oxford University Press, 1971).
61. Ibid.
62. Ibid.
63. Ibid.
64. For more on this, see Guyot-Réchard, *Shadow States*.
65. S. K. Chaube, *Hill Politics in Northeast India* (1968; Hyderabad: Orient Blackswan, 2012).
66. P. N. Kaul, *Frontier Callings* (New Delhi: Vikas Publishing House, 1976).
67. Ibid.
68. Verrier Elwin, *A Philosophy for NEFA* (1957; New Delhi: Isha Books, 2009).
69. Ibid.
70. 'Nehru Criticized for Inviting Chou', *The New York Times*, 17 February 1960.
71. Record of talks between P.M. [Jawaharlal Nehru] and Premier Chou En-lai [Zhou Enlai] held on 22nd April, 1960, from 4.30 p.m. to 7.45 p.m., Nehru Memorial Museum and Library, P. N. Haksar Papers, Wilson Center Digital Archive.
72. Shiv Kunal Verma, *1962: The War that Wasn't* (New Delhi: Aleph Book Co., 2016).
73. Ibid.
74. *Arunachal Pradesh: General Elections, Lok Sabha, March 1977: Statistical Report* (Itanagar: Chief Electoral Officer, Arunachal Pradesh, 1977).

9. SIKKIM AND THE COMPLETION OF REGION-MAKING

1. Details in Lal Bahadur Basnet, *Sikkim: A Short Political History* (New Delhi: S. Chand & Co., 1974).
2. Ibid.
3. H. H. Risley, *The Gazetteer of Sikkim* (1894; Delhi: Oriental Publishers, 1973).
4. Lal Bahadur Basnet, *Sikkim: A Short Political History* (New Delhi: S. Chand & Co., 1974).
5. J. W. Killigrew, 'Some Aspects of the Sino-Nepalese War of 1792', *Journal of Asian History* 13:1 (1979), 42–63. http://www.jstor.org/stable/41930319
6. Ibid.
7. For details, see Intelligence Branch, Army Headquarters, India, comp., *Frontier and Overseas Expeditions from India*, Vol. IV: *North and North-Eastern Frontier Tribes* (Simla: Government Monotype Press, 1907).
8. Ibid.
9. C. U. Aitchison, *A Collection of Treaties, Engagements and Sanads Relating to India and Neighbouring Countries*, Vol. XII: *The Treaties, &c, Relating to Jammu and Kashmir, Sikkim, Assam and Burma*, revised ed. (Calcutta: Government of India Central Publication Branch, 1931).
10. Ibid.
11. Ibid.
12. Ibid.
13. C.U. Aitchison, *A Collection of Treaties, Engagements and Sanads Relating to India and Neighbouring Countries, Vol XII* (Calcutta: Government of India, 1931).
14. P. R. Rao, *India and Sikkim, 1814–1970* (New Delhi: Sterling Publishers, 1972).
15. Ibid.
16. G. B. S. Sidhu, *Sikkim: Dawn of Democracy: The Truth Behind the Merger With India* (New Delhi: Penguin Viking, 2018).
17. Associated Press, 'Sikkim Votes to End Monarchy, Merge with India', *The New York Times*, 16 April 1975.
18. The Sanskrit shloka is 'Pragjyotishadhipah suro mlecchanamadhipo, Yavanaih sahito raja Bhagadatta maharathah', in the Sabha Parva of Mahabharata, cited in Dimbeswar Neog, *Introduction to Assam* (Bombay: Vora Publishers, 1947).
19. Devdutt Pattanaik, 'Good Deva-Bad Asura Divide Misleading', *The Times of India*, 27 February 2016.
20. Virag Pachpore, 'Vow to Make Akhand Bharat a Reality', Organiser, 23 August 2016, https://organiser.org/2016/08/23/68991/general/rcae6bdb6/
21. Catherine Clémentin-Ojha, '"India, that is Bharat …": One Country, Two Names', *South Asia Multidisciplinary Academic Journal* 10 (2014). https://doi.org/10.4000/samaj.3717
22. P.V. Kane, *History of Dharmasastra*, Vol. III (Poona: Bhandarkar Oriental Research Institute, 1946).

23. Benedict Anderson, *Imagined Communities: Reflections on the Origin and Spread of Nationalism* (1983; New Delhi: Rawat Publications, 2015).
24. Rahul Sagar, ed., *To Raise a Fallen People: How Nineteenth-Century Indians Saw Their World and Shaped Ours* (New Delhi: Juggernaut, 2022).
25. Ibid.
26. Sanjay Subrahmanyam, *Is Indian Civilization a Myth? Fictions and Histories* (Delhi: Permanent Black, 2013).
27. Details in E. W. Brown, *The Whole World Kin: A Pioneer Experience Among Remote Tribes, and Other Labours of Nathan Brown* (Philadelphia: Hubbard Brothers, 1890).
28. Quoted in Samrat Choudhury, *The Braided River: A Journey Along the Brahmaputra* (Gurugram: HarperCollins India, 2021).
29. Ibid.
30. James C. Scott, *The Art of Not Being Governed: An Anarchist History of Upland Southeast Asia* (New Haven, CT: Yale University Press), Kindle Edition, p. 61.

SELECT BIBLIOGRAPHY

Administration Report of the Manipur State for the Year 1937–38 (Imphal: State Printing Press, 1942).

Aitchison, C. U. *A Collection of Treaties, Engagements, and Sunnuds Relating to India and Neighbouring Countries*, Vol. I: *The Treaties &c., Relating to Bengal, Assam, Burmah, and the Eastern Archipelago*, revised by Lieutenant A. C. Talbot (Calcutta: Foreign Office Press, 1876).

——— *A Collection of Treaties, Engagements and Sanads Relating to India and Neighbouring Countries*, Vol. II: *The Treaties, &c, Relating to Burma, Nepal, Eastern Bengal and Assam, Bhutan, Sikkim, Tibet, Siam and the Eastern Archipelago* (Calcutta: Superintendent Government Printing India, 1909).

——— *A Collection of Treaties, Engagements and Sanads Relating to India and Neighbouring Countries*, Vol. XII: *The Treaties, &c, Relating to Jammu and Kashmir, Sikkim, Assam and Burma*, revised ed. (Calcutta: Government of India Central Publication Branch, 1931).

Allen, Charles. *A Mountain in Tibet: The Search for Mount Kailas and the Sources of the Great Rivers of India* (London: Andre Deutsch, 1982).

Anderson, Benedict. *Imagined Communities: Reflections on the Origin and Spread of Nationalism* (1983; New Delhi: Rawat Publications, 2015).

Annual Report on the Native States and Frontier Tribes of Assam, for the Year 1897–98 (Shillong: Assam Secretariat Printing Office [n.d.]).

Arunachal Pradesh: General Elections, Lok Sabha, March 1977: Statistical Report (Itanagar: Chief Electoral Officer, Arunachal Pradesh, 1977).

Asiatic Journal and Monthly Register for British and Foreign India, China, and Australasia 30 (London: Wm. H. Allen & Co., September–December 1839).

Auber, Peter. *Rise and Progress of the British Power in India*, 2 vols. (London: Wm. H. Allen & Co. and Calkin & Budd, Pall-Mall, 1837).

SELECT BIBLIOGRAPHY

Azad, Maulana Abul Kalam. *India Wins Freedom* (1958; Hyderabad: Orient Blackswan 1988).

Bailey, Lt Col F. M. *No Passport to Tibet* (London: Rupert Hart-Davis, 1957).

Banerjee, Anil Chandra. *The Making of the Indian Constitution, 1939–1947* (Calcutta: A. Mukherjee & Co., 1948).

Bareh, Hamlet. *Meghalaya* (Shillong: North-East India News & Feature Service, 1974).

Barpujari, H. K. *Assam in the Days of the Company, 1826–1858* (Gauhati: Lawyer's Book Stall, 1963).

Barpujari, H. K., S. K. Barpujari and A. C. Bhuyan, eds. *Political History of Assam*, Vol. I: *1826–1919* (Gauhati: Government of Assam, 1977).

Baruah, Sanjib. *India Against Itself: Assam and the Politics of Nationality* (Oxford: Oxford University Press, 2001).

Basnet, Lal Bahadur. *Sikkim: A Short Political History* (New Delhi: S. Chand & Co., 1974).

Bass, Gary J. *The Blood Telegram: Nixon, Kissinger, and a Forgotten Genocide* (New York: Alfred A. Knopf, 2013).

Bayfield, G. T. 'Narrative of a Journey from Ava to the Frontiers of Assam and Back, Performed between December 1836 and May 1837, under the orders of Lieutenant-Colonel Burney, Resident at Ava' (1873), reprinted in *Hill Tracts Between Assam and Burma: Selection of Papers* (Delhi: Vivek Publishing Co., 1978).

Benians, E. A., J. Butler and C. E. Carrington, eds. *The Cambridge History of the British Empire*, Vol. III: *The Empire-Commonwealth, 1870–1919* (New York: Cambridge University Press, 1959).

Bhaumik, Subir. *Insurgencies in India's Northeast: Conflict, Co-option and Change* (Washington: East-West Center, 2007).

——— 'Tripura: Ethnic Conflict, Militancy and Counterinsurgency', *Policies and Practices* 52 (Mahanirban Calcutta Research Group, 2012), 8–19.

Bhuyan, S. K., ed. and trans. *Tungkhungia Buranji, or A History of Assam, 1681–1826 A.D.* (London: Oxford University Press, 1933).

Bisheswar, N. *The Last Expression on my Death Bed* (Imphal: Pax Publications, 1986).

Bonney, P. Gracefulness. '*Syiemship* in Khasi Society: The *Syiemship* of Nongstoin', in *Revisiting Traditional Institutions in the Khasi-Jaintia Hills*, ed. Charles Reuben Lyngdoh (Newcastle upon Tyne: Cambridge Scholars Publishing, 2016), 80–92.

[Bordoloi, G. N.] *Constituent Assembly of India: North-East Frontier (Assam) Tribal and Excluded Areas Sub-Committee*, Vol. I: *(Report)* (New Delhi: Government of India Press, 1947).

Bower, Ursula Graham. *Naga Path* (London: John Murray, 1950).

Brown, E. W. *The Whole World Kin: A Pioneer Experience Among Remote Tribes, and Other Labors of Nathan Brown* (Philadelphia: Hubbard Brothers Publishers, 1890).

Bruce, C. A. *An Account of the Manufacture of the Black Tea as Now Practised at Suddeya in Upper Assam by the Chinamen Sent Thither for That Purpose. With Some Observations of the Culture of the Plant in China, and its Growth in Assam* (Calcutta: G. H. Huttmann, Bengal Military Orphan Press, 1838).

Burrell, A. 'Indian Tea Cultivation: Its Origin, Progress, and Prospects', *Journal of the Society of Arts* 25:1264 (9 February 1877), 199–215.

Butler, John. *A Sketch of Assam with some Account of the Hill Tribes* (London: Smith, Elder & Co., 1847).

Carey, Rev. William. *A Garo Jungle Book; or, The Mission to the Garos of Assam* (Philadelphia: Judson Press, 1919).

Cederlöf, Gunnel. *Founding an Empire on India's North-Eastern Frontiers, 1790–1840: Climate, Commerce, Polity* (Oxford: Oxford University Press, 2013).

Chakraborty, Deepayan. 'Situating the Historical Chronicles of Tripura in Traditional Indian Historiography', *Karatoya: North Bengal University Journal of History* 10 (March 2017), 60–81.

Chakravarti, Mahadev. 'Reorganization Question of Tripura (1949–62): Reactions of Different Political Parties', in *Reorganization of North-East India Since 1947*, ed. B. Datta Ray and S. P. Agrawal (New Delhi: Concept Publishing, 1996), 294–307.

Chasie, Charles. 'Nagaland', in *Sub-Regional Relations in the Eastern South Asia: With Special Focus on India's North Eastern Region*, ed. Mayumi Murayama, Kyoko Inoue and Sanjoy Hazarika (Chiba: Institute of Developing Economies, Japan External Trade Organization, 2005), 241–74.

Chasie, Charles, and Sanjoy Hazarika. *The State Strikes Back: India and the Naga Insurgency* (Washington: East-West Center, 2009).

Chatterji, Suniti Kumar. *The Origin and Development of the Bengali Language* (Calcutta: Calcutta University Press, 1926).

——— *Kirata-Jana-Krti* (1951; Calcutta: Asiatic Society, 1998).

Chaube, S. K. *Hill Politics in Northeast India* (1968; Hyderabad: Orient Blackswan, 2012).

Chaudhuri, Nalini Ranjan Roy. 'The Historical Past', in *Tripura: The Land and Its People*, ed. Jagadis Gan-Chaudhuri (Delhi: Leeladevi Publications, 1980), 13–43.

Chawngkunga, C. *Important Documents of Mizoram* (Aizawl: Art & Culture Department, Government of Mizoram, 1998).

Choudhury, Samrat. *The Braided River: A Journey Along the Brahmaputra* (Gurugram: HarperCollins India, 2021).

Choudhury, S. Dutta, ed., *Arunachal Pradesh District Gazetteers: Lohit District* (Shillong: Government of Arunachal Pradesh, 1978).

Clark, Mary Mead. *A Corner in India* (Philadelphia: American Baptist Publication Society, 1907).

Clémentin-Ojha, Catherine. '"India, that is Bharat ...": One Country, Two Names', *South Asia Multidisciplinary Academic Journal* 10 (2014). https://doi.org/10.4000/samaj.3717

Coupland, R. *The Future of India: Report on the Constitutional Problem in India* (Oxford: Oxford University Press, 1943).

——— *Indian Politics, 1936–42* (London: Oxford University Press, 1944).

Cross, Cecil Merne Putnam. *The Development of Self-Government in India, 1858–1914* (Chicago: University of Chicago Press, 1922).

Dalrymple, Sam. 'Gedu Mian and the Partition of Tripura', *Partition Studies Quarterly* 5 (January 2022). https://partitionstudiesquarterly.org/article/gedu-mian-and-the-partition-of-tripura/

Das, Durga, ed., *Sardar Patel's Correspondence*, Vol. V: *1945–50* (Ahmedabad: Navajivan Publishing House, 1973).

Dutta, J. C. *Malinithan: A Study on Iconography* (Itanagar: Government of Arunachal Pradesh, 1997).

Eliot, John. 'Observations of the Inhabitants of the Garrow Hills Made During a Public Deputation in the Years 1788 and 1789', *Asiatick Researches* 3 (1794), 21–45.

Elwin, Verrier *A Philosophy for NEFA* (1957; New Delhi: Isha Books, 2009).

Foster, William, ed. *Early Travels in India, 1583–1619* (London: Oxford University Press, 1921).

Fürer-Haimendorf, Christoph von. *The Naked Nagas: Head-Hunters of Assam in Peace and War* (1946; London: Spectrum Publications, 2004).

Gait, E. A. *Census of India, 1891: Assam*, Vol. I: *Report* (Shillong: Assam Secretariat Printing Office, 1892).

——— *A History of Assam* (1906; Guwahati: EBH Publishers, 2008).

Gan-Chaudhuri, Jagadis. 'Tripuri Political Consciousness', in *Tripura: The Land and Its People*, ed. Gan-Chaudhuri (Delhi: Leeladevi Publications, 1980), 153–8.

Gandhi, Rajmohan. *India After 1947: Reflections and Recollections* (New Delhi: Aleph Book Co., 2022).

Ghosh, B. 'Ethnicity and Insurgency in Tripura', *Sociological Bulletin*, 52:2 (2003), 221–43. http://www.jstor.org/stable/23620336

——— 'Religion and Politics in Bengal: The Noakhali Carnage, 1946–47', *Proceedings of the Indian History Congress* 72 (2011), 936–6. http://www.jstor.org/stable/44146785

Ghoshal, Anindita. 'Tripura: A Chronicle of Politicisation of the Refugees and Ethnic Tribals', *Development and Change* 14:2 (July 2017), 27–41.

Giri, Helen. *The Khasis Under British Rule, 1824–1947* (New Delhi: Regency Publications, 1998).

Gohain, Hiren. 'Chronicles of Violence and Terror: Rise of United Liberation Front of Asom', *Economic and Political Weekly* 42:12 (2007), 1012–18. http://www.jstor.org/stable/4419382

Grierson, George Abraham. *Linguistic Survey of India*, Vol. III, Part III (Calcutta: Government of India, 1904).

Grimwood, Ethel St Clair. *My Three Years in Manipur and Escape from the Recent Mutiny* (London: Richard Bentley & Son, 1892).

Guha, Amalendu. *Planter-Raj to Swaraj: Freedom Struggle and Electoral Politics in Assam, 1826–1947* (New Delhi: Indian Council of Historical Research, 1977).

Guha, Ramachandra. *India After Gandhi: The History of the World's Largest Democracy* (Delhi: Picador India, 2007).

Guite, Jangkhomang, '"Fighting the White Men Until the Last Bullet": The General Course of the Anglo-Kuki War', in *The Anglo-Kuki War, 1917–1919*, ed. Jangkhomang Guite and Thongkholal Haokip (London: Routledge India, 2018), 37–77.

Gupta, K., 'Distortions in the History of Sino-Indian Frontiers', *Economic and Political Weekly* 15:30 (1980): 1265–70. http://www.jstor.org/stable/4368898

Gurdon, Lt Col P. R. T. *The Khasis*, with an introduction by Sir Charles Lyall (London: Macmillan & Co., 1914).

Guyot-Réchard, Bérénice. *Shadow States: India, China and the Himalayas, 1910–1962* (Cambridge: Cambridge University Press, 2017).

Haksar, Nandita, and Sebastian M. Hongray. *Kuknalim: Naga Armed Resistance: Testimonies of Leaders, Pastors, Healers and Soldiers* (New Delhi: Speaking Tiger, 2019).

Harvey, G. E. *History of Burma* (London: Longmans, Green & Co., 1925).

Hersh, Seymour M. *The Price of Power: Kissinger in the Nixon White House* (New York: Summit Books, 1983).

Higgins, J. C. *Administration Report of the Manipur State for the Year 1911–1912* (Shillong: Assam Secretariat Printing Press, 1912).

Hluna, J. V. *Church and Political Upheaval in Mizoram: A Study of Impact of Christianity on the Political Development in Mizoram* (Aizawl: Mizo History Association, 1985).

Indian Franchise Committee. Vol. I: *Report of the Indian Franchise Committee, 1932* (London: His Majesty's Stationery Office, 1932).

Indian Statutory Commission. Vol. XIV: *Memorandum Submitted by the Government of Assam to the Indian Statutory Commission* (London: His Majesty's Stationery Office, 1930).

Intelligence Branch, Army Headquarters, India. *Frontier and Overseas Expeditions from India*, Vol. IV: *North and North-Eastern Frontier Tribes* (Simla: Government Monotype Press, 1907).

——— *Frontier and Overseas Expeditions from India*, Vol. VII: *Official Account of the Abor Expedition, 1911–1912* (1913; Delhi: Mittal Publications, 1983).

Johnstone, Major-General Sir James. *My Experiences in Manipur and the Naga Hills* (London: Sampson Low, Marston & Co., 1896).

Kakati, Satish C. 'The Man Who Saved India from Disaster', in *Lokpriya Gopinath Bordoloi: An Architect of Modern India*, ed. Lily Mazinder Baruah (New Delhi: Gyan Publishing House, 1992).

Kane, P. V. *History of Dharmasastra*, Vol. III (Poona: Bhandarkar Oriental Research Institute, 1946).

Kaul, P. N. *Frontier Callings* (New Delhi: Vikas Publishing House, 1976).

Killigrew, J. W. 'Some Aspects of the Sino-Nepalese War of 1792', *Journal of Asian History* 13:1 (1979), 42–63. http://www.jstor.org/stable/41930319

Kumar, Ram Narayan, and Laxmi Murthy. *Four Years of the Ceasefire Agreement Between the Government of India and the National Socialist Council of Nagalim: Promises and Pitfalls* (New Delhi: Other Media Communications, 2002).

Lalthangliana, B. *Culture and Folklore of Mizoram* (New Delhi: Publications Division, Ministry of Information and Broadcasting, Government of India, 2005).

Lees, W. Nassau. *Tea Cultivation, Cotton, and Other Agricultural Experiments in India: A Review* (London: Thacker, Spink & Co., 1863).

Leider, Jacques. 'On Arakanese Territorial Expansion: Origins, Context, Means and Practice', in *The Maritime Frontier of Burma*, ed. Jos Gommans and Jacques Leider (Leiden: KITLV Press, 2002), 127–50.

Lewis, Grace R. *The Lushai Hills: A Story of the Lushai Pioneer Mission* (London: Baptist Missionary Society, 1907).

Lindsay, Robert. 'Anecdotes of an Indian Life', in *Lives of the Lindsays; or, A Memoir of the Houses of Crawford and Balcarres*, Vol. IV (Wigan: C. S. Simms, 1840).

Lloyd, G. T. *Census of India, 1921*, Vol. III: *Assam*, Part I: *Report* (Shillong: Government Press Assam, 1923).

Lloyd, J. Meirion. *On Every High Hill* (Liverpool: Foreign Mission Office, 1952).

Long, Rev. James. *Analysis of the Rajmala or Chronicles of Tripura* [*Journal of the Asiatic Society of Bengal* (1850)] (Agartala: Tribal Research and Cultural Institute, Government of Tripura, 2008).

Lovett, Sir Verney. *A History of the Indian Nationalist Movement* (London: Frank Cass & Co. Ltd, 1968).

Ludden, David. 'The First Boundary of Bangladesh on Sylhet's Northern Frontiers', *Journal of the Asiatic Society of Bangladesh* 48:1 (June 2003), 1–54.

Lydall, E. F. *Administration Report of the Manipur State for the Year 1943–44* (Imphal: State Printing Press, 1945).

Mackenzie, Alexander. *History of the Relations of the Government with the Hill Tribes of the North-East Frontier of Bengal* (Calcutta: Home Department Press, 1884).

——— *The North-East Frontier of India* (Delhi: Mittal Publications, 1979).

Malik, Basudeb. 'The Sources for Reconstruction of the History of Arunachal Pradesh', *Journal of Ancient Indian History* 23 (2005–06), 33–40.

Malsawmliana, 'From Greater Autonomy to the Hill State With Reference to Mizoram', in *Politics of Regionalism in North-East India*, ed. Malsawmliana and Lalsangzela Pachuau (Delhi: Mittal Publications, 2015), 81–90.

Manipur Territorial Congress Committee. 'Memorandum Submitted to Smt. Indira Gandhi, Prime Minister of India, and Shri S. Nijalingappa, President, A.I.C.C.', in *Case of Manipur: Manipur Demands Statehood* (Imphal: Manipur Territorial Congress Committee, 1968).

Maxwell, Lieut. Col H. St P. *Administration Report of the Political Agency, Manipur, for the Year 1903–1904* (Shillong: Assam Secretariat Printing Office, 1904).

May, Andrew. *Welsh Missionaries and British Imperialism: The Empire of Clouds in North-East India* (Manchester: Manchester University Press, 2012).

McCall, Major Anthony Gilchrist. *Lushai Chrysalis* (London: Luzac & Co., 1949).

McCulloch, M. *Valley of Manipur* (Delhi: Gian Publications, 1980).

McSwiney, J. *Census of India, 1911*, Vol. III: *Assam*, Part I: *Report* (Shillong: Assam Secretariat Printing Office, 1912).

Means, Gordon P. *Tribal Transformation: The Early History of the Naga Hills*, ed. Achilla Imlong Erdican (New Delhi: Prestige Books International, 2013).

Menon, K. D., ed. *Tripura District Gazetteers: Tripura* (Agartala: Department of Education, 1975).

Menon, V. P. *The Transfer of Power in India* (Princeton: Princeton University Press, 1957).

Mills, A. J. M. *Report on the Khasi and Jaintia Hills, 1853* (1854; Shillong: North-Eastern Hill University Publications, c.1985).

——— *Report on the Province of Assam* (Calcutta: Thos. Jones, 'Calcutta Gazette' Office, 1854).

Mitri, Marco, and Dhiraj Neog. 'Preliminary Report on the Excavation of Neolithic Sites from Khasi Hills Meghalaya', *Ancient Asia: Journal of the Society of South Asian Archaeology* 7 (2016), 7. http://doi.org/10.5334/aa.119

Moon, Penderel. *Divide and Quit* (London: Chatto & Windus, 1961).

Mullan, C. S. *Census of India, 1931*, Vol. III: *Assam*, Part I: *Report* (Shillong: Government of India Central Publication Branch, 1932).

Nag, Sajal. *India and North-East India: Mind, Politics and the Process of Integration, 1946–1950* (New Delhi: Regency Publications, 1998).

Nath, Dr N. C., trans. *Sri Rajmala, Vol. I to IV* (Agartala: Tribal Research and Cultural Institute, Government of Tripura, 1999).

Neog, Dimbeswar. *Introduction to Assam* (Bombay: Vora Publishers, 1947).

Neufville, J. B. 'On the Geography and Population of Assam' (1828), in *India's North-East Frontier in the Nineteenth Century*, ed. Verrier Elwin (New Delhi: Gyan Books, 2019).

Nibedon, Nirmal. *Nagaland: The Night of the Guerrillas* (Delhi: Lancer, 1978).

Nichols-Roy, J. J. M. 'Note on the Khasi and Jaintia Hills', in *Memorandum Submitted by the Government of Assam to the Indian Statutory Commission* (Indian Statutory Commission, Vol. XIV) (London: His Majesty's Stationery Office, 1930).

Nongpluh, Bakyrmen. *Pioneering Indigenous Leadership: A Study of the Contribution of John Alla-ud-din Khan and James Joy Mohan Nichols-Roy in Establishing the Church of God in India, with Special Reference to Meghalaya* (Delhi: ISPCK, 2012).

Owen, Hugh F. 'Negotiating the Lucknow Pact', *Journal of Asian Studies* 31:3 (1972), 561–87. https://doi.org/10.2307/2052234

Parratt, John. *Wounded Land: Politics and Identity in Modern Manipur* (New Delhi: Mittal Publications, 2005).

Parratt, John, and Saroj Arambam Parratt. 'Hijam Irabot and the Radical Socialist Democratic Movement in Manipur', *Internationales Asienesforum* 31:3–4 (2000). https://doi.org/10.11588/iaf.2000.31.988

Parratt, Saroj Nalini Arambam. *The Court Chronicle of the Kings of Manipur: The Cheitharon Kumpapa* (London and New Delhi: Routledge, 2005).

——— *The Religion of Manipur: Beliefs, Rituals and Historical Development* (Calcutta: Firma KLM Pvt Ltd, 1980).

Parratt, Saroj N. Arambam, and J. Parratt. 'The Second "Women's War" and the Emergence of Democratic Government in Manipur', *Modern Asian Studies* 35:4 (2001), 905–19. http://www.jstor.org/stable/313195

Parry, N. E. 'Extract from a Note...dated 3rd March 1928', in *Memorandum Submitted by the Government of Assam to the Indian Statutory Commission* (Indian Statutory Commission, Vol. XIV) (London: His Majesty's Stationery Office, 1930).

Pataskar, H. V. *Report of the Commission on the Hill Areas of Assam 1965–66* (Delhi: Government of India, 1966).

Paul, Manas. *The Eyewitness: Tales from Tripura's Ethnic Conflict* (New Delhi: Lancer, 2009).

Pemberton, Captain R. Boileau. *Report on the Eastern Frontier of British India* (Calcutta: Government of India, 1835).

Philips, C. H., and M. D. Wainwright, eds. *The Partition of India: Policies and Perspectives, 1935–1947* (London: Allen & Unwin, 1970),

Pisharoty, Sangeeta Barooah. *Assam: The Accord, the Discord* (Gurugram: Penguin Random House India, 2019).

Porter, A. E. *Census of India, 1931*, Vol. V: *Bengal States and Sikkim* (Calcutta: Central Publications Branch).

Pudaite, Lal. 'Mizoram', in *Sub-Regional Relations in the Eastern South Asia: With Special Focus on India's North Eastern Region*, ed. Mayumi Murayama, Kyoko Inoue and Sanjoy Hazarika (Chiba: Institute of Developing Economies, 2005), 153–240.

Ralte, Benjamin. 'The Formation and Role of Eastern India Tribal Union in Hill Politics of North East India', in *Politics of Regionalism in North-East India*, ed. Malsawmliana and Lalsangzela Pachuau (Delhi: Mittal Publications, 2015), 91–104.

Rao, P. R. *India and Sikkim, 1814–1970* (New Delhi: Sterling Publishers, 1972).

Ray, Animesh. *Mizoram* (New Delhi: National Book Trust India, 1993).

Reid, A. Scott. *Chin-Lushai Land* (Calcutta: Thacker, Spink & Co., 1893).

Reid, Robert. *History of the Frontier Areas Bordering on Assam from 1883–1941* (1942; Guwahati: Bhabani Books, 2013).

——— 'The Excluded Areas of Assam', *The Geographical Journal* 103:1–2 (1944), 18–29. https://doi.org/10.2307/1789063

——— *Years of Change in Bengal and Assam* (London: Ernest Benn Ltd, 1966).

Report of the States Reorganisation Commission (New Delhi: Government of India Press, 1955).

Report on the Administration of Bengal, 1872–73, With a Statistical Summary (Calcutta: Bengal Secretariat Press, 1873).

Report on the Administration of Eastern Bengal and Assam, 1905–1906 (Shillong: Eastern Bengal and Assam Secretariat Press, 1907).

Risley, H. H. *The Gazetteer of Sikkim* (1894; Delhi: Oriental Publishers, 1973).

Robins, Nick. *The Corporation that Changed the World* (London: Pluto Press, 2012).

Robinson, W. *A Grammar of the Assamese Language* (Serampore: Serampore Press, 1839).

——— 'Descriptive Account of Assam' (1841), reprinted in *India's North-East Frontier in the Nineteenth Century*, ed. Verrier Elwin (New Delhi: Gyan Books, 2019).

Rustomji, Nari K. *Enchanted Frontiers: Sikkim, Bhutan and India's North-Eastern Borderlands* (Oxford: Oxford University Press, 1971).

Sagar, Rahul, ed. *To Raise a Fallen People: How Nineteenth-Century Indians Saw Their World and Shaped Ours* (New Delhi: Juggernaut, 2022).

Sangma, Milton S. *History and Culture of the Garos* (New Delhi: Books Today, 1981).

Scott, James C. *The Art of Not Being Governed: An Anarchist History of Upland Southeast Asia* (New Haven, CT: Yale University Press, 2009).

Selection of Papers Regarding the Hill Tracts between Assam and Burmah and on the Upper Brahmaputra (Calcutta: Bengal Secretariat Press, 1873).

Sema, Hokishe. *Emergence of Nagaland: Socio-Economic and Political Transformation and the Future* (New Delhi: Vikas Publishing House Pvt Ltd, 1986).

Sengupta, Nitish. *Land of Two Rivers: A History of Bengal from the Mahabharata to Mujib* (London: Penguin Books, 2011).

Shakespear, Major J. *Administration Report of the Political Agency, Manipur, for the Year 1904–05* (Shillong: Assam Secretariat Printing Press, 1905).

——— *History of Upper Assam, Upper Burmah and North-Eastern Frontier* (1914; Memphis: General Books, 2010).

——— *History of the Assam Rifles* (London: Macmillan & Co., 1929).

Sharma, S. K., and Usha Sharma, eds. *Documents on North East India: An Exhaustive Survey*, Vol. IV: *Assam (1936–1957)* (Delhi: Mittal Publications, 2006).

Sidhu, G. B. S. *Sikkim: Dawn of Democracy: The Truth Behind the Merger With India* (New Delhi: Penguin Viking, 2018).

Singh, Capt. M. K. Priyabrata. *Administrative Report of the Manipur State for the Year 1946–47* (Imphal: State Printing Press, 1948).

Singh, R. K. Jhalajit. *A Short History of Manipur*, 2nd ed. (Imphal: R. K. Jhalajit Singh, 1992).

Statistical Report on the General Election, 1972 to the Legislative Assembly of Tripura (New Delhi: Election Commission of India).

Statistical Report on the General Election, 1974 to the Legislative Assembly of Tripura (New Delhi: Election Commission of India).

Subrahmanyam, Sanjay. *Is Indian Civilization a Myth? Fictions and Histories* (Delhi: Permanent Black, 2013).

Sundar, N. 'Interning Insurgent Populations: The Buried Histories of Indian Democracy', *Economic and Political Weekly* 46:6 (2011), 47–57. http://www.jstor.org/stable/27918119

Syiemlieh, D. R. 'The Crown Colony [Plans]: The British and the Hill Areas of North-East India, 1945–46', *Proceedings of the Indian History Congress* 59, (1998), 691–8. http://www.jstor.org/stable/44147039

Tripura State Consolidated Administration Report for 1350, 1351 and 1352 T.E. (1940–1943 AD) (Agartala: Political Department, 1943).

Verma, Shiv Kunal. *1962: The War that Wasn't* (New Delhi: Aleph Book Co., 2016).

Ward, F. Kingdon. 'Botanical and Geographical Explorations in Tibet, 1935', *The Geographical Journal* 88:5 (1936), 385–410. https://doi.org/10.2307/1785960

Webster, J. E. *East Bengal District Gazetteers: Tippera* (Allahabad: Pioneer Press, 1910).

Wettstein, Marion. 'Origin and Migration Myths in the Rhetoric of Naga Independence and Collective Identity', in *Origins and Migrations in the Extended Eastern Himalayas*, ed. Toni Huber and Stuart Blackburn (Leiden: Brill, 2012), 213–38.

White, Major A. ed. *Memoir of the Late David Scott* (Calcutta: Baptist Mission Press, 1832).

Wilcox, Lt R. 'Memoir of a Survey of Assam and the Neighbouring Countries, Executed in 1825–6–7–8' (1832), reprinted in *Hill Tracts between Assam and Burma: Selection of Papers* (Delhi: Vivek Publishing Co., 1978). Originally published as *Selection of Papers Regarding the Hill Tracts between Assam and Burmah and on the Upper Brahmaputra* (1873).

Williams, Rev. W. 'A Visit to the Lushai Hills', *The Monthly Tidings* (August 1891).

Woodthorpe, R. G. *The Lushai Expedition, 1871–1872* (London: Hurst & Blackett, 1873).

Yambem, Sanamani. 'Nupi Lan: Manipur Women's Agitation, 1939', *Economic and Political Weekly* 11:8 (1976), 325–31. http://www.jstor.org/stable/4364388

Zorema, J. *Indirect Rule in Mizoram, 1890–1954* (New Delhi: Mittal Publications, 2007).

INDEX

INDEX

ABOUT THE AUTHOR

Samrat Choudhury is an author and journalist from Shillong, and a former editor of broadsheet newspapers in Delhi, Mumbai and Bengaluru. He currently divides his time between India and the Philippines and writes op-eds, analyses and occasional reportage for a number of national and international publications.

Samrat's previous book was *The Braided River: A Journey Along the Brahmaputra* (2021). He has earlier authored a novel, *The Urban Jungle*, which was nominated for the Man Asian Literary Prize. He also co-edited an anthology titled *Insider/Outsider* on Northeast India. His other projects include *Partition Studies Quarterly*, an online journal focused on the forgotten causes and experiences of the Partition of India in its Northeast, which he co-founded along with two others.

Samrat was the Asian Leadership Fellow from India at the International House of Japan in Tokyo in 2018 and a Chevening Scholar at the University of Westminster, London, in 2019.

30 Years *of*

HarperCollins *Publishers* India

At HarperCollins, we believe in telling the best stories and finding the widest possible readership for our books in every format possible. We started publishing 30 years ago; a great deal has changed since then, but what has remained constant is the passion with which our authors write their books, the love with which readers receive them, and the sheer joy and excitement that we as publishers feel in being a part of the publishing process.

Over the years, we've had the pleasure of publishing some of the finest writing from the subcontinent and around the world, and some of the biggest bestsellers in India's publishing history. Our books and authors have won a phenomenal range of awards, and we ourselves have been named Publisher of the Year the greatest number of times. But nothing has meant more to us than the fact that millions of people have read the books we published, and somewhere, a book of ours might have made a difference.

As we step into our fourth decade, we go back to that one word – a word which has been a driving force for us all these years.

Read.

Harper Collins

4th

HARPER PERENNIAL

HARPER BUSINESS

HARPER BLACK

हार्पर हिन्दी

HarperCollins *Children's Books*

HARPER DESIGN

HARPER VANTAGE

Harper Sport